The

GIVER'S

GUIDE

The
GIVER'S
GUIDE

Making Your
Charity Dollars Count

By Philip English Mackey

CATBIRD PRESS

No part of this book may be used or reproduced in any manner without written permission, except in the context of reviews. CATBIRD PRESS, 44 North Sixth Avenue, Highland Park, NJ 08904 201-572-0816. Our books are distributed to the trade by Independent Publishers Group.

Library of Congress Cataloging in Publication Data
Mackey, Philip English.
 The giver's guide : making your charity dollars count /
  by Philip English Mackey.
 Includes index.
  ISBN 0-945774-11-7 (paper) : $14.95
  1. Charities—United States—Handbooks, manuals, etc.
  2. Charities—United States—Societies, etc.—Handbooks,
    manuals, etc. 3. Charities—United States—
   Directories.
   I. Title
HV91.M25 1990
361.7'6'0973   90-39943
          CIP

ACKNOWLEDGMENTS

While accepting full responsibility for the final product, I wish to thank the following people who took time in their busy schedules to provide information or advice:

Robert Bothwell, Executive Director, National Committee for Responsive Philanthropy

Bennett Weiner, Vice President, Philanthropic Advisory Service of the Council of Better Business Bureaus

Sheila Williamson, Executive Director, Community Foundation of New Jersey

Joanetta Scruggs, Senior Associate, Public Relations, United Way of America

Larry Campbell, Registrar, Office of the Attorney General, Registry of Charitable Trusts, State of California

David E. Ormstedt, Assistant Attorney General, State of Connecticut

Cheryl Martin, Director, National Clearing House for Corporate Matching Gift Information, Council for Advancement and Support of Education

I also wish to thank Harvey Wolsh, CPA, for his review of materials relating to tax issues; Melissa Waldman for her editorial and other assistance; Patricia Lesnefsky for her word processing efforts; and reference librarians from New York to Seattle who were indispensable in assisting my research.

Special gratitude is due to Margery K. Heitbrink, Vice President for Research and Reports at the National Charities Information Bureau, who was the key to including vast amounts of that organization's materials in this book.

Finally, I would like to thank my brother Charles D. Mackey for his keen editorial eye, and my friend Barbara Hase for her support and patience during the long process of researching and writing this book.

Philip English Mackey

CONTENTS

American consumer, you're a puzzle. You study *Consumer Reports* before buying a new washer. You get quotes from four contractors before choosing one to remodel your downstairs bathroom. You shop in two supermarkets because the produce is better here and the meat there. You spend days making sure you get the best deal for your insurance dollar.

But when it comes to giving to charity, you are careless, indifferent and sometimes plain ignorant. You have never taken the time necessary to think out what sorts of charity you should, or want to, support and how you can best help them. So you give money without any consideration of what you want it to accomplish. You give money to people on the street, to people at your door, to people who send you letters "signed" by celebrities, to charities that may not represent your interests.

As a contributor to charities you're a consumer, whether you think you are or not. You spend money in order to purchase something—food for starving children, cancer research, upkeep of the church you attend or a new building at your alma mater. As a consumer of charitable causes, you should be concerned with the question that dominates the rest of your consuming activity: are you getting what you pay for?

We are all aware of the result of sloppy consumerism in the marketplace. You hire a roofer who comes to your door to tell you that your roof is worn and should be replaced. Two weeks after he is finished, the new roof leaks in more places than the old one. You obviously have wasted your money. You have rewarded an aggressive, but careless worker and encouraged him to continue his ways. And you have deprived a qualified worker of some business that would have helped him continue to provide quality workmanship.

The same thing happens in the charity marketplace. You give a small but respectable sum to an organization with a nice name and a promise to help cure the disease that killed your mother. You may never know it, but the charity spends most of its income on overhead and fund-raising activities. Despite your gift, the disease is no nearer eradication, you have rewarded a sham charity, and you have deprived an honest charity of money it would have put to good use.

This book offers you an alternative. It tells you how to find the names of charities active in the fields that interest you most. It explains how to evaluate charities to make sure you are getting the maximum for your charitable dollar. And it provides answers to many questions you may have about various aspects of giving.

Use this book to become a more sophisticated consumer of charity. Your more rational giving will help reward the most worthy charities, drive the fraudulent from the marketplace, and make all charities more responsive to givers and to the organizations that gather information about them.

THE STATE OF AMERICAN PHILANTHROPY

Charitable giving in the United States is a very big business. In 1989, Americans donated over $114 billion to charity. The American Association of Fund-Raising Counsel (AAFRC) puts this huge number in perspective in *Giving USA 1989* by pointing out that it is about half of what Americans spent on shoes and clothing that year. Or, to put it another way, for every $2 Americans spent to clothe themselves, they gave $1 to charity.

Where did that $114 billion come from? Well, corporations gave $5 billion of it. Foundations gave $6.7 billion. About $6.5 billion came from bequests. But the rest—all $96.4 billion of it—came from people just like you. A *lot* of people just like you. In a Gallup Poll conducted in November 1989, 85 percent of the American adults surveyed said they had given money to charity in the past twelve months. And they gave more than money. About 74 percent of them donated food, clothing or other property during the year. About 42 percent did volunteer work, with the average volunteer working six hours in the previous month. About 84 percent reported that, in the past year, they had contributed either money, property or time directly to a needy person without using a charitable organization as an intermediary.

This and previous Gallup surveys have found significant variations in the giving patterns of Americans:

- Church and synagogue members contribute more and volunteer more than non-members. In 1989, about 90 percent of church- and synagogue-goers gave money and 80 percent gave food, clothing or other property to charity. The corresponding figures for non-members were 70 percent and 67 percent.

- Non-whites are just as likely to give to charity as whites and a little more likely to give personal assistance to needy people. Not surprisingly, Americans with greater wealth tend to contribute more money, property and time than those with fewer resources. But the poor tend to contribute a greater portion of their income than do middle or high income groups.

- People who volunteer their time to charities tend to give more money than those who do not. In 1987, households with volunteers gave an average of $1021 or 2.4 percent of their income, while those with no volunteers gave an average of $489 or 1.3 percent.

- With respect to age groups, a 1989 *NonProfit Times*/Opinion Research Corp. survey reported that those most likely to give are 45-54 year-olds (81 percent), followed by the 55-64 group (76 percent), the 65+ group (72 percent), the 25-34 group (65 percent), the 35-44 group (63 percent) and the 18-24 group (61 percent).

All right, who got the $114 billion? AAFRC calculates that religious organizations received almost half of it, some $54.3 billion. Human services got $11.4 billion; education, $10.7 billion; health, $10 billion; arts, culture and humanities, $7.5 billion; public/society benefit, $3.6 billion; and various other sectors, $17.1 billion.

These gigantic sums are reduced to human scale in a 1988 Gallup Poll which shows the percentage of households reporting contributions to various types of charities in 1987 and their average contribution:

	Percent of Americans Giving	Average Contribution
Religion	52.5	$715
Human Services	23.9	210
Health	23.9	130
Youth Development	18.5	88
Education	15.1	293
Environment	10.8	87
Arts, Culture, Humanities	8.0	260
Public & Societal Benefit	6.5	153
Foundations	4.8	145
International/Foreign	4.2	281

The great amounts given to religious institutions should not be thought of as being spent for religious purposes alone. Another Gallup Poll, commissioned by Independent Sector and published in December 1988, found that nearly half of the approximately $41 billion contributed to religion in the year studied was spent on a wide range of programs and activities in the areas of human services, health, arts, education and societal improvement.

Well over 60 percent of the congregations in the survey supported or provided services such as housing, day care, food programs, medical care, health education, help for the disabled and international assistance. Between one-quarter and one-half of the congregations supported programs in civil rights and social justice, community development, arts instruction and performance, elementary and high school education, the environment or neighborhood improvement.

As for the setting of American philanthropy, Gallup reports that charity begins at home. About 58 percent of 1989 giving was to beneficiaries in the giver's own community, 15 percent to people in the same region of the country, 11 percent elsewhere in the United States and 12 percent in foreign countries.

The most frequent recipients of charity were young children, the elderly, the poor and the homeless (with over 60 percent of givers reporting such donations), followed by the sick (54 percent), the handicapped (51 percent), young adults (49 percent) and victims of crime, abuse or disaster (40 percent).

The primary motivation for all this largesse is Americans' conviction that they are giving to good causes and worthy organizations. About 37 percent of the Gallup sample cited the "good work" of charities as the reason they contribute. Far smaller percentages give primarily because of "spiritual reasons" (10 percent), because they are asked (9 percent), because they feel obligated (8 percent) and because of a family tradition (4 percent). Only 2 percent said they give primarily because it affords them a tax deduction.

Another survey, conducted for the *NonProfit Times* by Opinion Research Corp., provides greater detail about what persuades Americans to give. A large majority of the donors in this survey (about 67 percent) told researchers they had given at church. About 23 percent had made a contribution in response to a person-to- person request, 22 percent through an automatic paycheck deduction at work and 20 percent in response to a direct mail appeal. Relatively few givers had responded to a telephone solicitation (10 percent), a television or radio appeal (7 percent) or some other kind of request (6 percent). These figures add up to more than 100 percent because some people gave in more than one way.

Though the vast majority of Americans give to charity, many have an underlying concern about organizations that solicit funds. In a survey conducted by the Roper Organization for the National Charities Information Bureau (NCIB) in 1988, 77 percent of respondents who had made contributions in the previous year agreed that it was difficult to know which charitable organizations were responsible and legitimate. Over 70 percent said that they sometimes wanted to know more about charities than the charities told them and they wished there was an outside source of information. About 30 percent— almost one-third of all givers—admitted that they have contributed without even understanding what the charitable organization did.

When American givers try to find out more about charities they are considering donating to, the NCIB survey suggests they are most likely to rely on: the news media (74 percent) and friends and relatives (50 percent). Far fewer attempt to check out a charity by contacting an independent evaluating organization (29 percent) or by asking the charity itself for more information (27 percent).

It is clear that Americans want and need more information about the charities that approach them for money. The rest of the text portion of this book seeks to answer the questions Americans are asking—or ought to be asking—about charitable giving.

THE BASICS

Why Should You Give?

Why should I give?

That's for you to decide. But to help you think about the subject, consider what motivates the charity of your fellow citizens. According to professional fund-raisers, Americans give primarily because they feel that there are people and causes that need help and that those who possess the means have a moral obligation to provide assistance.

Americans also give because it makes them feel good about themselves. Some feel personal fulfillment when they see, or imagine, a handicapped child smile or people fishing in a once-polluted stream. For others, giving relieves guilt about not doing enough for humankind and fulfills an obligation some feel they owe to their religion, their country or an organization which has benefited them.

Another motivation for Americans' charity is the desire for recognition in the community. This can range from the need to be seen putting something in the Sunday collection basket to wanting the family name on the new wing of a hospital.

Finally, some Americans give for economic reasons. Giving may provide them with tax deductions, improved cash flow or preferment for business and other opportunities.

These reasons for giving are not distinct, of course. Several or all of them may be combined in a single act of giving.

How can I decide whom to give to?

This entire book is a long answer to that question. Its premise is that Americans—for all their lofty ideals about charity—frequently give carelessly and that what is needed is more deliberation about giving.

Start by doing a little thinking right now about what kinds of institutions you would like to give to. You may want to provide some support to organizations that benefit you personally and directly, such as your church, hospital, ambulance squad, volunteer fire company, library, neighborhood organization and public radio or television station. You may want to help organizations that benefit you in a more indirect way or that benefit people like you, such as environmental groups, colleges, museums, and medical research organizations. Both these forms of giving are sometimes referred to as "giving to yourself," because they tend to support your community and your values. Therefore, you may also wish to give to causes you believe in, even though they hold little or no direct benefit for you, your neighbors, your social class or even your species. Examples are help for disadvantaged groups in the United States, aid to developing countries and support for animal welfare organizations.

There are so many worthy causes. How can I narrow down the list?

Here are a few exercises that may help you sort out your thoughts and reach some conclusions.

- What will the country and world be like when your children, grandchildren or great-grandchildren are your age? Less beautiful? More dangerous? Less prosperous? More authoritarian? Less spiritual? More barren? Less fun? Will your descendants lack something that enriched your life? What can be done today to help make their world a better place to live in?

- Suppose visitors from Italy or Nigeria or Ecuador or Japan toured your area or the entire country. What would you be most proud of? Most ashamed of? What can people do today to protect the best and improve the worst?

- If you worked for a major foundation and were in charge of giving away tens of millions of dollars a year, how would you distribute the money?

IDENTIFYING CHARITIES

How can I find charities that specialize in my favorite causes?

You have part of the answer in the palm of your hand. Start with the Directory portion of this book and look up the area of the cause you have in mind—for world hunger, see International Relief; for aid to Native Americans, see Human Services or Education; for water pollution, see The Environment. Unless your cause is an unusual one, you'll find references to at least one, and in some cases many charities.

You'll need to go beyond this book if you want to consider more charities than those we list, if your cause is more obscure and isn't included here, or if you prefer giving to state or local organizations.

All right, suppose I don't find my favorite cause in this book? Where should I go for help?

Using the *Enyclo-pedia of Associations*

Go to the reference desk of your library and ask to see the *Encyclopedia of Associations*. This publication is one of the wonders of the world of books, a compilation so massive that you may find it daunting at first. But stick with it; it's really quite easy to use.

It comes in three parts. The three-volume *Encyclopedia of Associations: National Organizations of the United States* contains 21,500 entries. The one-volume *Encyclopedia of Associations: International Organizations* describes 4,000 organizations which are international in scope and headquartered outside the United States. And the seven-volume *Encyclopedia of Associations: Regional, State, and Local Organizations* contains information about 50,000 smaller organizations, plus regional, state and local chapters of national groups.

This treasury of information can be useful in two ways. It describes thousands of charities, familiar and obscure, national and local. And it lists thousands of other organizations which do not seek donations, but which may be able to provide you with information about those that do.

So, if I'm interested in, say, promoting business opportunities for minority women and don't know any organizations in the field, the *Encyclopedia of Associations* would identify some?

You bet. Here's what you would do. The *Encyclopedia* lists organizations topically, so you can scan the pages devoted to business or minority groups. There are so many of these, however, that you'd be better off going to the index and looking under "Minority, women" or "Women, minority." Here you would find at least three likely organizations: the Alliance of Minority Women for Business and Political Development, the Coalition of Minority Women in Business, and the National Association of Minority Women in Business. The text describes the programs and publications of each. It also provides the name, address and phone number of an executive, whose office can send you information or give you advice about how you might direct contributions to the field.

The *Encyclopedia* is also extremely helpful when you don't know much about a field and want to get a general picture of the types of charities within it. If you were interested in helping the disabled, for example, and wanted to consider various approaches to their problems, the *Encyclopedia*'s index would lead you to descriptions of over 100 organizations. Organizations that seek out and report employment opportunities, campaign for improved wheelchair access or help handicapped people enter and succeed in fields such as data processing, medicine and science. Organizations that specialize in learning disabilities, deafness or problems of people who have had their larynx removed. Organizations focusing on computer technology, legal action or trained dogs to help the disabled lead more active lives. Spend an hour with the *Encyclopedia* and you may get excited about a philanthropic approach you never thought of before.

OK, but are you saying that, no matter how obscure my topic, the *Encyclopedia* will tell me names of organizations in the field?

Are your interests more obscure than these?

The Antique Stove Association
Indoor Citrus and Rare Fruit Society
American Donkey and Mule Society
Club of the Friends of Ancient Smoothing Irons

American Fancy Rat and Mouse Society
Old Mine Lamp Collectors Society of America
Willkie Political Items Collectors
International League of Esperantist Radio Amateurs

They're all described in the *Encyclopedia*. But let's take some more likely examples. Is your interest arthritis research? The book describes the Arthritis Foundation in Atlanta. Urban education reform? The Delaware-based Cities in Schools may have the information you need. Environmental issues? There's the Coolidge Center for Environmental Leadership in Massachusetts. Higher education in Oregon and Washington? Maybe the Northwest Association of Schools and Colleges can help. Handicapped children? Call the Council for Exceptional Children in Washington, DC.

And all of these organizations can give me information about charities in their fields?

No, not exactly. All the organizations in the *Encyclopedia* have a special interest in their fields, and most of those with staff can probably provide you with at least some general information. If you ask them for suggestions about whom to give money to, some may be helpful and some may not. Some, also, may be self-serving and try to convince you to make a donation to them.

You should also keep in mind that the organization you call may have biases you don't agree with and may therefore give you unsuitable advice. The organizations you locate in the *Encyclopedia of Associations* can be a valuable resource, but you can't use them uncritically.

If my library doesn't have the *Encyclopedia of Associations*, is there any other reference book that will help?

Other Sources of Information

Nothing else really measures up to the *Encyclopedia*, so try a few other libraries if you can. A new reference work, the *National Directory of Nonprofit Organizations*, may be of some use. It lists over 140,000 nonprofits, indexed by geography, income and activity. The problem is that it provides very scant information about each charity, and the index to activities is incomplete, too general and often just plain incorrect (for example, the Council on Foreign Relations and the Greater Baton Rouge Chamber of Commerce are only two of the surprising entries under "Scientific research (diseases)"). Still, the book may be helpful in steering you to some charities you might otherwise not have found out about.

A reference book you will want to avoid totally is the inelegantly titled *Cumulative List of Organizations Described in Section 170(c) of the Internal Revenue Code,* or as its friends call it, "Publication 78." True, this two-volume U.S. Government publication contains a list of almost 450,000 organizations to which contributions are deductible. But there is no index to its densely packed 1550 pages, and the book is nothing more than an interminable list of organizations with no accompanying information. The book's only virtue is that if you know the exact name of an organization, it can tell you whether contributions to it are deductible. Even then, the book contains a warning that it is not all-inclusive.

There are two other publications which can be useful, though they should be a supplement to, not a substitute for, the *Encyclopedia.* They are the fund-raisers bible, the *Foundation Directory,* which contains indexes to steer you to foundations active in the area of charity that interests you, and the more complete *National Data Book of Foundations.* If your library doesn't have copies, you may wish to contact the books' publisher, The Foundation Center, and ask for assistance (79 Fifth Avenue, New York, NY 10003—212-620-4230).

You mean that foundations can help me find charities?

Some can. Here's what you would do. Let's say that you are interested in giving to American Indians. If you look in the index of the *Foundation Directory* (the 12th edition was published in 1989) under "Native Americans," you'll find references to thirty foundations with interests in that area. The body of the directory provides addresses and telephone numbers of these foundations; names of their trustees or directors; brief financial data; short descriptions of their purposes and activities; and comments about what sorts of programs they do and do not support.

Quick review of a few of the thirty foundations will show you that most include programs for Native Americans among a wide variety of causes they support, while a few concentrate their resources in the field. If these foundations are listed as having full-time staff, you might

Locating Charities
Through Foundations

try calling them to see if they can provide information about their grants and about where your contribution might have the most effect. Of course, they're more likely to spend time with you if you're contemplating a gift of $500 or $5000 than if you want to donate $50, but don't be afraid to call.

So far, much of what you've said has related to national charities. What if I prefer to give locally?

Looking for Local Charities

The regional edition of the *Encyclopedia of Associations* and the *National Directory of Nonprofit Organizations* may be of use to you here, but your best bet is to go at once to the old, reliable Yellow Pages. You'll find charities listed under such headings as Charitable Organizations, Foundations, Health Agencies and Associations, Health Services, Human Services Organizations, and Social Service Organizations. Of course, you won't find any descriptions in the Yellow Pages, but you can find out more about the organizations by checking with a local library or simply by calling the charity and asking them to send you some literature.

Another source for information about local charities is your local United Way, which publishes booklets with descriptions of its affiliated organizations. But remember that many charities are not affiliated with United Way, so the directory will be far from complete.

A third source of information in some areas—especially in cities—is the local community foundation, an organization dedicated to funding a variety of projects in a particular geographical area. Look in the *Foundation Directory* and your local phone book to see if there is a community foundation in your area. If you don't find anything listed, there are two organizations which may be able to help you. First, contact the Foundation Center (79 Fifth Avenue, New York, NY 10003—212-620-4230); if they don't report a community foundation near you, contact the Community Foundation Services Division of the Council on Foundations (1828 L Street, NW, Suite 300, Washington, DC 20036—202-466-6512).

OK. Now I've got a list of charities that are active in the fields I'd like to support. How do I decide which ones to give to?

Give to those that satisfy your personal criteria for what a charity should be. There are many criteria you could employ. Some, such as enthusiasm for the charity's basic mission, are obvious and universal. Others may be idiosyncratic. The whole purpose of this book is to encourage you to think about the subject, select some criteria which are meaningful to you, and act on them.

Three basic criteria are:

> Does the charity work for the ends you favor?
> Does the charity use means you approve of?
> Does the charity compare favorably with other charities in the same field?

I've already got a list of charities whose ends I favor, so can we talk about means?

Ends and Means

All right, but first an important point. All you have so far is a list of charities *that seem* to pursue the goals you favor. Be careful of giving too much weight to the name or the popular reputation of a nonprofit. Some highly reputable charities have names that are unintentionally misleading. Some not so reputable ones have names which are designed to mislead (be especially wary of organizations with names devised to be confused with major cancer and other popular charities). And some, though they truly work for the goals you want to support, may devote a large share of their funds to other causes you don't feel so strongly about or perhaps even dislike.

Now, let's talk about the means charities use to pursue their goals. Even if you love a charity's ends, you may not like its means. You may prefer some ways of approaching the problem to others, because you feel they are more likely to produce a solution or, in some cases, for ethical reasons. Let's say that you have decided you would like to contribute to an organization engaged in alleviating the problems arising from adolescent motherhood. You have done a little research and have a list of charities active in the field. How should you decide which ones to give to?

Consideration of means may shorten your list considerably. Charity A provides health services to babies born to young girls. Charity B counsels pregnant teenagers and makes sure they know that abortion is one of their options. Charity C concentrates on sexuality education in the public schools. Charity D campaigns for teenage chastity. Charity E distributes condoms to urban youth. Charity F supports research about health care for pregnant teens. Charity G counsels expectant teenagers against abortion.

I get the point. Obviously, I want to give money only to organizations that approach the problem in ways I approve and I think will be effective. Now, what about your third criterion, that the charity "compare favorably" with others?

Deciding how charities compare is where consumer skills come into play. You should try to determine which of the competing charities gives you the most for your investment, the most benefit for your buck. Some points you may want to consider:

- Which charity devotes the greatest percentage of its overall expenses to the ends and means you favor? Each of your potential recipients probably disburses its funds to several programs. If one devotes 20 percent of program expenditures to your pet cause and another allocates 45 percent, it is clear which charity is the "better buy."

- Which charity has the lowest percentage of "management and general" expenses or, conversely, the highest percentage of expenditures for its programs? While there may be perfectly good reasons for costs to differ, and while some charities manipulate figures to make themselves look better, the wise giver's choice will be influenced by which charity devotes the greatest share of its money to the purpose of the organization.

- Which charity has the lowest fund-raising costs? Think of it this way: some percentage of your donation to a charity merely pays the costs of getting the donation from you and thousands or millions of people like you. This is clear

Comparing Charities' Performance

when you help a charity by attending a dinner-dance, buying a chance on an expensive car or purchasing its T-shirts. But the same is true, though probably to a lesser degree, in virtually every charitable donation you make—the costs of the telethon, of the mass mailing, of organizing the canvassers. Again, be aware that some charities will play with the numbers to lower their fund-raising costs.

- Which charity has the best record of accomplishments in the area that interests you most? This may be difficult to compare, because it's not quantifiable; however, it might be the most important comparison you can make.

Who's got the time to do all this comparison shopping among charities?

If it's major national charities you're interested in, you'll be happy to know that the work has already been done for you. There are at least three organizations in America that have established their own criteria and that evaluate charities on a regular basis. Two, the National Charities Information Bureau (NCIB) and the Philanthropic Advisory Service of the Council of Better Business Bureaus (CBBB), have a mainstream perspective. The third, quite different, is a small organization called The Other Side, which rates charities from a Christian social-activist perspective.

Well, what criteria do these groups use?

To start with NCIB, the full text of its "Standards in Philanthropy" are reproduced in Appendix A. In brief, the organization believes that:

1. A charity's governing board should be an active, independent, volunteer body of at least five members who meet in-person at least twice a year to review the organization's policies, programs and operations. There should be no material conflicts of interest involving the board or the staff.
2. The charity's purpose, as approved by the board, should be formally and specifically stated.

NCIB Standards for
Evaluating Charities

3. The charity's activities should be consistent with its statement of purpose.
4. The charity should accurately describe its identity, purpose, programs and financial needs in its promotional material, fund-raising activities and public information.
5. Fund-raising practices should encourage voluntary giving and avoid intimidation; the charity should disclose, upon request, descriptive and financial information relating to its income and its revenue-generating activities; and the charity should make information available concerning any commercial activities conducted on its behalf.
6. At least 60 percent of the organization's annual expenses should be devoted to programs, as opposed to management/general and fund-raising expenses; and the charity's reserve funds generally should not exceed two times its annual expenditures.
7. Upon request, the organization should provide an annual report, including a narrative description of major activities, a list of board members and a comprehensive financial summary.
8. Complete financial statements should be prepared in conformance with generally accepted accounting principles.
9. The charity should prepare an annual budget consistent with the major classifications of its audited financial statements.

NCIB allows some flexibility in applying its standards to organizations less than three years old and to those with annual budgets of less than $100,000. Still, it maintains that the "spirit" of the standards is useful for all nonprofits.

Are the criteria of the other two organizations much different from NCIB's?

CBBB's standards (for the complete text, see Appendix B) are similar, although they are more specific regarding fund-raising solicitations. One significant difference has to do with a charity's allocation of funds. Whereas NCIB ties its standards to expenditures, CBBB focuses on income, holding that program activities should receive

Other Standards for Evaluating Charities

at least 50 percent of income. Thus, for charities that spend virtually all of what they collect, NCIB imposes stricter limitations on expenditures. With regard to fund-raising costs, however, CBBB's view, that they should not exceed 35 percent of related contributions, is more restrictive than NCIB's Standard 6.

The Other Side, with a constituency and a mission quite different from that of NCIB and CBBB, has distinctly different standards. The Other Side expects charities to be forthcoming with information; to spend no more than 25 percent of their cash income on fund-raising; to keep less than 30 days' cash and investments in reserve; to limit staff salaries, with top salaries under $15,000 as ideal; and to hire and promote women, people of color, gays, lesbians and people who share the commitments of the organization.

Everybody's criteria seem to stress the percent spent on fund-raising, but isn't that a questionable measure in some instances? For example, don't new organizations always have higher fund-raising costs?

Yes, new charities—and "unfashionable" or controversial causes—usually need to spend more to raise funds than better-known organizations, and they are far less likely to attract corporate grants or extensive volunteer help. Therefore, their management and fund-raising percentages are going to be higher than those of established, mainstream charities. Nonprofits will also show higher costs when they start a new kind of fund-raising, such as direct mail or telephone solicitation. An initial direct mail campaign is often called "donor prospecting" by professionals, because it covers many addressees in hopes of discovering the small percentage who will donate to the cause. That costs a lot of money, often more than the campaign brings in. Subsequent mailings are cheaper because they can concentrate on a selective audience of previous givers. Evaluating organizations, such as NCIB, take such factors into account when reporting fund-raising costs of new or changing charities.

Another reason why fund-raising percentages can be questionable as a criterion is the creative accounting that some charities use to make the percentages look lower than they really are. We'll talk more about this later.

Evaluating Fund-
Raising Costs

EVALUATING CHARITIES

Sources of Information

OK. I've formulated some criteria about charities. And I see that this book's Directory of Charitable Organizations answers a lot of my questions. But how can I get more information about the charities that interest me most?

The entries in this book's Directory are all drawn from the files of the National Charities Information Bureau, but not all the information could be included. If you would like additional information about any charity discussed here, write to NCIB at 19 Union Square West, New York, NY 10003-3395 or telephone them at 212-929-6300.

Founded in 1918, NCIB's purpose is to help "charities improve their performance and [inform] contributors about wise giving." The organization prepares and updates reports concerning 300 or so national philanthropic organizations that solicit contributions from the general public. It also publishes the periodical *Wise Giving Guide*, which lists all the charities the organization screens and reports their compliance, or lack of compliance, with NCIB's standards. At no charge, NCIB will send you the *Wise Giving Guide* and reports on three charities at a time.

And what if I want information about a national charity that's not listed in this book?

NCIB and CBBB

NCIB has files on some smaller charities that are not included in this book, so it may still be worthwhile to contact them. Another valuable resource is the Philanthropic Advisory Service of the Council of Better Business Bureaus, Inc. (CBBB), Dept. 024, Washington, DC 20042-0024—703-276-0100. CBBB "promotes ethical standards of business practices and protects consumers through voluntary self-regulation and monitoring activities." Its Philanthropic Advisory Service (PAS) seeks to educate donors "who are becoming increasingly aware that choosing which charities to support is an important 'buying' decision."

CBBB collects information on thousands of national nonprofits about which it has received inquiries, including more religious organizations than NCIB. Like NCIB,

CBBB publishes reports about leading national charities, including information about the organization's background, current programs, governing body, fund-raising practices, tax deductibility of contributions, finances and compliance with CBBB standards. You can get up to three free reports by writing to CBBB (enclose a self-addressed envelope and two first-class stamps). Or, for $2.00 and a self-addressed envelope, you can get the most recent issue of CBBB's periodical, *Give But Give Wisely,* which lists hundreds of prominent organizations and indicates whether they meet CBBB's standards.

What about The Other Side? I'd like to look at some of its reports too.

The Other Side, based in Philadelphia, publishes all its evaluations in its magazine of the same name. *The Other Side* describes itself, rather beguilingly, as "an independent, nonprofit, ecumenical magazine for Christians who take seriously the upside-down ways of Jesus." It seeks to stimulate commitment to "peace, justice, and Christian discipleship" and professes particular concern for "those who live on 'the other side' of the world's power and influence," including "struggling sisters and brothers in some of the poorest, most oppressed parts of the world."

It is from this perspective that *The Other Side* periodically evaluates about 125 charities. Not surprisingly, its comments are far more opinionated and provocative than those of the NCIB and CBBB. If you agree with *The Other Side*'s biases, you'll relish every page; even if you don't, you may find it fascinating reading.

To give you a flavor for its evaluations, here are a few excerpts, with the names omitted:

"Unfortunately, its support for oppressed peoples who are responding to violence with violence occasionally calls into question the depth of its own nonviolent commitment."

"Refused to reveal how high its salaries go. We find this snubbing of public openness rather bizarre."

"Money contributed to or through [A] probably goes farther than it does anywhere else."

"And the fact that most of its money and relief goods come via the U.S. government concerns us as well. Government aid is designed to advance U.S. interests, not the interests of the people being helped. [B] is often seen abroad as an informal arm of the U.S. government, which tends to undermine its credibility."

Such hunches and opinions may trouble you, but if you are serious about evaluating charities, and certainly if you share *The Other Side*'s viewpoint, you may want to consider what the magazine has to say and seek a response from the nonprofits it assails. You can contact the organization by writing to 300 West Apsley Street, Philadelphia, PA 19144, or telephoning 215-849-2178.

What about asking the charities themselves for information?

It may be a lot more biased than what you'd get from one of the evaluating organizations, but the information can be valuable. Ask for an annual report and recent financial statements. Stress your interest in the group's accomplishments in the last three or four years. If you have questions about what they send you, call again and ask for explanations.

Do government agencies have information about charities?

Information from
Government Agencies

Yes, some state governments have rich—and often underutilized—collections of information about charities in the office which registers or regulates nonprofits (see Appendix C for the office in your state). In most states, certain classes of charity must register and provide information about their activities. In every state, the data collected is public information and is available for your inspection.

Just what information you will find depends upon the state. Some collect data about finances, programs and boards of directors; fund-raisers and how much they are paid; pending or completed investigations and court actions; and complaints which have been filed against the organization. State offices are also often the best source for copies of IRS Form 990 (discussed below), a treasure trove of information about charities.

To give you an idea of the scale of operations of some of these offices, one large eastern state has extensive information, including Form 990s, on 3300 registered charities and at least some materials on 5500 additional nonprofits. New York State has a Charities Registration Office staff of 11, receives 500 phone calls a week and sends out 25,000 copies of charities' financial reports each year to givers both in and outside New York. New York maintains this remarkable volume largely because the state requires registered charities to notify potential donors that reports are available from the charity or from the New York state office.

What's so great about this Form 990?

It allows you to do your own evaluation of a charity. Form 990, "Return of Organization Exempt from Income Tax," is a definitive resource for those who want information about charitable and other nonprofit organizations, even the local organizations that can't or won't provide any background about their operations. Since 1982, virtually every such organization (religious groups and those with revenues under $25,000 are notable exceptions) has been required to file a Form 990 with the Internal Revenue Service, and this is also required by many states, sometimes with extensive supplements which provide additional information.

While the information on Form 990s varies in quality, many are rich in information about the groups you are considering. They will tell you:

- an organization's main sources of income
- how much revenue it derives from contributions, government grants, government contracts and services
- how much it spends in the program, fund-raising and management/general categories
- what it pays its top executives and consultants
- what its principal programs are
- whether its income exceeds its expenses
- how much volunteer help it receives

If your state is one of those that require charitable organizations to file supplements to Form 990, you may have much additional information at your command. New York State's supplements, for example, will inform you about:

- the amount of income the charity derives from each of its means of fund-raising: direct mail, telephone and door-to-door solicitations, special events, grants and so on

- the specific government agencies from which the organization receives its largest grants
- fund-raising operations, including the expenses and net proceeds for each fund-raising event and the amount of fees paid to professional fund-raisers
- the charity's practice of soliciting and selling used clothing, furniture, equipment, cars and other items

By requesting Form 990s for the past several years, you will also be able to draw conclusions about trends in the charity's financial data.

And if you want to compare several charities, it's far easier to do so using Form 990s than with annual reports or financial statements, because the tax form reports all data in the same format and on the same page.

Aren't Form 990s hard to interpret?

Not really. And if you need help, the National Charities Information Bureau publishes two valuable booklets to help you analyze them. They are *The 1, 2, 3 of Evaluation: An Introduction to Three Basic Tools* and *A Grantmaker's Guide to a New Tool for Philanthropy—Form 990.*

Where can I get a copy of an organization's Form 990?

How to Get
Form 990s

Nonprofits are required to make a copy available at their principal office, but this is only useful if you happen to live nearby. Some nonprofits have copies available in branch offices or will mail you one, perhaps charging you for duplication costs. If the charity can't or won't help you, contact your state office of charity regulation (see Appendix C) and ask if they have a form for the charity you have in mind. If they do, you can either go to the office and peruse the form or request a copy by mail. For the quickest service, call your state office and establish not only whether they have the forms you want, but what it will cost to have them duplicated and sent to you. When you send a check for the required amount, you should get the 990s you want within a few weeks.

If your state doesn't have Form 990s for the charities

that interest you, consider calling the regulatory office in a nearby state, especially if it is a populous one where charities are likely to be especially active. People in the charity regulation business say that California, Connecticut, Illinois, Massachusetts, Minnesota, New Jersey, New York, Oregon, Pennsylvania and Virginia have especially good collections of data, but others may also prove useful for your purposes.

If you try these avenues without success, the IRS can provide you with the forms you want, but it will take a month or two. Write the Internal Revenue Service Center that covers the region where the charity has its headquarters (to find out which office it is and its address, call your nearest IRS office). Make sure you use the precise name of the charity, because the IRS may have returns from many other groups with similar names. The IRS will inform you about duplicating costs and, when you send the appropriate amount, will mail you the form; for information, call 800-424-1040.

Is it much more difficult to evaluate local charities?

It's somewhat harder. NCIB and CBBB won't be able to assist you, but some of the 175 Better Business Bureaus and branches around the country may have the information you need. The individual bureaus and branches differ widely in this respect, but some have extensive information about local organizations. Even if your local Bureau isn't among them, it's still worth a call, because it is a likely source of information about any complaints that may have been received.

Residents of Minnesota have their own rich resource of information about national, state and local charities in the Charities Review Council. Founded over forty years ago, the Council collects information on over 2300 charities, evaluating them against such standards as a requirement that they spend at least 70 percent of revenues on programs. Minnesotans can get information over the phone (800-733-4484; or in Minneapolis-St. Paul, 870-0657) or request a listing of the status of the most active charities in the state.

If you can't get information from an outside source and your Better Business Bureau can't help, try getting it from the local charity itself. It may not be easy. Local charities are often shorthanded. They may not answer

Evaluating
Local Charities

your calls or letters and, when they do, may claim that they can't provide the information you request.

But remember, if they want a donation, you're the person in charge. You now know what to ask for. Tell the charity solicitor or employee that you won't give until you know fund-raising costs, amounts spent on the program you're interested in, the chief executive's salary and, above all, evidence of accomplishments. You won't always get the information you want, but they won't get your money either and your message will get across. When the charity encounters about twenty people like you, they'll start being more informative.

Your ace in the hole is the charity's Form 990 and other information that may be available at your state office of charity regulation. The charity's solicitor wants a donation for the annual circus benefit and says he just doesn't have time to get you figures about how much of the income actually goes to cancer victims? The Form 990 will show you that last year's benefit grossed $130,000, but had expenses of $121,000; state reports reveal that $28,000 of the expense was for the professional fund-raiser's fee. So you know that of every dollar contributed last year, less than seven cents went to cancer patients. *Now* decide whether you want to contribute to this or to some other organization.

You said a while back that religious organizations don't have to file a Form 990. Doesn't that make them hard to evaluate?

Evaluating Religious Organizations

Hard, but far from impossible. The Philanthropic Advisory Service of the Council of Better Business Bureaus can provide you with information about some religious organizations. And several groups of religious charities have organized to regulate themselves. Over 600 evangelical colleges, camps, and radio and television ministries have become members of the Evangelical Council of Financial Accountability, which requires adherence to strict standards and issues lists of the organizations that measure up. You can get a free copy of the latest list by calling 800-323-9473 or writing to P.O. Box 17456, Washington, DC 20041. Catholic charities belonging to the National Catholic Development Conference (NCDC) subscribe to its "Precepts of Stewardship" and the National Council of Catholic Bishops' "Principles and Guidelines for Fund Raising." NCDC does not publish a list of its members, but it would be a good idea to ask individual charities if they belong.

I just don't have time to evaluate charities. Aren't there ways to get around it?

Consulting this book or asking NCIB or CBBB for help takes very little time, but evaluating less renowned charities can be a problem. There are ways to avoid it, but they all have drawbacks. You can let someone else do your evaluating for you—by giving to an organization that gives to others—but you'll lose the privilege of directing money exactly where you want it to go. If you have substantial sums to donate, you can hire someone to advise you about suitable charities, but that will cost you some money.

Evaluation
Short Cuts

If you choose the former course, you can give money to a federated charity campaign which evaluates charities and makes priority decisions among them. Federated campaigns are not charities, but collection and allocation agencies organized to support charities linked to a core concern. Some familiar examples are United Way, United Jewish Appeal, Catholic Charities and United Negro College Fund; there are many others, some of which emphasize the environment, women's issues, health agencies and so forth. Keep in mind that every federated campaign, including United Way, specializes in certain types of charity, so make sure that the one you're giving to includes your favorite causes.

Another way to shift the evaluation process to others is to give money to a community foundation or a general foundation that is active in your region or area of interest. Use the *Foundation Directory* or the *National Data Book of Foundations* to identify appropriate foundations or, for community foundations, the Yellow Pages.

If your resources are sufficient to hire an advisor, make sure he or she is unattached to any particular charity and free to give you unbiased guidance. There is no clearinghouse for such advisors, but you may be able to get some names by talking to foundation or community foundation managers, financial advisors, attorneys or wealthy individuals in your community.

Those wealthy enough to hire an advisor may also be able to learn about worthy charities by conferring with other major givers. These givers may belong to an "affinity group," an organization of foundation and corporate managers interested in particular topics, such as arts, AIDS, the environment or voting rights. Or they may meet as a regional association of givers, like the Donors Forum of Chicago or the Northern California Grantmakers. The Council on Foundations (202-466-6512) can provide you with names, addresses and phone numbers of such groups.

GIVING MONEY

How Much to Give

What target should I set for how much money I give to charity each year?

Give whatever you think you can afford. If you're interested in comparisons, the average American giver has donated a little under 2 percent of his or her household income to charity over the past few decades, about $790 per household in 1987. On the other hand, there are people—including many devout Mormons and fundamentalists—who subscribe to the Old Testament standard of tithing, or giving away one-tenth of their income. Independent Sector, a coalition of nonprofit and corporate organizations, encourages giving 5 percent of your income, plus 5 hours of volunteer work per week. It's a reasonable target, but if you're going to increase your charitable giving, you owe it to yourself, and to the causes you believe in, to do your homework and give wisely.

When to Give

Is there a best time in the year to give?

From whose standpoint? The best time, from the charity's point of view, is early as possible, so the organization can benefit from the use of your money for the maximum time. From your point of view, the best time is probably late in the year, after you've had a chance to look over all the holiday appeals and to project the effect of giving on your income tax liability. In practice, the biggest months for donations are November and December.

Budgeting Your Giving

Do most people budget their charity?

Gallup Poll data suggest that only about 15 percent of Americans budget their charitable giving, and most of them do so only part of the time. But it's a good idea.

Without a budget, people with a generous nature may give away much more than they intend or can afford, and they may give it to the most demanding rather than the most worthy organizations. Some people who budget their giving keep half of it in reserve until the last few months of the year, when they receive the bulk of their charity solicitations. Others, who never respond to solicitations, give regularly to organizations they have evaluated and believe in. Even for these givers, it makes sense to delay some giving in case world or personal conditions give rise to new charitable urges as the year progresses.

Appendix E contains a contributions budgeting form, which you can duplicate for use each year, a sample budgeting form, and more information about the budgeting process. The budgeting form will help you review the various types of organizations you might want to give to and, if you stick with it, prove useful for income tax planning and filing.

How many charities should I give to? And is it OK to give in installments?

There's no right answer about the number of charities. In a recent survey, the average American reported giving to 3.2 organizations a year, but that shouldn't affect your giving. Just be aware that the more you give to, the less you give to each and the less impact you're having on any of them. Sending small amounts to many charities is also a little less efficient; the aggregate time that twenty charities spend processing and responding to your $30 gifts will be much greater than if you had mailed only six $100 checks. And let's not forget the time you spend on choosing, deciding amounts and writing checks. If you would like to donate to a wide range of organizations, you can save some of your and their time by giving them twice as much but half as often. In other words, if you want to give to twenty charities, give twice your normal amount to ten this year and again to another ten next year.

Installment giving? You raise the same problem of inefficiency if you send four small installments to your favorite charity rather than one payment. On the other hand, the charity will have the use of some of your money

How Many Charities to Give To

Installment Giving

earlier and will probably prefer installments to getting one check in December.

Which is better, to give to a national headquarters of a charity or to its local affiliate?

National Head-quarters and Local Chapters

No one can answer that question but you. And you should answer it only after you ask some other questions. What does the national office do with its donations? How much does it give to the affiliates? What kinds of financial and program information does the affiliate provide about its activities? And, given all this information, how and where do you want your money to be spent? The entries in this book will help answer these questions about major national charities; for others, contact CBBB, local Better Business Bureaus, state charity regulation offices or the organizations themselves.

I'd like to give $500 to the Fine Arts Department at my alma mater, but wouldn't I help out the school more by giving to their general fund?

Restricting Your Gifts

The cliché is that every institution wants unrestricted gifts to spend as it sees fit. That makes sense from the immediate economic point of view, but it may not be in the long-range interest of the organization, and many fund-raisers are aware of this. What they want is to engage your interest and your loyalty. So, start with a call to the alumni or development office. Tell the staff about your interest in fine arts and ask what their priorities are in the area. They may propose a use for your donation that will give you a feeling of real ownership. If so, it may not be long before you call them again.

The same goes for any charity. If you'd like to support a single program, rather than the organization at large, indicate your restriction on your check and in an accompanying note. To be most helpful, call first and discuss your intention and your interests with the appropriate staff members.

Is it possible—and is it ethical—to use a donation to encourage a charity to do something or not do something?

Using Donations as Leverage

It's certainly possible. If you place an order for $15,000 worth of, say, books, you can get special treatment unavailable to more typical $15 buyers. Similarly, if your potential contribution is large enough relative to its intended beneficiary, you can enter a whole new realm of charity, bargaining to encourage the kind of program you want. Is this ethical? Sure, so long as you make your offer openly and are willing to discuss pros and cons with the charity's management. The charity can accept your offer, decline it or persuade you to alter it. Where's the harm?

Here's how you might proceed. Let's say you would like to give $25,000 to help handicapped children learn job skills. You believe the students in a nearby school for the handicapped could be trained as data entry clerks, but the school's only computer is in the administrative office. Talk to the school administrators about the possibility of dedicating a classroom to data entry skills if you furnish computers and curricular materials. Now, maybe the educators can show you that your idea is unsound, but you owe yourself a try at getting what you want.

I want to give money anonymously. How can I do that?

It should be sufficient to request the charity to keep your contribution confidential. If you're giving money and don't want even the charity to know where it's coming from, have your bank send a cashier's check. Alternatively, you could ask a friend to write a check, or send cash by registered mail (with no return receipt requested, of course).

Giving Anonymously

I've heard that United Way has some challengers and the battle between them gets pretty tough at times. What's going on?

United Way has a long and distinguished history of collecting money for charities. The key to its success is its use of legions of volunteers to lower fund-raising costs. In 1989, the 2300 local United Ways collected $2.98 billion for over 40,000 health and human services agencies, with only about 10 percent going for fund-raising and administrative expenses. Data on sources of contributions in 1989 are not yet available, but 1988 figures show that, of the total for that year, 63.8 percent was donated by individual employees, 23.4 percent by corporations, 2.7 percent by small businesses, 2.6 percent by professionals, 1.4 percent by foundations and 6.1 percent by other contributors.

United Way has its detractors, however, who claim

Giving to United Way and Alternative Funds

that it is too conservative, too tied to corporations and too restrictive in the charities it supports. Its most vocal opponent is the National Committee for Responsive Philanthropy (NCRP), an advocacy group representing the interests of 100 alternative funds, many of which would like to break United Way's near monopoly on employee giving in most of the nation's workplaces. "Progressive charities have organized alternative funds to raise workplace charitable contributions," says NCRP's Executive Director Robert O. Bothwell, "because United Ways have locked them out. Few social action groups, few women's organizations, and *no* consumer, environmental, or peace groups are funded by United Ways." Other critics point out that United Way also excludes charities aimed at aiding people or institutions in foreign countries.

Some of the 100 alternative funds are traditional organizations such as the International Service Agencies, National Voluntary Health Agencies, combined health appeal drives and united arts funds. Non-traditional alternative funds, which NCRP refers to as "progressive," include three national funds—the Environmental Federation of America, National/United Service Agencies and the United Negro College Fund—and about fifty state and local funds representing social action, minority, environmental and women's organizations. NCRP estimates that these alternative funds will raise $105 million in 1989.

The primary battle between United Way and the alternative funds is being waged in workplaces, where the alternative funds seek equal access to employees in annual charity campaigns. The alternative groups have already won access to the mammoth Combined Federal Campaign, for U.S. Government employees, and to many state and local government workers. They have made less headway, however, in corporate charity drives.

United Way has acknowledged its challengers by promoting more donor choice. Some local United Ways already conduct campaigns that allow employees to contribute to United Way, to a group of charities in a particular field, such as health care, or to individual health or human service charities. United Way of America President William Aramony has saluted this model and proclaimed that, "We can no longer control the process the way we have done. . . . We've got to change."

Critics maintain, however, that even where United Way offers choices, it discourages employees from exercising them. They claim that if all charities were given equal access to workplace giving, the result would resemble the Combined Federal Campaign, in which only about 40 percent of all donations go to United Way.

What should you do when your boss puts pressure on you to give at work?

The standards of the U.S. Government's Combined Federal Campaign are suitable for employers everywhere. They forbid solicitations by direct supervisors; setting 100% participation goals; using contributor lists for any other purpose but routine collection and transmittal of money and pledges; establishing personal dollar or percentage goals and quotas; and developing and using lists of non-contributors.

If your employer engages in any of these practices, complain if you dare. If you think that might risk your job or chance for advancement, but still feel you have an obligation to challenge these activities, write to the organization for which the money is being raised—anonymously, if you feel you must—and describe what is happening. Charity officials know that unwilling givers donate little and are often turned off to giving in general. Chances are they'll ask your boss to relax the pressure for the long-range good of the cause.

I have a friend whose company makes matching donations to the charities she gives to. Do many companies do that?

Over 1000 do, and you may be working for one of them yourself. Contact your Personnel Office to find out. And don't assume that your employer is too small for such a program. Many of the 1000 are large corporations, but others have as few as four employees.

If your company has such a program, you have an especially effective way to make contributions. That's because your employer will double and in some cases even triple the size of your gift by matching it with company dollars. Some companies also match gifts of employees' spouses.

If my company doesn't have a matching gift program, how would I go about persuading management to start one?

Expert assistance is only a phone call away. The Council for Advancement and Support of Education (CASE) operates the National Clearinghouse for Corporate Matching Gift Information. If you call them at 202-328-5900, they will send you pamphlets you can use as you try to persuade your bosses that what makes sense for many of America's leading companies also makes sense for theirs. National Clearinghouse personnel are also available to discuss the issue with your company's managers.

Will companies match gifts to any charity I give to?

Only about 85 companies match gifts to virtually all nonprofits. The rest match only to certain types of charity. The most common beneficiaries of matching gift programs are educational institutions, especially colleges and universities. Others are museums, libraries, performing arts groups and public radio and television stations. Relatively few companies (in the area of 12 percent) match gifts to civic, social service or environmental organizations. Thus, you might find yourself with the uncomfortable choice of giving an unmatched gift to a cause you're really concerned about or a more valuable matched gift to charities that don't excite you.

Companies decide on their matching gift policies in different ways. In small firms, policies may merely reflect the personal interests of top executives; in most firms, however, committees carefully weigh the philosophy of the corporation and the needs of the community. Whatever the approach in your company, scrutinize its policy and see if it matches gifts to the organizations your charitable instincts and consumerist standards tell you to support.

Changing Corporate Policies

And if my company doesn't match gifts to my favorite charities, I guess you'd counsel trying to change the policy on that score, too?

Sure. Companies do make changes in the types of charity they support. CASE reports a tendency in recent years for more companies to match gifts to secondary education and cultural institutions. And even without employee pressure, some companies have decided that matching gifts only to colleges tends to exclude blue-collar workers. So, if your company's program is too restrictive for your tastes, make your case to management.

Here's an example of what you might do. Suppose your favorite cause is urban public education. Your corporation, like most, matches gifts to colleges and universities, but not to public secondary schools. Find out who makes the decisions in your company and write that person or committee a memo explaining why you feel it is important to encourage employee support of public secondary education. You might want to include statistics from CASE showing which companies are matching such gifts. Ask for a meeting with the responsible person or committee and try to convince some fellow workers to join you. Call the administrative offices of nearby school districts and seek help in preparing your case. Of course, you may not get what you want, but imagine the effect if you do. The addition of your favorite type of organization to the eligible recipients of a company with several hundred or several thousand employees could be an enormous boost to the cause you are trying to help.

I'd like to find out which companies in my area have matching gift programs. Do I have to call all their personnel offices?

No, there's a book that will tell you virtually everything you need to know on the subject. It is the annual *Matching Gift Details*, published by CASE and available at many libraries. If you wanted to know the policies of the Boeing Company, for example, you would discover that Boeing's Corporate Educational Gift Matching Program was established in 1978 and that the company matches gifts of all employees with over twelve months of continuous employment, plus those of retired employees and spouses of employees. *Matching Gift Details* would also tell you that beneficiaries eligible to receive Boeing's matching funds are all the accredited public and private educational institutions in the United States, from elementary schools to graduate and professional schools; art, historical and science museums; performing arts groups; libraries; and public radio and television stations. Boeing will match gifts of as little as

$25 and as much as $1000 per employee per institution per year, but will not give any institution more than $10,000 or all institutions combined more than $700,000 per year. *Matching Gift Details* also describes procedures for securing your company's gift and provides the name, address and telephone number of the person responsible.

How much money do all these matching gift programs provide to various charities?

For 1988-89, the Council for Aid to Education estimates that companies provided matching gifts of over $228 million, $172 million of it to colleges and universities. The total amount received by the charities, of course, was approximately double that amount.

This is a huge sum, but the potential of matching gifts is far greater. The amazing thing about these programs is how few employees take advantage of them, only about 10 percent of those eligible. There are several possible explanations. Employees may not know about the existence or extent of their companies' programs. They may not want to make donations to the eligible charities. They may erroneously believe that securing a matching gift is a time-consuming or complicated process. Or they may have simply never reflected on what their participation could mean to worthy charities. You could do a lot for a number of worthy causes by becoming your company's official or unofficial champion of matching gift donations.

I hear a lot about "planned giving," but I don't really know what it means.

Planned Giving

Planned giving, sometimes called "deferred giving," refers to the many ways of giving beyond simple donations of cash, including bequests, life income gifts, life insurance and pooled income funds. These gifts are "planned" because they follow thorough examination of the giver's assets and needs and seek maximum advantage to both the giver and the charity. If you study the subject, you may be amazed at the many advantages that can spring from your planned giving.

I've always planned to leave money to charity in my will. What advice do you have on bequests?

There are several ways to give to charitable organizations in your will. You can bequeath a specific amount of money, a percentage of your estate, a particular piece of real property, or all or part of the residue (the amount remaining after distribution of your specific bequests and payment of debts).

But before you start drafting a new will, consider some of the drawbacks of giving by bequest. It's not very advantageous from the charity's point of view. Even when you tell the organization's staff about your intention—and you should always do so—they won't be able to count on it, because wills are revocable. So a bequest means less to a charity than other forms of giving that make irrevocable commitments. Even if you don't revoke your bequest, its benefits may be diluted after your death by administrative and probate costs and by the lengthy delays which sometimes accompany the probate process. You may also be troubled by the public nature of a bequest. Probated wills are public information, so you may give posthumous offense to family members who feel that your money should have been placed in their hands. If you'd rather not let the world know about your gift, put it in a trust document rather than in your will.

On the other hand, the revocability of wills is an advantage if you don't feel you can commit to a large donation during your lifetime. And they provide an unlimited estate tax deduction, which can put your estate in a lower tax bracket. If charitable bequests reduce your taxable estate (including insurance proceeds) below $650,000, your estate will not be subjected to federal estate taxes at all.

I've heard about ways you can give to charity and still keep getting income from the gift. Does that work only for the rich?

No indeed. You're talking about life income agreements, which truly allow you to give away your cake and eat it too. Life income agreements combine the benefits of a gift with those of a bequest; they take many forms, but generally provide an income tax deduction and security during your lifetime, while providing an eventual benefit to your favorite charity.

One way to do this is with a gift annuity, which is partly a charitable gift and partly a purchase of an annuity that will pay you an income for as long as you live. To establish a gift annuity, you contract with a charity to give it money now, in return for a fixed income for life, a portion of which will be tax-free. A variation is the deferred gift annuity, which delays the income payments for some period of time, for example until you retire. It has many of the virtues of an Individual Retirement Account (IRA) or a Keogh Plan and, in some cases, fewer restrictions.

Another form of life income agreement is the charitable remainder trust, in which you transfer assets to a trust established to provide you with income as long as you and other designated beneficiaries live. When all beneficiaries are dead, the trust "remainder" goes to a designated charity. These trusts allow you to take an immediate tax deduction based on the value of the donation, the age of the beneficiaries and the amount of the payout.

There are three other forms of life income agreement. With an annuity trust, you transfer assets to a trustee, probably the charity itself, and receive annual payments of a fixed percentage of the initial fair market value as long as you live. A charitable remainder unitrust offers you a flexible annual income, since payments are based on a fixed percentage of the changing market value of the property. A pooled income fund may be attractive to you if you like the idea of remainder trusts, but have limited resources. Property you transfer to the charity becomes part of its pooled fund, which pays you a pro-rated share of its earnings while you live; at your death, your portion of the principal becomes property of the charity. Because charitable remainder trusts don't provide for your heirs, you may wish to use some of your tax savings to make them beneficiaries of life insurance in the amount of the principal. When you die and the trust becomes property of the charity, the insurance benefits will replace the assets as a source of wealth for them. This could give you a great advantage over leaving them the same amount of money, since the insurance payment is not subject to estate tax.

So a charitable remainder trust can be used for retirement planning purposes?

Yes. Here's how it might work. Suppose you're approaching retirement and you're thinking about selling stock you have owned for thirty years and investing the proceeds for income. The trouble is that your capital gain is so great that you're going to lose a good chunk of the sales price in taxes. Strange to say, if you gave your stock away, you might be able to do much better.

In conjunction with a planned-giving officer at a major charity, you establish a charitable remainder trust and donate your stock to it. You take a tax deduction for the charitable gift and apply it to your high pre-retirement income. The trust sells your stock, without incurring any capital gains tax liability, and invests the proceeds in high-yielding instruments. Your income will be greater than if you had sold the stock yourself. Before entering into any such transaction, however, make sure you check what the effect will be on your alternative minimum tax liability.

If you're concerned about a relative who would have received the proceeds from the sale of your stock when you died, use some of the money you saved in taxes to buy an insurance policy for the same amount as the sales price. When you die, both the charity and your relative will receive the value of the stock.

I've also read about trusts that give the income to the charity. What good does that do the giver?

You're probably talking about charitable lead trusts. You would only consider creating one if you were financially secure and didn't need the income from a portion of your assets. You would place the assets in a trust that would provide income to the charity either for a set number of years or for your lifetime. Upon your death, the trust would distribute the assets to beneficiaries you have named. And what about the charity that now has lost the income from your money? In all likelihood, it has bought a life insurance policy on you for the amount of the assets in trust. When you die, the charity will use the insurance money to replace your trust as a source of income. The particular benefit here is that you can transfer assets to your beneficiaries outside of your estate and therefore outside the reach of estate taxes.

Aren't there charities that let you set up small foundations within their structure?

Yes, they're called supporting foundations. Setting up your own independent, private foundation can involve a lot of fees, record-keeping and reporting. Establishing a supporting foundation in conjunction with a qualified charity is far less burdensome and can start with relatively small sums. Ask your favorite charity or your community foundation about minimum amounts and procedures. If you form such a relationship, you or your designee will sit on the board of your "advised fund," as it is called, and participate in, but not control, decisions about how funds are invested and proceeds are allocated.

A similar arrangement, known as a "pooled common fund," may require a larger initial donation, but has more of the feel of a real foundation. Here, though your money is pooled with other people's funds for investment purposes, you alone choose the recipients of grants which are issued in your name. The charity that helps you establish one of these "mini-foundations" will probably insist on receiving a certain percentage of your fund's income, but the rest may be assigned to other charities if you like. A conventional private foundation is perpetual, but your pooled common fund will be liquidated and its assets distributed to charity upon your death.

Some people donate life insurance policies to charities, don't they?

Yes, the two possibilities here are to sign over an existing policy to a charitable institution or to buy a new policy and make the charity a beneficiary. In either case, you can take a deduction for the premiums you pay each year. And the charity is assured of an immediate, major gift upon your death.

This is all pretty confusing. How can I figure out if any of these plans are suitable for me?

Your confusion is understandable. All of these forms of giving differ in their benefits to the charity, their suitability for you, and their tax consequences. If any seem attractive to you, one good way to proceed is to call or write to the charities you favor and ask which form of gift, bequest, or trust they recommend. A large charity may have a "planned-giving officer," or some other expert on staff or on call, who can recommend the form of gift that best suits the interests of the charity and your particular circumstances. Of course, you should make sure that your accountant, attorney or financial advisor agrees with the charity's recommendation.

Two notes of caution. Be sure to establish your

Donating Life Insurance Policies

planned-giving relationship with a reputable charity and not with some outfit which is out to exploit tax dodges today and may be gone tomorrow. Also, if you plan to put a restriction of any kind on your gift, be sure to discuss it with your intended beneficiary; the organization may have bylaws provisions prohibiting it from accepting your restricted gift.

How can I make my donations produce the biggest tax break?

That topic is too complicated—and too subject to change—to discuss here in full. Suffice it to say that, if you itemize deductions, the United States government encourages charitable giving to qualified organizations by allowing you to deduct every dollar of your gift, subject to caps of 20 percent, 30 percent or 50 percent of your adjusted gross income, depending on the type of gift and the type of organization you give it to. And if your contributions exceed the cap, you can carry over the excess amount and deduct it in any of the next five years.

But be careful. The tax laws also provide for a stiff alternative minimum tax to discourage you from sheltering too much of your income. If you plan to contribute major sums, you should do some calculations to see whether your gift might make you subject to this tax and its significantly higher tax liability. If it does, or even if it might, find another way of making the donation, such as spreading it out over two or more years. If these calculations are beyond your ability or would take too much time, consult with an accountant, attorney or financial planner before making a donation that might come back to haunt you.

You say I can only claim a deduction for a gift to a "qualified" organization. How do I know who's "qualified" ?

In broad terms, qualified organizations are those that are religious, charitable, educational, scientific or literary in purpose or those dedicated to preventing cruelty to children or animals. Gifts are not deductible if they are made to political organizations, foreign organizations, homeowners associations, social clubs, labor unions, chambers of commerce, individuals, or groups whose purpose is to lobby for changes in laws.

Costs of raffle, bingo or lottery tickets are not de-

The Charitable
Deduction

Tax Deductibility

• 39 •

ductible, regardless of how worthy the charity they support. Donations are also not deductible if they are only substitutes for fees, dues or tuition. You cannot, for example, give your fraternal order a donation in lieu of dues and expect to deduct that expense.

For specific charities, if they are large national organizations, look them up in this book to see if contributions are tax deductible. In some cases, you will find that the parent organization is not qualified, perhaps because it lobbies for changes in laws, but that a subsidiary organization is. An example is the American Civil Liberties Union (ACLU), which has established the ACLU Foundation to attract tax-deductible contributions.

If you want to know the status of charities not listed in this book, look over their literature for statements on the subject or give them a call. If you have any reason to distrust them, ask that they send you a copy of their "determination letter" from the IRS. Be careful of organizations that say they are "tax-exempt." That means they don't pay taxes, but it does *not* mean that contributions to them are tax deductible. You can also consult the IRS publication *Cumulative List of Organizations Described in Section 170(c) of the Internal Revenue Code,* which can be found at many large libraries and IRS offices.

Deducting When You Get Something Back

If I buy a ticket to a $200-per-couple charity dinner-dance, can I deduct the entire amount for tax purposes?

No, you can only deduct the amount that represents an outright gift; some of your $200 is going to pay for your meals and some for the dance. That portion is not a gift, but a purchase. Your ticket may state what portion of the price is deductible. If it doesn't, the charity can tell you.

If you buy a ticket, but are unable to attend the charity function, you may deduct the entire amount, which now represents a gift and nothing more. To be on the safe side—and to help out the sponsoring organization—let them know in advance, so they can resell your ticket or at least cancel your meal.

What about the situation where I get a premium, such as a T-shirt or a coffee mug, from my public television station, in response to my cash gift?

The Internal Revenue Service has recently ruled that contributions are fully deductible where the premium is of token value. For 1990, this means that, when claiming a deduction, you can ignore premiums if its fair market value is no more than 2 percent of the donation or $50, whichever is less. These figures will change with the inflation rate, so you'll need to check the IRS instructions each year to know the exact rules.

My aunt refuses to take deductions for charitable giving because she thinks it ruins the spirit of charity. Any comments?

Your aunt is welcome to do what she wants, of course. She seems to be siding with those who think that taking the deduction is an underhanded, mercenary act, as opposed to those who maintain it is merely an honest way in which our government encourages charitable giving. If your aunt is willing to listen, why don't you show her that she doesn't have to keep the money she saves on taxes by claiming the deduction; she can add it to next year's gifts to her favorite charities.

I'm planning on selling some gold coins next year and giving the proceeds to the local historical society. But the coins have gone way up in value since I bought them, and the capital gains tax is going to eat up a lot of my profit. Will the IRS forgive some of that tax so I can make a bigger contribution?

No, but there's a much better solution for your problem. Don't sell the coins; give them to the historical society. You'll avoid fees, you'll avoid capital gains taxes, and the charity will get that much more money. And you'll get an income tax deduction equal to the fair market value of the coins, so long as the historical society uses them as part of its charitable purpose. If it doesn't, and accepts the coins only to sell them, you may deduct only what you paid for them.

GIVING PROPERTY

Where to Give Property

I can't afford to give much money. What else can I do?

Money is only one part of charitable giving. You have possessions which, though superfluous to you, can be a great benefit to others. You can, in fact, save lives and not spend a dime.

In our economically stratified society, one man's trash is another man's treasure. The winter jacket we never take from the closet could save the life of a homeless person. And the old tires, furniture and toys we leave at the curb could be useful to families in neighborhoods not far away.

Remember that everybody, no matter how poor, has something of value to donate to a charity. What about a gift of your blood? Or of your bone marrow (which, like blood, soon regenerates)?

I've got lots of things in my basement and garage that I never use. How can I find charities to give them to?

Your donations will be welcomed by churches and synagogues, centers for the homeless, abused women, or senior citizens, the Salvation Army and other relief groups, and the American Red Cross and other emergency relief organizations. You can find other possibilities by looking in the classified telephone directory under such headings as "Furniture, Used," "Resale Shops," "Thrift Shops" and "Second-Hand Shops." But don't take your goods to the first person who expresses interest. First, establish that the store is a nonprofit (and that donations to it are tax deductible, if that is important to you) and that it benefits a charity that you want to support. If you have several to choose from, see if one might have a pick-up service for your bulky items. You might also try calling your nearest United Way office; it may run a used-goods clearinghouse of its own or be able to refer you to one.

If it's books you want to donate, call nearby libraries, many of which hold periodic used book sales as fund-raisers; if they don't want them, try a hospital or senior citizen organization. If you'd like your books to go to underdeveloped countries, call the International Book Bank (800-874-7268) and ask about its programs.

One nationwide chain of nonprofit thrift stores that may have a location in your area is Goodwill Industries, donations to which are doubly beneficial. Not only will the store devote proceeds from your items to helping disabled and vocationally disadvantaged people; it also hires such individuals to fix and prepare items for resale. If you don't find a listing in your local phone book, write or call Goodwill Industries of America (9200 Wisconsin Avenue, Bethesda, MD 20814—301-530-6500) and ask for the location nearest you.

You'd better ask some good consumer questions before you make your donation to any of these organizations, though. There have been instances where charities pick up goods, but sell them for pennies to for-profit thrift stores, considerably reducing the impact of the gift.

If you can't find a charity to pick up your used items, consider another route. Hold a garage sale, pay someone to cart off what won't sell, and donate the net proceeds to your favorite cause.

Some of the things I'd like to donate are fairly valuable—some china and several paintings, for example. I'd hate to see them get sold for a few dollars in some thrift shop.

Better check the thrift shop to see if it sells such items and at what price. You might also speak to the shop manager about the items. If your visit leaves you with doubts, consider other recipients. Alternatives to thrift stores are charity auctions, where high quality items are sold, often at generously high prices, to benefit the sponsoring organization. By donating your cut glass bowl to a charity auction, you may generate two gifts, the value of the piece itself and the amount that the bidder overpays for it.

Any sort of charity may sponsor an auction. To find one, start by calling your favorite organizations; if they don't run an auction and can't suggest a suitable nonprofit that does, ask thrift stores, museums, shop-owners and appraisers in your area for leads.

What are these bargain sales I've heard about?

A bargain sale occurs when you sell something to a charity for less than it's worth. You are, in effect, giving

Charity Auctions

Bargain Sales

**Tax Deductions
for Gifts of Property**

the organization the difference between your sale price and the fair market value. There are often tax advantages in following this course rather than selling the property at market value, incurring capital gains tax and donating the proceeds.

How do I decide how big a tax deduction to claim for property I give to charities?

The IRS rule is that you can deduct the "fair market value" of whatever you donate. The IRS defines fair market value as "the price at which property would change hands between a willing buyer and a willing seller, neither being required to buy or sell, and both having reasonable knowledge of all the necessary facts." This is sometimes hard to arrive at and you may be tempted to guess. But be careful. A lot of givers intentionally or unintentionally overestimate the value of goods they donate, and some of them get penalized for their mistakes.

For gifts of real estate, fair market value is based on the traditional method of studying "comparable sales." For stamp and coin collections, there are catalogs which may be available at your local library. For cars, the IRS recommends using the "blue book" price, adjusted for unusual equipment, mileage and condition. For used clothing, furniture or books, a good way to establish fair market value is to note the sale price of similar used goods at about the same time as your donation. In other words, you might look around the thrift store when you deliver your old furniture and establish the price of similar pieces.

If you can't find goods for sale like the ones you are donating, the safe course is to have the items appraised or to claim a deduction you are sure is on the low side. This is because in an IRS review of your tax return, the burden will be on you to establish that you have claimed no more than fair market value.

Don't be foolish enough to assign a high fair market value based on the willingness of a thrift store employee to sign off on your exaggerated price. The IRS won't accept the employee's opinion as definitive. And don't make the mistake of claiming the amount your donated items bring in at a charity auction. People pay all kinds of inflated prices at such affairs, and the IRS will not accept their exuberant generosity as establishing fair market value. Buyers, in fact, can claim the amount they pay over fair market value as *their* charitable gift.

For gifts of appreciated property—paintings, collections, stocks, furniture, land—remember that you can deduct the full appreciated value only if the charity uses the gift for the purpose or function for which it was granted tax-exempt status. That is, if the museum keeps the painting you donate, you can deduct the appreciated fair market value; but if the museum sells the work, you may be able to deduct only your "tax basis," the amount you paid for it. Obviously, the lower deduction amount applies for any gift you make to a charity auction. Clearly, if you care about tax advantage, it's in your interest to find a recipient for your property who will use it for its tax-exempt purpose.

By the way, if you offer use of your property, such as a week's stay in your vacation home, as an item for sale at a charity auction, don't attempt to deduct anything. In nearly all cases, you may claim deductions only if you contribute your "entire interest" in the property.

When you establish the fair market value of goods you are donating, make a careful record of your findings and get the charity to sign a statement that it received the items. The most efficient way to proceed is to make two copies of a list of the books you are giving to your local library or of the clothes you are donating to the senior citizen home. Include comments about the condition and value of each item. Then ask an official of the charity to sign your list as a receipt. In practice, of course, the local librarian won't sort through three boxes of dusty books before signing a receipt, but the copy you leave with the donation will provide the staff with a chance to review the list later. And the values you assign may alert the librarians to books they may wish to sell for cash, rather than place on their shelves.

Do I need to do anything special to claim deductions for gifts of property?

Not if you claim a total of $500 or less. Over that amount, you'll need to file Form 8283. Deductions of over $5000 per item or group of similar items will require that you provide appraisals and acknowledgments by an official of each charitable organization to which you donate property.

Giving Cars and Equipment

Are there charities that might take my son's old car off my hands? The transmission is shot, so it's just taking up space in our driveway.

There are charities in some areas that will accept an old car as a donation, but they generally require that you deliver it to them. Some of these charities actually operate used car lots or automobile junkyards; others will sell your car and devote the proceeds to their programs. Check your Yellow Pages and call a few local charities to see if you have one of these rarities in your vicinity.

My company has to get rid of some old models of its office equipment products. I'd like to give them to public schools. What's the procedure?

It depends on how many items you're talking about and how much you want to spread them around. If you'd like to give everything to one school or school district, call the superintendent's office, describe the gift and see if the district is interested. The school board will probably have to pass a resolution accepting the gift before you can make delivery. If you don't have any particular district in mind, call your state's department of education or school boards association and ask for recommendations of districts that are especially in need. They will probably be willing to advertise the availability of the items. They may even help distribute them.

There is also a national clearinghouse for such donations, which can warehouse your surplus equipment and distribute it throughout the country. It is the National Association for the Exchange of Industrial Resources (NAEIR), 560 McClure Street, Galesburg, IL 61401—309-343-0704. NAEIR will take floor tile, welding guns, art supplies, computer software, scientific instruments and virtually anything else that conceivably could be used in a school or college. The organization then publishes a thick catalog, which it distributes to its members, who choose which items they want.

Donating Real Estate

Isn't it possible to donate your house to a charity, but go on living in it?

Absolutely. If you're property rich and cash poor, you might consider agreeing to donate your home or farm to the organization at a future date, while reserving the right to enjoy the property for your lifetime, for the lives of you and your children, or for a set number of years. You'll get significant tax advantages now, yet go on using the property for the rest of your life.

A friend told me that it's possible to donate the development rights to your land and to take a tax deduction for it. Have I got that right?

Yes. You can guarantee that all or part of your land will remain undeveloped forever and get a tax deduction in the process. The only cost to you will be that your remaining interest in the land will be worth less if you should want to sell it.

Here's how it works. Let's say you have thirty acres of farmland you would like to protect against future development. You call your county and find out that it has a program for preserving open space. You grant to the county what is called an "enforceable open space easement in perpetuity" on the land, guaranteeing that it will never be developed. And you can deduct the fair market value of the donation, that is, the difference between what the land in your area is worth with and without development rights.

You mentioned giving blood and bone marrow. What do I do if I want to give my body organs when I die?

Sign a Uniform Donor Card, indicating your desire to have your organs made available to help others when you are dead. But that's not enough, because if your next of kin objects, the operation won't be carried out even if your intent is clear. So discuss the issue with your closest relatives and make sure they understand your wishes. For information and copies of the Uniform Donor Card, contact the United Network for Organ Sharing, P.O. Box 13770, Richmond, VA 23225 — (800) 24-DONOR.

Donating
Development Rights

Giving
Body Organs

GIVING YOUR TIME

As a recent college graduate, I just can't afford to give money to charity, and the only possessions I own are things I use. Is there some other way I can help?

Even if you have no money or goods to give away, you still have something of enormous value to the charity of your choice. It is what Emerson called the greatest gift: "a piece of thyself," your time in the form of voluntary assistance.

If you volunteer, you'll be joining a lot of your fellow citizens. A Gallup Poll conducted for Independent Sector in 1988 found that 45 percent of adult respondents had volunteered during 1987, about 80 million people nationwide. The average volunteer gave 4.7 hours a week, a total of about 19.5 billion hours or about $150 billion worth of time.

Of course, the primary reason to volunteer is to help others, but you will receive a personal reward in return. Giving money is, for the most part, a very impersonal act; in most instances you put your check in the mail and occasionally reflect on the child it may be feeding or the scientist it may be training. Giving goods is only a little more personal in that you can picture your computer, your land or your books in use. When you give time, though, you enter the picture. You relate with like-minded people and with the people you want to help, bringing a whole new human dimension to your charitable giving.

Among the other benefits you may receive are new friendships, new skills and opportunities, academic credit, new business contacts, first-hand knowledge of the charity's operations, and a chance to influence the organization, whether through simple suggestions or through a role in its governance. Some senior citizen organizations maintain that volunteering has another beneficial effect: it prolongs the active life of the elderly.

I've never volunteered because I don't want to get stuck addressing envelopes or filing forms. Are there any enjoyable or creative jobs for volunteers?

Depending on your qualifications and your geographic location, you can volunteer to do almost any job you can imagine. As a volunteer, you can:

> build houses
> coach basketball
> provide employment counseling
> serve as a member of a board of directors
> read to the blind or elderly
> teach just about anything
> write fund-raising appeals
> design posters or advertisements
> give legal advice
> supervise children's games
> perform as a clown, magician or comedian
> lobby legislators
> take photographs or videos
> fight fires
> write or deliver speeches
> take care of injured or lost animals
> play or teach a musical instrument
> act in or direct plays
> run a nonprofit shop
> assist nurses, lawyers or librarians
> provide accounting, budgeting or investment advice
> operate computers
> design parks and playgrounds
> be a disk-jockey
> repair electronics
> counsel recovering alcohol or drug abusers
> drive a truck

In short, virtually anything you can do for work or for fun, you can do as a volunteer.

OK, volunteer jobs can be interesting, but don't a lot of nonprofits treat volunteers like untrained labor?

Apparently not. Over 70 percent of the volunteers interviewed by Gallup researchers in November 1989 said they enjoyed their activities "a great deal." The reason, in part, is that nonprofit managers are beginning to understand the great value of volunteers in an era of increasing competition for limited resources. And they are taking a whole new approach to their volunteers. Managers now understand that volunteers must be developed, just the way employees are. Volunteers relegated to addressing envelopes two afternoons a week for a year are likely to become demoralized and disenchanted with the organization. They are likely to find something better to do with their time, perhaps volunteering for another nonprofit which shows an interest in their skills, their comfort, and their personal and professional growth.

Is it possible to spend my vacations helping charitable organizations in foreign countries or other parts of the U.S.?

Combining
Volunteering
with Vacations

Yes, you can "get away from it all" and do good at the same time. There are organizations that want volunteers, even for short periods, to provide medical care, distribute food, build houses, maintain hiking trails, excavate ancient ruins and do lots of other tasks. Why not try it for one vacation and see how you like the experience. You may come home more refreshed and renewed than if you had spent the two weeks lying on a beach. And, if you read on, you'll discover that there are tax advantages, too.

If you're interested, check with individual charities or professional groups, churches or unions in your field to see if they run such programs. If your interest is in providing housing and you would like to work in an overtly Christian organization, you may wish to contact Habitat for Humanity, with headquarters at Habitat & Church Streets, Americus, GA 31709—912-924-6935 and regional centers throughout the country. Minnesota-based Global Volunteers coordinates volunteer activities in third world countries and can help you make the necessary arrangements (2000 American National Bank Building, St. Paul, MN 55101—612-228-9751). For other organizations in the field, see Bill McMillon's book, *Volunteer Vacations: A Directory of Short-Term Adventures That Will Benefit You . . . and Others.*

College students can perform similar services, especially during spring breaks. You can get information about volunteering or about setting up a volunteer program by contacting Vanderbilt University, a leader in the field (University Chaplain Office, Box 6311, Station B, Nashville, TN 37235—615-343-7878), or the Campus Outreach Opportunity League (386 McNeal Hall, University of Minnesota, St. Paul, 55108—612-624-3018). The League has published a book, *Break Away: A Guide to Organizing an Alternative Spring Break,* which can help students establish a program on their campus.

For high school students, there are summer camps that specialize in service to charitable organizations, although it costs money to attend them. For names of such camps near you, call the National Camp Association (800-966-2267) or the American Camping Association (800-777-2267), which publishes an annual *Guide to Accredited Camps.* Church officials in your community may also be able to direct you to such camps.

I don't have a lot of spare money to give, but I do have a skill that some charity could use: I make professional audio-visual presentations for businesses.

You're in an enviable position. And so are professionals in fields such as public relations, advertising, graphics, fund-raising, management consulting and virtually any endeavor which can serve small or large businesses. You may not be able to donate $20,000 to a charity, but a few days of your time might be worth that much and more to them. By all means, do a little study, pick a few worthy charities and speak to the top staff people about your skills. Don't let anybody assign you to licking stamps; it's in the charity's interest and your interest to exploit your most valuable talents.

What tax breaks are there for volunteers?

Not many. To settle the most obvious question, the IRS is not crazy enough to let you deduct the value of the time you contribute. Not only would this be enormously expensive in lost tax revenues, but it would be virtually impossible to regulate.

You may, however, deduct unreimbursed costs relating to time you donate to a "qualified organization." These costs include transportation expenses; uniforms; and meals and lodging, if your volunteer work takes you away from home overnight. Yes, this includes expenses of travel to do charity work in foreign countries, so long as there is "no significant element" of recreation or vacation involved; check IRS Publication 526 for details. You can also deduct costs of telephone calls, attending a convention as the "chosen representative" of a nonprofit and so forth. You may not include the costs of hiring someone

Tax Deductibility of Volunteering

to watch your kids while you do your volunteer work, and remember, to deduct anything, you have to keep good records.

As long as we're discussing "what's in it for me," volunteering can provide unique benefits for people who want to improve their working lives. Volunteering can prepare you for a new position or a whole new career by giving you experience you wouldn't be able to acquire otherwise. Your volunteer supervisor may be able to provide you with a valuable reference. Who knows? You might end up working for the agency you volunteer for.

Volunteerism has a similar benefit for high school students. When the only job opportunities are at fast food franchises, volunteering, with the experience and contacts it brings, may be the best way for students to further their college or employment goals. A high school student could volunteer as a nurse's aide, for example, and earn a letter of recommendation for the pre-med program she wants to enter. Another might become a volunteer firefighter and gain contacts to help him get his first job. Volunteer work in a legal aid office could help a college student gain admission to law school. These experiences can be so valuable to teens that parents might consider subsidizing their children's volunteer work so they won't feel compelled to take paying, but mind-numbing jobs at the local strip mall. High schools also give credit for volunteering, in some instances.

How can I find out who needs volunteers?

The need is so great that there are lots of volunteer clearinghouses around. You may have a state, county or local office of volunteerism in your area, so check your phone book under "Volunteers" or "Voluntary." If you don't find something there, call your city hall, your library, the nearest community foundation office or a nearby United Way office. Students should check their schools and colleges to see if they have clearinghouses. Also be on the lookout for Volunteer Fairs, often held in conjunction with National Volunteer Week in late April. If you work for a sizeable company, your employer may be able to help locate volunteer opportunities or may have a clearinghouse for employees. Some large companies feel so strongly about participation in community activities that they give time off or provide transportation

Benefits of Volunteer Work

How to Find Out Who Needs Your Skills

to help employees pursue their volunteer activities. A few even support employee volunteers by making automatic contributions to every nonprofit they serve.

If all else fails, you can resort to calling individual charities you might like to help and asking what sort of volunteer needs they have. Use the same techniques we discussed above in the section on identifying charities.

Keep in mind that you may be able to do volunteer work for a distant charity; even if your ideal nonprofit is located a continent away, call them to see if they could use your help in making phone calls, writing, using a computer, organizing a local chapter or providing information about local conditions or local potential donors.

A reference book that can be very helpful in identifying volunteer opportunities is *Volunteerism: The Directory of Organizations, Training and Publications*, now in its third edition. Your library should have a copy. As its name suggests, *Volunteerism* provides information on thousands of volunteer organizations, both national and local, and can help you locate groups seeking volunteers to assist AIDS victims, the homeless, the handicapped, senior citizens and many other causes.

I work for a medium-sized company that doesn't encourage volunteerism in any way I know of. Maybe I could persuade them to.

If you do, you'll have made a tremendous contribution to your community. Suggest the idea to the company's managers and *volunteer* to help plan and operate a clearinghouse for company volunteers. The hours you spend may be multiplied hundreds or thousands of times over as your fellow employees respond to the opportunities and discover the fun and fulfillment of volunteering. If you need information to help persuade your bosses to move in this direction, contact VOLUNTEER - The National Center, 1111 North 19th Street, Arlington, VA 22209—703-276-0542.

If there are so many volunteering opportunities, it might be hard to decide where to spend my time.

That's true. It's more complicated than choosing a charity to give money to, because there are so many personal factors involved. You need to reflect not only on whom you want to help, but on what volunteer tasks you want to perform and what conditions you want to work under. It's really a lot like looking for a job, but with the interesting twists that salary is of no importance and the mission of the organization is paramount. (Wouldn't it be interesting if volunteering could teach us to treat our regular job searches more like volunteer job searches?)

Deciding Where to Volunteer

So don't give your precious time away to the first charity that asks, any more than you would give your entire charity budget to the first worthy cause you see. Be a wise consumer; shop around to find a charity that will give you the most for your volunteer hour, both with regard to what it does for the cause and what it does for you.

Of course, you should start by evaluating charities, so you'll know which ones you are willing—or better, which you are *eager*—to work for. Consult the entries in this book; contact NCIB, CBBB, your local BBB or your state charity regulation office, as appropriate; read The Other Side; ask the charity for information. Then make some preliminary calls to find out if your chosen charities need your skills during the hours you have available. Be sure to ask them how long it would take before they could process you and get you started. If the wait is too long, you may want to ask if they know of a similar charity that can use you sooner.

How do I set up my voluntary relationship with a charity?

Approaching the Charity

You should interview for the volunteer position just as you would for a regular job. Request a written job description. Ask exactly what you will be doing, when and with whom. Find out if it is possible to work the hours that are most convenient for you. Ask if you will be trained and if there are "job growth" opportunities. Visit the location where you will spend your volunteer hours. Check to see if you will have to bear costs for travel, materials, meals and so forth. If you don't like what you hear and see—or if your consumerist questions are met with hostility or incredulity—look elsewhere.

If you find a job you think you will like, make a short-term trial commitment and ask for an agreement in writing about the "terms and conditions" of your work. Include a provision for regular meetings with the volunteer coordinator and your supervisor to review your efforts, trade suggestions for improvement and extend the commitment.

By the way, an alternative to volunteering during your off-hours is full-time employment with a nonprofit. It may be an act of charity, to some extent, because the pay may not be as good as what you could command elsewhere. But it might be a lot more gratifying than your present job. Instead of making a lot of money to enable you to be happy, maybe you could make a little less and get that happiness seven or more hours every day.

You should see the amount of charity mail I get, at least one piece every day. I throw 99 percent of it out, so they're wasting their money and my time. How can I stop the flow?

It's not going to be easy. You probably get so much charity mail because you have been generous in the past. You haven't given to all the groups who send to you, of course, but some of them have obtained your name and address from organizations you have contributed to, clubs you belong to, magazines you subscribe to and mail order houses you have bought from. This means that it's going to be very difficult to stop the stream of mail pouring into your mailbox.

There are several useful steps you can take, though. The easiest and most effective is to write to the Mail Preference System, Direct Marketing Association, 11 West 42nd Street, P.O. Box 3861, New York, NY 10163-3861, and ask that your name be deleted from mailing lists of the commercial direct mail marketing firms which subscribe to the service. In your request, include every variation of your name (including misspellings you see on your mail) and specify whether you want your name removed from commercial lists, nonprofit lists or both. Such a request has the potential of decreasing your unwanted mail by hundreds of items each year, but you'll continue to get mail from charities that maintain their own mailing lists. To stop this mail, make a form letter requesting removal of your name, send it to the executive directors of the organizations and enclose your address from their mailings. As for the charities you want to continue hearing from, write and ask them not to rent your name to anyone else.

But don't expect these measures to solve the problem completely. Even if a charity removes you from its lists, it may rent your name again in a few months and unwittingly put you right back into its computer. At some point, you may conclude that you're fighting the inevitable and just decide to keep tossing those unwanted mailings into the wastebasket, soothed by the knowledge that they aren't costing the sender much. If the waste of paper bothers you, your best course may be to donate to a charity that plants or protects trees.

Duplicate Mailings

I was getting so much charity mail from one organization that I started counting it. They sent me twelve appeals in a year! Aren't they wasting a lot of money this way?

Fund-raisers know that whether you respond to a mailing or not depends on your mood, recent news, the time of year and other changing factors. That's why many of them send multiple mailings, increasing their chances of hitting you when the time is ripe. Many nonprofits remove names of unresponsive addressees from their lists after a certain number of appeals. Some do not.

If appeals come within a few days of each other, it is probably a matter of duplicate mailings, perhaps because the charity has acquired your name from several different sources. The spelling or your name or address might be slightly different, confusing the computer's purging programs that eliminate only exact duplicates.

If you see that this is happening, do the charity, your mailman and yourself a favor. The next time a piece of mail comes in from the offending organization, put it aside for a week or so until the duplicates have all arrived. Then clip the duplicate mailing labels, mark the one that is most accurate, and send them back to the charity with a brief note. To its credit, a New York City public television station, WNET, recently launched its own attack on the problem by sending all its supporters a brochure emblazoned with the words, "We are not asking for money." The mailing provided a postage-paid form for reporting duplicates and drew tens of thousands of responses.

Occasionally I get a charity appeal that contains a "gift"—note cards, decorative stamps, decals, return address stickers; one even contained a nickel. Doesn't this cost the charity a lot of money?

You can usually bet that the fund-raisers know what they're doing. You remember those mailings, don't you, while you've forgotten hundreds of others. In a sense, the gift presents you with a dilemma: if you don't send a donation, it feels like cheating to use the gift, but it also seems a shame to throw it out. In short, the gifts are calculated to make you feel guilty if you don't donate. They tend to work, too. If they didn't usually produce more money than they cost, no one would send them.

Of course, you are never under any obligation to pay for unordered merchandise. If you are ever billed for such items, notify your state charity regulation office and the nearest Better Business Bureau.

So what should you do with the beautiful note cards? If you want to support the organization, do so. But if not, don't accept the guilt trip. The charity is making an investment in sending you the gift, but they know and you know that all investments don't pay off. Use the cards or throw them out, but don't worry about the great sacrifice of the poor charity that sent you the gift.

Did I understand you to say that when I send money to a charity, it rents my name to other charities?

It's a common practice; one estimate is that about 75 percent of nonprofits either rent or exchange mailing lists. Whether you like the idea or not, you'll have to admit that it makes economic sense from the charity's point of view.

Direct mail fund-raising campaigns are expensive; naturally, charities want to send mailings to those people who are most likely to respond. It is a tenet of the fund-raising business that the most likely giver is someone who has given before, either to the same charity or to one with similar aims or similar supporters. Therefore, Charity A is willing to pay for the use of the names and addresses of contributors to kindred Charity B. Then too, selling your name and address is a way for your favorite charity to pick up a little more income.

Some charities pick up a lot more income by renting their lists not only to other charities, but also to commercial businesses. One national veterans organization earned over $16 million in a twelve-year period by renting names to both categories.

So you can see why charities sell or exchange names. But should they? A common view is they have the right to do what they want with your name unless you object. The Direct Marketing Association urges nonprofits to tell donors if their names may be rented or exchanged and to inform them how they can avoid the process. Some charities provide a space on their donation forms where you can indicate your wishes. You might want to encourage your favorite charities to do something similar.

Sometimes I see solicitations saying that corporation, foundation or wealthy benefactor has challenged the charity to raise, say, $100,000 and will match any contribution I make. If I send money and the charity doesn't raise the entire $100,000, will I get my money back?

Matched Gifts

You raise a significant point, and there is a related question of what happens if your contribution arrives after the challenge has been met. Both questions relate to the charity promising to match your donation and then not being able to do so. NCIB's view is that charities have the obligation to specify the total amount to be matched and to give the contributor the option of having the donation returned if the challenge is not met. In practice, some charities adhere to this standard, while others do not. If you are concerned about the issue, send a note with your check, expressing your support for the NCIB standard and asking to be informed if your gift is not matched; if you're not the trusting type, maybe you should also call six months later to see what happened.

Is it just my imagination or are sweepstakes getting much more common as a fund-raising device?

Sweepstakes

It's not your imagination. The American public has a weakness for "get-rich-quick" schemes, so it's natural that charity fund-raisers and other direct mail promoters try to exploit it. Beware of organizations that require a contribution to enter their sweepstakes (that's totally illegal) and those that announce in a direct mail piece that you have already won a prize (which is probably worth no more than a few cents).

Some of the charity mail I get is awfully heavy-handed, full of crying children and big-name signatures. What are the ethics of direct mail fund-raising?

Both the National Charities Information Bureau and the Council of Better Business Bureaus have standards on the subject (see Appendices A and B). The views of nonprofit professionals can be seen in the results of an informal poll conducted by columnist Jerry Huntsinger and reported in the September 1989 *NonProfit Times*. Of the 500 respondents, most of whom were associated with nonprofits and some of whom were themselves fund-raisers, over two-thirds disapproved of using fictitious signatures or claims of false financial crises in direct mail appeals. Smaller percentages opposed words like "official" or "urgent" on envelopes; the use of doctored or purchased photographs; the use of celebrity endorsements without any real commitment by the celebrity; a description of the worst case as if it were a typical case; the use of phrases like "I am writing you this personal appeal" in a mass-mailing; and wording letters to make non-givers feel guilty.

Over two-thirds of the respondents thought charities have the obligation to inform potential givers about the availability of financial statements; the market value of premiums offered in response to gifts; the probability of winning a sweepstakes (and in full-size print); the use of a "representative" case history, rather than an actual one; the likely disposition of surveys included in the mailing (in some cases, they are never even read); and the use to which donations will be put if the appeal produces more money than needed for the need described. Remarkably, 68 percent also said that donor names should not be traded, rented or sold without the donor's consent, even though this practice is very common.

Whatever your view of fund-raising ethics, don't expect a crusade to transform the industry. A study conducted by Robert F. Carbone, of the Clearinghouse for Research on Fund-Raising at the University of Maryland, found little agreement among fund-raisers about what is ethical, and little hope that ethical lapses will be punished. Carbone found that only 34 percent of fund-raisers thought their colleagues were "intimately aware" of ethics

The Ethics of Direct Mail Fund-Raising

in their field and a mere 5 percent thought that violators of professional ethics received any punishment. Small wonder that "objectionable" practices seem so common, even among those who sometimes disapprove of them.

Do you have any special advice about responding to in-person or telephone solicitations?

In-Person and Telephone Solicitations

The most obvious caveat is not to give anything to solicitors unless they identify themselves, their employer and their relationship to the benefiting organization. If you encounter solicitors in the street or at your front door, they may also need a permit from your municipality. Why don't you also ask what portion of your donation will go to the charity and what the money will be used for? The solicitor may not know or may not want to tell you. But the charity and the fund-raising firm will get the message that people are starting to ask tough questions and that they'd better start providing answers, verbally or in writing.

Probably the best response to in-person or telephone solicitors is to ask them to send you information, including answers to the questions above. Tell them that only then will you consider including their organization in your giving for the year.

If you give more than a few dollars on the street or at your door, give a check rather than cash. This will help you claim a tax deduction and also make it more difficult for an unscrupulous solicitor to convert the gift to his or her own use.

For what a solicitor must tell you, see your state's solicitation disclosure requirements in Appendix C.

Pledging

Telephone solicitors, telethons and public radio and television stations are always asking for "pledges." Just what is a pledge and how does it differ from a donation?

In the solicitation of large gifts, charities or their fund-raisers often ask for pledges, rather than cash, because the donor does not have the money on hand or has indicated a desire to give at a future date or in installments. When telephone solicitors and telethon hosts ask you to "make a pledge," it is more of a marketing device, designed to commit you to an action that cannot be completed on the phone. If you make a pledge, you will soon receive a letter or bill, citing your promise and asking you to remit the appropriate amount. Of course, you should honor your commitments, but beware the unscrupulous solicitors who send letters or bills about pledges you did not make. If you receive such a letter, do the charity a favor and *don't* send a donation. Instead, call or write the organization's executive director to say that, through carelessness or design, its solicitors are risking its reputation.

Charities differ in their accounting practices regarding pledges. Some organizations, including many in the health and welfare field, record pledges as soon as the commitment is made. Other organizations, including many colleges, universities and hospitals, wait until they actually receive the money.

Sometimes I encounter solicitors who ask me to buy something to support a charity and I often wonder how much of my purchase price the charity gets.

You should do more than wonder. You should *ask:* whom the solicitor works for, what the charity is, where you can get written information, and what percentage the charity will receive. And don't reach for your wallet unless you get answers that satisfy you. If the solicitors can't respond to your questions, you can give the charity a second chance by asking that information be sent to you in the mail.

In this case, as in others we have discussed here, there's a value in asking even if you're pretty sure the solicitor doesn't have the information. It gets the message out—to the solicitors, to their bosses and to any bystanders who hear your question—that the issue is important and that answers *should* be provided.

What percentage of the cost of the book, or the greeting cards or the circus ticket goes to the charity? It can be as much as 100 percent if the goods have been donated and volunteers are used to sell them. Or it can be minuscule if some for-profit business has simply latched on to a charitable cause to help it market a product.

What should I do when I'm sympathetic to a cause, but completely turned off by the style or behavior of the people soliciting for it?

Easy! Give to the charity, but not through the solicitor. Get the charity's address, omit any special designation, such as "Department D6," which may identify the solicitor, and send a check. Not only will the obnoxious solicitors not get credit for your donation; if they're being paid on a percentage basis, they'll miss out on a financial reward, too. You can do something similar in response to a mail solicitation. Ignore the envelope and form provided, and just send a check on your own (remembering to omit the "Department D6," or whatever, in the address you use). Of course, you can always complain to a charity about its fund-raisers, and you should do it whenever you think it's warranted.

Should I give money to panhandlers?

Giving to
Panhandlers

Well, one approach is to apply the same tests you would to a charity solicitation. At least you don't have to worry about administrative and fund-raising costs diluting the effect of your contribution. On the other hand, there may be serious problems about the charity's stated mission and its record of spending its revenues on programs which address that mission.

Whatever your doubts about helping, it is difficult to turn down an appeal on the streets. Even those who steel themselves to say no or just keep walking, often confess to a gut-wrenching feeling of guilt—sometimes mixed with fear—as they do so. You may feel better if you reflect that many government and charity officials discourage giving to beggars because it encourages the activity and keeps some of them away from the social services which can address the causes, as well as the symptoms, of their distress. Your philanthropic urges may be better directed to the providers of these services than to the individuals they are intended to serve.

Panhandlers will become easier to face if an idea already at work in Los Angeles, New York City, and Portland, Oregon, becomes more widespread. In Los Angeles, the Weingart Center Association, a nonprofit service organization in the city's Skid Row area, printed thousands of coupons entitling the bearer to a free meal at its cafeteria. Then Weingart sold the coupons to businesses for $2.50 each. The businesses distributed the coupons to their employees to give to beggars they encounter on the streets.

The effect was a win-win-win situation: the Center used the money it received as support for its cafeteria and other services; panhandlers got nutritious meals; and employees could make a contribution to beggars, without worrying that it might be misspent. There were other benefits, too. Businesses and their employees became familiar with the work of the Center and were more likely to support it in conventional ways. And panhandlers who showed up for food became aware of the Center's other services.

Instead of complaining about beggars or giving them small change, maybe you can make a big change by championing a similar program in the community where you live or work. Why not talk to an agency that provides meals to the poor and volunteer to help establish a meal coupon program? The Weingart Center, 566 South San Pedro Street, Los Angeles, CA 90013—213-627-9000 can provide you with information.

Are there really charities that are scams?

You bet there are. Any time people hand over money and are not around to see how it is spent, there are going to be some unscrupulous characters who will try to take advantage of the situation. Of course, the overwhelming majority of charities are untainted by impropriety, but it still pays to be wary.

There are various kinds of fraudulent or unethical charities. A very few are established for the sole purpose of benefiting the founders and have no real interest in the cause they pretend to espouse. Others may have perfectly legitimate goals and a record of real accomplishment, yet allow practices that are questionable or downright dishonest. In some cases, the fault may lie with fund-raisers hired by the charity; the charity may or may not know about the unethical fund-raising techniques.

Here are just a few examples of charity scams in recent years:

- A Wisconsin charity was charged with raising over $300,000 for anti-drug and other services, but spending less than $15,000 on these activities.

- A Virginia fund-raising firm raised enough money to send 21,000 handicapped children to a concert, but distributed only 700 tickets

- Pennsylvania fund-raisers were charged with collecting over a million dollars for senior citizens and needy children, keeping over 75 percent as their fee and turning over as little as one percent to their client charities

- An Ohio animal shelter received only $2500 of the $400,000 raised for it by professional fund-raisers

- A Florida charity was reported to have raised over $1.5 million to help find missing children, but to have spent most of the money on administrative salaries and expenses—and to have "lost" $70,000 from an office headed by two employees identified as crack-cocaine addicts.

- Charities were formed, not to aid cancer and heart disease victims, as their names implied, but to provide profits for a commercial fund-raising firm.

- New York State officials have charged some police federations with having raised $5.5 million and contributed only $14,000 to charity.

- A cancer fund paid its fund-raisers 80 percent of the $7.7 million they collected and spent less than 3.5 percent on its programs.

- According to the Washington State attorney-general's office, some local charities collected funds, but devoted no money—none!—to charitable purposes.

- A national organization collected over $450,000 in the name of a children's charity, which knew nothing about it, and gave the charity a meager $10,000.

- A state of Washington campaign encouraging donations of goods to a national charity turned over the goods to for-profit thrift stores, which gave the charity a paltry 80 cents per item, even for major appliances.

- And who can forget television evangelist Jim Bakker, sentenced to jail for mail fraud and conspiracy, who directed $3.7 million in contributions to his personal use?

Outrageous. Why don't authorities crack down on these people?

It's more complicated than it seems at first. There is, for example, the little problem of the United States Constitution and its First Amendment guarantees of free speech. For example, the U.S. Supreme Court in 1982 struck down a Washington state law imposing a limit on fund-raisers' fees. In a 1988 decision, the same court invalidated a North Carolina statute that, among other restrictions, required fund-raisers to tell potential donors how much of the money raised would actually go to the charity. In 1989, a federal court of appeals struck down a Virginia law that required solicitors to submit scripts to state reviewers before using them in fund-raising campaigns.

Left with little authority to control what solicitors say to potential donors, state charity regulators have scrambled to shape new laws that would respect First Amendment rights at the same time they afford protection against abuses. One practice that has survived the scrutiny of the courts is requiring charities to register with and provide certain information to the states where they operate (although some observers claim that the worst offenders solicit without registering). Another practice is requiring solicitors to inform donors that financial information is available, or requiring them to disclose information to donors who request it.

Another avenue clearly open to regulators is the use of consumer protection statutes against errant charity solicitors. Florida, Iowa, Maryland and Tennessee are some of the states that have enacted new laws stressing penalties for fund-raising violations.

Regulatory Responses

But won't a lot of people be deceived and defrauded before the violators are identified?

There will be some problems, but keep in mind that only a tiny fraction of charity solicitations are deceptive or fraudulent. We need to balance the need for regulation of a few "bad apples" with the legitimate rights and interests of the many honest charities and fund-raisers that do so much good in our society. Of course, we could cut down on fraud if we forced every charity to submit mailings and telephone scripts for prior approval and required them to tell potential donors all kinds of consumer protection information before asking for money. But it would create expensive regulatory bureaucracies and curtail revenues to many legitimate charities.

So that's it? We have to resign ourselves to the fact that sleazy operators will go on deceiving and cheating people?

No, you're assuming that we have to rely on government to combat charity fraud. What about citizen power? Consider "sneaker fraud" for a minute. Most sneakers sold in this country are of reasonable quality relative to their price. A few brands may not live up to the claims of advertisements and of salespeople. The government holds out the threat of prosecuting manufacturers or retailers guilty of consumer fraud, and we exercise due caution when we shop.

It should be the same with charity fraud, but what's missing is the smart shopping. We tend to treat charity salespersons and advertisements differently. We don't ask questions; we don't maintain a healthy skepticism; we don't do basic consumer research. If we did, it wouldn't solve all the problems, but with the threat of punishment for proven violators, it could go a long way toward regulating the market. So, in the face of news about charity fraud, don't stop giving; start *thinking*.

Some state offices of charity regulation are moving to support consumer efforts to curtail fraud. As a New York official recently told a meeting of state charity regulators, "Criminal prosecution is not a substitute for public awareness." Maryland uses part of the revenue from charity registration fees to fund a public education campaign, including dissemination of materials to schools, libraries and the media, and the creation of a

What You Can Do to Prevent Charity Fraud

toll-free line to help citizens get answers and report abuses. Minnesota, Connecticut and other states have begun publishing financial data about charities and informing citizens about the availability of the information. These states have decided that the best way to combat fraud is to help create an educated citizenry.

What should I do if I encounter a scam charity or if someone tries to pressure me into giving?

Notify your state office of charities regulation (list in Appendix C), the local police and your local Better Business Bureau. If the scam involves the mails, also report the circumstances to your nearest postal inspector; ask your local post office for information. Of course, get the best evidence you can to back up your accusation, for example, witnesses to, or tape recordings of, a fraudulent pitch or a threat.

Don't charities have an obligation to police their own fund-raisers and insure that their solicitations are accurate and fair?

Policing
Fund-Raisers

Certainly they do. CBBB standards call for charities to sign contracts with their professional fund-raisers, establishing the organization's oversight and control over all activities carried out on their behalf. Among other things, such contracts provide for the charity to screen and approve all materials and telephone solicitation scripts the fund-raisers plan to use. CBBB also recommends that charities hire fund-raising professionals only after considering the quality as well as the success of their previous solicitations.

I've heard that you have to be especially careful about appeals for funds from police and firefighter groups. I would think they would be the most honest charities of all. What's up with them?

Police and Firefighter
Solicitations

Such warnings are usually made not about police officers and firefighters themselves, but about organizations that claim to represent them, organizations that use the respect you have for these professions as a means of invading your wallet. Devices they use may include: selling hundreds of tickets so needy or handicapped children can attend circuses or variety shows, but admitting only a few children; selling ads in benefit publications which are printed, if at all, in extremely limited editions; and soliciting ads with letters designed to look like invoices.

Occasionally, they may even suggest that you will get special consideration from police and firefighters if you donate, or hint at disadvantages if you don't. These campaigns sometimes return a very low percentage of donations and sales to the charity.

In the face of such abuses, exercise special caution when asked to donate to such charities. Ask hard questions and don't give unless you get satisfactory answers. If you give, make your check out to the cause you intend to benefit, not to the individual solicitor or the event organizer. And if any threat or improper promise is made, report it to your state attorney general's office.

All of these charity bingo games and other uses of gambling to help charities, are they on the level?

They seem to be spreading like wildfire, and there are serious concerns about them. While they provide important revenues to some charities, especially church organizations, they often have extremely high fund-raising costs, with an average of 86 percent of revenues absorbed by operations, prizes and other expenses. Moreover, they are subject to the corrupting influences that accompany gambling wherever it exists. Law enforcement officials report numerous cases of manipulation, skimming money off the top and other abuses. One charity reported that its revenues suddenly increased from $1,000 to $11,000 a night when it took over "casino" operations from a professional gambler who had been running them.

Players probably feel that if they win at one of these games, great, and if they lose, at least the money goes to a good cause. But an average of 86 percent of it doesn't go to a good cause at all. Play the games if you want to, but you probably should think of them as ways to satisfy your gambling rather than your charitable instincts.

I never put money in those canisters next to cash registers because I wonder if the money ever gets to where it's supposed to go. Am I being too suspicious?

Your caution is well-founded. The use of canisters is notoriously difficult to control. If a store clerk or a light-fingered customer doesn't invade the canister, the person who collects it may take a legal or illegal cut of its contents. Instead of feeding the canisters, write a check to the charities of your choice. If you are a retailer, don't agree to display any canisters unless you are satisfied that a reasonable percentage of the donations will get to the charity.

Why do some charities have names that are so much alike? It would be easier for us if they chose names that were less confusing.

Unfortunately, confusing you may be the whole idea. In recent years there has been a proliferation of "sound-alike" charities, new groups which have adopted names similar to those of well-known organizations. New charities can't be prohibited from using names similar to those of more established institutions. Your only defense is to pay close attention to names and, perhaps, to use this book to distinguish the players.

Can you really trust the figures that charities put out about their fund-raising costs and so forth?

Not entirely. There are ways in which creative accountants can make a charity look better with respect to administrative costs, fund-raising costs and other figures. A common way to lower reported fund-raising costs, for example, is to write off as a public education expense a major portion of the costs of a fund-raising mailing. Experts say that even professionals have trouble seeing through the smokescreen raised by creative accountants. National Charities Information Bureau reports, and the shortened versions of those reports presented in this book, attempt to adjust for such practices.

Some charity regulators argue that citizens are better advised to examine reports of program activity than financial reports. They maintain that you should ask the charity to provide figures on how many children they feed, how many grants they award, how many acres they reclaim, and then judge them on that basis.

My father got a call recently from a financial advisor who offered to help him get a big tax break in return for a major gift to charity. Does that sound like it's on the level?

There are two concerns about such an offer. The more obvious one is that the caller may be a con artist and the charity he "locates" for your father may be part of the scam. Make sure your father does a lot of inves-

Can You Trust
Charity Statistics?

Offers of Big
Tax Breaks

tigating into any organization he's thinking about giving big bucks to.

The other problem is that the caller, even if he locates a worthy charity, seems to be subordinating charitable giving to tax advantages. This practice, sometimes accompanied by a large finder's fee from the charity to the person who lands the gift, has acquired some notoriety. It has recently been denounced in a statement signed by 55 planned giving officers, fund-raisers, consultants and attorneys involved in planned giving activities. The signers express their disapproval of "promotions" that seem to be "selling" charitable gift arrangements as tax shelters and promoters who charge high fees for making the arrangements. They strengthen their case by recommending that the charities they represent decline gifts connected to "unreasonable" fees.

Charity Executive Salaries

Don't some nonprofit executives get disgracefully high salaries while their organizations are helping the poor?

It's a controversial topic these days. A *NonProfit Times*/Opinion Research Corp. survey reports that most Americans object to charitable organizations that pay their executives high salaries. About 53 percent of adult Americans say they would be less likely to give to a major charity if they knew its chief executive earned over $100,000 a year.

The problem with these findings is that they are out of touch with reality. According to a survey conducted by TPF&C, a division of the Towers Perrin management consulting firm, the median salary for executives of 215 major nonprofits in 1989 was $127,200.

That's a lot of money. But is it a reason to give or not to give?

It depends on the charity and on your standards. In some cases, top salaries of $100,000 or more are quite understandable. Charities that engage in research, operate "think tanks," or are active in fields requiring specialized, scientific knowledge need to pay high salaries to secure the labor of talented people in short supply. Those with budgets in the tens or hundreds of millions of dollars need to compete with private enterprise to hire executives capable of managing large enterprises. Would you consider a charity more successful or more moral if it saved money on executive salaries and, as a result, raised less money or achieved less with the money it had available? Then too, executive salaries should not be thought of as strictly administrative costs, since the personnel in question may devote significant portions of their time to fund-raising and program services.

On the other hand, you may choose to avoid giving to small charities, with limited resources and programs, which pay high salaries to their executives. There are instances where nonprofits have seemingly been established primarily to provide high salaries to their staff and secondarily to run programs. Do a little research to make sure you're not supporting such a "con-game."

I've heard it said that Americans are the most generous people on earth. Is that so?

Americans certainly have that reputation, and virtually all experts agree that we have few or no rivals. It's difficult to cite hard statistics, however, because every country has its own conditions and definitions, making it almost impossible to compare "apples to apples." A reasonably accurate comparison of British and American givers in 1985-86 found that the average American household gave seven times as much money to charity as the average British household. In terms of their ability to donate, the average American household gave 2.4 percent of its gross household income, while the average British household contributed only .63 percent of its income. Small wonder that British and other countries' charities envy and admire their American counterparts.

But remember that the governments of other developed countries bear a much higher proportion of the costs of what Americans consider charitable activities, including health, education, the arts, religion and welfare. In effect, the American government pays for most charitable activities by subsidizing its citizens' choices (at least those of citizens who itemize) through the means of the charitable deduction, while many other governments directly subsidize a much greater proportion of charitable activities.

My grandfather used to say, "Never give a dime if you can't see how it's spent." What other rules and sayings about giving are there?

There's a lot of "folk wisdom" about charitable giving. Here are some examples, gathered from people all over the country. Some contradict others; some are probably irrational; some may be worth adopting. You decide which are which:

Folk Wisdom on Giving

- Give to small organizations; they need your money more and what you give will have more impact.

- Support charities which other people shun. Everyone gives to the popular, the sympathetic and the fashionable. Make your contributions to the causes that only you and a small percentage of your fellow citizens believe in.

- Contribute to charities which don't offer tax deductibility, since most people avoid them.

- Give to what you don't live. As a doctor, you already make your contribution to medicine. Don't put all your eggs in one basket. Contribute to needs beyond your profession, your neighborhood and your everyday concerns.

- Donate to organizations that don't receive government assistance. Those with government help have "arrived." They have friends in high places. They don't need you as badly as those that fail to attract or that reject government assistance.

- Don't give all your money to organizations which support middle-class people and values. Devote at least some of your charity to other cultures, other social classes. In however small a way, help build a transfer of wealth from the "haves" to the "have-nots" of the United States and the world.

- Contribute to organizations with low fund-raising costs, not to nonprofits that send you ten lavish appeals each year.

- Support those who rely on contributions as opposed to revenues from memberships, publications, products and services.

- Help those that help themselves; support charities that are aggressively seeking to build revenues by selling goods and services.

- Donate to organizations that provide services in third world countries; your dollar will buy a lot more there than it could in the United States.

- Don't give to nonprofits that get a lot of money from corporations. They've got rich friends, so they don't need you, and they may be too careful about offending their corporate supporters.

- If you work for a corporation that matches gifts, donate at least some money to eligible charities; the leverage you get is just too good to pass up.

I feel I should support charities that depend most on personal giving, the ones that government agencies don't give to and that don't raise income from their programs or sales efforts. What do you think of that plan?

It's fine if you've considered all the facts and decided that's what you want to do. People have widely variant views on this topic. Some look on government support with suspicion, convinced that the receiving charity is collaborating with some government policy they don't like. Others see government support as a "seal of approval," guaranteeing the charity's integrity and quality.

Some look askance at charities that sell books, magazines, articles of clothing, greeting cards, mailing lists and information services, on the ground that these charities focus too much of their attention on their businesses or compete unfairly with for-profit enterprises. Others consider such activities forward-looking and prudent, especially because they give the charity more stability at times when bad economic conditions or other circumstances cause donations to slacken. One thing is certain: as government support has decreased in the past decade, most charities with the potential for entrepreneurial activity have moved in that direction.

**Helping Charities
With No Other
Means of Support**

Buying Goods from Charities

How much am I helping a charity, such as a museum, when I buy products in its gift shop or through its catalog?

In general, such sales amount to a small percentage of a charity's income, but most charities are in a situation where every dollar counts, so the money can be very important. In essence, a museum shop or a public radio network's mail order catalog is a business operating within the nonprofit organization. Formally or informally, that business has to pay all the costs a similar for-profit pays, except that it may benefit from volunteer assistance and it is exempt from income taxes on those activities "substantially related" to its charitable purpose. So every time you buy a product from a charity, only the profit margin on the item is supporting the organization.

While the profit is generally small, the total revenue of shop and catalog sales can reach impressive proportions. New York City's Metropolitan Museum of Art raised almost $70 million in 1989, nearly half of its total revenues, from sales through its four catalogs and nine gift shops (not all of them in New York).

Giving Via Credit Card Purchases

I've heard that I can support charities through my credit card purchases. How does that work?

So-called "affinity" credit cards pay a small percentage of the amount of your purchases, or a small amount for each time you use the card, to nonprofits that have struck deals with the card issuers. It's a painless way to give, and there are no fund-raising costs for the charity.

You may want to call your favorite charity to see if it benefits from any credit card program. Or consider the Working Assets card. Working Assets Funding Service is a nonprofit organization that receives five cents every time you use its card. Each year, cardholders nominate charities to receive the resulting funds and, after they are screened for effectiveness, vote how to allocate funds among 32 of them. In 1989, the major beneficiaries were Greenpeace, the National Abortion Rights Action League, the National Gay and Lesbian Task Force, the Environmental Defense Fund, Amnesty International, and Habitat for Humanity. Working Assets also offers other arrangements which give "progressive" nonprofits one percent of your long-distance phone charges and two percent of the cost of your travel purchases. You can get more information by calling Working Assets at 800-522-7759.

You get no tax deduction for credit card charity, because you are not actually making a donation. An alternative, if you're eligible, is to get one of the cards that gives you a one-percent credit on your purchases. At the end of the year, you can write a tax-deductible check to your favorite cause in the amount of the total credits you have received.

Last Christmas, I got a card from a business friend saying she'd contributed to an animal welfare group in my name. Is this practice common?

Not yet, but it's certainly on the increase. You know the feeling of trying to figure out what to give someone who has everything? Or someone with whom you've been trading dumb presents for years? Some people, and some businesses, are now forsaking nature calendars and bottles of liquor in favor of cards announcing a gift in the recipient's name. Some report a warm response from the recipient and a feeling on both sides that this is closer to what Christmas is all about. Charities report instances where the gift cards have prompted recipients to send in a donation of their own. An increasing number of charities are encouraging the trend by offering attractive holiday cards to announce the gift. It's a healthy trend which will probably grow as more charities promote the concept. Of course, the same idea can work for you on any occasion that normally calls for a card or gift: a birthday, wedding, anniversary, birth, illness or death.

When earthquakes, hurricanes or famines occur, what's the best way to get help to victims?

First, find out what organizations are providing assistance, then perform a quick evaluation to determine which one you should support. Newspapers often list organizations active in relief efforts in areas hit by natural disasters. Check the list against the charities described in this book or against information you get from other sources. You may want to stick to established relief organizations and avoid ad hoc groups with no track records.

How much money do I need to set up my own foundation?

There's no minimum amount. Some people with quite modest means establish private foundations. However, there are legal costs and paperwork, so don't plunge into it without some careful consideration of the pros and cons. A good start would be to read the latest edition of John Edie's *First Steps in Starting a Foundation,* published by the Council on Foundations. Contact the Council, 1828 L Street, NW Suite 300, Washington, DC 20036 —202-466-6512, to purchase a copy or to request additional information. Also discuss the idea with an accountant or financial planner to make sure it is in your financial interest. The indispensable next step is to hire experienced legal counsel. As an alternative to your own foundation, consider establishing a "pooled common fund" or a donor-advised fund in conjunction with your favorite charity or your community foundation (discussed above).

What charities are most successful at raising funds?

It depends on what funds you mean. The Young Men's Christian Association had the highest income of any nonprofit in America in 1988, but much of that income came not from contributions, but from membership fees. Following the YMCA in terms of total income, according to information compiled by the *NonProfit Times*, were Lutheran Social Ministry Organizations, American Red Cross, Salvation Army, Catholic Charities, U.S. Committee for UNICEF, Goodwill Industries of America, Shriners Hospital for Crippled Children, Boy Scouts of America and United Jewish Appeal. The *NonProfit Times'* complete list of the 100 "biggest" charities in America is presented in Appendix D, with a breakdown of sources of income into public support, government, membership fees and other categories.

What's the difference between charities that ask for contributions and those that offer memberships?

Sometimes the difference is real and sometimes it isn't. For some charities, membership makes you part of the governing process; you will be asked to vote for officers and members of the board of directors and perhaps on priorities for the coming year. If there are local chapters, membership may entitle you to participate in their governance and activities. For many charities, membership means that you receive a magazine, a book or, in some cases, a card entitling you to various discounts. Occasionally, membership is no more than a card stating that you are a member; here it is purely a marketing device, calculated to make you feel more bonded to the organization. Except in this last instance, it costs the organization money to provide you with the privileges of membership and the cause is receiving less than if you simply made a donation. So if you never get around to reading the magazine, consider asking the charity to withhold it in your case.

Why do charities sponsor events such as formal balls? It seems to me they must be very expensive to run and probably produce little revenue for the cause.

It's true that the fund-raising expenses of dinner-dances, fashion shows and golf-tennis outings are sometimes high. Of course, a charity benefits more from a straight donation of $200 than from your purchase of a $200 ticket to a charity ball. But special events have other attractions for charities. They can be public relations bonanzas that bring the organization to the attention of thousands of people. They can educate attendees by introducing them to the charity's clientele or programs (for example, the organization for retarded citizens that intersperses its clients among guests at its swank dinner-dance). And they can forge a bond between attendees and the charity, which can yield volunteer assistance and major gifts long after the event is over. So, there can be far more to such events than is revealed by a fund-raising percentage.

On the other hand, there are some special events that don't bring these benefits, that are held because "well, we've always done it." Charities should engage in periodic evaluations to gauge whether the money and volunteer time invested in the annual dinner-dance might produce more results if spent on other kinds of fund-raising or directly on programs.

If you're interested in helping a charity that seems to be tied to unproductive special events, don't just go on donning your formal wear. Ask for an evaluation of

Charity Events

the last few events. If the evaluation doesn't convince you—or, more likely, if it doesn't exist—you have two excellent ways to express your concerns. The simplest is to write a letter explaining that you don't care to attend the $200-per-couple ball, and to enclose a $200 contribution. More time-consuming, but also more likely to change the charity's policy, is to volunteer to help the organization evaluate its special events and consider alternative means of accomplishing its goals.

Those celebrities who appear in ads for charities, do they actually work for or give money to them, or do they just lend their names?

Charity Celebrities

There are thousands of "charity celebrities" and, of course, they have widely differing relationships with charities. Some do nothing more than lend their names—though in many cases, that is a very valuable "gift." Some take an active role in telethons and other time-consuming fund-raisers. Others volunteer to do everything from pounding nails to serving on boards of directors to testifying before Congress. There's even a nonprofit Celebrity Outreach Foundation, which matches notables with charities they would like to help.

One celebrity, actor Paul Newman, has used his fame to help a number of charities in a unique way. He helped create two food companies, Newman's Own, Inc. and Salad King, Inc., which contribute 100 percent of their profits to charities. Since 1982, the companies, which produce salad dressing, spaghetti sauce, popcorn and lemonade, have given $28 million to a wide variety of charitable institutions.

How can I find out about giving to charities in foreign countries?

Giving Overseas

First consult that old standby, the *Encyclopedia of Associations,* to see if there are any American or international organizations dedicated to the country that interests you. For many countries, you will find several associations that may be able to advise you about the kind of giving you have in mind. Another source of information is the country's embassy or consulate, but be aware that you may not get much help if you want to give to social welfare or environmental groups that might be considered anti-government or anti-establishment.

For giving in Canada, the process is simpler. The

Canadian Council of Better Business Bureaus and some of its branches have Philanthropic Advisory Services similar to the U.S. organization. For the national office, call 416-669-1248, or write 2180 Steels Avenue West, Suite 219, Concord, ON, Canada L4K 2Z5. And the Charities Division of Revenue Canada can provide copies of a registered charity's "Public Information Return."

You may want to think twice about giving directly to a foreign charity, however. They are difficult to evaluate and they provide you with no tax break. A better course is to give a restricted donation to a U.S. charity that conducts the kinds of programs you favor in the country you have in mind. Given the number and variety of our charitable organizations, you are almost certain to find an appropriate one. In several cases, you can give to an American affiliate of a foreign charity. Ask the embassy or consulate, an expatriate or social organization, for information.

Apparently, some charities pay their fund-raisers a flat fee, while others pay a percentage of the money they raise. Which way is better?

There is no easy answer to this question. Percentage-based fees have passionate detractors and proponents. Arguments against percentage fees are that they encourage questionable claims and high-pressure solicitations, ignore the long-term interests of the charity, discourage contributors and provide unfair profits to fund-raisers. They may also harm fund-raising in a broader sense, because they contribute to an attitude of "let the fund-raiser do it," instead of to the kind of cooperation which is the key to successful campaigns. On the other hand, small nonprofits sometimes extol percentage fees as a no-risk arrangement for organizations that can't afford to pay flat fees.

The National Society of Fund Raising Executives (NSFRE) has recently altered its view on the issue. Its ethics code barred percentage fees until 1989, but now permits them. The change came about at least in part because of fears that the ban constituted a "restraint of trade" in violation of federal antitrust laws.

Flat Fee vs. Percentage Fund-Raising

Endowment Funds

I'm not sure that I completely understand endowment funds, but I think I'd rather give money that a charity will put to use right away, rather than have it stashed away in some savings account. Any advice?

Every charity, like every family, ought to have a rainy day fund, perhaps one that will yield some interest for everyday expenses. That's the idea of an endowment; it is money that is set aside and will not be used for current purposes. Endowment money *is* put to use right away in a sense, though, because it starts earning interest for the charity on the day it is invested. So it's perfectly reasonable and appropriate to give to an endowment campaign or to earmark a regular donation for endowment, but it is equally reasonable to restrict your donation to current programs. If you have strong feelings either way, just tell the charity how you want your money to be spent — and, to be safe, write it on your check. Before you decide one way or the other, you might want to call the staff of the charity and ask their views.

Government Support for Charities

Did the big federal spending cutbacks of the Reagan years hurt charities or did the private sector pick up the slack?

There were huge cutbacks, all right. According to Johns Hopkins University's Institute for Policy Studies, federal assistance to nonprofits, excluding Medicare and Medicaid payments, dropped 20% between 1980 and 1988, amounting to about $30 billion, adjusted for inflation. At the same time, other cuts caused an increased demand for nonprofit services. While there was brave talk about the private sector assuming the burden, there were also tax changes making contributions less attractive. Changes in the business world, such as the mergers, acquisitions and leveraged buyouts that have transformed the corporate landscape, also hurt nonprofits by eliminating some giving programs and limiting others. As a result of a number of such factors, the private sector made up for only about one third of the government cuts.

This loss has produced several changes in the way nonprofits operate, some of which you have probably seen signs of. There is more emphasis on volunteers, managerial efficiency and sophisticated fund-raising.

There is increasing use of marketing research techniques to target services and sharpen messages. And there is a rise in the number of charities entering into cooperative marketing arrangements with private enterprises. In most of these ventures, the charity agrees to let a corporation use its name to help sell a product, for which it receives money in proportion to the amount sold.

Aren't there a lot of charities that support the same causes, and wouldn't it be more efficient if they merged?

With almost 450,000 charities in the United States, there are bound to be many with overlapping purposes and services. That's not necessarily a bad thing. Many have specializations which, at least to their adherents, justify their separate existence. Animal welfare groups are a good case in point. There are literally thousands, but many have goals and methods which distinguish them: some attack all forms of hunting, while others promote it; some oppose all animal experimentation, while others urge that it be more humane; some fund zoos, while others seek to abolish them; some champion vegetarianism; some specialize in a single breed of dog; some condone lawbreaking; and some simply limit their activities to a city or region.

Even where groups have identical aims, there may be value in their separate existence. A new, small organization may produce innovative ideas, fresh approaches and novel ways to attract funds which would never be considered by an established charity.

There are ways to produce more efficiency without discouraging the benefits that come from small size and new approaches. It might be in the interests of some charities to merge, especially where two organizations provide similar services in different geographical areas. Other nonprofits—even those with completely different aims—could save considerable sums by sharing facilities, equipment and perhaps even some staff. If you feel strongly about the need for such cooperation, of for a merger, volunteer to help your favorite small charity by studying the possibilities and reporting to the board of directors. They might not like the idea at first, but they should at least be willing to hear your conclusions. If you don't want to get that involved, or if the organization

Redundancy and Efficiency Among Charities

declines your offer, put your case in writing and, if you're so inclined, tell them that you'll give your money to more efficient charities.

My gifts seem so puny in the face of all the world's problems. Any suggestions about how I can magnify my efforts?

Magnifying Your Efforts

Several. We've already discussed matching gift programs and how you might be able to persuade your employer to start or expand such a program. Also at work, you might time your efforts with the annual federated campaign. Maybe you can get some colleagues to join you in a committee to study the list of federated agencies and select a few especially efficient and effective charities as objects of your gifts. Or, where the campaign allows you to write in names of charities, do some research and suggest particularly worthy candidates to your fellow employees. At other times of the year, when news events—famine, earthquakes, hurricanes, health issues or problems at a nearby cultural institution—cause sudden interest among your co-workers, you might offer the names of organizations you believe are the best vehicles for assistance.

Apart from your place of employment, you might attempt to organize or improve the giving program of your Junior League, Lions, Rotary, Kiwanis or other such organization. Or you might form a group of friends, relatives or associates in your neighborhood, club or congregation. Discuss your ideas about charity and advocate giving in concert. Remember, as you put down this book and go forth as a consumer-minded giver, that you have something to teach your friends. Expand the good you can do by helping them examine their giving habits and maximize the impact of their charity dollars.

Introducing Children to Charitable Giving

I'd like to raise my children to care about charity. Any suggestions?

Sure, though they all relate to the obvious advice to set a good example. The best way to introduce young people to charity is through volunteerism. As soon as your children are old enough to be helpful, take them with you to a soup kitchen or an environmental clean-up project. When they get a little older, consider sending them to a summer camp which specializes in volunteer activities and encourage them to go off on volunteer projects of their own.

To encourage your children to give money to charities and to be thoughtful about it, involve them in the process of looking over appeals for contributions and discuss with them the relative merits of various organizations. When they reach an appropriate age, you can give them a small amount of money and let them decide how to distribute it, or suggest that they use it put on a small show or carnival, with the proceeds going to the charity of their choice. Finally, when the kids graduate from high school or college, you might consider establishing a small supporting foundation or pooled common fund in their names. By providing such a background, you'll have opened the door to a lifetime of systematic giving.

The following information on 382 leading national charities has been extracted from reports prepared by the National Charities Information Bureau (NCIB). NCIB is a nonprofit organization founded in 1918, with the mission of helping contributors give wisely and encouraging charities to meet basic standards in their operations and reporting. NCIB initiates a report when it receives a significant number of inquiries about an organization and revises reports periodically or when there are substantial changes, especially in the charity's adherence to NCIB standards. The status of all charities on which NCIB reports is summarized in NCIB's periodical *Wise Giving Guide*. You can obtain a free copy of the *Wise Giving Guide* and up to three reports on individual charities by contacting NCIB at 19 Union Square West, New York, NY 10003-3395—212-929-6300.

It is important to emphasize that NCIB reports are accurate as of the date they are released, but that all information is subject to change as charities alter their programs and practices. If you have a strong interest in a specific charity, read the report in this book, then call or write NCIB to see if more recent information is available. Or contact the Philanthropic Advisory Service of the Council of Better Business Bureaus (Dept. 023, Washington, DC 20042-0023—703-276-0100), which may have information on the same organization.

This book presents information on all the charities identified by NCIB as having current reports as of July 1, 1990. NCIB focuses on national organizations that have stimulated broad contributor interest. NCIB does not generally report about religious, fraternal or political organizations, or about local institutions. A charity's absence from this book or from the NCIB's report files has no negative significance whatsoever.

Some of the entries in this directory are incomplete, for one of several reasons. Where the NCIB was, at press time, revising its report, the editor has decided that circumstances may have changed to such an extent that an entry might be seriously misleading. In other cases, a partial report has been given when the most recent NCIB report is based on 1985 figures or earlier, because the information may be out of date. And smaller charities, with expenditures under $1 million as of the latest report, have been given only partial entries.

An important feature of NCIB's reports is the evaluation of charities according to its standards. The current standards are reprinted in Appendix A and summarized on page 15-16 of this book. Prior to July 1, 1988, NCIB used a slightly different set of standards, also reprinted in Appendix A.

The entries that follow present only a portion of the information provided in the corresponding NCIB reports. NCIB played no role in determining what information would be included in our entries and how it would be expressed. Additional details about finances, programs, structure, governance and staffing may be obtained by reading the original reports.

Here's what you need to know about the information presented in the entries that follow:

- **Order of Entries** - Charities are grouped according to their chief function under headings based on those used by NCIB. Cross-references will guide you to related charities included under other headings, and the alphabetical index makes it easy to find any organization in the book.

- **Name of Charity** - The formal name of the organization is presented as it appears in NCIB listings. Consult the index for references to other versions of the name. Reports on charities that have changed their names since 1986 show the former name immediately following the current name.

- **Year of Data** - The fiscal year of the data NCIB used for its report. If this information seems dated in some cases, it is often because audited financial statements are not available until long after the close of the fiscal year.

- **Expenditures** - The total cash expenditures of the organization in the year reported. The value of distributed supplies and equipment is excluded from this figure.

- **Percent to Program** - The percentage of total cash expenditures which is devoted to programs of the organization, as opposed to those expenditures devoted to management/general and fund-raising costs. Where NCIB believes that information submitted by a charity portrays program expenditures inappropriately, NCIB recalculates the figures.

- **Fund-raising Cost**s - The amount of fund-raising expenditures as a percentage of related *support/revenue* (not as a percentage of *expenditures*, as in the Percent to Program statistic; these percentages are unrelated and do not add up to 100%). NCIB sometimes averages this cost over a number of years to present a fairer picture. Where NCIB believes that information submitted by a charity portrays fund-raising costs inappropriately, NCIB recalculates the figures. NCIB advises that proper allocation and evaluation of fund-raising costs can be complex and suggests that contributors place more emphasis on a charity's Percent to Program figure.

- **Contributions Deductible** - Whether the organization's tax status allows you to claim a charitable deduction for your contribution.

- **Top of Staff Salary Range** - The maximum salary permitted by the organization's salary policy, as reported by the charity in the year indicated. NCIB asks charities to report the dollar value of salary, deferred compensation and such benefits as housing, but some may not be scrupulous in submitting complete information in these areas. In some instances, therefore, the figure presented here may underrepresent the total compensation package of any employees who are paid the maximum salary in the range.

- **Meets NCIB Standards** - Organizations that meet all standards are reported with a "Yes." Organizations that have provided NCIB with insufficient information to evaluate them are reported with a "?". Organizations that fail to meet one of the standards are reported with a "No," followed by the numbers of the standards failed. A question mark after a number indicates that NCIB raises questions, but has not reached a conclusion, about adherence to that standard. See the Comments section for NCIB's reasons for classifying standards as failed or questioned. Following the report on compliance is the date of NCIB's most recent report; because the numbering of standards changed with the introduction of revised standards on July 1, 1988, it is important to note whether NCIB's report was issued before or after that date and to refer to the appropriate version of the standards in Appendix A.

- **Purpose** - A succinct statement of the charity's purpose, either quoted or paraphrased from the organization's literature.

- **Program** - A brief description of the charity's program activities in the year indicated, with the percentage of *total* cash expenditures devoted to each program (note that the percentages are of the total of program, management/general and fund-raising expenditures; therefore, they will not add up to 100%, but should instead approximate the Percent to Program figure). Programs consuming less than 5 percent of the organization's total expenditures are not reported.

- **Comments** - Extracts of NCIB reports relating to the charity's organizational structure, its adherence to NCIB standards, its sources of income, and the quality of its financial and program reporting.

The abbreviation "N/A" in any category means that the necessary information was not available, generally because the charity did not provide it to NCIB.

CONTENTS
Directory of Charitable Organizations

ANIMAL-RELATED

animal protection, wildlife preservation

AFRICAN WILDLIFE FOUNDATION, INC.

1717 Massachusetts Avenue, NW
Washington, DC 20036
(202) 265-8393

> Year of Data: 1987
> Expenditures: $1,363,997
> Percent to Program: 74.8%
> Fund-raising Costs: 14%
> Contributions Deductible: Yes
> Top of Staff Salary Range: $98,000 (1988)
> Meets NCIB Standards: Yes (1/11/89)

Purpose: To "promote the conservation of the wildlife resources of Africa, primarily through a program of education designed to develop a trained African leadership technically qualified in wildlife management and related skills"

Program: Fiscal 1987 activities included:

• Conservation Education and Training (37%) - support for youth hostels in national parks, education centers and activities of over 1000 Wildlife Clubs in Africa; support for educational activity at a Tanzanian college and a Kenyan university; workshops for incorporating a conservation curriculum into a Kenyan literacy program

• Aid to Parks and Reserves (25%) - support of managers of national parks and reserves throughout Africa; supply of radios, uniforms, vehicles and other items

• Field Operations (13%) - operation of an office in Kenya, from which visiting scientists and conservation experts may carry out their projects

Comments: NCIB recommends improvements in AWF's annual report and audited financial statements.

AMERICAN HUMANE ASSOCIATION

9725 East Hampden Avenue
Denver, CO 80231
(303) 695-0811

> Year of Data: 1988
> Expenditures: $2,834,827
> Percent to Program: 80%
> Fund-raising Costs: 10.3%
> Contributions Deductible: Yes
> Top of Staff Salary Range: $70,000 (N/R)
> Meets NCIB Standards: Yes (4/7/89)

Purpose: "To prevent neglect, abuse, cruelty and exploitation of children and animals and to assure that their interests and well-being are fully, effectively and humanely guaranteed by an aware and caring society"

Program: Fiscal 1988 activities included:

• Animal Protection (47%) - provision of expertise and guidance to local humane societies, municipal animal control departments and government agencies; consultative services on animal-related topics; advocacy for animal protection activities; training programs for animal care and control personnel; humane education materials for children and adults; publications include a bimonthly newsletter and a quarterly magazine

• Child Protection (33%) - development of a child sexual abuse curriculum for social workers; development of a data base of child protection policies in the states and territories; support for efforts to assess and correct child and spouse maltreatment in the military; response to information requests; publications include a bimonthly newsletter and a quarterly magazine

Comments: AHA's Child Protection program is funded primarily by government grants and contracts, and by income from investments, trusts and bequests. In fiscal 1988, AHA received $166,765 in royalty payments for marketing endorsements of commercial products, such as Cats Pride Premium Kitty Litter. NCIB recommends improvements in AHA's audited financial statements and budget.

ANIMAL PROTECTION INSTITUTE OF AMERICA

6130 Freeport Boulevard
P.O. Box 22505
Sacramento, CA 95822
(916) 422-1921

Purpose: To educate "the public regarding the alleviation of cruelty toward animals, the preservation of animal lives in a natural environment, and the alleviation of problems connected with an over-population of unwanted pets and abandoned and neglected animals and wildlife"

Comments: NCIB is currently preparing a new report on this organization.

ANIMAL WELFARE INSTITUTE

P.O. Box 3650
Washington, DC 20007
(202) 337-2332

Year of Data: 1988
Expenditures $439,633
Percent to Program: 76%
Fund-raising Costs: 7%
Contributions Deductible: Yes
Top of Staff Salary Range: N/A
Meets NCIB Standards: Yes (7/14/89)

Purpose: "To promote the welfare of all animals and to reduce the total of pain and fear inflicted on animals by man"

Comments: The editor deemed this organization too small (under $1 million in expenditures in the most recent year reported) to be given a complete listing.

DEFENDERS OF WILDLIFE

1244 19th Street, NW
Washington, DC 20036
(202) 659-9510

Purpose: To "preserve the natural abundance and diversity of native wild animals and plants, and to protect the habitats on which they depend"

Comments: NCIB is currently preparing a new report on this organization.

DUCKS UNLIMITED, INC.

One Waterfowl Way
Long Grove, IL 60047
(708) 438-4300

Year of Data: 1986
Expenditures: $54,306,655
Percent to Program: 67.3%
Fund-raising Costs: 30.6%
Contributions Deductible: Yes
Top of Staff Salary Range: N/A
Meets NCIB Standards: Yes (6/23/88)

Purpose: "To help restore and rehabilitate prime waterfowl breeding grounds in Canada, where over 70 percent of North America's waterfowl are hatched" and throughout North America

Program: Fiscal 1986 activities included:
- Transfer to Ducks Unlimited Canada (42%) - DU's funds comprised 85% of DU Canada's total revenues in 1986; DU Canada used the funds to develop over 50,000 acres of new habitat, conduct engineering surveys of new project sites, conduct "preliminary reconnaissance surveys" and evaluate 2,600 marshes
- United States Habitat (8%) - matching aid to help states acquire and enhance wetlands
- Conservation Education (6%) - publication of a bimonthly magazine and educational efforts, including films, brochures and symposiums

Comments: NCIB's report is primarily about Ducks Unlimited, Inc. (U.S.), but contains some information about two separately incorporated organizations, Ducks Unlimited Canada and Ducks Unlimited de Mexico, which are largely funded by DU. The report does not include information about DU's 3,600 chapters and committees. In 1988, DU reported having 576,000 members. NCIB does not consider DU's fund-raising cost percentage as a material deviation from its standard of 30%. NCIB recommends improvements in DU's annual report.

FRIENDS OF ANIMALS, INC. and COMMITTEE FOR HUMANE LEGISLATION, INC.

30 Haviland Street
Norwalk, CT 06856
(203) 866-5223

Year of Data: 1987
Expenditures: $3,116,457
Percent to Program: 89.1%
Fund-raising Costs: 8.2%
Contributions Deductible: FOA: Yes; CHL: No
Top of Staff Salary Range: $30,000 (1987)
Meets NCIB Standards: Yes (8/12/88)

Purpose: To prevent cruelty to and exploitation of animals through education and programs "to humanely limit animal births through the spaying of the female cat and dog and through other humane methods as they become available;" the Committee for Humane Legislation's purpose is "To educate the public and lobby on behalf of animals"

Program: Fiscal 1987 activities included:

- Spaying Costs (73%) - support for a large-scale spaying program which subsidizes the spaying and altering of about 60,000 to 70,000 cats and dogs per year; FOA sells discount spaying certificates to the public and arranges with over 800 veterinarians in 46 states to accept the certificates as payment in full for spaying operations; veterinarians send certificates to FOA for payment
- Public Information and Animal Protection (16%) - including publications; grants to a wildlife sanctuary and to an organization studying ways to limit the use of animals in medical research

Comments: FOA has chapters in New York, New Jersey and New England. It maintains thrift shops in New Jersey, Florida and Connecticut. In fiscal 1987, proceeds from animal spaying services provided 46% of the organization's total revenues. FOA has described CHL as its "legislative arm." FOA did not provide an annual report for NCIB's review, though it stated its intention of producing one for fiscal 1988. NCIB recommends improvements in FOA's budget presentation. FOA places donation canisters in retail stores as part of its fund-raising efforts. NCIB points out that such campaigns are generally difficult to administer and control and suggests that potential contributors request information about how money is distributed. In the case of one of FOA's efforts, about 30% of the money collected in canisters was paid to the persons who collected them.

THE FUND FOR ANIMALS, INC.

200 West 57th Street
New York, NY 10019
(212) 246-2096

Year of Data: 1987
Expenditures: $1,288,376
Percent to Program: 73%
Fund-raising Costs: 8.5%
Contributions Deductible: Yes
Top of Staff Salary Range: $15,000 (1987)
Meets NCIB Standards: Yes (8/1/88)

Purpose: "To promote the alleviation of fear, the prevention of pain and the relief of suffering of animals everywhere and to foster humane conduct toward animals and encourage and support the cooperation among all persons interested in humane activities"

Program: Fiscal 1987 activities included:

- Animal Rescue and Protection (47%) - rescue of animals in danger and operation of facilities in Texas and California which provide shelter for burros and other animals that have been abused, injured or "destined for slaughter houses and laboratory experimentation;" also included are grants to "allied organizations"
- Humane Education (23%) - publication and distribution of pamphlets and a newsletter

Comments: NCIB recommends improvements in FA's annual report.

HUMANE SOCIETY OF THE UNITED STATES

2100 L Street, NW
Washington, DC 20037
(202) 452-1100

Year of Data: 1988
Expenditures: $10,286,885
Percent to Program: 65.8%
Fund-raising Costs: 23.3%
Contributions Deductible: Yes
Top of Staff Salary Range: $140,000 (1988)
Meets NCIB Standards: ?: 1, 8 (8/30/89)

Purpose: To "prevent and eliminate the abuse and suffering of animals." Major goals include reducing overbreeding of cats and dogs; exposing and eliminating the suffering of animals used in biomedical research, competitive events and blood sports; correcting inhumane conditions for animals in zoos, circuses, pet shops and kennels; and stopping cruelty to animals that are mass produced for food.

Program: HSUS's reporting of its expenditures does not allow a detailed breakdown of its spending on individual programs. In general, the organization's activities in 1988 included: campaigns to discourage purchase of furs and to encourage spaying and neutering household pets; efforts to make cockfighting illegal; legal action to apply sanctions against Iceland for killing whales and to embargo purchase of tuna from countries that do not protect dolphins from fishing nets; lobbying Congress for the discontinuation of releasing pound animals for research and for passage of legislation protecting marine mammals, elephants and other endangered species; and evaluating shelters for counties and municipalities. HSUS reports that its investigations in 22 states uncovered cruelties in horse and dog racing, puppy mills, pet shops, auctions, zoos and animal shelters. HSUS publishes a periodical with a circulation of almost 300,000 and a number of pamphlets; in 1988, it also produced two video programs.

Comments: In 1987, a committee of HSUS's Board approved purchase of a house as part of its president's compensation package and, because of legal restrictions, accepted a donated property by putting the title in the name of an executive vice president. These transactions were not reported to the full Board of Directors at its next meeting and were not accurately reported in the organization's 1987 audited financial statements. These actions led NCIB to question whether the Board had exercised its trustee and management responsibilities and whether HSUS had adhered to Standard 1, particularly 1g, and Standard 8.

INTERNATIONAL FUND FOR ANIMAL WELFARE

NCIB reports that, as of July 1, 1990, this organization has not, over a period of several years, furnished requested information sufficient to prepare a report.

NATIONAL ANTI-VIVISECTION SOCIETY

53 West Jackson Boulevard, Suite 1550
Chicago, IL 60604-3795
(312) 427-6065

Year of Data: 1989
Expenditures: $1,434,189
Percent to Program: 68%
Fund-raising Costs: 7%
Contributions Deductible: Yes
Top of Staff Salary Range: $58,750 (1989)
Meets NCIB Standards: No: 1e (5/2/90)

Purpose: To "teach methods and means of combating vivisection and inhumane treatment of animals"

Program: NAVS's reporting of financial and other data does not allow a detailed breakdown of its expenses and programs. Fiscal 1989 activities included public awareness programs (production of brochures; advertisements; participation in debates, lectures, rallies and interviews; production of videos, catalogues and brochures); children's programs (stickers, petitions and postcards relating to chimpanzees and an educational film); science programs (support for development and implementation of scientifically valid alternatives to the use of live animals in research, testing and teaching); a small grants program; and activity related to legislation affecting animals.

Comments: NCIB faults NAVS for paying fees to its board members (Standard 1e) and recommends improvements in NAVS's annual report and budget presentation.

NATIONAL HUMANE EDUCATION SOCIETY

NCIB reports that, as of July 1, 1990, this organization has not, over a period of several years, furnished requested information sufficient to prepare a report.

NATIONAL WILDLIFE FEDERATION

1412 16th Street, NW
Washington, DC 20036
(202)797-6800
or
8925 Leesburg Pike
Vienna,VA 22184
(703) 790-4000
(800) 432-6564 (for membership)

Year of Data: 1987
Expenditures: $49,426,000
Percent to Program: 63%
Fund-raising Costs: 28.5%
Contributions Deductible: Yes
Top of Staff Salary Range: $170,000 (1988)
Meets NCIB Standards: Yes (2/13/89)

Purpose: "To encourage the intelligent management of the life-sustaining resources of the earth—its productive soil—its essential water sources—its protective forests and plantlife—and its dependent wildlife—and to promote and encourage the knowledge and appreciation of these resources, their interrelationship and wise use, without which there can be little hope for a continuing abundant life"

Program: Fiscal 1987 activities included:
- Education programs (24%) - including administrative costs of education programs, energy and toxic effects studies, a raptor effects study, legislative activities and legal proceedings
- Nature Education Materials (19%) - costs of producing and marketing books, games, records, cards and other materials with nature and conservation themes
- Associate Member Program (14%) - publication and distribution of various magazines to about 865,000 members
- Ranger Rick Membership (12%) - publication and distribution of a magazine to about 722,000 members, ages 6-12
- Your Big Backyard and NatureScope (6%) - publication and distribution of a magazine to about 430,000 young

children and of a curriculum guide for elementary school teachers

Comments: NCIB's report is about the NWF and the NWF Endowment and does not include state affiliates, autonomous organizations which raise their own funds and conduct their own programs. In fiscal 1987, about 42% of NWF's total revenues came from memberships and 31% from program-related sales. NCIB recommends improvements in NWF's annual report, budget presentation and audited financial statements.

NORTH SHORE ANIMAL LEAGUE, INC.

750 Port Washington Blvd.
Port Washington, NY 11050
(516) 883-7575

Purpose: To operate an animal shelter and provide medical services to animals, primarily in its local area, and to promote animal adoption and spaying through the media nationally

Comments: NCIB is currently preparing a new report on this organization.

PEOPLE FOR THE ETHICAL TREATMENT OF ANIMALS

Box 42516
Washington, DC 20015
(202) 726-0156

Purpose: To "educate the public against speciesism and human chauvinist attitudes towards animals through documentary films and pictures of current conditions in slaughterhouses and experimental laboratories"

Comments: NCIB is in the process of preparing its first report on this organization.

WILDLIFE PRESERVATION TRUST INTERNATIONAL, INC.

34th Street and Girard Avenue
Philadelphia, PA 19104
(215) 222-3636

Year of Data: 1988
Expenditures: $639,011
Percent to Program: N/A
Fund-raising Costs: N/A
Contributions Deductible: Yes
Top of Staff Salary Range: $42,000 (1988)
Meets NCIB Standards: No: 7b, 7c?, 8 (3/2/90)

Purpose: Promoting "education and research in the natural sciences, particularly zoology, with a view to the preservation and conservation of those species of fauna in danger of extinction in the wild state"

Comments: The editor deemed this organization too small (under $1 million in expenditures in the most recent year reported) to be given a complete listing.

WORLD WILDLIFE FUND

1250 24th Street, NW
Washington, DC 20037
(202) 293-4800

Purpose: To "promote conservation, restoration and wise management of living things on Earth, and the common natural environment they share"

Comments: NCIB is currently preparing a new report on this organization.

- **CENTER FOR MARINE CONSERVATION** (see THE ENVIRONMENT)
- **NATIONAL AUDOBON SOCIETY** (see THE ENVIRONMENT)
- **WILDERNESS SOCIETY** (see THE ENVIRONMENT)

ARTS AND HUMANITIES

music, dance, historic preservation, television, theater

ACTION FOR CHILDREN'S TELEVISION

20 University Road
Cambridge, MA 02138
(617) 876-6620

Year of Data: 1986
Expenditures $162,189
Percent to Program: 75.1%
Fund-raising Costs: 4.7%
Contributions Deductible: Yes
Top of Staff Salary Range: $17,500 (1987)
Meets NCIB Standards: Yes (9/4/87)

Purpose: "To encourage and persuade broadcasters and advertisers to provide programming of the highest possible quality designed for children of different ages...; To encourage the development and enforcement of appropriate guidelines relating to children and the media...; To encourage research, experimentation and evaluation in the field of children's television"

Comments: The editor deemed this organization too small (under $1 million in expenditures in the most recent year reported) to be given a complete listing.

AMERICAN SYMPHONY ORCHESTRA LEAGUE

777 14th Street, NW
Washington, DC 20005
(202) 628-0099

Year of Data: 1988
Expenditures: $3,025,317
Percent to Program: 72%
Fund-raising Costs: 25%
Contributions Deductible: Yes
Top of Staff Salary Range: $120,000 (1988)
Meets NCIB Standards: Yes (1/12/90)

Purpose: To ensure the artistic excellence and administrative effectiveness of its member orchestras

Program: Because ASOL's annual report described fiscal 1988 activities under different headings than those used in its audited financial statements, it is not possible to provide detailed information about the organization's program expenditures. Activities included maintenance of a reference library housing orchestra industry data as well as orchestral scores, books and periodicals; consulting services and technical assistance to orchestras in such areas as long-range planning, fund-raising, volunteer management and ticket sales; monitoring legislative activity of concern to the industry; a national conference for 1,800 attendees; seminars, workshops and advanced training courses on orchestra management and other subjects; support for a full year on-the-job training fellowship in orchestra management for seven individuals; and maintenance of an Orchestra Library Information Service, a database of 4,000 compositions for symphony and chamber orchestras.

Comments: The League is primarily a membership organization, with hundreds of symphony orchestras as voting members. Associate or non-voting memberships are available to individuals (including musicians, conductors, music critics, musicologists and members of orchestra boards) and such organizations as educational institutions, libraries and music-related businesses. In fiscal 1988, about 26% of ASOL's total revenues came from membership dues. NCIB recommends improvements in ASOL's annual report.

NATIONAL CORPORATE FUND FOR DANCE

NCIB reports that, as of July 1, 1990, this organization has not, over a period of several years, furnished requested information sufficient to prepare a report.

NATIONAL TRUST FOR HISTORIC PRESERVATION

1785 Massachusetts Avenue, NW
Washington, DC 20036
(202) 673-4000

Year of Data: **1985**
Expenditures $18,538,851
Percent to Program: 78.7%
Fund-raising Costs: 29%
Contributions Deductible: Yes
Top of Staff Salary Range: $120,000 (1986)
Meets NCIB Standards: Yes (6/26/86)

Purpose: To identify and act on national preservation issues by initiating demonstration projects and model programs, advocating preservation policies in legislative, judicial, administrative and private forums, aiding local groups through providing preservation expertise, technical advice and financial assistance, working with Congress for a national preservation agenda, and offering educational programs for organizations and private citizens

Comments: The editor deemed NCIB's information about this organization too dated (1985 data or before) to give the organization a complete listing.

THE STATUE OF LIBERTY - ELLIS ISLAND FOUNDATION, INC.

52 Vanderbilt Avenue
New York, NY 10017
(212) 883-1986

Year of Data: 1987
Expenditures: $106,430,188
Percent to Program: 91.6%
Fund-raising Costs: 14.7%
Contributions Deductible: Yes
Top of Staff Salary Range: $101,000 (1987)
Meets NCIB Standards: Yes (7/22/88)

Purpose: "Restoration and preservation of the Statue of Liberty and Ellis Island"

Program: Fiscal 1987 activities included:
- Restoration and Preservation (53%) - activities to restore, preserve and protect the Statue of Liberty National Monument
- Public Awareness and Education (39%) - efforts to stimulate public interest in and knowledge of the history of the Statue of Liberty, including costs of the Liberty Weekend Centennial Celebration (see comments)

Comments: NCIB advises contributors that SLEIF is raising money for only the northern portion of Ellis Island. SLEIF's Liberty Weekend Centennial Celebration, on July 4, 1986, had expenses of $38.6 million, but revenues of only $22.4 million, a $16.1 million loss. In fiscal 1987, about 45% of SLEIF's support came from surcharges on sales of commemorative coins by the U.S. Treasury Department.

- **HELP HOSPITALIZED VETERANS** (see HEALTH-GENERAL)
- **MARTIN LUTHER KING, JR. CENTER FOR NONVIOLENT SOCIAL CHANGE** (see SOCIAL ACTION)

CHILD SPONSORSHIP

international relief ; fund-raising by means of sponsoring children

- **CHILDREN, INCORPORATED** (see INTERNATIONAL RELIEF)
- **CHILDREN INTERNATIONAL** (see INTERNATIONAL RELIEF)
- **CHRISTIAN CHILDREN'S FUND, INC.** (see INTERNATIONAL RELIEF)
- **COMPASSION INTERNATIONAL, INC.** (see INTERNATIONAL RELIEF)
- **FUTURES FOR CHILDREN, INC.** (see INTERNATIONAL RELIEF)
- **PLAN INTERNATIONAL (U.S.A.)** (see INTERNATIONAL RELIEF)
- **SAVE THE CHILDREN FEDERATION, INC.** (see INTERNATIONAL RELIEF)
- **WORLD VISION, INC.** (see INTERNATIONAL RELIEF)

COMMUNITY IMPROVEMENT

beautification, housing and development, community centers, local government

CENTER FOR COMMUNITY CHANGE

NCIB reports that, as of July 1, 1990, this organization has not, over a period of several years, furnished requested information sufficient to prepare a report.

NATIONAL CIVIC LEAGUE
55 West 44th Street
New York, NY 10036
(212) 730-7930

Year of Data: 1984
Expenditures $833,998
Percent to Program: 70.4%
Fund-raising Costs: 24.3%
Contributions Deductible: Yes
Top of Staff Salary Range: $65,000 (1985)
Meets NCIB Standards: Yes (5/14/86)

Purpose: To "multiply the number, harmonize the methods and combine the forces of those who are interested in developing citizens who know how to work together for progressive improvement of our system of government with special attention to the need for more vigorous and responsible state and local institutions"

Comments: The editor deemed this organization too small (under $1 million in expenditures in the most recent year reported) to be given a complete listing.

UNITED WAY OF AMERICA

701 North Fairfax Street
Alexandria, VA 22314-2045
(703) 836-7100

Year of Data: 1986
Expenditures $24,539,044
Percent to Program: 93.7%
Fund-raising Costs: 1.4%
Contributions Deductible: Yes
Top of Staff Salary Range: $230,000 (1987)
Meets NCIB Standards: Yes (11/24/87)

Purpose: To "aid and assist [local United Ways] ... and other similar agencies, organizations and institutions exempt from Federal income taxes ... in their efforts to solicit, collect and otherwise raise, manage and dispose of money for patriotic, charitable, social, philanthropic, eleemosynary and benevolent services of every nature ... [and] to encourage and stimulate planning and cooperation regarding health, welfare and recreation problems and services...."

Program: Fiscal 1986 activities included:
- Management Improvement Services (39%) - includes training, personal and leadership development, executive/staff development and placement, intern training, management and community studies, venture grant programs, regional assistance and maintenance of a reference library
- Campaign Support (29%) - includes technical support for local campaigns, workplace presence activities, corporate development, government relations, development of material for national media, compilation and reporting of fund-raising statistics and production of film and campaign materials
- Communications (14%) - includes marketing research, public relations and advertising, video communications, technical assistance, sponsorship of communications contests and publications
- Planning (10%) - includes centennial programs, health planning, energy planning, community problem solving, community resources development, information and referral, technical assistance, liaison with other United Way organizations, long-range strategic planning activities, needs assessment and development of management information systems

Comments: Approximately 2,200 local United Ways raised about $2.5 billion and supported 37,000 service organizations in 1986. About 72% of UWA's total support in 1986 came from "Membership Support" of local United Ways. UWA does not control or direct the allocations or activities of locals. NCIB's report concerns only the national organization, including its regional offices. NCIB recommends improvements in UWA's annual report.

- **AMERICA THE BEAUTIFUL FUND** (see THE ENVIRONMENT)
- **AMERICAN FORESTY ASSOCIATION** (see THE ENVIRONMENT)
- **LOCAL INITIATIVE SUPPORT CORPORATION** (see HOUSING)
- **NATIONAL URBAN COALITION, INC.** (see HUMAN SERVICE)
- **UNITED NEIGHBORHOOD CENTERS OF AMERICAN** (see HUMAN SERVICE)

CONSUMER PROTEC- TION, LEGAL AID

HALT, INC. (HELP ABOLISH LEGAL TYRANNY)
1319 F Street, NW, Suite 300
Washington, DC 20004
(202) 347-9600

Year of Data: 1988
Expenditures: $2,723,128
Percent to Program: 33.3%
Fund-raising Costs: 66.9%
Contributions Deductible: Yes
Top of Staff Salary Range: $41,500 (1988)
Meets NCIB Standards: No: 6a, 8? (5/21/90)

Purpose: "Public education regarding the law, legal procedures, and legal services; the development and support of alternative means for resolving legal disputes; and the general reduction of the cost and improvement of the quality of available legal services"

Program: Most of HALT's program spending in fiscal 1988 (63% of total expenditures) was for public education, largely for multipurpose direct mail campaigns, but also for appearances on local and national media, distribution of a quarterly newsletter and a conference.

Comments: NCIB points out that HALT's major activity, in terms of expenses, is conducting a direct mail campaign, which, in 1988, accounted for over half the organization's expenditures. HALT considers this campaign primarily as a means of informing people about its message and treats 75% of the costs as program expenditures. NCIB disagrees and calculates HALT's program expenditures as only 33% of total expenses, in violation of Standard 6a. NCIB also questions whether HALT's financial statements accurately reflect its program and supporting service expenses (Standard 8).

NATIONAL LEGAL AID AND DEFENDER ASSOCIATION
1625 K Street, NW, 8th Fl.
Washington, DC 20006
(202) 452-0620

Year of Data: **1985**
Expenditures $1,359,865
Percent to Program: 62.1%
Fund-raising Costs: 10%
Contributions Deductible: Yes
Top of Staff Salary Range: $62,800 (1985)
Meets NCIB Standards: Yes (10/3/86)

Purpose: To "promote and develop legal aid and defender work; to encourage the formation of new legal aid and defender organizations, wherever they may be needed, whose purpose shall be to render legal services without charge, if necessary, to all who may appear to be entitled thereto, and who are unable to procure such assistance elsewhere, and to promote measures for their protection"

Comments: The editor deemed NCIB's information about this organization too dated (1985 data or before) to give the organization a complete listing.

PACIFIC LEGAL FOUNDATION
NCIB reports that, as of July 1, 1990, this organization has not, over a period of several years, furnished requested information sufficient to prepare a report.

PUBLIC CITIZEN
NCIB reports that, as of July 1, 1990, this organization has not, over a period of several years, furnished requested information sufficient to prepare a report.

WASHINGTON LEGAL FOUNDATION
NCIB reports that, as of July 1, 1990, this organization has not, over a period of several years, furnished requested information sufficient to prepare a report.

- **MORALITY IN MEDIA** (see CRIME PREVENTION)
- **NATIONAL HEAD INJURY FOUNDATION** (see HEALTH-GENERAL)

CRIME PREVENTION, PUBLIC PROTECTION

crime prevention, drug usage, obscenity, highway safety, child abuse

CHILDREN'S LEGAL FOUNDATION
(formerly Citizens for Decency Through Law)

2845 E. Camelback Road, Suite 740
Phoenix, AZ 85016
(602) 381-1322

Purpose: To eliminate "material which violates our nation's obscenity laws; inform the public of the problems associated with pornography; and demand and assist enforcement of the law"

Comments: NCIB is currently preparing a new report on this organization.

FORTUNE SOCIETY, INC.

39 West 19th Street
New York, NY 10011
(212) 206-7070

Year of Data: **1983**
Expenditures $747,787
Percent to Program: 72.1%
Fund-raising Costs: 13.7%
Contributions Deductible: Yes
Top of Staff Salary Range: $45,000 (1985)
Meets NCIB Standards: Yes (2/13/85)

Purpose: "To create a greater public awareness of the prison system in America today; to help the public understand the problems and complexities confronting inmates during their incarceration and when they return to society; to work with released prisoners on a one-to-one basis, helping them in their adjustment to society; to develop community involvement with crime-prevention programs by creating alternatives for the released convict"

Comments: The editor deemed NCIB's information about this organization too dated (1985 data or before) to give the organization a complete listing.

JUST SAY NO INTERNATIONAL
(formerly Just Say No Foundation)
(Preliminary Report)

1777 North California Blvd., Suite 210
Walnut Creek, CA 94596
(415) 939-6666 or (800) 258-2766

Year of Data: 1987
Expenditures: $1,041,866
Percent to Program: 66.6%
Fund-raising Costs: 27.7%
Contributions Deductible: Yes
Top of Staff Salary Range: $60,840 (1988)
Meets NCIB Standards: No Determination (5/4/88)

Purpose: To foster and reinforce "an attitude of intolerance toward drugs and drug use; [promote] healthy lifestyles and constructive alternatives to the use of dangerous drugs; [provide] children and teenagers with the information, skills, and support they need to resist peer pressure and other influences to use drugs"

Program: JSNI reported that its fiscal 1987 activities included provision of free or low-cost books, pamphlets and "training modules" to support Just Say No Clubs or encourage their formation.

Comments: About 41% of JSNI's total support for 1987 was in government grants. JSNI was so new at the time of NCIB's report that it had not yet produced an annual report or audited financial statements. Consequently, NCIB deferred judgment concerning JSNI's adherence to standards.

MORALITY IN MEDIA

475 Riverside Drive
New York, NY 10115
(212) 870-3222

Year of Data: 1986
Expenditures: $1,016,933
Percent to Program: 63.1%
Fund-raising Costs: 29.3%
Contributions Deductible: Yes
Top of Staff Salary Range: $75,000 (1987)
Meets NCIB Standards: Yes (11/20/87)

Purpose: "To educate and alert parents and community leaders to the problem of, the scale of, and the danger in distribution of obscene material. To encourage communities to express themselves in a unified, organized way (a) to legitimate media requesting responsibility and (b) to law enforcement officials urging vigorous enforcement of obscenity law in the case of out-and-out smut peddlers."

Program: Fiscal 1986 activities included:

- Public Education (31%) - efforts to inform the public about "the danger pornography brings to community standards," including a National Conference on Pornography
- Research and Publications (25%) - publication of literature on obscenity for the general public
- Newsletter (7%) - publication and distribution of a newsletter, with a circulation of 50,000

Comments: In 1987, MIM had seven statewide affiliates and 19 chapters in 12 states. Chapters and affiliates pay no dues to the national headquarters. MIM provided information only about the national headquarters to NCIB; contributors interested in program and financial activities of the organization, should examine the activities of affiliates and chapters in their local area. NCIB recommends improvements in MIM's annual report.

MOTHERS AGAINST DRUNK DRIVING

669 Airport Freeway, Suite 310
Hurst, TX 76053
(817) 268-6233 or (800) GET-MADD

Year of Data: 1988
Expenditures: $26,827,239
Percent to Program: 23.1%
Fund-raising Costs: 61.5%
Contributions Deductible: Yes
Top of Staff Salary Range: $60,000 (1988)
Meets NCIB Standards: No: 4, 6a, 8? (12/7/89)

Purpose: "To aid the victims of crimes performed by individuals driving under the influence of alcohol or drugs, to aid the families of such victims, and to increase public awareness of the problem of drinking or drugged drivers and to otherwise reduce the number of injuries or death as a result of drinking or drugged drivers"

Program: Fiscal 1988 activities included:

- Public Awareness (52%) - a campaign involving 13 million letters, plus telemarketing, print and radio public announcements, poster and essay contests for young people and distribution of educational materials; over 9 million

of the letters included personalized address stickers, key chains, ball point pens, baseball cards, calendars and bumper stickers; NCIB allocates only about 23% of these costs to public awareness and the rest to fund-raising

- Chapter Development (8%) - support services for chapters, including organizing, program information, assistance with resolution of conflicts, regional development conferences and workshops on local issues and programs
- Victim Service (6%) - including publication of a magazine and training for 120 people in victim counseling techniques, victim advocacy within the criminal justice system and public policy

Comments: In addition to its national office, MADD has 384 chapters including affiliates in four foreign countries. NCIB reports that MADD's major activity, in terms of its expenditures, is conducting direct mail and telemarketing campaigns. Its failure to acknowledge this in its annual report and solicitations is misleading, in NCIB's view, and violative of Standard 4. NCIB questions MADD's accounting practices as regards allocations of the expenses of multi-purpose mailings (Standard 8). If MADD's allocations were used, the organization's programs expenses would be 65% of total expenses. In NCIB's calculations, however, MADD's program expenditures are far less than that, perhaps as low as 23% of total expenses, in violation of Standard 6a.

NATIONAL COMMITTEE FOR PREVENTION OF CHILD ABUSE

332 S. Michigan Avenue, Suite 1600
Chicago, IL 60604
(312) 663-3520

Year of Data: 1988
Expenditures: $1,946,122
Percent to Program: 81.1%
Fund-raising Costs: 10.5%
Contributions Deductible: Yes
Top of Staff Salary Range: $62,000 (1989)
Meets NCIB Standards: Yes (8/10/89)

Purpose: To provide "coordination between state and local organizations and advocacy and technical assistance to professionals and organizations" in order to prevent child abuse

Program: Fiscal 1988 activities included:
- Chapter Activities (25%) - programs to encourage formation and development of volunteer-based chapters, including provision of assistance in administration, board development and public education
- Research and Demonstration (20%) - costs of research and demonstration programs held in locations throughout the country
- Publications and Education (15%) - publication and distribution of over 45 publications for professionals and the general public
- Public Awareness/Relations (14%) - costs of an ongoing public relations campaign to educate the American public about the problem of child abuse and its prevention

Comments: NCPCA has 67 chapters in 50 states; they raise funds independently of the national office, and NCPCA does not control or direct their financial transactions. NCIB's report concerns only the national organization. NCIB recommends improvements in NCPCA's annual report.

NATIONAL COUNCIL ON CRIME AND DELINQUENCY

685 Market Street, Suite 620
San Francisco, CA 94105
(415) 896-6223

Year of Data: 1988
Expenditures: $1,773,657
Percent to Program: 79.2%
Fund-raising Costs: 14.0%
Contributions Deductible: Yes
Top of Staff Salary Range: $65,000 (1988)
Meets NCIB Standards: No: 1d (8/10/89)

Purpose: To "improve the criminal justice system and to maximize the effectiveness and efficiency of law enforcement, juvenile and criminal courts, and correctional institutions.... [and] to stimulate and develop community-based programs for the prevention, treatment and control of delinquency and crime"

Program: Fiscal 1988 activities included:
- Research (48%) - development of new knowledge that can be applied to the criminal justice process
- Consultation (17%) - assistance to com-

munities, private organizations and governmental units in developing sound criminal justice policies, based on the best available research-based knowledge
- Public Education (10%) - presentations, conferences, press releases and publications

Comments: In fiscal 1988, about 59% of NCCD's support came from government grants. NCIB faults NCCD for poor attendance at its board of directors meetings (Standard 1d). NCIB recommends improvements in NCCD's annual report.

NATIONAL CRIME PREVENTION COUNCIL

1700 K Street, NW, 2nd Fl.
Washington, DC 20006
(202) 466-6272

Year of Data: 1987
Expenditures: $3,626,145
Percent to Program: 94%
Fund-raising Costs: 11.5%
Contributions Deductible: Yes
Top of Staff Salary Range: $87,648 (1988)
Meets NCIB Standards: Yes (12/13/88)

Purpose: To "enable people to prevent crime and build safe, caring communities...."

Program: NCPC's reporting of its activities does not allow a detailed breakdown of its programs. Fiscal 1987 activities included a public service advertising campaign, featuring McGruff, "the trench-coated spokesdog," and focusing on citizen involvement in community crime prevention programs and educating children about drug abuse; a video on children and drug abuse; a high school program to reduce teen victimization and increase the use of teens as crime prevention and community resources; consultation, training, seed grants and other assistance to local programs involving teens in addressing community needs; a "Corporate Partnerships Initiative" to involve business in the work of reducing crime and re-establishing the country's sense of community; operation of a resource center; and a publications program, including a newsletter.

Comments: In fiscal 1987, about 72% of NCPC's support came from the U.S. Department of Justice. NCIB recommends improvements in NCPC's audited financial statements.

NATIONAL FEDERATION FOR DECENCY

NCIB reports that, as of July 1, 1990, this organization has not, over a period of several years, furnished requested information sufficient to prepare a report.

- **AMERICAN HUMANE ASSOCIATION** (see ANIMAL-RELATED)
- **CHILDHELP USA** (see HUMAN SERVICE)
- **UNITARIAN UNIVERSALIST SERVICE COMMITTEE, INC.** (see INTERNATIONAL RELIEF)

EDUCATION

scholarship funds, fellowships, literacy, minority education, graduate study, seminars

AMERICA'S FUTURE, INC.

NCIB reports that, as of July 1, 1990, this organization has not, over a period of several years, furnished requested information sufficient to prepare a report.

AMERICAN INDIAN GRADUATE CENTER (formerly American Indian Scholarships, Inc.)

4520 Montgomery Blvd. NE, Suite 1-B
Albuquerque, New Mexico 87109
(505) 881-4584

Year of Data: 1988
Expenditures: $1,809,113
Percent to Program: 88.5%
Fund-raising Costs: 26.0%
Contributions Deductible: Yes
Top of Staff Salary Range: $36,700 (1988)
Meets NCIB Standards: Yes (1/20/89)

Purpose: "To help open the doors to graduate education for American Indians and Alaska Natives by providing fellowship support. Also to help meet the professional manpower needs of Indian tribes and Alaska Native communities by promoting graduate education for Indians in such critical areas as business, education, natural resources, law and health and engineering."

Program: AIGC's reporting of its activities does not allow a detailed breakdown of its programs. In general, AIGC provides financial assistance to students pursuing graduate degrees at the masters, doctoral and law degree levels, with priority given to the fields of law, health, engineering, business, education and natural resources. During the 1986-87 academic year, the organization awarded $1,529,387 in fellowships to 92 masters degree candidates and 154 Ph.D. candidates. Recipients represented 84 Indian tribes and Alaska Native groups from 21 states. In addition to awarding fellowships, AIGC contracted with the Bureau of Indian Affairs to administer its Special Higher Education Program.

Comments: In fiscal 1988, 95% of AIGC's total support came from government grants. NCIB recommends improvements in AIGC's budget presentation.

ASPIRA OF AMERICA, INC.
1112 16th Street, NW, Suite 340
Washington, DC 20036
(202) 835-3600

Purpose: To "motivate, orient and assist Hispanic youth toward enhancing their intellectual and leadership development; foster a commitment among Hispanic youth to dedicate their leadership skills toward the resolution of socioeconomic problems within the community; and increase access to quality education for Hispanic youth through advocacy programs"

Comments: NCIB is currently preparing a new report on this organization.

A BETTER CHANCE, INC.
419 Boylston Street
Boston, MA 02116
(617) 421-0950

Year of Data: 1987
Expenditures: $1,628,654
Percent to Program: 59.0%
Fund-raising Costs: 29.7%
Contributions Deductible: Yes
Top of Staff Salary Range: $82,000 (1987)
Meets NCIB Standards: No: 7c, 6a? (10/14/88)

Purpose: "To develop programs and services to assist and further the education of students from disadvantaged circumstances in order to enable them to realize their personal potential...."

Program: Fiscal 1987 activities included:
- Student Recruitment, Placement and Support (26%) - costs of recruiting 1,762 "talented and highly motivated minority students," placing 333 of them in 161 public and private secondary schools and counseling them and their families
- Research and Alumni Programs (24%) - studies documenting student growth and postgraduate accomplishments;

developing and modifying programs; publicizing activities.
- Special Projects (5%) - programs to test new methods of recruiting and selecting students for placement.

Comments: NCIB faults ABC for failing to include a financial summary in its annual report (Standard 7c) and questions ABC's percent of total expenses devoted to program (Standard 6a). NCIB recommends improvements in ABC's annual report.

CITIZENS' SCHOLARSHIP FOUNDATION OF AMERICA, INC. and DOLLARS FOR SCHOLARS
1505 Riverview Road
P.O. Box 297
St. Peter, MN 56082
(507) 931-1682

Year of Data: 1987
Expenditures: $9,410,404
Percent to Program: 95%
Fund-raising Costs: 7.5%
Contributions Deductible: Yes
Top of Staff Salary Range: $78,000 (1988)
Meets NCIB Standards: Yes (4/8/88)

Purpose: To stimulate "student financial aid opportunities in the private sector"

Program: Fiscal 1987 activities included:
- Student Aid Management Services (93%) - administration of scholarship programs for 199 corporations, foundations and associations throughout the country; CSFA's services to scholarship sponsors included designing programs and preparing and distributing application materials, processing applications, selecting recipients, notifying recipients and non-recipients, and providing sponsors with annual reports

Comments: "Dollars for Scholars" is a "community scholarship effort that enlists the participation of individuals, organizations, merchants, corporations, and foundations to provide annual support for resident students with ability and need who wish to pursue virtually any kind of higher education opportunity." In 1988, CSFA provided advisory and support services to its 320 chapters in 30 states. Chapters do not solicit funds in the name of the national organization and CSFA does not control or direct the chapters' financial transactions. NCIB's report concerns only the national organization and does not include local "Dollars for Scholars" affiliates.

CONSORTIUM FOR GRADUATE STUDY IN MANAGEMENT

One Brookings Drive
Box 1132
St. Louis, MO 63130
(314) 889-6364

Year of Data: 1988
Expenditures: $2,436,210
Percent to Program: 89.3%
Fund-raising Costs: 6.8%
Contributions Deductible: Yes
Top of Staff Salary Range: $56,200 (1988)
Meets NCIB Standards: Yes (6/12/89)

Purpose: To "hasten the entry of minority men and women (Blacks, Hispanics, Native Americans) into management careers in business via the Masters of Business Administration Degrees"

Program: CGSM's reporting of its activities does not allow a detailed breakdown of its programs. CGSM awarded 310 Fellowships in 1987 and 1988, 65% to Blacks, 32% to Hispanics and 3% to Native Americans. Consortium Fellows, who must be U.S. citizens, receive full tuition and fees, plus stipends. They also participate in a three-day orientation program before beginning full-time graduate study. In fiscal 1989, using former Fellows as role models, CGSM piloted a program to encourage minority youth to stay in the educational system through college. About 78% of CGSM's expenditures go to "Student Costs" and about 6% to Orientation Programs; smaller percentages are spent on recruiting, alumni relations and placement services.

Comments: The Consortium is a joint effort of nine graduate schools offering MBA programs: Indiana University, University of Michigan, New York University, University of North Carolina at Chapel Hill, University of Rochester, University of Southern California, University of Texas at Austin, Washington University in St. Louis and University of Wisconsin. NCIB recommends improvements in CGSM's annual report and budget presentation.

COUNCIL FOR BASIC EDUCATION

725 15th Street, NW
Washington, DC 20005
(202) 347-4171

Year of Data: 1986
Expenditures: $1,633,711
Percent to Program: 78.4%
Fund-raising Costs: 11.9%
Contributions Deductible: Yes
Top of Staff Salary Range: $58,200 (1987)
Meets NCIB Standards: Yes (3/31/88)

Purpose: "Strengthening of teaching and learning in American Schools," by promoting (1) the "basic intellectual disciplines" of English, mathematics, science, history, geography, government, foreign languages, and the arts; (2) opportunity for all students to develop their abilities to the fullest extent; and (3) use of clear standards of achievement to measure progress and govern promotion

Program: Materials submitted by CBE to NCIB did not fully describe programs related to expenditure categories. Major expenditure categories in fiscal 1986 were Independent Study in the Humanities (43%), a program of eight-week fellowships for high school teachers to pursue studies in the humanities; Mathematics/Science Institutes (17%), a series of university-based institutes aimed at enriching high school teachers' subject matter knowledge and teaching skills; and Urban Schools (15%), efforts to help professional development in selected urban districts.

Comments: CBE describes itself as a "national organization without local affiliates" and as a membership organization with school administrators, teachers, university professors and interested citizens as members. About 30% of CBE's revenues for fiscal 1986 came from government grants. NCIB recommends improvements in CBE's annual report and audited financial statements.

COUNCIL ON SOCIAL WORK EDUCATION, INC.

1600 Duke Street, Suite 300
Alexandria, VA 22314
(703) 683-8080

Year of Data: 1987
Expenditures: $1,598,272
Percent to Program: 64.9%
Fund-raising Costs: 9.3%
Contributions Deductible: Yes
Top of Staff Salary Range: $98,000 (1988)
Meets NCIB Standards: Yes (6/14/88)

Purpose: To "give leadership and service to social work education in the United States"

Program: CSWE's reporting of its financial materials does not allow a detailed breakdown of its programs and expenses. Fiscal 1987 program activities included conducting an annual meeting for faculty members and leaders of voluntary and government agencies "to determine the direction of social work education for the year;" sponsoring regional conferences and faculty development seminars; "accreditation of graduate and undergraduate schools of social work;" preparing and disseminating curriculum and training materials to academic institutions; monitoring national issues and legislation relating to social work; and publishing periodicals and reports.

Comments: In fiscal 1987, 46% of CSWE's support was from membership dues, 27.4% from government agencies and 22.6% from program service revenues; only about 2% came from public support. CSWE was unable to provide NCIB with an annual report. NCIB recommends improvements in CSWE's audited financial statements.

ETHICS RESOURCE CENTER

600 New Hampshire Ave., NW
Suite 400
Washington, DC 20037
(212) 333-3419

Year of Data: 1987
Expenditures $907,507
Percent to Program: 89.2%
Fund-raising Costs: 11.2%
Contributions Deductible: Yes
Top of Staff Salary Range: $72,000 (1988)
Meets NCIB Standards: Yes (7/29/88)

Purpose: "To restore public trust in government, business, education and the other institutions of our society by strengthening their ethical practices"

Comments: The editor deemed this organization too small (under $1 million in expenditures in the most recent year reported) to be given a complete listing.

FOUNDATION FOR CHILDREN WITH LEARNING DISABILITIES

99 Park Avenue, 6th Fl.
New York, NY 10016
(212) 687-7211

Year of Data: 1987
Expenditures $994,373
Percent to Program: 74.9%
Fund-raising Costs: 14.2%
Contributions Deductible: Yes
Top of Staff Salary Range: $45,000 (1988)
Meets NCIB Standards: Yes (5/16/88)

Purpose: "To assist people everywhere in understanding the special needs and potentials of children with learning disabilities and to support programs for children with learning disabilities and their families"

Comments: The editor deemed this organization too small (under $1 million in expenditures in the most recent year reported) to be given a complete listing.

FOUNDATION FOR ECONOMIC EDUCATION

NCIB reports that, as of July 1, 1990, this organization has not, over a period of several years, furnished requested information sufficient to prepare a report.

FREEDOMS FOUNDATION AT VALLEY FORGE

Route 23
Valley Forge, PA 19481
(215) 933-8825

Year of Data: 1986
Expenditures: $2,315,509
Percent to Program: 69.1%
Fund-raising Costs: 9.1%
Contributions Deductible: Yes
Top of Staff Salary Range: $60,000 (1987)
Meets NCIB Standards: Yes (1/6/88)

Purpose: "To carry out national programs of information and education that preserve our heritage of free government and traditional American values"

Program: Fiscal 1986 activities included:

* Education (43%) - conferences for elementary, junior high and high school students; graduate credit seminars and graduate history workshops
* American Heritage Programs (14%) - including administration of awards; publications; operations of a Center for Responsible Citizenship; and costs of the Medal of Honor Grove, a grove of trees, each dedicated to a U.S. Medal of Honor recipient
* Awards Programs (12%) - awards to high school and college teachers for excellence in private enterprise education; awards to recognize individuals, organizations, corporations and schools for contributions to responsible citizenship and strengthened understanding "of freedom and the traditions of our free society"

Comments: FFVF has about 40 chapters in 22 states. NCIB recommends improvements in FFVF's annual report and audited financial statements.

INSTITUTE FOR HUMANE STUDIES

1210 Roberts Road
Fairfax, VA 22030
(703) 323-1055

Year of Data: 1987
Expenditures $845,386
Percent to Program: 80.6%
Fund-raising Costs: 3.7%
Contributions Deductible: Yes
Top of Staff Salary Range: $60,000 (1988)
Meets NCIB Standards: Yes (10/3/88)

Purpose: "To contribute to the establishment and preservation of a society of free individuals and specifically develop the intellectual foundations of such a society;" "discovering, developing, and placing the best scholars dedicated to the classical liberal values of liberty, private property, free enterprise, free trade, and peace"

Comments: The editor deemed this organization too small (under $1 million in expenditures in the most recent year reported) to be given a complete listing.

INVEST-IN-AMERICA NATIONAL COUNCIL

2400 Chestnut Street, Suite 3308
Philadelphia, PA 19103
(215) 568-7311

Purpose: To "increase understanding and appreciation of the U.S. free market system to the degree that there are no territorial limits to its interests or efforts"

Comments: NCIB is in the process of preparing its first report on this organization.

JOINT COUNCIL ON ECONOMIC EDUCATION

432 Park Avenue South
New York, NY 10016
(212) 685-5499

Year of Data: 1988
Expenditures: $2,984,520
Percent to Program: 74.7%
Fund-raising Costs: 7.1%
Contributions Deductible: Yes
Top of Staff Salary Range: $95,000 (1988)
Meets NCIB Standards: Yes (2/28/89)

Purpose: To "increase the quantity and improve the quality of economic education in the nation's schools ... by providing teacher training programs and developing quality materials for the kindergarten through the college level curriculum"

Program: About 54% of JCEE's fiscal 1988 expenditures were for restricted program services listed in audited financial statements as "DEEP [Developmental Economic Education Program] Expansion Projects," "Tax Whys II," "At Risk Project" and "Other Restricted Projects." Other activities, each involving less than 5% of total expenditures, included services to 1,650 school districts; economic training for teachers; programs contributing to a network of 50 Affiliated State Councils on Economic Education and 295 university Centers for Economic Education; publications, including an advanced placement course in economics and a curriculum guide on international trade; public information programs; and promotion of research on the teaching and learning of economics at all levels.

Comments: NCIB recommends improvements in JCEE's annual report.

LAUBACH LITERACY INTERNATIONAL

1320 Jamesville Avenue, Box 131
Syracuse, NY 13210
(315) 422-9121

> Year of Data: 1987
> Expenditures: $4,907,819
> Percent to Program: 88.6%
> Fund-raising Costs: 19.5%
> Contributions Deductible: Yes
> Top of Staff Salary Range: $75,800 (1988)
> Meets NCIB Standards: Yes (11/8/88)

Purpose: To "enable illiterate adults and older youth to acquire the listening, speaking, reading, writing, and mathematics skills they need to solve the problems they encounter in their daily lives; to take full advantage of opportunities in their environment; and to participate fully in the transformation of their society"

Program: Fiscal 1987 activities included:

- Publishing (64%) - publications from New Readers Press, the publishing division of LLI, including books on writing skills and instructional videos to promote reading and math skills
- United States Program (16%) - under the name Laubach Literacy Action, provision of services to state and local groups to help organize literacy programs; training for 37,000 volunteer tutors and certification for 700 trainers; production of two video training packages
- International Program (7%) - supervision, coordination and financial support of literacy programs in foreign countries, especially Colombia, India and Mexico

Comments: About 81% of LLI's fiscal 1987 support came from sales of its publications.

CHARLES A. LINDBERGH FUND INC.

708 South 3rd Street, Suite 110
Minneapolis, MN 55415
(612) 338-1703

> Year of Data: 1988
> Expenditures $332,781
> Percent to Program: 76.8%
> Fund-raising Costs: 7.6%
> Contributions Deductible: Yes
> Top of Staff Salary Range: $40,000 (N/A)
> Meets NCIB Standards: No: 1d, 6b? (1/9/90)

Purpose: To provide financial assistance in the form of Lindbergh fellowships and grants to individuals, primarily undergraduate and graduate students, in fields which were of concern to Charles Lindbergh such as aeronautical research, conservation, exploration and wildlife preservation

Comments: The editor deemed this organization too small (under $1 million in expenditures in the most recent year reported) to be given a complete listing.

LITERACY VOLUNTEERS OF AMERICA, INC.

5795 Widewaters Parkway
Syracuse, NY 13214-1846
(315) 445-8000

> Year of Data: 1987
> Expenditures $951,696
> Percent to Program: 78.8%
> Fund-raising Costs: 23.1%
> Contributions Deductible: Yes
> Top of Staff Salary Range: $40,000 (1988)
> Meets NCIB Standards: Yes (4/6/88)

Purpose: "To promote and foster increased literacy in the United States and Canada through teaching of and aid to the illiterate and to train, encourage and aid individuals and other groups or organizations desiring to increase literacy through voluntary programs"

Comments: The editor deemed this organization too small (under $1 million in expenditures in the most recent year reported) to be given a complete listing.

NATIONAL ACTION COUNCIL FOR MINORITIES IN ENGINEERING, INC.

3 West 35th Street
New York, NY 10001
(212) 279-2626

> Year of Data: 1989
> Expenditures: $4,290,055
> Percent to Program: 82%
> Fund-raising Costs: 8%
> Contributions Deductible: Yes
> Top of Staff Salary Range: $110,000 (1989)
> Meets NCIB Standards: Yes (5/25/90)

Purpose: To "achieve a substantial increase in the number of underrepresented minorities—Blacks, Hispanics (especially Mexican Americans and Puerto Ricans) and

Native Americans—who receive baccalaureate degrees in engineering"

Program: Fiscal 1989 activities included:

- Incentive Grants Program (55%) - grants of $2,099,612 to 141 participating colleges and universities to help fund the education of about 3,120 minority engineering students, who met NACME's eligibility criteria
- Retention (7%) - support to a limited number of engineering institutions to enhance retention services and to allow NACME to record, analyze and disseminate data helpful in improving the retention rate of minority engineering students

Comments: In fiscal 1989, NACME expressed the intention of providing continuing support for participating students until they complete their undergraduate education.

NATIONAL COMMITTEE FOR CITIZENS IN EDUCATION, INC.

10840 Little Patuxent Parkway, Suite 301
Columbia, MD 21044
(301) 997-9300

Year of Data: 1987
Expenditures $630,292
Percent to Program: 84.1%
Fund-raising Costs: 6.7%
Contributions Deductible: Yes
Top of Staff Salary Range: $70,000 (1987)
Meets NCIB Standards: Yes (1/15/88)

Purpose: "To improve the education of children by mobilizing and assisting citizens—including parents—to strengthen public schools"

Comments: The editor deemed this organization too small (under $1 million in expenditures in the most recent year reported) to be given a complete listing.

NATIONAL FUND FOR MEDICAL EDUCATION

35 Kneeland Street
Boston, MA 02111
(617) 482-5501

Year of Data: 1987
Expenditures: $1,350,243
Percent to Program: 79.3%
Fund-raising Costs: 9.6%
Contributions Deductible: Yes
Top of Staff Salary Range: $130,000 (1988)
Meets NCIB Standards: Yes (11/9/88)

Purpose: "To promote the best possible health care for the American people through improvement in medical education...."

Program: Fiscal 1987 activities included:

- Grants (62%) - over $600,000 for grants and fellowships, including 9 "Innovative Grants" for such topics as nonverbal communication, bridging racial and class differences in patient-doctor communications and ambulatory training for medical students in the management of chronic diseases; 2 grants to introduce proven innovations into new settings; and 20 small grants to encourage dissemination of new teaching methods among medical schools
- SmithKline Beckman Medical Perspectives Fellowships (11%) - 28 fellowships to medical students for research in such subjects as community-based child abuse prevention, health care systems for black South Africans and attitudes toward sexual assault victims among male and female examiners

Comments: NCIB recommends improvements in NFME's budget presentation.

NATIONAL HISPANIC SCHOLARSHIP FUND

P.O. Box 748
San Francisco, CA 94101
(415) 892-9971

Year of Data: 1987
Expenditures: $2,078,736
Percent to Program: 88%
Fund-raising Costs: 2%
Contributions Deductible: Yes
Top of Staff Salary Range: $68,000 (1989)
Meets NCIB Standards: Yes (7/12/89)

Purpose: "To establish and maintain a national funding agency for the development and promotion of Hispanic academic achievement and research"

Program: Fiscal 1987 activities included:
- Scholarships (58%) - $1.2 million in scholarships of $400-$1,000 to 1,526 graduate and undergraduate students of Hispanic American background
- Awareness Project (30%) - costs of 30 dinners and receptions held in cities with significant Hispanic population, to increase awareness of the organization's activities and increase support

Comments: In fiscal 1987, about 43% of NHSF's total support was from a single corporate source, the Anheuser-Busch Companies. NCIB recommends improvements in NHSF's budget presentation and audited financial statements.

NATIONAL MEDICAL FELLOWSHIPS, INC.

254 West 31st Street, 7th Fl.
New York, NY 10001
(212) 714-0933

Year of Data: 1987
Expenditures: $1,798,173
Percent to Program: 71.1%
Fund-raising Costs: 26.3%
Contributions Deductible: Yes
Top of Staff Salary Range: $80,000 (1988)
Meets NCIB Standards: Yes (6/13/88)

Purpose: To assist minority medical students through grants awarded on the basis of financial need, in order to increase the number of minority students in medical school

Program: NMF's reporting of its activities does not allow a detailed breakdown of its programs. Fiscal 1987 activities included award of $1.3 million in scholarships, fellowships and special merit awards to 889 minority medical students, about 73% of whom were black, 26% Hispanic and 1% American Indian. NMF also administers grant awards under 11 special programs, such as the Commonwealth Fund Fellowship Program, which provides stipends to at least 20 students per year to conduct 8-12 weeks of research under the supervision of biomedical scientists.

Comments: NCIB recommends improvements in NMF's annual report and audited financial statements.

NATIONAL MERIT SCHOLARSHIP CORPORATION

One Rotary Center
Evanston, IL 60201
(708) 866-5100

Year of Data: 1986
Expenditures: $29,812,817
Percent to Program: 95.9%
Fund-raising Costs: 2.3%
Contributions Deductible: Yes
Top of Staff Salary Range: $100,000 (N/A)
Meets NCIB Standards: No: 3 (6/15/87)

Purpose: To identify and honor academically talented students in the nation's secondary schools through its two annual competitions, the National Merit Scholarship Program and the National Achievement Scholarship Program for Outstanding Negro Students

Program: NMSC's reporting of its activities does not allow a detailed breakdown of its programs. NMSC administers "The Merit Program," a national competition for about 6,000 merit scholarships. About a third of these are National Merit Scholarships, the selection process for which begins with national administration of the Preliminary Scholastic Aptitude Test/National Merit Scholarship Qualifying Test. The top 35,000 scorers receive Letters of Commendation and the top 15,000 (about one half of one percent of the nation's high school seniors) qualify as scholarship semifinalists. After taking the Scholastic Aptitude Test and documenting high academic performance, about 90% of the semifinalists qualify as finalists and receive a Certificate of Merit. Actual scholarship recipients are chosen by a committee of college admissions officers and high school counselors. The 1,800 winners receive a one-time $2,000 award. In 1986, the "Merit Program" also included award of $16.7 million for 1,341 corporate-sponsored scholarships, 1,179 "Special Scholarships" and 2,885 college-sponsored scholarships. NMSC also administers "The Achievement Program," which provides recognition and encouragement for promising black high school students. In 1986, $2.6 million in scholarships were awarded.

Comments: NCIB faults NMSC for building its assets available for use to 2.5 times its fiscal 1986 operating budget (Standard 3). NCIB recommends improvements in NMSC's budget presentation and audited financial statements.

NATIONAL SCHOOLS COMMITTEE FOR ECONOMIC EDUCATION

86 Valley Road, P.O. Box 295
Cos Cob, CT 06807-0295
(203) 869-1706

Year of Data: 1987
Expenditures $93,006
Percent to Program: 64.2%
Fund-raising Costs: 13.4%
Contributions Deductible: Yes
Top of Staff Salary Range: $40,000 (1988)
Meets NCIB Standards: Yes (12/5/88)

Purpose: "To extend the teaching of private enterprise principles and values in schools"

Comments: The editor deemed this organization too small (under $1 million in expenditures in the most recent year reported) to be given a complete listing.

NATIONAL URBAN FELLOWS, INC.

55 West 44th Street, Suite 600
New York, NY 10036
(212) 921-9400

Year of Data: 1987
Expenditures: $1,202,605
Percent to Program: ?
Fund-raising Costs: 5.9%
Contributions Deductible: Yes
Top of Staff Salary Range: $85,800 (1988)
Meets NCIB Standards: Yes (9/13/88)

Purpose: To "meet the need for competent, experienced, local and state government administrators, particularly women and

minority groups, by providing a program combining academic and [hands-on experience]"

Program: NUF's reporting of its activities does not allow a detailed breakdown of its programs. Fiscal 1987 activities included selection of 55 minority and female mid-career professionals to participate in its 14-month National Urban Fellowship and National Rural Fellowship programs; fellowships involve four months of education and a 10-month assignment as a special assistant to an experienced urban or rural administrator of a government or other public agency; fellows receive a Masters degree in regional planning or rural economic development. NUF also administers a Corporate Executive Fellowship, a 24-month program which earns the fellow an MBA degree.

Comments: Though NUF's financial reporting did not allow a precise calculation of program service expenses, NCIB concludes that those expenses appear to be well within the requirements of Standard 6a. NCIB recommends improvements in NUF's budget presentation.

PUSH FOR EXCELLENCE (OPERATION PUSH)

NCIB reports that, as of July 1, 1990, this organization has not, over a period of several years, furnished requested information sufficient to prepare a report.

READING IS FUNDAMENTAL, INC.

600 Maryland Avenue, S.W., Suite 500
Washington, DC 20024
(202) 287-3371

Year of Data: 1986
Expenditures: $6,823,518
Percent to Program: 97%
Fund-raising Costs: 11%
Contributions Deductible: Yes
Top of Staff Salary Range: $65,145 (1987)
Meets NCIB Standards: Yes (8/7/87)

Purpose: To "promote the establishment of local RIF projects throughout the country in order to give impetus to reading motivation at an early age by making inexpensive books, particularly paperbacks, accessible to children for personal ownership"

Program: RIF reported all its fiscal 1986 program services in a single category. Activities included distribution of inexpensive books, operation of national projects and provision to local RIF programs of such services as workshops and training materials for volunteers; discounts negotiated with 355 publishers and distributors; technical assistance; and public service announcements. During the year, 3,152 RIF projects operated in 10,151 locations and served over two million children; 86,000 volunteers distributed over 6.5 million books.

Comments: Local RIF projects rely on the national organization's assistance, but are run by such independent groups as schools, PTAs and civic groups. In fiscal 1986, about 86% of RIF's support came from government contracts. NCIB advises contributors of unrestricted funds that, in fiscal 1986, about 26% of such funds went to program services and 26% to supporting services; there was an excess of unrestricted support over expenses of $371,269 or about 48%. NCIB recommends improvements in RIF's annual report.

RED CLOUD INDIAN SCHOOL

NCIB reports that, as of July 1, 1990, this organization has not, over a period of several years, furnished requested information sufficient to prepare a report.

ST. JOSEPH'S INDIAN SCHOOL

NCIB reports that, as of July 1, 1990, this organization has not, over a period of several years, furnished requested information sufficient to prepare a report.

ST. LABRE INDIAN SCHOOL EDUCATIONAL ASSOCIATION

St. Labre Indian School
Ashland, MT 59004
(406) 784-2200

Year of Data: 1988
Expenditures: $11,969,557
Percent to Program: 68%
Fund-raising Costs: 31.8%
Contributions Deductible: Yes
Top of Staff Salary Range: $50,000 (1988)
Meets NCIB Standards: No: 6b, 8 (1/5/90)

Purpose: Provides educational services to Native Americans on the Northern Cheyenne and Crow reservations

Program: Fiscal 1988 activities included:
- Instructional (36%) - costs of three schools, which also provide two or three meals a day and medical services to their students
- Community Services (13%) - operation of a health clinic, alcoholism programs, a cafeteria and provision of employment and low-income housing services for community residents

Comments: SLISEA is owned by and operated under the corporate title of the Roman Catholic Bishop of Great Falls, Montana. NCIB faults SLISEA because its balance sheet does not report any asset amount for its holdings of land, building and equipment (Standard 8) and because its available assets, at the end of fiscal 1988, were about 2.6 times its fiscal 1989 budget (Standard 6b). NCIB recommends improvements in SLISEA's budget presentation.

STARR COMMONWEALTH SCHOOLS/STARR COMMONWEALTH FOR BOYS

13725 Starr Commonwealth Road
Albion, MI 49224
(517) 629-5591

Year of Data: 1986
Expenditures: $11,311,903
Percent to Program: 87.7%
Fund-raising Costs: 29.5%
Contributions Deductible: Yes
Top of Staff Salary Range: $74,500 (1987)
Meets NCIB Standards: Yes (6/9/87)

Purpose: To maintain and operate "homes for homeless, neglected and delinquent" children to instruct them "in the mechanical trades and professions and vocations of life...."

Program: Virtually all of SCS's fiscal 1986 program expenditures (about 81% of total expenditures) were devoted to residential, educational and counseling services to 547 children with emotional and behavior problems.

Comments: NCIB recommends improvements in SCS's annual report.

UNITED NEGRO COLLEGE FUND

500 East 62nd Street
New York, NY 10021
(212) 644-9600

Year of Data: 1987
Expenditures $41,290,789
Percent to Program: 76.1%
Fund-raising Costs: 18.9%
Contributions Deductible: Yes
Top of Staff Salary Range: $78,461 (1987)
Meets NCIB Standards: Yes (2/11/88)

Purpose: To "raise general operating funds for its member institutions ... [provide] educational programs and services of mutual benefit to the member institutions ... [and serve] as a center of information concerning the higher education of blacks in the United States"

Program: UNCF's reporting of its activities does not allow a detailed breakdown of its programs. In fiscal 1987, it distributed $29.5 million to "member and non-member institutions." It also funded programs to build endowments at 37 colleges and to help 18 colleges increase endowments by matching Federal Challenge Grant money with private contributions.

Comments: UNCF raises funds for 42 black colleges, with a combined enrollment of about 45,000 students. Of the funds collected, 50% is divided equally among all member colleges, 40% is divided on the basis of the colleges' income from gifts, grants and endowments and 10% is divided on the basis of enrollment. The colleges do not engage in any other solicitations for operating funds, except to their alumni and trustees. NCIB recommends improvements in UNCF's annual report and audited financial statements.

WORLD RESEARCH, INC.

NCIB reports that, as of July 1, 1990, this organization has not, over a period of several years, furnished requested information sufficient to prepare a report.

- **AFS INTERCULTURAL PROGRAMS**
  (see INTERNATIONAL)

- **AIESEC-UNITED STATES, INC.**
  (see INTERNATIONAL)

- **AFRICAN-AMERICAN INSTITUTE**
  (see INTERNATIONAL)

- **AMERICAN FUND FOR DENTAL HEALTH** (see HEALTH - GENERAL)

- **AMERICAN HUMANICS, INC.** (see YOUTH DEVELOPMENT)

- **ASSOCIATION ON AMERICAN INDIAN AFFAIRS** (see SOCIAL ACTION)

- **CENTER FOR POPULATION OPTIONS**
  (see HEALTH-GENERAL)

- **COUNCIL FOR AID TO EDUCATION**
  (see PHILANTHROPY)

- **COUNCIL ON CAREER DEVELOPMENT FOR MINORITIES** (see EMPLOYMENT)

- **EXPERIMENT IN INTERNATIONAL LIVING** (see INTERNATIONAL)

- **FATHER FLANAGAN'S BOYS' HOME**
  (see YOUTH DEVELOPMENT)

- **FOREIGN POLICY ASSOCIATION**
  (see INTERNATIONAL)

- **FOUNDATION FOR INDEPENDENT HIGHER EDUCATION** (see PHILANTHROPY)

- **FREEDOM HOUSE, INC. and WILLKIE MEMORIAL OF FREEDOM HOUSE, INC.** (see INTERNATIONAL)

- **INSTITUTE OF INTERNATIONAL EDUCATION** (see INTERNATIONAL)

- **INTERNATIONAL PEACE ACADEMY**
  (see INTERNATIONAL)

- **MARTIN LUTHER KING, JR. CENTER FOR NONVIOLENT SOCIAL CHANGE, INC.** (see SOCIAL ACTION)

- **MEDICAL EDUCATION FOR SOUTH AFRICAN BLACKS** (see INTERNATIONAL)

- **NAACP LEGAL DEFENSE AND EDUCATIONAL FUND and EARL WARREN LEGAL TRAINING PROGRAM, INC.** (see SOCIAL ACTION)

- **NAACP SPECIAL CONTRIBUTION FUND** (see SOCIAL ACTION)

- **NATIONAL ALLIANCE OF BUSINESS, INC.** (see EMPLOYMENT)

- **RECORDING FOR THE BLIND** (see HEALTH-VISUAL HANDICAPS)

- **ROSEBUD EDUCATIONAL SOCIETY/ ST. FRANCIS INDIAN MISSION/LITTLE SIOUX** (see HUMAN SERVICE)
- **SER/JOBS FOR PROGRESS, INC.** (see EMPLOYMENT)
- **YOUTH FOR UNDERSTANDING** (see INTERNATIONAL)

EMPLOYMENT

job training, career development, jobs for the disabled, the young and the aging

COUNCIL ON CAREER DEVELOP- MENT FOR MINORITIES, INC.
1341 W. Mockingbird La., Suite 412-E
Dallas, Texas 75247
(214) 631-3677

Year of Data: 1986
Expenditures $319,561
Percent to Program: 75%
Fund-raising Costs: 4.2%
Contributions Deductible: Yes
Top of Staff Salary Range: $55,000 (1986)
Meets NCIB Standards: Yes (3/26/87)

Purpose: To "improve the career awareness and employability of under-represented minority students, to upgrade the career counseling and job referral services provided to these students, and to aid employers in the employment, retention and advancement of minority college graduates"

Comments: The editor deemed this organization too small (under $1 million in expenditures in the most recent year reported) to be given a complete listing.

GOODWILL INDUSTRIES OF AMERICA, INC.
9200 Wisconsin Avenue
Bethesda, MD 20814
(301) 530-6500

Year of Data: 1986
Expenditures: $4,861,240
Percent to Program: 74.1%
Fund-raising Costs: 3.9%
Contributions Deductible: Yes
Top of Staff Salary Range: $103,000 (1986)
Meets NCIB Standards: Yes (11/6/87)

Purpose: "To expand the vocational opportunities of disabled people in order to help them achieve full participation in society" and to provide "leadership, support and guidance" to member local Goodwill Industries

Program: Fiscal 1986 activities included:

- Support Services to Membership (37%) - assistance in the development of national and local public relations materials; consultations for the implementation and development of job opportunities for the handicapped
- Direct Services to Membership (34%) - consultations, executive placement, training seminars and data processing services
- General Counsel, Governing Meetings & Other Services (5%) - legal and legislative activities; governance meetings; liaison with Goodwill Industries Volunteer Services and other "special projects"

Comments: In 1986, GIA reported 175 member Goodwill Industries in the United States and Canada and 44 affiliated members in 30 foreign countries. Goodwill Industry members are autonomous corporations to which GIA provides various services. NCIB's report concerns the national organization only and does not include member local Goodwill Industries. In 1986, GIA received about 52% of its revenues from "Membership dues," about 30% from "Fees and grants from government agencies," about 15% from "Program service fees" and only about 2% from contributions, bequests and foundation grants. NCIB recommends improvements in GIA's annual report and audited financial statements.

NATIONAL ALLIANCE OF BUSINESS, INC.

1201 New York Ave., NW, Suite 700
Washington, DC 20005
(202) 289-2888

Year of Data: 1986
Expenditures: $9,733,438
Percent to Program: 64.6%
Fund-raising Costs: 5.8%
Contributions Deductible: Yes
Top of Staff Salary Range: $200,000 (1985)
Meets NCIB Standards: Yes (5/20/87)

Purpose: "To supply job training policy input at the national level, to encourage business to join in the partnership, and to promote the continued improvement of the job training system nationwide"

Program: Fiscal 1986 activities included:

- Training and Technical Assistance to the JTPA System (34%) - costs of aiding local job training programs funded by the Job Training Partnership Act of 1982, including training and consulting services to business volunteers, assistance to Private Industry Councils (PICs) in determining training needs and negotiating with organizations to run specific programs
- Special Program Activity (16%) - programs to replicate the Boston Compact, a school/business partnership for educational improvement, based on the business community's pledge of employment opportunities for all students attaining certain educational goals
- Public Information and Policy Development (13%) - support of legislative action to strengthen remedial education programs for at-risk youth and increase funding for job-training; distribution of 25,000 copies of a report on demographic and economic predictions and resulting employment and training issues; sponsorship of a conference on at-risk youth
- Services and Relationships with Employers (9%) - efforts to attract business support, especially at the local level, for efforts to train and find jobs for the disadvantaged

Comments: In fiscal 1986, about 58% of NAB's support came from the United States Department of Labor. NCIB recommends improvements in NAB's annual report and audited financial statements.

OPPORTUNITIES INDUSTRIALIZATION CENTERS OF AMERICA, INC.

100 West Coulter Street
Philadelphia, PA 19144
(215) 951-2200 or (800) 352-6427

Year of Data: 1986
Expenditures: $3,894,647
Percent to Program: 88.7%
Fund-raising Costs: 20.3%
Contributions Deductible: Yes
Top of Staff Salary Range: $82,100 (1986)
Meets NCIB Standards: ?: 3 (12/23/87)

Purpose: To "provide technical assistance and guidance to local communities in establishing OIC centers and afford appropriate service and resources to such OICs when formed in enabling them to establish programs for the development and utilization of technical skills, thereby assisting individuals to qualify for better job opportunities through job development and training, without regard to race, creed or color"

Program: Fiscal 1986 activities included:
- Technical Assistance (45%) - assistance to OIC affiliates to improve the quality and quantity of the services they deliver
- Transportation (18%) - implementation of a vehicular maintenance training program in various cities for underemployed transit workers and selected unemployed minorities
- New York High Tech Center (8%) - operation of a center which offers training in word processing and advanced office equipment, plus job search, counseling and interviewing assistance

Comments: OICA recently reported 78 independently incorporated and governed affiliates and developing groups. Affiliates receive technical assistance, but do not remit funds to, or receive funds from, the national organization. OICA does not control or direct the affiliates' financial transactions. NCIB's report concerns only the national organization. In fiscal 1986, about 62% of OICA's support came from government contracts. Government support has declined from an annual average of about $10,160,000 in fiscal 1981-82 to about $1,890,000 in fiscal 1983-86. OICA's expenditures have dropped from $12,648,000 in fiscal 1981 to about $3,895,000 in fiscal 1986. NCIB questions OICA's continued deficit unrestricted fund balance as of June 30, 1986 (Standard 3).

NCIB recommends improvements in OICA's annual report.

SER/JOBS FOR PROGRESS, INC.

1355 River Bend Drive, Suite 240
Dallas, TX 75247
(214) 631-3999

Year of Data: 1986
Expenditures: $3,837,445
Percent to Program: 76.6%
Fund-raising Costs: 0%
Contributions Deductible: Yes
Top of Staff Salary Range: $67,500 (1987)
Meets NCIB Standards: No: 3 (2/23/88)

Purpose: To "formulate and advocate initiatives that result in the increased development and utilization of America's human resources, with special emphasis on the needs of Hispanics, in the areas of education, training, employment, business and economic opportunities"

Program: Fiscal 1986 activities included:
- Job Corps (52%) - direct training and supportive services for youth
- Training and Technical Assistance (20%) - assistance to SER local affiliates
- Minority Business/Training (8%) - technical assistance to minority business persons in such areas as contract procurement, loan packaging and financial analysis; recruitment of minority college students for entrepreneurship; recruitment and training of dislocated workers
- High School Equivalency Program (7%) - assistance to students, whose family are engaged in migrant or seasonal farm work, to obtain equivalent or actual secondary education

Comments: SER recently reported that it operates 107 training centers in 77 cities in 15 states and that its autonomous affiliates have a total of 111 offices. Affiliates receive technical assistance, but do not remit funds to, or receive funds from, the national organization. SER does not control or direct the affiliates' financial transactions. NCIB's report concerns only the national organization. In fiscal 1986, about 88% of SER's support came from government grants. NCIB advises contributors of unrestricted funds that their funds have been used for supporting services, including generating government funding. NCIB faults SER for its continued deficit unrestricted fund balance (Standard 3c). NCIB recommends improvements in SER's annual report.

- **ASSOCIATION FOR RETARDED CITIZENS OF THE UNITED STATES** (see HEALTH-GENERAL)
- **FAMILY SERVICE ASSOCIATION** (see HUMAN SERVICE)
- **NATIONAL COUNCIL ON THE AGING** (see HUMAN SERVICE)
- **NATIONAL RIGHT TO WORK LEGAL DEFENSE FOUNDATION** (see SOCIAL ACTION)
- **PUSH FOR EXCELLENCE** (see EDUCATION)
- **VOLUNTEERS OF AMERICA** (see HUMAN SERVICE)

THE ENVIRONMENT

environmental protection, resources management and conservation, energy use and conservation, wildlife preservation, land use

AMERICA THE BEAUTIFUL FUND
219 Shoreham Building
Washington, DC 20005
(202) 638-1649

Year of Data: 1989
Expenditures: $269,159
Percent to Program: 72%
Fund-raising Costs: 11.5%
Contributions Deductible: Yes
Top of Staff Salary Range: $35,000 (1989)
Meets NCIB Standards: Yes (5/14/90)

Purpose: To "promote, develop and assist citizens' activities designed to improve the quality of life," by providing free vegetable and flower seeds, along with technical assistance, to charitable and civic groups

Comments: The editor deemed this organization too small (under $1 million in expenditures in the most recent year reported) to be given a complete listing.

AMERICAN FARMLAND TRUST
1920 N Street, NW, Suite 400
Washington, DC 20036
(202) 659-5170

Year of Data: 1988
Expenditures: $2,183,194
Percent to Program: 68.2%
Fund-raising Costs: 17.4%
Contributions Deductible: Yes
Top of Staff Salary Range: $75,000 (1989)
Meets NCIB Standards: Yes (10/16/89)

Purpose: "To promote, support and effectuate the preservation of American agricultural land and to disseminate information concerning the importance to the nation of this critical natural resource"

Program: AFT's reporting of its activities does not allow a detailed breakdown of its programs. In general, AFT helps government agencies and land protection groups conserve land for agriculture and, to a lesser extent, protects farmland through private sector techniques applied to land acquisition, financing and sale. In 1988, AFT reported aiding passage of land-saving programs, which it helped design, in California and Pennsylvania. These programs protect farmland through the purchase of development rights from farmers. AFT also reports that it inspired the federal government's Conservation Reserve Program, which compensates farmers for removing highly erodible land from crop production. AFT distributes information about threats facing farmland through mailings, workshops, conferences, newsletters and a video.

Comments: NCIB recommends improvements in AFT's annual report.

AMERICAN FORESTRY ASSOCIATION

1516 P Street, NW
Washington, DC 20005
(202) 667-3300

Year of Data: 1986
Expenditures: $1,822,451
Percent to Program: 77.2%
Fund-raising Costs: N/A
Contributions Deductible: Yes
Top of Staff Salary Range: $70,000 (1987)
Meets NCIB Standards: ?: 7 (8/20/87)

Purpose: To promote "intelligent management and use of our forests, soil, water, wildlife, and all other natural resources" and "enlightened public appreciation of natural resources, and the part they play in the social, recreational and economic life of the nation"

Program: Fiscal 1986 activities included:

• Magazine (27%) - costs of publishing a bimonthly magazine
• Membership Services and Promotions (14%) - not described in AFA's annual report
• Trail Riders (12%) - costs of "trips and tours for outdoor education"
• Urban Forestry (11%) - promotion of urban forestry through a conference, coordination of the National Urban Forest Council and distribution of 8000 copies of "The National Urban Forest Forum"
• Other activities included working with

Congress on sections of the Tax Reform Bill relating to forestry, promoting a volunteer program in conservation for teenagers and promoting tree planting by community groups.

Comments: Over 41% of AFA's total support comes from membership dues. AFA states that $15 of its $24 dues charge is tax deductible. Because of the way AFA reported its financial data, NCIB raised a question about its adherence to Standard 7 and was unable to determine whether it met Standard 4.

CENTER FOR MARINE CONSERVATION, INC.

1725 DeSalles Street,NW Suite 500
Washington, DC 20036
(202) 429-5609

Purpose: To "protect endangered and threatened species and their marine habitats, and to conserve marine ecosystems and resources"

Comments: NCIB is currently preparing a new report on this organization.

THE CONSERVATION FOUNDATION

1250 24th Street, NW, Suite 500
Washington, DC 20037
(202) 293-4800

Year of Data: 1986
Expenditures: $3,581,037
Percent to Program: 76.6%
Fund-raising Costs: 5.0%
Contributions Deductible: Yes
Top of Staff Salary Range: $135,000 (1986)
Meets NCIB Standards: Yes (6/12/87)

Purpose: "To promote greater knowledge about the earth's resources—its waters, soils, minerals, plant and animal life; to initiate research and education concerning these resources and their relation to each other; to ascertain the most effective methods of making them available and useful to people; to assess population trends and their effect upon environment; ... to encourage human conduct to sustain and enrich life on earth"

Program: Materials submitted by CF to NCIB did not fully describe programs related to expenditure categories. Program expenditure categories in fiscal 1986 were Land, Heritage and Wildlife (17%), Environmental Trends and

Institutions (13%), Communications (12%), General Program (11%), Water, Energy and Minerals (9%), Economics and Environment (8%), and Pollution Control and Public Health (7%). Recent activities include development of recommendations for allocating governmental responsibilities for protecting groundwater; publication of a study on economic impact of soil erosion; identifying future water resource conflicts; production of a study assessing the U.S. national park system; surveying and research for a similar study of state parks; co-sponsorship of a symposium on land use in the southern states; organization of and support for "dialogue groups" for addressing resource and environmental disputes; training for EPA regional staff in dispute resolution; coordination of participation of public interest groups in controlling hazardous chemicals; staff and administrative support for the U.S. representative to the World Commission on Environment and Development; identification and study of new dimensions of environmental and resource problems; and publication of newsletters, books, reports and research papers on a variety of topics.

Comments: CF formally affiliated with the World Wildlife Fund, Inc. in October 1985, forming a common board of directors and sharing some staff, but remaining separate legal entities with separate financial records. NCIB recommends improvements in CF's annual report.

CONSERVATION INTERNATIONAL FOUNDATION

1015 18th Street, NW, Suite 1000
Washington, DC 20036
(202) 429-5660

Year of Data: 1988
Expenditures: $3,811,542
Percent to Program: 66%
Fund-raising Costs: 14%
Contributions Deductible: Yes
Top of Staff Salary Range: $95,000 (1989)
Meets NCIB Standards: Yes (9/26/89)

Purpose: "To help sustain biological diversity and the ecosystems and ecological processes that support life on earth;" "to build national indigenous conservation capacity, country by country, throughout the world, beginning in tropical America"

Program: Fiscal 1988 activities included:
- Country Programs (36%) - development of conservation programs in Bolivia, Costa Rica and Mexico, involving work with governments and private organizations
- Science (14%) - including work to develop improvements in geographic information systems technology in Latin America; assistance in production of a national-level overview of biological resources of Mexico and Costa Rica; and helping to establish conservation data centers in Latin America
- Communications (8%) - publications, including a quarterly report for CI members
- Strategic Planning (6%) - development of a study, "Ecosystem Conservation and the Strategic Vision of Conservation International"

Comments: NCIB reports that attendance at CI's board of directors meetings in fiscal 1989 was technically just short of meeting Standard 1, but, because of the borderline situation, reserved judgement until its next review. NCIB recommends improvements in CI's annual report.

THE COUSTEAU SOCIETY, INC.

930 W. 21st Street
Norfolk, VA 23517
(804) 627-1144

Year of Data: **1984**
Expenditures $9,947,606
Percent to Program: 72.2%
Fund-raising Costs: 28.9%
Contributions Deductible: Yes
Top of Staff Salary Range: $90,000 (1984)
Meets NCIB Standards: No: 1 (8/7/86)

Purpose: To seek "conservation of natural resources and protection of all elements of the environment" through its research films, publications, lectures and exhibits

Comments: The editor deemed NCIB's information about this organization too dated (1985 data or before) to give the organization a complete listing.

ENVIRONMENTAL ACTION FOUNDATION

1525 New Hampshire Avenue, NW
Washington, DC 20036
(202) 745-4870

Purpose: To serve as a resource for concerned citizens and organizations in the areas of energy policy, toxic substances and solid waste reduction

Comments: NCIB is in the process of preparing its first report on this organization.

ENVIRONMENTAL DEFENSE FUND

257 Park Avenue South
New York, NY 10010
(212) 505-2100 or (800) CALL-EDF

Year of Data: 1988
Expenditures: $7,789,860
Percent to Program: 80%
Fund-raising Costs: 16%
Contributions Deductible: Yes
Top of Staff Salary Range: $90,000 (1989)
Meets NCIB Standards: Yes (9/21/89)

Purpose: "To encourage and support the conservation of natural resources and the enhancement of environmental quality; To receive and administer funds for scientific, educational and charitable purposes and to conduct such research and disseminate the results of such research by means of seminars, conferences, [and] publications...."

Program: Fiscal 1988 activities included:

- Wildlife and Water Resources (26%) - including work on drafting provisions for the Endangered Species Act; aid to states in developing programs to protect rare wild plants; advocacy and research to protect Antarctic marine animals; legal action to support the Marine Mammal Protection Act
- Education, Legislative Action and Membership Activities (23%) - outreach activities to inform members and public about EDF's work and about environmental issues; legislative activities to strengthen the protection of the environment
- Toxic Chemicals (20%) - efforts to reduce lead in gasoline, reduce dioxin pollution and maintain standards regarding exposure to radiation
- Energy and Air Quality (12%) - research

on acid rain; computer support of energy planning and conservation; research and policy action on ozone depletion; assistance in drafting state laws and regulations to reduce sulfur dioxide emissions

Comments: NCIB recommends improvements in EDF's annual report.

FRIENDS OF THE EARTH, INC. and FRIENDS OF THE EARTH FOUNDATION

218 D Street, SE
Washington, DC 20003
(202) 544-2600

Purpose: FOE: To "promote understanding and appreciation of the need for, and otherwise further, the preservation, protection and restoration of the natural resources and beauty of the United States and other area of the world, and the enhancement and rational use of all other aspects of man's environment;" FOE Foundation: To "engage in a scientific, educational and literary program that pertains to preservation, restoration and rational use of the earth"

Comments: NCIB is currently preparing a new report on this organization.

GREENPEACE USA

NCIB reports that, as of July 1, 1990, this organization has not, over a period of several years, furnished requested information sufficient to prepare a report.

INFORM, INC.

381 Park Avenue South
New York, NY 10016
(212) 689-4040

Year of Data: 1987
Expenditures: $1,081,264
Percent to Program: 77.6%
Fund-raising Costs: 6.2%
Contributions Deductible: Yes
Top of Staff Salary Range: $45,000 (1988)
Meets NCIB Standards: Yes (5/31/88)

Purpose: To conduct research about "the social and environmental effects of industrial activities; compare the underlying problems confronting individual companies, their efforts to resolve them, the costs and results; define practical and constructive alternatives for improving business performance and identify exemplary corporate programs that may serve as models; describe federal and state laws and regulations and analyze ways to make regulation more effective"

Program: All 1987 program spending (78% of total expenditures) was devoted to Research and Public Education, including examination and evaluation of 15 U.S. garbage-burning plants; research on the relative merits of methanol and natural gas as replacements for gasoline as motor fuels; study of more efficient methods of irrigation management in California and Colorado; conferences to inform public about research; publications on such topics as Hudson River pollution, toxic wastes, acid rain, garbage management and independent workers' clinics.

Comments: NCIB recommends improvements in Inform's audited financial statements.

KEEP AMERICA BEAUTIFUL, INC.

Mill River Plaza
9 West Broad Street
Stamford, Connecticut 06902
(203) 323-8987

Purpose: "To promote public education against the discarding of litter on public roadsides, parks, recreational and similar areas, and to encourage and voluntarily assist in the elimination of such litter by any other lawful means, thereby making such roadsides and areas more attractive and their use by the public more enjoyable"

Comments: NCIB is currently preparing a new report on this organization.

NATIONAL AUDUBON SOCIETY

950 Third Avenue
New York, NY 10022
(212) 832-3200

Year of Data: 1988
Expenditures: $30,978,725
Percent to Program: 70.2%
Fund-raising Costs: 21.9%
Contributions Deductible: Yes
Top of Staff Salary Range: $140,000 (1989)
Meets NCIB Standards: Yes (7/6/89)

Purpose: To "conserve plants and animals and their habitats, to further the wise use of land and water, to promote rational energy strategies, to protect life from pollution, and to seek solutions to global environmental problems"

Program: Fiscal 1988 activities included:
- Environmental Education and Information (21%) - programs to educate the public on conservation and ecological issues, including nature centers, camps and publications for the general public
- Membership and Publishing (21%) - costs of membership renewal and fulfillment of member subscriptions to magazines and other publications; costs of publishing two bimonthly magazines, which discuss conservation, ecological and wildlife preservation issues
- Wildlife Preservation and Conservation (16%) - operation of sanctuaries; legal action to forestall activities the society deems detrimental to natural habitats; activities initiating or responding to legislative actions affecting conservation laws
- Scientific and Field Research (7%) - programs seeking to maintain a high level of technical competence among the Society's field representatives, instructors and wardens; includes such activities as ecology systems analysis, environmental sciences, feeding studies and migration studies
- Chapter Activities (6%) - programs to encourage chapter members to participate in priority issues of the society

Comments: NAS has over 500 affiliated chapters and about 500,000 members who pay a national membership fee, part of which is returned to chapters for local purposes. NCIB's report concerns the national organization only. In fiscal 1988, about 30% of NAS's total support came from member dues. NCIB recommends improvements in NAS's annual report.

NATIONAL PARKS AND CONSERVATION ASSOCIATION

1015 31st Street, NW, 4th Fl.
Washington, DC 20007
(202) 944-8530

Year of Data: 1987
Expenditures: $3,516,699
Percent to Program: 82%
Fund-raising Costs: 13%
Contributions Deductible: Yes
Top of Staff Salary Range: $90,000 (1988)
Meets NCIB Standards: Yes (8/17/89)

Purpose: "To protect and improve the quality of our national park system and to promote an understanding, appreciation and sense of personal commitment to parklands"

Program: Fiscal 1987 activities included:
- Public Education (51%) - including publication of a bimonthly magazine; publication of a "comprehensive plan for the future of the National Park System;" about 42% of the expenses reported in this program category were for costs of "membership solicitations, renewal, maintenance and contribution drive"
- Field Program (7%) - efforts by NPCA's Alaska, Rocky Mountain and Southwest/California regional offices and its New York State chapter to help protect and expand national parks
- Natural Resources (5%) - including investigation of how the National Park System's research program "could better provide the scientific information needed for wise management of park resources;" involvement in establishing South Moresby National Park Preserve in British Columbia; organizing the first session of the International Parks Forum of the Americas and the Caribbean; efforts to limit park aircraft overflights; and efforts to reintroduce the wolf to Yellowstone National Park
- Grassroots Activities (5%) - including support for conferences for "park-watchers," concerned citizens who "keep NPCA apprised of threats to parks in their vicinity"

Comments: NCIB recommends improvements in NPCA's budget presentation. NCIB has asked NPCA for details about its relationship to the New York Parks and Conservation Association, a chapter of NPCA with its own board of directors.

NATURAL RESOURCES DEFENSE COUNCIL, INC.

40 W. 20th Street, 11th Fl.
New York, NY 10011
(212) 727-2700

Year of Data: 1987
Expenditures: $9,230,736
Percent to Program: 69.3%
Fund-raising Costs: 20.9%
Contributions Deductible: Yes
Top of Staff Salary Range: $115,000 (1988)
Meets NCIB Standards: Yes (5/2/88)

Purpose: To protect "the environment for the general welfare of the public by collecting and making available information relating to environmental protection and taking whatever legal steps may be appropriate to assure that the environment is protected"

Program: NRDC's reporting of its activities does not allow a financial breakdown of its programs. Fiscal 1987 activities included:
- Public Lands and the Coast - including initiatives to restrict tax subsidies for conversion of erodible lands and wetlands; appealing a Forest Service plan to expand clearcutting and construction of logging roads; signing an agreement with the Department of Interior ensuring that environmental factors are considered prior to issuance of coal mining leases
- Public Health and the Environment - advocacy of a 50% reduction in acid rain- causing pollution; campaigning for air quality improvements in New York City; filing suit to force the Environmental Protection Agency to ban a carcinogenic plant growth regulator; monitoring the Clean Water Act; publication of a handbook on water quality standards
- Nuclear Program - extension of a previous agreement with the Soviet Academy of Sciences to permit NRDC seismologists to monitor underground Soviet nuclear tests from stations inside the USSR; efforts to bring outmoded Department of Energy reactors into compliance with federal environmental

laws; publication of two volumes of a series on nuclear weapons

- Global Environment - helping to draft legislation requiring the Agency for International Development to spend $2.5 million each year on wildlife conservation, to improve tropical rain forest conservation and to fund assistance efforts to help maintain the natural resource base in sub-Saharan Africa

Comments: NCIB recommends improvements in NRDC's annual report and audited financial statements.

THE NATURE CONSERVANCY

1815 North Lynn Street
Arlington, VA 22209
(703) 841-5300 or (800) 628-6860

Year of Data: 1988
Expenditures: $58,899,000
Percent to Program: 74.2%
Fund-raising Costs: 8.8%
Contributions Deductible: Yes
Top of Staff Salary Range: $99,000 (1988)
Meets NCIB Standards: Yes (3/24/89)

Purpose: To acquire, protect and maintain tracts of land "so that the natural character of the land endures"

Program: Fiscal 1988 activities included:
- "Saving the Best and the Rarest" (41%) - securing protection of natural settings, by purchase, easements or agreements with owners
- Managing Species and Communities (18%) - management aid to preserves and other natural areas, workshops and training programs, prescribed burning, restoring buffer lands, controlling weeds and brush, monitoring natural communities and leading field trips
- Setting Priorities for Conservation (16%) - creation of three new conservation data centers in Panama, Venezuela and Canada; completion of a Biological and Data Conservation System for faster accessibility of information, facilitating legal and protection activities

Comments: In 1989, NC consisted of a national/international office, four regional offices in the United States and 88 other chapter, field and preserve offices; NC reported membership of 475,000. NCIB recommends improvements in NC's audited financial statements.

RESOURCES FOR THE FUTURE, INC.

1616 P Street, NW
Washington, DC 20036
(202) 328-5000

Year of Data: 1987
Expenditures: $6,510,179
Percent to Program: 61.4%
Fund-raising Costs: 6.2%
Contributions Deductible: Yes
Top of Staff Salary Range: $160,000 (1988)
Meets NCIB Standards: No: 1e, 6b (1/24/89)

Purpose: To "advance the development, conservation, and use of natural resources and to improve the quality of the environment through programs of research and education"

Program: Fiscal 1987 activities included:
- National Center for Food and Agricultural Policy (17%) - examines public policy issues involving agriculture, food and nutrition, international trade, natural resources and environmental quality; awards small grants and fellowships
- Quality of the Environment (13%) - research into such topics as benefit-cost analyses of environmental and other health and safety regulations; natural resources valuation; strategies for management of toxic wastes; groundwater contamination; regional resource management models; and analyses of industry's response to government regulation
- Renewable Resources (11%) - research focusing on policy issues involving forestry; agriculture; water and climate resources; and pesticide use
- Energy and Materials (8%) - research on such topics as economic dimensions of oil price shocks; regulatory issues in natural gas and electricity; shifts in industrial metals and materials requirements; and analysis of outer space as an economic resource
- Education and Communication (8%) - publication of books and studies on radioactive waste, asbestos control, metallic mineral exploration, recreation,

mining, regulatory agencies, pollution control laws and nuclear nonproliferation; publication of a quarterly magazine and production of a weekly radio program

Comments: NCIB faults RFF for compensating its board members for attendance at executive committee meetings (Standard 1e) and for having assets available for use which were 2.6 times its fiscal 1988 budget (Standard 6b). NCIB recommends improvements in RFF's audited financial statements.

SAVE-THE-REDWOODS LEAGUE

114 Sansome Street, Room 605
San Francisco, CA 94104
(415) 362-2352

Year of Data: 1986
Expenditures: $3,035,497
Percent to Program: 84.3%
Fund-raising Costs: 8.0%
Contributions Deductible: Yes
Top of Staff Salary Range: $80,000 (1987)
Meets NCIB Standards: No: 3 (10/2/87)

Purpose: To "encourage and support reforestation and conservation of California Redwood forest areas"

Program: SRL's reporting of its activities does not allow a detailed breakdown of its programs. Fiscal 1986 activities included purchase of over 4,000 acres of forest land in order to enlarge four parks, transfer of $1.6 million in land to the State of California and grants to the state for its purchase of additional lands. Other grants supported reforestation, creation or replacement of exhibits and maintenance at various parks.

Comments: SRL seeks to preserve and protect redwoods in 31 California Redwood State Parks and Redwood National Park, largely through land acquisition and transfer to the state. The state matches League contributions. The park system is now about 70% complete and the League plans to purchase about 150,000 additional acres. NCIB faults SRL for having assets available for use which, by NCIB's accounting, were 3 times its total expenses in 1986 (Standard 3). NCIB recommends improvements in SRL's annual report and budget presentation.

SIERRA CLUB

730 Polk Street
San Francisco, CA 94109
(415) 776-2211

Year of Data: 1988
Expenditures: $24,453,300
Percent to Program: 61%
Fund-raising Costs: 46%
Contributions Deductible: No
(see Sierra Club Foundation)
Top of Staff Salary Range: $87,000 (1988)
Meets NCIB Standards: Yes (11/9/89)

Purpose: To "explore, enjoy and protect the wild places of the earth"

Program: Fiscal 1988 activities included:
* Studying and Influencing Public Policy (19%) - lobbying, research and legal policy development by staff volunteers; the Sierra Club Legal Defense Fund contributed an additional $3.3 million in legal services
* Information and Education (18%) - publication of books (20-25 each year) and a bimonthly magazine
* Outdoor Activities (9%) - foreign or domestic trips for members who may help clean, maintain or restore trails, camps or wilderness areas; "Inner City Outings" provide recreational and educational wilderness experiences
* Membership Services (6%) - support for chapters and groups and the development of membership

Comments: In 1989, SC reported 57 chapters, 350 "Groups" and 490,000 members; 18% of all membership dues received by the national organization is returned to local chapters. NCIB recommends improvements in SC's annual report and budget presentation.

THE SIERRA CLUB FOUNDATION

730 Polk Street
San Francisco, CA 94109
(415) 776-2211

Year of Data: 1986
Expenditures: $3,946,352
Percent to Program: 67.7%
Fund-raising Costs: 27.1%
Contributions Deductible: Yes
Top of Staff Salary Range: $57,000 (1986)
Meets NCIB Standards: Yes (8/28/87)

Purpose: To "preserve and enhance the natural environment"

Program: All of SCF's fiscal 1986 program expenditures were devoted to grants to the Sierra Club and other organizations. Grants to the Sierra Club funded such projects as a library of materials on conservation, environmental policy, natural history and other outdoor activities; information services; the "Inner City Outings" program; protection of ecosystems near Everglades National Park; and training programs for citizens of the Great Lakes area. Grants to other organizations included support for Sierra Club chapters in Hawaii and West Virginia, for maintaining a bike trail in Wisconsin, a pollution prevention conference in Alabama and a film on Texas ecology.

Comments: SCF, a tax-deductible arm of the Sierra Club, provides grants to the Club and to other conservation organizations. NCIB recommends improvements in SCF's annual report.

SIERRA CLUB LEGAL DEFENSE FUND

2044 Fillmore Street
San Francisco, CA 94115
(415) 567-6100

Year of Data: **1985**
Expenditures $2,854,986
Percent to Program: 72.6%
Fund-raising Costs: 25.3%
Contributions Deductible: Yes
Top of Staff Salary Range: $86,500 (1985)
Meets NCIB Standards: Yes (8/28/86)

Purpose: "To provide legal representation for public interest groups and conservation-minded individuals in environmental litigation and administrative proceedings"

Comments: The editor deemed NCIB's information about this organization too dated (1985 data or before) to give the organization a complete listing.

UNION OF CONCERNED SCIENTISTS

26 Church Street
Cambridge, MA 02238
(617) 547-5552

Year of Data: 1987
Expenditures $3,456,866
Percent to Program: 68.6%
Fund-raising Costs: 31.4%
Contributions Deductible: Yes
Top of Staff Salary Range: $60,850 (1987)
Meets NCIB Standards: Yes (12/21/88)

Purpose: To advocate "sensible policies concerning national energy, national security and nuclear power safety through research, public education, lobbying and litigation"

Program: Fiscal 1987 expenditures were allocated to research and dissemination of results concerning nuclear arms (53% of total expenditures); research and dissemination of results regarding nuclear plant safety (19%); and legislative activities (7%). Activities included a campaign on nuclear plant safety; a successful court challenge to the Nuclear Regulatory Commission, requiring it to mandate certain safety measures; a campaign to keep arms reduction and safe energy issues before the public and candidates through 1988; a conference on the Strategic Defense Initiative; and production of a video/slide program advocating deep reductions in nuclear weapons. Publications included books and a quarterly journal, with a circulation of 130,000.

Comments: NCIB recommends improvements in UCS's annual report, budget presentation and audited financial statements.

WILDERNESS SOCIETY

1400 Eye Street, NW
Washington, DC 20005
(202) 842-3400

Purpose: To "preserve wilderness and wildlife, protect America's prime forests, parks, rivers and shorelands, and foster an American land ethic"

Comments: NCIB is currently preparing a new report on this organization.

WORLD RESOURCES INSTITUTE and WORLD RESOURCES INSTITUTE FUND

1709 New York Ave., NW, Suite 700
Washington, DC 20006
(202) 638-6300

Year of Data: 1986
Expenditures $4,061,213
Percent to Program: 75.7%
Fund-raising Costs: 6.3%
Contributions Deductible: Yes
Top of Staff Salary Range: $85,000 (1986)
Meets NCIB Standards: Yes (4/24/87)

Purpose: WRI's purpose is to "help governments, international organizations, the private sector, and others address a fundamental question: How can we meet basic human needs and nurture economic growth without undermining the natural resources and environmental integrity on which life, economic vitality, and international security depend?" WRIF's purpose is to "perform development and other functions for the benefit of WRI."

Program: Fiscal 1986 activities included:
- Communication and Public Affairs (18%) - communicating and marketing the results of research programs, through publications, media contacts, briefings and speaking engagements
- Resources and Environmental Information (16%) - including $331,000 in grants for an annual report on international conditions and trends in population, resources and the environment
- Institutions, Governance and Economics (13%) - including $221,000 in grants for "promoting sustainable growth," an economic and environmental analysis of resource subsidies and price controls; assessing and valuing natural resource and ecological services; and defining U.S. economic and political interests in the global environment
- Conserving Forest and Biological Diversity (10%) - including $225,000 in grants for implementing an international plan of action for conserving tropical forests
- Energy and Climate (8%) - including $125,000 in grants for studies of technologies and policies for sustainable energy and greenhouse gases and climate change

Comments: In fiscal 1986, about 69.5% of WRI's support came from a MacArthur Foundation grant. NCIB recommends improvements in WRI's audited financial statements.

- **DEFENDERS OF WILDLIFE** (see ANIMAL-RELATED)
- **DUCKS UNLIMITED, INC.** (see ANIMAL-RELATED)
- **CHARLES A. LINDBERGH FUND, INC.** (see EDUCATION)
- **NATIONAL WILDLIFE FEDERATION** (see ANIMAL-RELATED)
- **POPULATION INSTITUTE** (see SOCIAL ACTION)
- **RURAL ADVANCEMENT FUND OF THE NATIONAL SHARECROPPERS FUND** (see SOCIAL ACTION)
- **WILDLIFE PRESERVATION TRUST INTERNATIONAL** (see ANIMAL-RELATED)
- **WORLD WILDLIFE FUND** (see ANIMAL-RELATED)
- **ZERO POPULATION GROWTH** (see SOCIAL ACTION)

HEALTH - GENERAL AND REHABILITATION

*research, care and rehabilitation,
medical education, parenthood*

ACTION ON SMOKING AND HEALTH

2013 H Street, NW
Washington, DC 20006
(202) 659-4310

Purpose: To "take legal actions with regard to the problems of smoking and serve as the voice of nonsmokers and those concerned with the problems of smoking"

Comments: NCIB is currently preparing a new report on this organization.

ALS ASSOCIATION (AMYOTROPHIC LATERAL SCLEROSIS)

21021 Ventura Boulevard, Suite 321
Woodland Hills, CA 91364
(818) 340-7500 or (800) 782-4747

Year of Data: 1989
Expenditures: $2,063,952
Percent to Program: 76%
Fund-raising Costs: 12%
Contributions Deductible: Yes
Top of Staff Salary Range: $100,000 (1988)
Meets NCIB Standards: Yes (9/21/89)

Purpose: To support research and, through its affiliates, provide services in the areas of patient support, information dissemination and public awareness related to the cause, prevention and cure of Amyotrophic Lateral Sclerosis (ALS)

Program: Fiscal 1989 activities included:
- Patient Services (28%) - grants, awards and an annual volunteer leadership conference on "new resources and techniques [of patient support], government actions ... and the latest in clinical and basic ALS research"
- Research (26%) - support of 21 ongoing or completed ALS-specific research projects and approval of eight new grants
- Public Information and Education (22%)

- co-sponsorship of a conference and publications, including a bimonthly newspaper

Comments: Financial information about ALSA's local affiliates was not included in the organization's annual report and is absent from the NCIB report; NCIB recommends improvements in ALSA's annual report.

ALZHEIMER'S DISEASE AND RELATED DISORDERS ASSOCIATION

70 East Lake Street, Suite 600
Chicago, IL 60601-5997
(312) 853-3060
(800) 621-0379 outside IL
(800) 572-6037 in IL

Year of Data: 1987
Expenditures: $14,642,153
Percent to Program: 76%
Fund-raising Costs: 14%
Contributions Deductible: Yes
Top of Staff Salary Range: $135,000 (1988)
Meets NCIB Standards: Yes (3/31/89)

Purpose: "To provide guidance and support for the afflicted and their families primarily through member Chapters and Affiliates; to encourage and support research into causes, improved diagnosis, therapy, cures for and prevention of Alzheimer's disease and related brain disorders; to publicize the medical, social, psychological and financial needs of the affected and to strive for public education to ameliorate the problems"

Program: Fiscal 1987 activities included:
- Research (20%) - award of 56 research grants, including 35 grants supporting new research initiatives, 18 grants supporting established Alzheimer's disease researchers and 3 awards of salary support for "promising young investigators"
- Member Services (18%) - local chapter assistance to over 1,000 local support groups, which help victims and their families cope with Alzheimer's disease, provide information and referral and participate in grassroots advocacy
- Public Awareness and Education (16%) - development of nine topical brochures, provision of educational materials to 55,000 requestors and response to 38,500 telephone calls requesting information and support

- Chapter Services (8%) - assistance to chapters and training workshops

Comments: NCIB's report is based on ADRDA's audited financial statements for its national headquarters and unaudited combined financial statements for 151 of its 188 chapters.

AMERICAN DIABETES ASSOCIATION, INC.

1660 Duke Street
Alexandria, VA 22314
(703) 549-1500 or (800) 232-3472

Year of Data: 1988
Expenditures: $46,260,682
Percent to Program: 80%
Fund-raising Costs: 20.6%
Contributions Deductible: Yes
Top of Staff Salary Range: $150,000 (1988)
Meets NCIB Standards: Yes (2/15/90)

Purpose: To "find a preventive and cure for diabetes and to improve the well-being of all people with diabetes and their families"

Program: For fiscal 1988, the ADA reported combined expenditures for the national headquarters and chapters under the categories of Patient Activities (28% of total expenditures), Research Activities (20%), Public Activities (15%), Professional Activities (9%), and Community Activities (7%). ADA's description of its programs used different categories:

- Patient Education - provision of "special-topic literature" and other information to benefit diabetes victims; costs of conducting an annual Youth Leadership Conference and sponsorship of 60 youth summer camps; lectures, discussion groups and other activities sponsored by affiliates and chapters
- Professional Education - costs of annual Scientific Sessions, attended by more than 8,600 scientists, physicians and health professionals; provision, by affiliates, of information, symposia and training to local health professionals; publication of two professional periodicals
- Public Education - costs of seminars for science writers, media awards, public service announcements and an American Diabetes Alert Day public

education campaign; support for legislation benefiting diabetes victims
- Research - award of $7,147,573, including grants to encourage young scientists to enter diabetes-related research and to give scientists opportunities to gather preliminary data to qualify for major support from other funding agencies

Comments: In fiscal 1988, ADA had 56 affiliates and 800 chapters nationwide and reported 230,000 general members and 8,600 professional members. Certain contributions to affiliates are shared with the Association and certain contributions to the Association are shared with the appropriate affiliate. NCIB reports that ADA's fund-raising methods recently included door-to-door solicitations, walk-a-thons and the sale of cards and other items, activities which are "generally difficult to administer and control." NCIB objects to ADA's use of "matching check" solicitations which do not give contributors the option of having their donations returned if the matching check challenge is not met. NCIB recommends improvements in ADA's budget presentation.

AMERICAN FOUNDATION FOR AIDS RESEARCH

5900 Wilshire Boulevard
2nd Floor, East Satellite
Los Angeles, CA 90036
(213) 857-5900
        or
1515 Broadway, Suite 3601
New York, NY 10036-8901
(212) 719-0033

Year of Data: 1987
Expenditures: $9,368,468
Percent to Program: 82.7%
Fund-raising Costs: 8.8%
Contributions Deductible: Yes
Top of Staff Salary Range: $100,000 (1988)
Meets NCIB Standards: Yes (4/5/89)

Purpose: "To support research on AIDS and its complications" and to provide public information and education about AIDS

Program: Fiscal 1988 activities included:
- Research Awards (69%) - grants for purposes including "studying the structure of the virus and examining how it kills cells;" "vaccines to prevent infection and drugs that will arrest it;" "exploring the complications of AIDS, including

opportunistic infections, viral cofactors and neurological aspects of the disease;" and "weighing the ethical implications of society's response to the epidemic"
* Public Information and Education (14%) - publications, including a monthly newsletter distributed to scientists and physicians; appearances before congressional committees and other governmental bodies; response to requests for information and materials from the media and others

Comments: AFAR's total revenues increased 65% from fiscal 1987 to fiscal 1988.

AMERICAN FUND FOR DENTAL HEALTH

211 East Chicago Avenue
Chicago, IL 60611
(312) 787-6270

Year of Data: 1988
Expenditures: $1,759,300
Percent to Program: 74%
Fund-raising Costs: 15.3%
Contributions Deductible: Yes
Top of Staff Salary Range: $80,000 (1988)
Meets NCIB Standards: Yes (5/3/90)

Purpose: To "improve the health of the nation by supporting programs and projects in education, research, and service which will expand knowledge of dental and general health, improve the prevention and treatment of dental disease, and augment dental education"

Program: Fiscal 1988 activities included grants and awards to dental schools and dental organizations (22% of total expenditures); grants to support a "Study for Identification of Children At High Risk for Dental Caries" (16%); a "Face of Dentistry" film project (13%); scholarships and fellowships (10%); and a program of seminars for senior dental students (7%).

Comments: AFDH states that its board members "represent entire constituencies of the dental community, including the American Dental Association, American Association of Dental Schools, American Dental Trade Association and dental laboratory industries."

AMERICAN HEALTH ASSISTANCE FOUNDATION

15825 Shady Grove Road, Suite 140
Rockville, MD 20850
(301) 948-3244; (800) 227-7998

Purpose: "Funding scientific research of age-related and degenerative diseases [and] educating the public about Alzheimer's disease, coronary heart disease, and glaucoma." In fiscal 1988, the AHAF board of directors approved a new program "for financial assistance to caregivers and to patients suffering from Alzheimer's disease." Includes the following programs: Alzheimer's Disease Research Program; Coronary Heart Disease Research Project; National Glaucoma Research Program.

Comments: NCIB is currently preparing a new report on this organization.

AMERICAN HEART ASSOCIATION

7320 Greenville Avenue
Dallas, TX 75231
(214) 373-6300
(800) 527-6941 outside TX

Year of Data: 1988
Expenditures: $196,887,000
Percent to Program: 77%
Fund-raising Costs: 16%
Contributions Deductible: Yes
Top of Staff Salary Range: $181,000 (1989)
Meets NCIB Standards: Yes (5/5/89)

Purpose: To "reduce premature death and disability from cardiovascular diseases and stroke"

Program: Fiscal 1988 activities included:
* Research (33%) - over $61 million in grants and awards, including support for 1,388 research projects, 687 fellowships and 102 other research awards
* Public Health Education (19%) - materials for media and public use concerning good nutrition, high blood pressure, and the dangers of smoking; programs for pre-schoolers; special efforts to discourage smoking by teenagers
* Community Services (15%) - including work by volunteers to certify or recertify 2.7 million people in life support courses and to screen 700,000 people for high blood pressure

- Professional Education and Training (9%) - "scientific sessions" for over 25,000 professionals; ten conferences; sponsorship of or participation in 20 postgraduate courses; issuance of 13 medical statements

Comments: ACS reports about 200,000 members, one-third of whom are medical professionals, and 2.4 million volunteers. Twenty-five percent of contributions to affiliates go to the national center. NCIB reports that AHA uses such special events as "jump-a-thons" to raise funds and calls such methods "generally difficult to administer and control." NCIB recommends that interested contributors request local financial statements and look for separate reporting of such special fund-raising activities.

AMERICAN KIDNEY FUND

6110 Executive Blvd., Suite 1010
Rockville, MD 20852
(301) 881-3052

Purpose: To "provide financial assistance to help victims of kidney disease, particularly those who have end-stage renal disease and who are being treated by means of the artificial kidney and kidney transplant

Comments: NCIB is currently preparing a new report on this organization.

AMERICAN LEPROSY MISSIONS

1 Broadway
Elmwood Park, NJ 07407
(201) 794-8650
(800) 543-3131 outside NJ

Year of Data: 1988
Expenditures: $8,051,467
Percent to Program: 59.2%
Fund-raising Costs: 33.5%
Contributions Deductible: Yes
Top of Staff Salary Range: $62,000 (1988)
Meets NCIB Standards: Yes (8/9/89)

Purpose: To "present the Gospel of the Lord Jesus Christ by word and deed to those with leprosy," to encourage medical and social treatment of leprosy patients and to work with other organizations toward the eradication of leprosy

Program: ALM's reporting of its activities does not allow a detailed breakdown of its

programs. ALM reports that it supports about 1,000 hospitals, clinics and dispensaries in about 25 countries; recruits and trains leprosy workers overseas; provides patients with medicine, medical and surgical treatment, physical therapy, vocational training, food, shelter and clothing; and supports leprosy research. It cooperates "with national churches to foster evangelism and spiritual growth" and seeks to educate the American public about leprosy and the needs of its victims through films, literature and television documentaries. ALM publishes a newsletter nine times a year. Fiscal 1988 program activities included Drug Therapy (36%), Public Education (14%), and Training of Professionals (11%).

Comments: NCIB considers ALM's expense ratios as "reasonable," even though its expenditures for program are just short of NCIB's Standard 6. NCIB recommends improvement in ALM's annual report, balance sheet and budget.

AMERICAN LIVER FOUNDATION

1425 Pompton Avenue
Cedar Grove, NJ 07009
(201) 256-2550

Year of Data: 1988
Expenditures: $1,321,747
Percent to Program: 84.6%
Fund-raising Costs: 7.7%
Contributions Deductible: Yes
Top of Staff Salary Range: $60,000 (1989)
Meets NCIB Standards: Yes (9/7/89)

Purpose: "To improve understanding, prevention and cure of all liver diseases, especially viral hepatitis, cirrhosis, alcohol-related liver diseases, liver disorders in children, cancer of the liver, and gallstones, and to reduce the economic burden of liver diseases in America...."

Program: Fiscal 1988 activities included:
- Public Education (35%) - preparation and dissemination of literature and media information, including publication of a quarterly newsletter
- Transplant Patient Support (27%) - not described in materials available to NCIB
- Research (19%) - award of 16 postdoctoral and 13 student research fellowships, plus additional scholarships and awards

Comments: ALF recently consisted of a national headquarters, 26 chapters and an affiliate, the Dean Thiel Foundation, which raises funds on behalf of itself and ALF. NCIB recommends improvements in ALF's annual report and audited financial statements.

AMERICAN LUNG ASSOCIATION

1740 Broadway
New York, NY 10019-4374
(212) 315-8700

Year of Data: 1988
Expenditures: $13,676,816
Percent to Program: 80%
Fund-raising Costs: 17.6%
Contributions Deductible: Yes
Top of Staff Salary Range: $125,274 (1989)
Meets NCIB Standards: Yes (11/22/89)

Purpose: The "conquest of lung disease and the promotion of lung health"

Program: Fiscal 1988 activities included:
- Lung Disease (48%) - including $2.5 million in awards and grants; development of professional education materials about emphysema and a video news release on flu and pneumonia; cosponsorship of a conference on asthma education; development of recommendations for comprehensive health care for HIV-AIDS patients
- Community Health and Program Support (12%) - including provision of a health education program to over a million students in 5,600 schools; publication of a brochure about lung disease among minorities
- Smoking and Health (10%) - development of a smoking cessation package for the workplace and a poster campaign aimed at expectant mothers and black youth; legislative support for a higher cigarette excise tax, the Comprehensive Health and Safety Act and a ban on smoking on airline flights of less than two hours' duration

Comments: ALA has 59 state or large city constituent associations and 76 "affiliated lung associations." Constituents and affiliates raise funds in their own names, but pay ALA for the use of its trademarks, such as Christmas Seals, and pay ALA 10% of their "shareable income." In fiscal 1988, about 54% of ALA's support came from shareable income. ALA does not control or direct the constituents' or affiliates' financial transactions. NCIB's report concerns only the national organization. Since 90% of contributions are retained by affiliates, NCIB suggests that contributors study their finances, focus, fund-raising practices and quality of programs.

AMERICAN PARKINSON'S DISEASE ASSOCIATION

116 John Street
New York, NY 10038
(800) 223-2732

Purpose: To "ease the burden and find the cure to Parkinson Disease through medical research and information and referral services to patients, families, medical personnel and the public"

Comments: NCIB is currently preparing a new report on this organization.

AMERICAN SOCIAL HEALTH ASSOCIATION

P.O. Box 13827
Research Triangle Park, NC 27709
(919) 361-2742

Year of Data: 1986
Expenditures: $1,653,742
Percent to Program: 77.8%
Fund-raising Costs: 7.2%
Contributions Deductible: Yes
Top of Staff Salary Range: $69,349 (1986)
Meets NCIB Standards: Yes (3/23/88)

Purpose: To prevent and control "sexually transmissible diseases (STDs) and their damaging social and economic consequences"

Program: Fiscal 1986 activities include:
- Information and Education (54%) - provision of information about sexually transmissible diseases and referral to community health care resources through a toll-free national telephone hotline; operation of a Herpes Resource Center, which sponsors about 100 local self-help groups and publishes a newsletter; operation of a National AIDS Information Center, which responded to about 2,000 calls per day and sent out about 300 information packets per day; development of an instructional packet for high school stu-

dents and an education project to teach high school students about AIDS

- Research (8%) - including awards of four two-year postdoctoral fellowships, totalling $75,000
- Public Policy (6%) - presentation of testimony and other advocacy about STDs and their impact on "almost every facet of American life"

Comments: ASHA's planned expenditures for 1987 were more than double its 1986 expenditures, mostly for expansion of the National AIDS Hotline; ASHA projected that these increases would be funded primarily from "Fees and grants from government agencies." NCIB recommends improvements in ASHA's annual report.

ARTHRITIS FOUNDATION

1314 Spring Street, NW
Atlanta, GA 30309
(404) 872-7100
(800) 283-7800 infoline

Year of Data: 1987
Expenditures: $50,199,668
Percent to Program: 74%
Fund-raising Costs: 16.6%
Contributions Deductible: Yes
Top of Staff Salary Range: $120,800 (1988)
Meets NCIB Standards: Yes (12/12/88)

Purpose: To provide services in the areas of research, education and community/patient services related to the prevention, cure and treatment of arthritis and rheumatoid diseases, including osteoarthritis, rheumatoid arthritis, gout, systemic lupus erythematosus, ankylosing spondylitis, scleroderma, juvenile arthritis and polymyasitis

Program: Fiscal 1987 activities included:

- Public Health Education (29%) - costs of the telethon and the national office's direct mail campaign; production of news releases, radio and television programs, films and brochures; operation of a toll-free information service; publication of a bimonthly magazine
- Patient and Community Service (20%) - development of an exercise program, a seven-week self-help course for people with systemic lupus, a videotape and a program to train lay people to provide support to arthritis victims
- Research (18%) - $7.9 million in grants

and awards, including support for 47 arthritis research centers and 146 research scientists; many chapters award additional research grants

- Professional Education (7%) - seminars for professionals; provision of literature, slides, films and a bimonthly bulletin

Comments: AF consists of 72 chapters and divisions, a national office, a professional section and a section concerned with childhood arthritis. The American Rheumatism Association, an affiliate until 1986, is now an independent medical society. AF conducts a nationwide telethon which raised over $9 million in 1987, though AF did not report related expenses. NCIB reports that AF uses such special events as "skate-a-thons" and golf tournaments to raise funds and calls such methods "generally difficult to administer and control." NCIB recommends that interested contributors request local financial statements and look for separate reporting of such special fund-raising activities. NCIB recommends improvements in AF's budget presentation.

ASSOCIATION FOR RETARDED CITIZENS OF THE UNITED STATES

2501 Avenue J
P.O. Box 6109
Arlington, TX 76005
(817) 640-0204

Year of Data: 1987
Expenditures: $265,589,913
Percent to Program: 87.5%
Fund-raising Costs: 23.6%
Contributions Deductible: Yes
Top of Staff Salary Range: $107,102 (1986)
Meets NCIB Standards: Yes (4/12/89)

Purpose: To promote "the improvement of the quality of life of all people with mental retardation, the prevention of this handicapping condition and the search for cures"

Program: Fiscal 1987 activities of ARC's national headquarters included:

- Community and Patient Services (65%) - direct assistance and services to affiliates, such as research and analysis on legislative issues and job placement for mentally retarded persons
- Professional Health, Education and Training (8%) - seminars, materials to educate employers about employment

of the mentally retarded and a conference to develop "principles for operating corporate guardianship programs"

- Public Health Education (7%) - provision of information and assistance to requestors; implementation of a public awareness media campaign concerning "finding cures for mental retardation;" publication of six issues of a newsletter
- Research (6%) - research awards and grants; efforts in bioengineering to develop devices to assist retarded or handicapped persons, for example a "computerized voice activated environmental control system"

Comments: Of ARC's total expenses in 1987, 98.1% was spent by affiliates. In 1987, ARC reported that it had 1,300 local and state chapters and 160,000 members. There are some Associations for Retarded Citizens which are not ARC affiliates, however. Every affiliated chapter pays an affiliation fee, plus a $6.00 fee for each member. In fiscal 1987, ARC and its affiliates received $193,486,911, or about 71% of their total revenue, in government grants and fees. NCIB recommends improvements in ARC's audited financial statements, annual report and budget.

ASSOCIATION FOR VOLUNTARY SURGICAL CONTRACEPTION (formerly Association for Voluntary Sterilization)

122 East 42nd Street
New York, NY 10168
(212) 351-2500

Purpose: To "promote and support voluntary surgical contraception programs throughout the world"

Comments: NCIB is currently preparing a new report on this organization.

ASTHMA AND ALLERGY FOUNDATION OF AMERICA

1717 Massachusetts Ave., NW, Suite 305
Washington, DC 20036
(202) 265-0265

Purpose: To "unite the public, the medical profession, research scientists and public health workers in a campaign to solve the health problems posed by the allergic diseases"

Comments: NCIB is currently preparing a new report on this organization.

CENTER FOR POPULATION OPTIONS

1025 Vermont Ave., NW, Suite 210
Washington, DC 20005
(202) 347-5700

Year of Data: 1988
Expenditures: $1,486,018
Percent to Program: 77%
Fund-raising Costs: 4.4%
Contributions Deductible: Yes
Top of Staff Salary Range: $69,450 (1989)
Meets NCIB Standards: Yes (6/27/89)

Purpose: To "enhance opportunities for young people in key decision-making areas of their lives: continuing their education, planning their families, obtaining needed health and social services, and attaining productive employment.... [with special emphasis on] interconnections between family formation and other 'life actions'"

Program: Fiscal 1988 activities included:
- Support for School-Based Clinics (13%) - technical assistance and training to school-based clinics in such areas as program design, implementation strategies, evaluation, fund-raising and public relations; sponsorship of national conference; publications, including quarterly newsletter
- Media Project (13%) - efforts to educate and inform the entertainment industry on "ways to present a more responsible, socially relevant view of sexuality," including seminars, creation of an entertainment industry task force and awards to meritorious television programs
- Research Program (12%) - study of operations and effects of school-based clinics
- Partnership Program (11%) - work with

youth-serving organization to promote "awareness of issues surrounding teen pregnancy and related concerns, such as AIDS;" assistance to groups concerning AIDS education; sponsorship of an AIDS conference; publications

- Public Education and Resource Center (10%) - provision of information about adolescent pregnancy to reporters and the public; maintenance of a specialized library
- International Clearinghouse on Adolescent Fertility (10%) - collection and dissemination of information about promising teen pregnancy prevention efforts from around the world; start-up funding and consultation to eight projects in developing countries

Comments: None.

CENTER FOR SCIENCE IN THE PUBLIC INTEREST

1501 16th Street, NW
Washington, DC 20036-1499
(202) 332-9110

Year of Data: 1989
Expenditures: $3,470,767
Percent to Program: 75.4%
Fund-raising Costs: 26.8%
Contributions Deductible: Yes
Top of Staff Salary Range: $55,000 (1989)
Meets NCIB Standards: Yes (4/25/90)

Purpose: "research, education and advocacy on nutrition, diet, and related health issues"

Program: CSPI's reporting of its financial and other data does not allow a detailed breakdown of its expenses and programs. Fiscal 1989 activities included research and evaluation of scientific issues and communication of results to the public; publication of a nutrition newsletter; advocacy for more preventative approaches to alcohol abuse problems; efforts to improve the health status of blacks, latinos and other minority populations; promotion of increased production and availability of food that is free of chemical and other contaminants; efforts to investigate accuracy of food and beverage advertising and monitor industry compliance with food safety laws; and initiation of litigation on nutrition.

Comments: In fiscal 1989, about 63% of the CSPI's total revenues came from membership dues. NCIB suggests that CSPI's fund-raising/development costs are somewhat high. NCIB recommends improvements in CSPI's annual report.

CITY OF HOPE

1500 E. Duarte Road
Duarte, CA 91010
(818) 359-8111

Purpose: To "support advanced research, treatment and medical education in catastrophic diseases, including cancer, leukemia, blood, heart and lung diseases, certain hereditary maladies, and metabolic disorders, such as diabetes" at the National Pilot Medical Center and the Beckman Research Institute

Comments: NCIB is in the process of preparing its first report on this organization.

CYSTIC FIBROSIS FOUNDATION

6931 Arlington Road
Bethesda, MD 20814
(301) 951-4422 or (800) FIGHT CF

Year of Data: 1987
Expenditures: $31,450,108
Percent to Program: 77.7%
Fund-raising Costs: 12.3%
Contributions Deductible: Yes
Top of Staff Salary Range: $130,000 (1987)
Meets NCIB Standards: Yes (11/14/88)

Purpose: "To find the means for the prevention, control and effective treatment of Cystic Fibrosis"

Program: Fiscal 1987 program activities included:

- Medical Programs (43%) - grants to over 120 cystic fibrosis care centers; grants to scientists engaged in research; and fellowships to support training of scientists establishing careers in the field
- Public and Professional Information and Education (26%) - programs designed to improve the knowledge of medical personnel and the general public about the disease, its symptoms and its treatments
- Community Services (9%) - including programs to help the general public in detection of the disease; provision of referral services; processing of inquiries

Comments: CFF operates through a national headquarters and about 58 local chapters, some of which have branches. CFF's total revenues increased 36% from 1986 to 1987; its 1988 budget is 33% higher than 1987 expenses. NCIB faults CFF for its fund-raising solicitations which asked recipients to make a contribution, purchase a book or check a box declaring, "No, I'm sorry but I can't afford to send even $3.00." CFF later reported removing the offending statement. NCIB recommends improvements in CFF's annual report.

DEAFNESS RESEARCH FOUNDATION

9 East 38th Street
New York, NY 10016
(212) 684-6556

Year of Data: 1987
Expenditures: $1,710,762
Percent to Program: 73.9%
Fund-raising Costs: 11.4%
Contributions Deductible: Yes
Top of Staff Salary Range: $63,000 (1987)
Meets NCIB Standards: Yes (5/24/88)

Purpose: "To sponsor research into the causes and improved means of treatment and prevention of deafness and other ear disorders; to encourage young scientists to enter the field of otologic research; ... to encourage ear examinations, and to encourage individuals with ear disorders to bequeath their inner ear structure to the Temporal Bone Banks Program for Ear Research"

Program: Fiscal 1987 activities included:
- Research (61%) - grants totaling $1,014,666
- Public Education (12%) - distribution of brochures and televised public service announcements in efforts to educate the public about the impact of deafness and related ear impairments

Comments: NCIB recommends improvements in DRF's annual report.

DIABETES TRUST FUND, INC.

1034 S. 23rd Street, Suite 202
P.O. Box 55785
Birmingham, AL 35255
(205) 856-7519

Purpose: To support "diabetes research, education and treatment" programs
Comments: NCIB is currently preparing a new report on this organization.

DYSAUTONOMIA FOUNDATION

20 East 46th Street, Room 302
New York, NY 10017
(212) 949-6644

Year of Data: 1986
Expenditures $434,468
Percent to Program: 87%
Fund-raising Costs: 5.8%
Contributions Deductible: Yes
Top of Staff Salary Range: $40,000 (1987)
Meets NCIB Standards: Yes (10/16/87)

Purpose: "To stimulate and promote medical research into familial dysautonomia [a genetic disorder of the autonomic nervous system] ... and to provide information to the public, both lay and medical, about the disease"

Comments: The editor deemed this organization too small (under $1 million in expenditures in the most recent year reported) to be given a complete listing.

EPILEPSY FOUNDATION OF AMERICA

4351 Garden City Drive, Suite 406
Landover, MD 20785
(301) 459-3700 or (800) 332-1000

Year of Data: 1986
Expenditures: $19,502,432
Percent to Program: 68.6%
Fund-raising Costs: 29.8%
Contributions Deductible: Yes
Top of Staff Salary Range: $125,000 (1988)
Meets NCIB Standards: Yes (8/29/88)

Purpose: "Prevention and control of epilepsy and improving the quality of life of people affected by the condition and their families"

Program: NCIB's report uses EFA's fiscal 1987 activity descriptions, but 1986 expenditure figures, because combined audited financial statements for 1987 were not yet available. Activities included:

- Patient Services (41%) - including legal advocacy, legal information services and publications; employment services; information and referral services; and minority services involving a media campaign for minority audiences
- Public Health Education (11%) - including media campaigns and publication and distribution of a periodical and a series of pamphlets
- Community Services (9%) - including affiliate services to people with epilepsy and their families; cooperation with government agencies

Comments: EFA has described itself as a "national spokesman, advocate and ombudsman" for persons with epilepsy, "defining their myriad problems and devising specific detailed programs to solve them." In addition to its national headquarters, EFA recently reported 86 chapter/affiliate organizations and 11,000 individual members. In 1986, about 42.9% of combined revenues and 44.4% of combined expenses were attributed to the national headquarters. In the same year, 25.5% of combined revenue was from government grants, most of them to the affiliates.

52 ASSOCIATION, INC.
350 Fifth Avenue, Room 1829
New York, NY 10118
(212) 563-9797

Year of Data: **1982**
Expenditures $297,829
Percent to Program: 66.6%
Fund-raising Costs: 16.4%
Contributions Deductible: Yes
Top of Staff Salary Range: $50,000 (1983)
Meets NCIB Standards: Yes (1/11/84)

Purpose: "Building confidence in the more severely disabled" and "working with the handicapped on a rehabilitation through sports concept"

Comments: The editor deemed NCIB's information about this organization too dated (1985 data or before) to give it a complete listing.

HELP HOSPITALIZED VETERANS
2065 Kurtz Street
San Diego, CA 92110
(619) 291-5846,5791,3793

Year of Data: 1987
Expenditures: $5,921,315
Percent to Program: 44.6%
Fund-raising Costs: 52.7%
Contributions Deductible: Yes
Top of Staff Salary Range: $48,000 (1988)
Meets NCIB Standards: No: 4 (6/30/88)

Purpose: "Distributing crafts kits containing arts and crafts materials to patients and occupational therapy departments in military and veterans' hospitals"
Program: Fiscal 1987 activities consisted of distribution of 796,000 craft kits to 250 Veterans Administration and military hospitals.
Comments: HHV failed to meet NCIB's Standard 4 because, in 1987, its program expenses were low and its fund-raising expenses were high. NCIB also faults HHV's failure to mention the costs of its fund-raising activities in its annual report and its exaggerated valuation of the craft kits it distributes.

HUNTINGTON'S DISEASE SOCIETY OF AMERICA, INC.
140 West 22nd Street
New York, NY 10011
(212) 242-1968 or (800) 345-HDSA

Year of Data: 1987
Expenditures $716,777
Percent to Program: 81.9%
Fund-raising Costs: 9.6%
Contributions Deductible: Yes
Top of Staff Salary Range: $50,000 (1987)
Meets NCIB Standards: Yes (5/23/88)

Purpose: "To serve as a clearinghouse for public education and information regarding Huntington's Disease; to support and encourage medical and scientific research in Huntington's Disease; to assist persons and families 'at risk' to Huntington's Disease with respect to availability of professional care and patient services...."
Comments: The editor deemed this organization too small (under $1 million in expenditures in the most recent year reported) to be given a complete listing.

JUVENILE DIABETES FOUNDATION INTERNATIONAL

432 Park Avenue South
New York, NY 10016-8013
(212) 889-7575 or (800) 223-1138

Year of Data: 1988
Expenditures: $25,154,061
Percent to Program: 73%
Fund-raising Costs: 24%
Contributions Deductible: Yes
Top of Staff Salary Range: $100,000 (1989)
Meets NCIB Standards: Yes (12/12/89)

Purpose: "Supporting and advancing research in the field of Diabetes and particularly Juvenile Diabetes throughout the world and providing material of an educational and informational nature to persons throughout the world who are interested in and affected by Juvenile Diabetes"

Program: Fiscal 1988 activities included:
- Research Support (54%) - 209 grants, 86 postdoctoral fellowships, 5 research career development awards and 16 summer student research awards
- Public Education (19%) - efforts to inform the public about the treatment of and the need for a cure for diabetes, via magazines, pamphlets, films, visual aids and public service announcements

Comments: JDFI recently consisted of a national headquarters, 131 chapters and an international associate chapter in Canada. There are also international affiliates in nine foreign countries. Chapters remit all net proceeds to the national headquarters. NCIB reports that JDFI uses such special events as walk-a-thons to raise funds and calls such methods "generally difficult to administer and control." NCIB recommends that interested contributors request local financial statements and look for separate reporting of such special fund-raising activities. NCIB recommends improvements in JDFI's annual report and budget presentation.

LUPUS FOUNDATION OF AMERICA, INC.

1717 Massachusetts Ave., NW, Suite 203
Washington, DC 20036
(202) 328-4550

Year of Data: 1986
Expenditures: $2,369,661
Percent to Program: 84.7%
Fund-raising Costs: 10.4%
Contributions Deductible: Yes
Top of Staff Salary Range: $75,000 (1987)
Meets NCIB Standards: Yes (1/22/88)

Purpose: "To encourage research to discover the causes and improve methods of treating, diagnosing, curing and preventing Lupus Erythematosus...; To promote programs of public education about lupus; To provide patient education and encourage moral support and understanding for lupus patients and their families...."

Program: Fiscal 1986 activities included:
- Public Awareness and Information (29%) - costs of a public relations campaign in conjunction with 30 women's organizations; preparation of public service announcements for radio and television; distribution of press releases; publication of a tri-annual newsletter, with a circulation of 52,000; and response to 14,000 requests for information
- Patient Education and Support (27%) - preparation of books, pamphlets and fact sheets for lupus patients, professionals and the general public
- Research (20%) - award of 18 research grants of $10,000 each and ten student summer fellowships of $1,500 each

Comments: LFA has 102 chapters nationwide, with at least 35 members each; chapters, which are separate legal entities, maintain their own financial records and pay dues to the national organization. NCIB's report concerns expenditures and programs of the national organization and its chapters combined. NCIB recommends improvements in LFA's annual report, budget and audited financial statements.

MARCH OF DIMES BIRTH DEFECTS FOUNDATION

1275 Monomeric Avenue
White Plains, NY 10605
(914) 428-7100

Year of Data: 1986
Expenditures: $115,242,000
Percent to Program: 67.4%
Fund-raising Costs: 27.6%
Contributions Deductible: Yes
Top of Staff Salary Range: $143,176 (1986)
Meets NCIB Standards: Yes (2/19/88)

Purpose: To support "diagnosis, treatment, and prevention of birth defects through programs of research, professional education, public education, and support of medical care"

Program: Fiscal 1986 activities included:
- Community Services (22%) - cooperation with community organizations to educate women and girls about health and nutrition during pregnancy
- Public Health Education (20%) - including 377 grants to schools, hospitals, churches and other community agencies to inform and motivate the public concerning "maternal and newborn health;" production of health education materials, including pamphlets and radio and film spots, to educate the public about health care and nutrition during pregnancy
- Research (12%) - 506 grants and awards to support basic research, clinical (human) research, "starter" grants to young researchers, social and behavioral science research; including a $1,200,000 grant to the Salk Institute, to which MOD has given about $50 million over the years
- Professional Health Education (7%) - including 503 grants and awards to professional schools, hospitals and universities for in-service training of medical professionals; conferences and publications for professionals
- Medical Services (6%) - including 520 grants to medical schools, hospitals and other health care institutions; and assistance to individuals, such as past polio patients and persons suffering from the effects of birth defects

Comments: Fifty percent of MOD's income is retained for use by its 243 local chapters. NCIB suggests that prospective contributors request financial statements from local chapters, particularly with regard to special fund-raising activities, such as door-to-door solicitations, walk-a-thons and sports events, which are "generally difficult to administer and control." NCIB recommends improvements in MOD's audited financial statements.

MAYS MISSION FOR THE HANDICAPPED

NCIB reports that, as of July 1, 1990, this organization has not, over a period of several years, furnished requested information sufficient to prepare a report.

MEDIC ALERT FOUNDATION INTERNATIONAL

P.O. Box 1009
Turlock, CA 95381
(209) 668-3333 or (800) 344-3226

Year of Data: 1986
Expenditures: $5,742,774
Percent to Program: 79.9%
Fund-raising Costs: 25%
Contributions Deductible: Yes
Top of Staff Salary Range: $95,565 (1986)
Meets NCIB Standards: Yes (10/26/87)

Purpose: To "provide information to assist in diagnosing and treating individuals with hidden medical problems in emergency medical situations"

Program: Fiscal 1986 activities included:
- Member Services (66%) - costs of registering members, processing reorders and updating member records
- Volunteer Program and Public Information (5%) - costs of a print media program and public service announcements on radio and television

Comments: The Medic Alert system that MAFI promotes involves metal emblems, in the form of bracelets or necklaces, and wallet cards, which inform emergency medical personnel about members' hidden medical problems, and a 24-hour information service for people to call collect to inquire about a member's medical condition. About 57% of MAFI total support for 1986 came from memberships, the cost of which includes purchase of the Medic Alert emblem. MAFI also makes free memberships available to those who are unable to pay. MAFI states that it has a worldwide membership of over 2.5 million people. NCIB recommends improvements in MAFI's annual report.

MUSCULAR DYSTROPHY ASSOCIATION, INC.

810 Seventh Avenue
New York, NY 10019
(212) 586-0808

Year of Data: 1987
Expenditures: $95,067,747
Percent to Program: 74.8%
Fund-raising Costs: 17.7%
Contributions Deductible: Yes
Top of Staff Salary Range: $167,308 (1988)
Meets NCIB Standards: Yes (10/28/88)

Purpose: "To foster and promote the cure and alleviation of ... muscular dystrophy" and other neuromuscular diseases, such as amyotrophic lateral sclerosis (ALS), myasthenia gravis and Charcot-Marie-Tooth disease

Program: Fiscal 1987 activities included:
- Patient and Community Services (40%) - including comprehensive diagnostic examinations; testing and clinical follow-up; assistance in acquisition of 32,000 orthopedic appliances and devices, respiratory therapy equipment, etc.; physical, occupational and respiratory therapy assistance to 20,000 individuals; summer camps for young patients and weekend retreats for adults
- Research (20%) - including 550 research grants, special grants and postdoctoral fellowships relating to basic research, clinical studies and drug screening; administration of a clinical fellowship program; publication of *Muscular Dystrophy Abstracts*
- Professional and Public Health Education (15%) - publication and distribution of a magazine and of about 2.8 million brochures on 30 topics; a symposium for professionals

Comments: MDA consists of a national headquarters, 170 chapters and 230 hospital-affiliated clinics. The national headquarters receives all contributions and expends all the funds. MDA conducts the annual Jerry Lewis Labor Day Telethon as part of its fund-raising

activities. In 1987, expenditures for the telethon were $8,940,922 and income was $33,329,360. NCIB recommends improvements in MDA's audited financial statements.

MYASTHENIA GRAVIS FOUNDATION

53 West Jackson Blvd., Suite 1352
Chicago, IL 60604
(312) 427-6252

Year of Data: 1986
Expenditures: $1,301,304
Percent to Program: 76.8%
Fund-raising Costs: 18.9%
Contributions Deductible: Yes
Top of Staff Salary Range: $63,000 (1987)
Meets NCIB Standards: Yes (2/1/88)

Purpose: To "foster, coordinate and support research in the cause, prevention, alleviation and cure of Myasthenia Gravis and to provide health care professionals and the general public with information about the disease"

Program: Recent activities included:
- Research Grants and Related Activities (25%) - award of 23 grants and fellowships; cosponsorship of a symposium for physicians and researchers
- Public Health Information and Education (24%) - preparation of articles, advertisements and public service announcements; participation in health fairs; presentations and displays
- Patient and Community Services (19%) - support for clinics and treatment centers, counseling and support groups, reduced-cost "drug banks"
- Professional Information and Education (9%) - publication and distribution of special manuals for physicians and nurses; seminars for physicians and nurses

Comments: MGF has 53 chapters nationwide; in fiscal 1986, 75% of its support came from these affiliates. MGF did not provide NCIB with its annual report for 1986. NCIB recommends improvements in MGF's budget.

NATIONAL COUNCIL ON ALCOHOLISM, INC.

12 West 21st Street, 8th Fl.
New York, NY 10010
(212) 206-6770

Year of Data: 1986
Expenditures: $1,561,104
Percent to Program: 66.7%
Fund-raising Costs: 8.1%
Contributions Deductible: Yes
Top of Staff Salary Range: $98,000 (1986)
Meets NCIB Standards: Yes (10/27/87)

Purpose: To "promote education and science by encouraging scientific research, studies, and investigation in all fields of learning with particular reference to the problems of alcoholism and alcohol addiction...." NCA recently expanded its mission to include educating the public on drug-related problems.

Program: NCA's reporting of its activities does not allow a detailed breakdown of its programs. Fiscal 1986 activities included a prevention campaign aimed at children ages 8-14; work with the Association of Junior Leagues to help reduce alcohol problems among women; study of state use of federal moneys to improve prevention and treatment services for women; and publication of papers and information sheets.

Comments: NCA recently had 191 independently incorporated state and local affiliates. Affiliates do not solicit funds in the name of the national organization, and NCA does not control or direct the affiliates' financial transactions. NCIB's report concerns only the national organization. NCIB recommends improvements in NCA's audited financial statements.

NATIONAL DOWN SYNDROME SOCIETY

141 Fifth Avenue
New York, NY 10010
(212) 460-9330 or (800) 221-4602

Year of Data: 1986
Expenditures $220,466
Percent to Program: 77.2%
Fund-raising Costs: 12.8%
Contributions Deductible: Yes
Top of Staff Salary Range: $49,000 (1987)
Meets NCIB Standards: Yes (3/24/87)

Purpose: "To promote better understanding of mental retardation and Down Syndrome in particular"

Comments: The editor deemed this organization too small (under $1 million in expenditures in the most recent year reported) to be given a complete listing.

NATIONAL EASTER SEAL SOCIETY

2023 West Ogden Avenue
Chicago, IL 60612
(312) 243-8400

Year of Data: **1985**
Expenditures $6,864,560
Percent to Program: 85.6%
Fund-raising Costs: 0%
Contributions Deductible: Yes
Top of Staff Salary Range: $115,492 (1986)
Meets NCIB Standards: Yes (10/23/86)

Purpose: National Service Center only: "To assist persons with disabilities and their families in finding and making effective use of resources that will help them in developing their abilities and in living purposeful lives; to assist communities in development of necessary and appropriate services for persons with disabilities; to establish and maintain services which meet the needs of persons with disabilities...."

Comments: The editor deemed NCIB's information about this organization too dated (1985 data or before) to give it a complete listing.

NATIONAL EMERGENCY MEDICINE ASSOCIATION, INC. and NATIONAL HEART RESEARCH

306 West Joppa Road
Baltimore, MD 21204
(301) 494-0300 or (800) 332-6362

Year of Data: 1988
Expenditures: $8,117,462
Percent to Program: 32%
Fund-raising Costs: 57.8%
Contributions Deductible: Yes
Top of Staff Salary Range: $95,000 (1989)
Meets NCIB Standards: No: 6a, 7, 3?, 4? (8/11/89)

Purpose: To "promote, fund and support the improvement of emergency medical care and emergency room facilities and operations, through research as to skills, techniques, procedures, and devices, in order that the public may be benefited by improved standards of emergency medical care, and ... to conduct seminars and to publish for the benefit of the public, studies, test results and research." In 1986, NEMA announced a National Heart Research special project to fund research and educational efforts for prevention and emergency treatment for heart attack victims.

Program: In fiscal 1988, virtually all of program spending (29% of total expenditures) was devoted to public health education, including production of a nationally broadcast radio program; publication of a quarterly newsletter and mailing 21.4 million letters with information about heart, trauma and emergency care. A small percentage went to grant programs.

Comments: NCIB advises contributors that NEMA is raising funds currently to finance grants awarded in prior years. It also advises that, by the terms of NEMA's contract with its professional fund-raiser, contributions are not available for research or other program use until the fund-raiser's expenses are met. NCIB faults NEMA for its low program and high fund-raising expenditures (Standard 6a) and for failure to include a list of its board members or a financial summary in its annual report (Standard 7). NCIB questions NEMA's practice of expending most of its program service funds for grants unrelated to heart disease, while soliciting funds primarily for its National Heart Research program (Standard 3 and 4).

NATIONAL FOUNDATION FOR ILEITIS AND COLITIS, INC.
444 Park Avenue South
New York, NY 10016
(212) 685-3440

Year of Data: 1987
Expenditures: $4,677,620
Percent to Program: 70.4%
Fund-raising Costs: 15.2%
Contributions Deductible: Yes
Top of Staff Salary Range: $85,000 (1987)
Meets NCIB Standards: ?: 3 (6/15/88)

Purpose: To support research and education related to inflammatory bowel diseases—ileitis and colitis

Program: Fiscal 1987 activities included:
• Research (40%) - including $1.6 million to fund 45 grants and awards for scien-

tific and clinical research studies and to encourage talented young investigators to devote their careers to related research; sponsorship of conferences and specialized workshops
• Health Professional Education and Public Information (30%) - including programs to increase patient and public awareness of ileitis and colitis; patient-education meetings sponsored by local chapters; workshops for primary care physicians; distribution of pamphlets

Comments: NCIB questions NFIC's deficit fund balance as of September 30, 1987 (Standard 3). NCIB reports that the deficit is primarily due to NFIC's practice of making grant commitments in excess of available funds, in the expectation that necessary funds will be raised in subsequent years.

NATIONAL HEAD INJURY FOUNDATION, INC.
333 Turnpike Road
Southboro, MA 01772
(617) 879-7473

Year of Data: 1986
Expenditures $972,861
Percent to Program: 84.2%
Fund-raising Costs: 8.7%
Contributions Deductible: Yes
Top of Staff Salary Range: N/A
Meets NCIB Standards: Yes (7/27/87)

Purpose: "Prevention of head injury through support of activities and legislation related to prevention and highway safety to reduce occurrence of head injuries and fatalities; development of support programs for head injury survivors and for their families; assisting in the establishment of rehabilitation programs for the head-injury population; and achieving recognition by the public, health care professionals and governmental agencies of the problem of head injury and the needs of those who have suffered head injuries"

Comments: The editor deemed this organization too small (under $1 million in expenditures in the most recent year reported) to be given a complete listing.

NATIONAL HEALTH COUNCIL, INC.

350 Fifth Avenue, Suite 1118
New York, NY 10118
(212) 268-8900

Year of Data: 1986
Expenditures $602,366
Percent to Program: 81.4%
Fund-raising Costs: 8.9%
Contributions Deductible: Yes
Top of Staff Salary Range: $98,000 (1987)
Meets NCIB Standards: Yes (9/4/87)

Purpose: To "enable its member organizations to work together effectively to promote the health of all Americans with a strong sense of human concern especially for vulnerable people;" "to stimulate greater public awareness of health and health related concerns;" "to strengthen cooperative efforts among health related private sector organizations, and between the private and governmental sectors;" and "to foster collaborative activities among voluntary health agencies that will provide accountability and public confidence in their programs"

Comments: The editor deemed this organization too small (under $1 million in expenditures in the most recent year reported) to be given a complete listing.

NATIONAL HEMOPHILIA FOUNDATION

110 Greene Street, Room 406
New York, NY 10012
(212) 219-8180

Year of Data: 1986
Expenditures: $6,712,626
Percent to Program: 81.6%
Fund-raising Costs: 13.1%
Contributions Deductible: Yes
Top of Staff Salary Range: $63,000 (1986)
Meets NCIB Standards: ?: 7 (1/13/88)

Purpose: To "promote opportunities for improving the quality of life for all affected by hemophilia and related disorders so that each can fulfill his or her ultimate potential. The ultimate aim is a cure."

Program: Fiscal 1986 activities included:
• Patient Services (55%) - patient assistance primarily carried out by chapters
• Research (8%) - over $200,000 in fellowships and grants, including matters relating to the safety and efficacy of

blood products and hemophilia and AIDS
• Community Services (7%) - support for comprehensive treatment centers and counseling about finances, employment, scholarships and medical support services
• Public Health Education (6%) - general information to the public and comprehensive education for patients and their families

Comments: In 1986, NHF reported 52 affiliated chapters in the U.S.; the above expenditure figure is the total for the national headquarters and 39 affiliates. Of this total, about 16% was spent by the national headquarters. About 20% of contributions received by chapters are shared with the national headquarters. NCIB questions NHF's inconsistent and incomplete financial statements (Standard 7). NCIB recommends improvements in NHF's budget presentation.

NATIONAL HOSPICE ORGANIZATION

1901 North Fort Myer Drive, Suite 307
Arlington, VA 22209
(703) 243-5900

Year of Data: 1986
Expenditures $836,845
Percent to Program: 69.6%
Fund-raising Costs: 24%
Contributions Deductible: Yes
Top of Staff Salary Range: $53,255 (1986)
Meets NCIB Standards: Yes (2/29/88)

Purpose: To provide "palliative services for terminally ill people and their families. Hospice emphasizes pain and symptom control provided by a team of professionals.... The majority of hospice services are delivered in the home with inpatient care available as needed."

Comments: The editor deemed this organization too small (under $1 million in expenditures in the most recent year reported) to be given a complete listing.

NATIONAL JEWISH CENTER FOR IMMUNOLOGY AND RESPIRATORY MEDICINE

380 East Colfax Avenue
Denver, CO 80206
(303) 388-4461

Year of Data: **1985**
Expenditures $39,559,500
Percent to Program: 65.4%
Fund-raising Costs: 30.9%
Contributions Deductible: Yes
Top of Staff Salary Range: $102,900 (1984)
Meets NCIB Standards: Yes (12/30/86)

Purpose: "Treating and studying respiratory diseases and disorders of the immune system"

Comments: The editor deemed NCIB's information about this organization too dated (1985 data or before) to give it a complete listing.

NATIONAL KIDNEY FOUNDATION, INC.

30 East 33rd Street
New York, NY 10016
(212) 889-2210 or (800) 622-9010

Year of Data: 1988
Expenditures: $13,719,763
Percent to Program: 78.6%
Fund-raising Costs: 9.8%
Contributions Deductible: Yes
Top of Staff Salary Range: $117,500 (1989)
Meets NCIB Standards: Yes (10/18/89)

Purpose: "Total eradication of all diseases of the kidney and urinary tract" and quality care and assistance for those suffering from these diseases

Program: Fiscal 1988 activities included:
- Patient and Community Services (35%) - including informational programs, screening and early detection programs, drug banks, transportation services, exercise programs and emergency short-term financial aid for patients and their families; summer camp programs for 1,500 young dialysis and transplant patients
- Public Education (17%) - distribution of over 420,000 educational brochures and of 200,000 organ donor cards; publication of a bimonthly newsletter; provision of promotion kits and public service announcements to affiliates; operation of a toll-free telephone information service
- Research (16%) - including $1.6 million for 42 postdoctoral research fellowships
- Professional Education (9%) - newsletters, journals and other publications for medical professionals
- Program Assistance to Affiliates (5%) - consultation and other assistance to affiliates

Comments: NKF consists of 49 affiliates with 200 chapters nationally; affiliates are asked to support the national headquarters with 25% of their net contributions income. NCIB recommends improvements in NKF's budget presentation.

NATIONAL MULTIPLE SCLEROSIS SOCIETY

205 East 42nd Street
New York, NY 10017-5706
(212) 986-3240 or (800) 227-3166
(800) 624-8236 tape-recorded

Year of Data: 1987
Expenditures: $45,745,039
Percent to Program: 71.8%
Fund-raising Costs: 21.7%
Contributions Deductible: Yes
Top of Staff Salary Range: $140,000 (1987)
Meets NCIB Standards: Yes (6/30/88)

Purpose: To provide services in the areas of education and community services and to support research relating to the prevention, cure and treatment of multiple sclerosis (MS)

Program: Fiscal 1987 activities included:
- Patient Services (24%) - operation of 81 chapter-supported treatment centers around the United States, which offer diagnostic, treatment and management services in neurology and varied medical specialities; other services may include vocational rehabilitation, physical therapy, counseling and occupational therapy
- Research and Research Fellowships (17%) - grants to support studies to find cures or alleviations of MS
- Public Education (15%) - informing the general public about MS and its manifestations
- Community Services (11%) - planning

and improving community health practices; supporting clinics and other public health facilities; promoting detection of MS

- Professional Education and Training (6%) - keeping professionals informed and engaged in health work by keeping them abreast of new diagnostic techniques

Comments: In early 1988, NMSS had 97 chapters and 48 branches and was affiliated with 81 MS clinics; general membership totaled 370,000. Local chapters receive 40% of all contributions to direct mail and "Students Against MS" appeals and 60% of all other undesignated monies donated to NMSS. NCIB recommends improvements in NMSS's annual report, budget presentation and audited financial statements.

NATIONAL OSTEOPOROSIS FOUNDATION

1625 Eye Street, NW, Suite 822
Washington, DC 20006
(202) 223-2226

Year of Data: 1987
Expenditures $645,940
Percent to Program: 75%
Fund-raising Costs: 7.2%
Contributions Deductible: Yes
Top of Staff Salary Range: $80,000 (1988)
Meets NCIB Standards: Yes (3/16/89)

Purpose: "Increasing public awareness and knowledge, educating physicians and health care professionals, and supporting research activities concerning osteoporosis and related areas"

Comments: The editor deemed this organization too small (under $1 million in expenditures in the most recent year reported) to be given a complete listing.

NATIONAL PSORIASIS FOUNDATION

6443 S.W. Beaverton Highway, Suite 210
Portland, OR 97221
(503) 297-1545

Year of Data: 1989
Expenditures: $613,392
Percent to Program: 86.6%
Fund-raising Costs: 5.4%
Contributions Deductible: Yes
Top of Staff Salary Range: $60,000 (1989)
Meets NCIB Standards: Yes (2/14/90)

Purpose: To "promote public awareness of psoriasis, to improve the well-being of those with psoriasis, and to support psoriasis research"

Comments: The editor deemed this organization too small (under $1 million in expenditures in the most recent year reported) to be given a complete listing.

NATIONAL SUDDEN INFANT DEATH SYNDROME FOUNDATION

10500 Little Patuxent Pkwy., Suite 420
Columbia, MD 21044
(301) 964-8000

Year of Data: 1986
Expenditures $844,933
Percent to Program: 80.3%
Fund-raising Costs: 6.4%
Contributions Deductible: Yes
Top of Staff Salary Range: $43,500 (1987)
Meets NCIB Standards: Yes (12/1/87)

Purpose: "To provide support through education and direct contact to families following the loss of a child to Sudden Infant Death Syndrome (SIDS) and to support research into the diagnosis, treatment, and prevention of SIDS"

Comments: The editor deemed this organization too small (under $1 million in expenditures in the most recent year reported) to be given a complete listing.

PARALYZED VETERANS OF AMERICA

801 18th Street, NW
Washington, DC 20006
(202) USA-1300 or (800) 424-8200

Year of Data: 1987
Expenditures: $25,749,124
Percent to Program: 51.5%
Fund-raising Costs: 38.5%
Contributions Deductible: Yes
Top of Staff Salary Range: $130,000 (1988)
Meets NCIB Standards: No: 6a (5/4/89)

Purpose: "To provide medical and vocational assistance to paraplegics, to support research for the treatment of spinal cord injuries and for the development of rehabilitative methods and devices, and to educate the public in the problems of paraplegics"

Program: Fiscal 1987 activities included:

- Memberships and Benefit (30%) - operation of regional service offices which assist veterans in submitting claims and securing service-related benefits; sponsorship, with the chapters, of sports and educational activities for the handicapped; publication, with the chapters, of monthly magazines and newsletters
- Public Affairs (12%) - advocacy programs to promote special needs of the handicapped, including accessibility issues; publicity for activities and publications
- Research (9%) - grants for medical and technological research into treatment of spinal cord injuries and for development of rehabilitative methods and devices

Comments: PVA has 11,000 members in 31 local affiliated chapters, each of which is a separate corporation. NCIB's report is about the national headquarters only; prospective contributors interested in local chapters may wish to examine their programs and finances. PVA's percent of program expenditures was below the 60% level of NCIB Standard 6a. NCIB recommends improvements in PVA's annual report and audited financial statements.

PARKINSON'S DISEASE FOUNDATION

William Black Medical Research Bldg .
Columbia University Medical Center
650 West 168th Street
New York, NY 10032
(212) 923-4700

Year of Data: 1989
Expenditures: $1,629,640
Percent to Program: 82%
Fund-raising Costs: 4%
Contributions Deductible: Yes
Top of Staff Salary Range: $53,490 (1989)
Meets NCIB Standards: ?: 1g (2/14/90)

Purpose: To "plan, undertake, support and promote the investigation and study of Parkinson's Disease and allied diseases"

Program: Fiscal 1989 activities included:
- Research (69%) - award of $1,088,380 in grants and fellowships, $782,910 of it in research grant allocations to the William Black Research Building, which provides laboratories for research in the

neurosciences, and to the wards and out-patient departments of the Neurological Institute and Vanderbilt Clinic, all at Columbia University Medical Center; additional research grants were awarded to departments at other universities and hospitals; $204,333 in student and post-doctoral fellowships was also awarded
- Public Information/Patient Information Referral (14%) - including publication of pamphlets, participation in professional meetings and presentations to lay groups

Comments: NCIB questions PDF's payment of $55,000, in fiscal 1989, to a firm with which a board member was associated (Standard 1g).

LINUS PAULING INSTITUTE OF SCIENCE AND MEDICINE

NCIB reports that, as of July 1, 1990, this organization has not, over a period of several years, furnished requested information sufficient to prepare a report.

PLANNED PARENTHOOD FEDERATION OF AMERICA, INC.

380 Second Avenue
New York, NY 10010
(212) 777-2002

Year of Data: **1985**
Expenditures $224,316,960
Percent to Program: 80.4%
Fund-raising Costs: 29.8%
Contributions Deductible: Yes
Top of Staff Salary Range: $113,000 (1985)
Meets NCIB Standards: Yes (9/25/87)

Purpose: To provide leadership "in making effective means of voluntary fertility regulation, including contraception, abortion, sterilization, and infertility services, available and fully accessible to all as a central element of reproductive health care; in achieving, through informed individual choice, a U.S. population of stable size in an optimum environment; in stimulating socio-economic, and demographic research; in developing appropriate information, education, and training programs...."

Comments: The editor deemed NCIB's information about this organization too dated (1985 data or before) to give it a complete listing.

WILL ROGERS MEMORIAL FUND

785 Mamaroneck Avenue
White Plains, NY 10605
(914) 761-5550

Year of Data: 1988
Expenditures $2,132,935
Percent to Program: 83.6%
Fund-raising Costs: 9.7%
Contributions Deductible: Yes
Top of Staff Salary Range: $80,000 (1988)
Meets NCIB Standards: No: 1d, 6b (1/13/89)

Purpose: To provide medical assistance to entertainment industry personnel with pulmonary or other diseases, to conduct research on pulmonary diseases and the effects of nutrition on dementia, and to create media announcements to educate the public about illness prevention

Program: Fiscal 1988 activities included:

- Research (41%) - pulmonary research and studies of the effects of nutrition on Alzheimer's disease; award of over $714,000 in fellowships for the study of various pulmonary diseases and of AIDS
- Health Education (30%) - information to the public concerning such topics as drug abuse, stress, cholesterol, smoking, seat belt use, choking rescue, AIDS, child safety and stroke; creation of about 12 new public service announcements
- Medical Care (13%) - payment for professional and hospital services for members of the entertainment/communications industry

Comments: NCIB faults WRMF for having assets available for use of about 2.3 times its fiscal 1989 budget (Standard 6b) and poor attendance at its executive committee meetings (Standard 1d). NCIB reports that WRMF receives about 66% of its total support from canister collections in movie theaters across the country and calls such methods "generally difficult to administer and control." NCIB recommends that interested contributors request local financial statements and look for separate reporting of such special fund-raising activities. NCIB recommends improvements in WRMF's annual report and budget presentation.

SHRINERS HOSPITAL FOR CRIPPLED CHILDREN

NCIB reports that, as of July 1, 1990, this organization has not, over a period of several years, furnished requested information sufficient to prepare a report.

STARLIGHT FOUNDATION

10920 Wilshire Blvd., Suite 1640
Los Angeles, CA 90024
(213) 208-5885

Year of Data: 1989
Expenditures: $1,629,452
Percent to Program: 80%
Fund-raising Costs: 13.2%
Contributions Deductible: Yes
Top of Staff Salary Range: $58,000 (1989)
Meets NCIB Standards: Yes (4/20/90)

Purpose: Grants wishes to critically, chronically and terminally ill children, ages 2 1/2 through 18 years

Program: SF's only program expense for fiscal 1989 (80% of its total expenditures) was its Children's Wish program, which grants an average of $800-$1,000 to arrange for a celebrity or sports hero visit, a specific event or trip or some tangible goods for about 100 children per month. SF encourages wishes that involve the children's families and coordinates the wish-granting process with doctors, social workers and family.

Comments: In fiscal 1989, SF had nine chartered chapters in the United States, England and Australia and was planning to add five more, including three in Canada. SF conducts its programs in cooperation with 104 participating hospitals in 14 states, the United Kingdom and Australia.

SUNSHINE FOUNDATION

4010 Levick Street
Philadelphia, PA 19135
(215) 335-2622

> Year of Data: 1988
> Expenditures: $2,029,866
> Percent to Program: 59%
> Fund-raising Costs: 26%
> Contributions Deductible: Yes
> Top of Staff Salary Range: $50,000 (1988)
> Meets NCIB Standards: Yes (1/26/90)

Purpose: To "fulfill dreams and wishes of terminally and chronically ill children"

Program: SF's only program expense for fiscal 1988 (59% of its total expenditures) was to "fulfill dreams" of children; its activities included sending children and their families to Disney World, the Pocono Mountains in Pennsylvania or the New Jersey seashore.

Comments: SF consists of 41 affiliated chapters in the United States, plus a thrift shop and a travel agency, a wholly-owned subsidiary. All funds raised by chapters and the thrift shop are remitted to the Foundation. NCIB recommends improvements in SF's annual report.

UNITED CEREBRAL PALSY ASSOCIATIONS, INC. and UNITED CEREBRAL PALSY RESEARCH AND EDUCATIONAL FOUNDATION, INC.

7 Penn Plaza Suite 804
New York, NY 10001
(212) 268-6655

Purpose: To "promote research in cerebral palsy and promote treatment, education and rehabilitation of persons with cerebral palsy, their families," the medical profession and the public

Comments: NCIB is currently preparing a new report on this organization.

LEONARD WOOD MEMORIAL - AMERICAN LEPROSY FOUNDATION

11600 Nebel Street, Suite 210
Rockville, MD 20852
(301) 984-1336

> Year of Data: 1988
> Expenditures $548,720
> Percent to Program: 83.9%
> Fund-raising Costs: 11.9%
> Contributions Deductible: Yes
> Top of Staff Salary Range: $33,000 (1988)
> Meets NCIB Standards: Yes (9/28/89)

Purpose: "To carry on, maintain and support laboratory investigation, clinical observation and all manner of research with respect to the disease of leprosy...."

Comments: The editor deemed this organization too small (under $1 million in expenditures in the most recent year reported) to be given a complete listing.

- **AFRICARE** (see INTERNATIONAL RELIEF)
- **ALSAC - ST. JUDE'S CHILDREN'S RESEARCH HOSPITAL** (see HEALTHCANCER)
- **AMERICARES FOUNDATION, INC.** (see INTERNATIONAL RELIEF)
- **CHILD WELFARE LEAGUE OF AMERICA, INC.** (see HUMAN SERVICE)
- **DISABLED AMERICAN VETERANS** (see HUMAN SERVICE)
- **FATHER FLANAGAN'S BOYS' HOME** (see HUMAN SERVICE)
- **MAP INTERNATIONAL** (see INTERNATIONAL RELIEF)
- **MEDICAL EDUCATION FOR SOUTH AFRICAN BLACKS, INC.** (see INTERNATIONAL)
- **NATIONAL COUNCIL ON THE AGING** (see HUMAN SERVICE)
- **NATIONAL FUND FOR MEDICAL EDUCATION** (see EDUCATION)
- **NATIONAL MEDICAL FELLOWSHIPS, INC.** (see EDUCATION)
- **THE PATHFINDER FUND** (see SOCIAL ACTION)

- **PROJECT CONCERN INTERNATIONAL** (see INTERNATIONAL RELIEF)
- **PROJECT HOPE/PEOPLE-TO-PEOPLE HEALTH FOUNDATION** (see INTERNATIONAL RELIEF)
- **SPECIAL OLYMPICS INTERNATIONAL** (see RECREATION)
- **UNITED STATES OLYMPIC COMMITTEE** (see RECREATION)
- **WORLD REHABILITATION FUND, INC.** (see INTERNATIONAL RELIEF)

HEALTH - VISUAL HANDICAPS

research and care, braille and recorded literature, self-help, guide dogs

AMERICAN BROTHERHOOD FOR THE BLIND

1800 Johnson Street, Suite 300
Baltimore, MD 21230
(301) 659-9314

Purpose: To "provide services to the blind, including the distribution of 'Twin Vision' books to children, counsel, resource and advocacy services, and scholarships to blind students"

Comments: NCIB is currently preparing a new report on this organization.

AMERICAN COUNCIL OF THE BLIND

NCIB reports that, as of July 1, 1990, this organization has not, over a period of several years, furnished requested information sufficient to prepare a report.

AMERICAN FOUNDATION FOR THE BLIND, INC.

15 West 16th Street
New York, NY 10011
(212) 620-2000

Year of Data: 1989
Expenditures: $13,836,000
Percent to Program: 80.8%
Fund-raising Costs: 21.3%
Contributions Deductible: Yes
Top of Staff Salary Range: $120,000 (1989)
Meets NCIB Standards: No: 6b (1/22/90)

Purpose: To advocate, develop and provide "programs and services that help blind and visually impaired people achieve independence with dignity in all sectors of society"

Program: Because AFB's annual report described fiscal 1989 activities under different headings than those used in its audited financial statements, it is not possible to provide detailed information about the organization's program expenditures. Activities included grants and awards totalling $339,000; public meetings concerned with improving employment opportunities for blind and visually impaired people; support for statewide public education projects on diabetic retinopathy; provision of information in response to about 2,000 telephone calls per month; maintenance of a library for use by the visually impaired; and the publication of monographs, manuals, texts, brochures and periodicals. AFB also developed and sold aids and appliances designed to help blind people participate more fully in the activities of the sighted world.

Comments: In fiscal 1989, about 33% of AFB's total revenues came from sales of publications and of various aids and appliances. NCIB faults AFB because, on June 30, 1989, it had assets about 2.4 times its expenses in the year just ended and 2.3 times its fiscal 1990 budget (Standard 6b). NCIB recommends improvements in AFB's annual report and budget presentation.

AMERICAN PRINTING HOUSE FOR THE BLIND

1839 Frankfort Avenue
Louisville, KY 40206
(502) 895-2405

> Year of Data: 1987
> Expenditures: $14,981,195
> Percent to Program: 80.6%
> Fund-raising Costs: 25.3%
> Contributions Deductible: Yes
> Top of Staff Salary Range: $86,358 (1988)
> Meets NCIB Standards: Yes (5/5/89)

Purpose: "To provide visually handicapped people with educational and recreational literature in braille, large type and recorded form and to manufacture the learning aids, special tools and special supplies necessary for their education"

Program: APH's reporting of its activities does not allow a detailed breakdown of its programs. In general, APH's major activities are:

- Manufacture of Books and Aids for the Blind - APH contracts with other non-profit agencies and individuals to manufacture books and aids for dis-

tribution to the blind at cost or less, usually free
- Newsweek Talking Magazine Fund for the Blind - this recorded version of *Newsweek* costs subscribers $38.00 for a year's subscription and is distributed to over 9,000 recipients
- Fund for Braille and Recorded Editions - provides braille and recorded editions of *Reader's Digest* to blind and physically handicapped individuals, libraries, nursing homes and other institutions

Comments: APH solicits contributions for its general fund and for two special funds, "Fund for Braille and Recorded Editions - Reader's Digest" and "Newsweek Talking Magazine Fund." A totally separate non-profit organization, The Reader's Digest Fund for the Blind, Inc., does not solicit contributions. APH receives an annual federal government appropriation for its manufacturing operations; in fiscal 1987, the government allocated $5,510,000 for these purposes. NCIB recommends improvements in APH's annual report.

BLINDED VETERANS ASSOCIATION

477 H Street, NW
Washington, DC 20001
(202) 371-8880

Purpose: To "promote the welfare of blinded veterans so that they may take their rightful place in the community, and to preserve and strengthen a spirit of fellowship among blinded veterans"

Comments: NCIB is currently preparing a new report on this organization.

CHRISTIAN BLIND MISSION INTERNATIONAL

NCIB reports that, as of July 1, 1990, this organization has not, over a period of several years, furnished requested information sufficient to prepare a report.

CHRISTIAN RECORD SERVICES, INC. (formerly Christian Record Braille Foundation, Inc.)

4444 South 52nd Street
Lincoln, NE 68506
(402) 488-0981

Year of Data: 1987
Expenditures: $5,474,894
Percent to Program: 71.9%
Fund-raising Costs: 23.3%
Contributions Deductible: Yes
Top of Staff Salary Range: $28,787 (1988)
Meets NCIB Standards: Yes (1/20/89)

Purpose: To provide "charitable, educational, religious and missionary" aid and assistance to blind, visually and physically handicapped persons

Program: Fiscal 1987 activities included:

- Personal Services (23%) - efforts to seek out blind and handicapped persons and provide them with visitation, counseling and referral services; recruitment and training of personnel for these efforts
- Other Direct Services (18%) - operation of national camps for the blind, gifts, scholarships, production and distribution of Bible correspondence courses, glaucoma clinics and interpreting for the deaf
- Public Information and Education (14%) - to inform the general public about needs and wants of blind and physically handicapped persons
- Production of Periodicals (12%) - production of five braille, three recorded and two large print publications, plus simplified reading materials for the deaf
- Lending Library (5%) - purchase or production of books, programs and music in braille, on record, cassettes and in large print; circulation of the collection

Comments: CRS's by-laws refer to it as "the agency of the seventh-day Adventist Church to physically handicapped persons."

GUIDE DOG FOUNDATION FOR THE BLIND, INC.

371 East Jericho Turnpike
Smithtown, NY 11787
(516) 265-2121

Year of Data: 1986
Expenditures $748,442
Percent to Program: 74.2%
Fund-raising Costs: 17.6%
Contributions Deductible: Yes
Top of Staff Salary Range: $53,299 (1987)
Meets NCIB Standards: Yes (6/4/87)

Purpose: "To provide greater mobility to the blind through the use of trained guide dogs; To provide further aid and assistance to the handicapped through the use of appropriately trained dogs"

Comments: The editor deemed this organization too small (under $1 million in expenditures in the most recent year reported) to be given a complete listing.

GUIDING EYES FOR THE BLIND, INC.

611 Granite Springs Road
Yorktown Heights, NY 10598
(914) 245-4024

Year of Data: 1986
Expenditures: $2,271,842
Percent to Program: 64.6%
Fund-raising Costs: 27.5%
Contributions Deductible: Yes
Top of Staff Salary Range: $62,000 (1987)
Meets NCIB Standards: Yes (2/8/88)

Purpose: "To provide greater mobility for qualified visually handicapped people through the raising and training of guide dogs and the training of these individuals in their use"

Program: Fiscal 1986 activities included:

- Guide Dog Training (44%) - three to six months of training for Labrador Retrievers, Golden Retrievers and German Shepherds; and 26-day classes for 130 blind students
- Breeding Farm (13%) - breeding of dogs and raising them to an age of six to eight weeks
- Other (9%) - including refresher classes for graduates, accommodations and transportation of students, training of some students in their home communities and public education activities

Comments: NCIB recommends improvements in GEB's annual report and audited financial statements.

HOPE SCHOOL

NCIB reports that, as of July 1, 1990, this organization has not, over a period of several years, furnished requested information sufficient to prepare a report.

INTERNATIONAL EYE FOUNDATION

7801 Norfolk Avenue
Bethesda, MD 20814
(301) 986-1830

Year of Data: 1987
Expenditures: $1,471,823
Percent to Program: 72.8%
Fund-raising Costs: 16.3%
Contributions Deductible: Yes
Top of Staff Salary Range: $58,000 (1988)
Meets NCIB Standards: Yes (8/22/88)

Purpose: To promote "peace through the prevention and cure of blindness worldwide...through a program of fellowships, surgical teaching missions, research and distribution of ocular tissues...and other educational, scientific, and charitable projects...."

Program: IEF's reporting of its expenditures does not allow a detailed breakdown of its programs. In general, 1987 activities included work to survey and improve eye care facilities in Honduras, Haiti, Guinea, Malawi, Egypt, Puerto Rico and the Ivory Coast and special projects in Malawi, Grenada, Ethiopia and the Caribbean.

Comments: In 1987, about 49% of IEF's cash support came from restricted government grants. In addition to cash support, IEF received and distributed donated medical supplies valued at over $410,000. NCIB recommends improvements in IEF's annual report and audited financial statements.

HELEN KELLER INTERNATIONAL, INC.

15 West 16th Street
New York, NY 10011
(212) 807-5800
(800) 842-3333 for donations

Year of Data: 1986
Expenditures: $3,756,549
Percent to Program: 77.5%
Fund-raising Costs: 30.7%
Contributions Deductible: Yes
Top of Staff Salary Range: $100,000 (1987)
Meets NCIB Standards: Yes (8/3/87)

Purpose: To "prevent blindness, particularly among pre-school children in developing countries; to restore sight to cataract victims; to educate blind children, with emphasis on their studying side-by-side with sighted children in regular schools; and to rehabilitate blind adults in order that they may lead independent, useful lives in their homes and in their communities"

Program: Fiscal 1986 activities included:
• Rehabilitation, Education and Prevention (64%) - consultation, training and assistance for programs related to vitamin A deficiency concentrated in Bangladesh, Indonesia and the Philippines; assistance to Peru, Sri Lanka, Indonesia, Tanzania, Morocco and Fiji to integrate an eye-care component in existing health care systems; training of health workers, nurses and physicians to detect, treat and make referrals for a range of eye diseases and disorders, especially the major blinding diseases, xerophthalmia, trachoma and cataract
• Public Education (13%) - preparation of articles for magazines and professional journals; work with ABC-TV to produce a feature on effects of vitamin A on blindness

Comments: HKI has directed particular attention to xerophthalmia, a blinding disease caused by vitamin A deficiency. In fiscal 1986, about 37% of HKI's support came from government grants. Although HKI's fund-raising costs were slightly higher than the 30% allowed by Standard 4, NCIB rates it as meeting the standard in view of the decline from a 42.7% figure in 1985.

NATIONAL ACCREDITATION COUNCIL FOR AGENCIES SERVING THE BLIND AND VISUALLY HANDICAPPED

232 Madison Avenue, Suite 907
New York, NY 10016
(212) 779-8080

Year of Data: 1988
Expenditures $456,090
Percent to Program: 80.3%
Fund-raising Costs: 12.5%
Contributions Deductible: Yes
Top of Staff Salary Range: $80,000 (1988)
Meets NCIB Standards: Yes (7/11/89)

Purpose: "To promote the development of modern, effective and sound programs of services for blind and visually handicapped children and adults primarily through accreditation" and to "develop and periodically review standards for professional services and administration for agencies which are concerned with education, health, recreation, rehabilitation and social welfare services...."

Comments: The editor deemed this organization too small (under $1 million in expenditures in the most recent year reported) to be given a complete listing.

NATIONAL ASSOCIATION FOR VISUALLY HANDICAPPED

22 West 21st Street
New York, NY 10010
(212) 889-3141
or
3201 Balboa Street
San Francisco, CA 94121
(415) 221-3201

Year of Data: 1988
Expenditures $423,631
Percent to Program: 89.4%
Fund-raising Costs: 6.2%
Contributions Deductible: Yes
Top of Staff Salary Range: $37,500 (1989)
Meets NCIB Standards: Yes (8/4/89)

Purpose: "To advance the welfare of the visually handicapped; to research and provide standards for editing reading materials and texts in such form as may be used by visually handicapped persons; to promote the publication of reading, educational and text materials available to schools, school districts, libraries, social institutions and individuals...."

Comments: The editor deemed this organization too small (under $1 million in expenditures in the most recent year reported) to be given a complete listing.

NATIONAL BRAILLE ASSOCIATION, INC.

1290 University Avenue
Rochester, NY 14607
(716) 473-0900

Year of Data: 1986
Expenditures $124,493
Percent to Program: 79.7%
Fund-raising Costs: 38.8%
Contributions Deductible: Yes
Top of Staff Salary Range: $16,900 (1987)
Meets NCIB Standards: Yes (8/18/88)

Purpose: To unite "volunteers and professional workers for the visually impaired in one national organization to develop, provide and coordinate volunteer services in the production and distribution of reading materials in all media: braille, recording and large type"

Comments: The editor deemed this organization too small (under $1 million in expenditures in the most recent year reported) to be given a complete listing.

NATIONAL FEDERATION OF THE BLIND

1800 Johnson Street, Suite 300
Baltimore, MD 21230
(301) 659-9314

Purpose: To "improve and assure the civil rights of blind persons throughout the country"

Comments: NCIB is currently preparing a new report on this organization.

NATIONAL RETINITIS PIGMENTOSA FOUNDATION, INC.

1401 Mt. Royal Avenue
Baltimore, MD 21217
(301) 225-9400 or (800) 638-2300

Year of Data: 1987
Expenditures: $3,237,035
Percent to Program: 83.6%
Fund-raising Costs: 8.0%
Contributions Deductible: Yes
Top of Staff Salary Range: $110,250 (1988)
Meets NCIB Standards: Yes (12/22/88)

Purpose: "Discovery of the cause, treatment and prevention of Retinitis Pigmentosa and other retinal degenerations"

Program: The only major program expenditure in fiscal 1987 (64% of total expenditures) was for research; under this program, NRPF awarded $1.8 million for 11 grants to research centers, 8 genetic studies, 4 blood limpid studies, 4 individual research grants, 6 postdoctoral fellowship/career development awards and 2 animal models.

Comments: In 1988, NRPF reported 60 affiliates in the United States and 21 foreign countries; affiliates remit funds received to the national headquarters, which advances money to them to cover expenses. NCIB recommends improvements in NRPF's annual report and audited financial statements.

NATIONAL SOCIETY TO PREVENT BLINDNESS

500 East Remington Road
Schaumburg, IL 60173-4557
(708) 843-2020
and

FIGHT FOR SIGHT RESEARCH DIVISION

160 East 56th St. 8th Fl.
New York, NY 10022
(212) 751-1118

Year of Data: 1988
Expenditures: $9,556,601
Percent to Program: 73.8%
Fund-raising Costs: 17.3%
Contributions Deductible: Yes
Top of Staff Salary Range: $25,000 (1986)
Meets NCIB Standards: Yes (7/13/89)

Purpose: NSPB's purpose is to "study causes, direct or indirect, of blindness and defective vision; to promote public and profes-

sional education; and to promote all measures, including legislative ones, which might lead to the elimination of the causes of blindness." FFS's primary purpose is "stimulating and financing research in ophthalmology and its related sciences."

Program: NSPB and FFS activities for fiscal 1988, with percentages of combined total expenditures, included:

- Community Services (26%) - sponsoring and promoting screening programs for eye problems among children and adults; promoting vision safety, including occupational, home and school safety incentive programs
- Public Health Education (24%) - informing the public about basic facts concerning eye care, health and safety, through publications, mass media and response to inquiries from the public
- Professional Education and Training (16%) - provision of information to eye care professionals, nurses, scientists, teachers, social workers and others
- Research (7%) - 10 grants to support basic and clinical vision research; statistical and applied research in the nature and extent of blindness and vision loss

Comments: In 1988, FFS became a separately incorporated research division and subsidiary of NSPB. NCIB's reports on their separate activities prior to their merger and concludes that the merged organization meets all NCIB standards. NSPB reports having 25 affiliates, two divisions and a subsidiary, located in 27 states and Puerto Rico. FFS has 12 local leagues, located in Florida, New Jersey, New York and Pennsylvania, which are fund-raising arms of the national organization. NCIB recommends improvements in NSPB/FFS's annual report.

NEW EYES FOR THE NEEDY, INC.
549 Millburn Avenue
Short Hills, NJ 07078
(201) 376-4903

Year of Data: 1987
Expenditures $304,632
Percent to Program: 75.1%
Fund-raising Costs: 0%
Contributions Deductible: Yes
Top of Staff Salary Range: $19,000 (1988)
Meets NCIB Standards: Yes (11/2/88)

Purpose: To purchase new prescription eyeglasses and artificial eyes for those who cannot afford them in the United States and to send tested reusable plastic eyeglasses to missions and hospitals overseas

Comments: The editor deemed this organization too small (under $1 million in expenditures in the most recent year reported) to be given a complete listing.

RECORDING FOR THE BLIND
20 Roszel Road
Princeton, NJ 08540
(609) 452-0606

Year of Data: 1988
Expenditures: $6,432,959
Percent to Program: 71%
Fund-raising Costs: 14.8%
Contributions Deductible: Yes
Top of Staff Salary Range: $87,500 (1988)
Meets NCIB Standards: Yes (4/24/89)

Purpose: To provide "print-handicapped people with the reading tools to educate themselves in competition with their sighted peers"

Program: RFB's reporting of its activities does not allow a detailed breakdown of its programs. Fiscal 1988 activities included supplying over 136,000 taped books to 24,000 borrowers in 50 states and 37 foreign countries. RFB's library contains over 71,800 taped books.

Comments: RFB is an academically-oriented library service; it has 22 local units which operate recording studios where volunteers record the texts of educational books for distribution on cassette tape to the blind. NCIB recommends improvements in RFB's annual report and budget presentation.

RESEARCH TO PREVENT BLINDNESS, INC.
598 Madison Avenue
New York, NY 10022
(212) 752-4333

Year of Data: **1984**
Expenditures $2,985,753
Percent to Program: 94%
Fund-raising Costs: 1%
Contributions Deductible: Yes
Top of Staff Salary Range: $90,000 (1985)
Meets NCIB Standards: No: 3 (6/24/86)

Purpose: To act as a catalyst between the eye research scientist and those sources of economic and social support that are necessary to eliminate inadequacies which have adversely affected the development of a dynamic national eye research effort

Comments: The editor deemed NCIB's information about this organization too dated (1985 data or before) to give it a complete listing.

- **AMERICAN HEALTH ASSISTANCE FOUNDATION (see HEALTH-GENERAL)**

HEALTH - CANCER

ALSAC - ST. JUDE CHILDREN'S RESEARCH HOSPITAL

One St. Jude Bldg.
P.O. Box 3704
Memphis, TN 38173-0704
(800) USS-JUDE

Purpose: "To raise funds for the maintenance of St. Jude Children's Research Hospital in Memphis, Tennessee, a national institution dedicated to the care, research, and cure of leukemia, other related blood diseases, childhood cancer, muscular dystrophy, malnutrition, and all other catastrophic diseases under study. To aid and assist in the care, treatment, and cure of children stricken with ... [these diseases], without regard to race, creed, or color, and to aid and assist in research for the cure of said diseases"

Comments: NCIB is currently preparing a new report on this organization.

AMC CANCER RESEARCH CENTER

1600 Pierce Street
Denver, CO 80214
(303) 233-6501

Year of Data: 1986
Expenditures: $8,763,815
Percent to Program: 77.5%
Fund-raising Costs: 29.0%
Contributions Deductible: Yes
Top of Staff Salary Range: $138,000 (1985)
Meets NCIB Standards: Yes (4/1/87)

Purpose: To "advance knowledge of cancer prevention, detection, diagnosis and treatment through major programs of laboratory, clinical, and community cancer control research and service activities across the nation"

Program: Fiscal 1986 activities included:
- Laboratory Cancer Program (35%) - laboratory research, operating laboratories in such areas as biochemistry, molecular biology, cell biology, immunology and experimental therapeutics
- Clinical Cancer Program (22%) - clinical cancer research, involving nuclear mag-

netic resonance imaging, ultrasound, radiological and clinical laboratory units, with special emphasis on optimizing cancer therapy, improving diagnostic modalities and developing improved cancer screening technologies
- National Community Cancer Control Programs (21%) - developing and maintaining cancer control research programs and services

Comments: In 1987, AMC reported that it had 12,000 auxiliary volunteers "organized into 70 chapters and councils;" it also had 13 "Area Boards," which deliver programs of cancer control to their communities. NCIB recommends improvements in AMC's annual report.

AMERICAN CANCER SOCIETY

1599 Clifton Road, NE
Atlanta, GA 30329
(404) 320-3333
(800) 227-2345 medical info

Year of Data: 1987
Expenditures: $295,526,000
Percent to Program: 76.2%
Fund-raising Costs: 16.9%
Contributions Deductible: Yes
Top of Staff Salary Range: $175,000 (1988)
Meets NCIB Standards: Yes (12/14/88)

Purpose: Dedicated "to eliminating cancer as a major health problem by preventing cancer, saving lives from cancer and diminishing suffering from cancer through research, education and service"

Program: Fiscal 1987 activities included:
- Research (28%) - including over $75 million in grants and awards, primarily to individually developed projects involving scientists already working in established medical institutions; with the exception of its epidemiological work, ACS neither hires staff researchers nor operates its own laboratories
- Public Education (18%) - programs to inform people about cancer, tell them what they can do to protect themselves and demonstrate related health habits and lifestyles; emphasis on smoking control, the relationship between diet, nutrition and cancer and the importance of periodic checkups and tests
- Patient Services (13%) - programs to arrange visits to cancer patients by

people who have experienced the same type of cancer; programs to help women adjust to the particular problems associated with breast cancer; laryngectomy and ostomy rehabilitation programs; production of pamphlets, booklets and audiovisual presentations for cancer patients
- Professional Education (10%) - national conferences, clinical fellowships, materials, professorships and scholarships which provide information on the prevention, early detection and treatment of cancer and on rehabilitation of patients; includes costs of a cancer journal for physicians, with a circulation of 470,000, and a second periodical for specialists
- Community Services (7%) - including operation of a toll-free information system and cooperation with the American Heart Association and American Lung Association resulting in the ban on smoking during airline flights of two hours or less

Comments: ACS consists of a national headquarters, 57 chartered divisions, most of them representing states, and 3232 county-level units, all of which enroll a total of 2.5 million volunteers. NCIB reports that ACS uses such special events as "jail-a-thons" and daffodil sale days to raise funds and calls such methods "generally difficult to administer and control." NCIB recommends that interested contributors request local financial statements and look for separate reporting of such special fund-raising activities.

AMERICAN INSTITUTE FOR CANCER RESEARCH

759 R Street, NW
Washington, DC 20009
(202) 328-7744

Purpose: To "provide funding support for researchers exploring the relationship between nutrition, diet and cancer, and to expand public knowledge of the results of such recent research"

Comments: NCIB is currently preparing a new report on this organization.

CANCER CARE, INC. (NATIONAL CANCER CARE FOUNDATION, INC.)

1180 Avenue of the Americas
New York, NY 10036
(212) 221-3300

Year of Data: 1988
Expenditures: $7,260,595
Percent to Program: 66.3%
Fund-raising Costs: 30.6%
Contributions Deductible: Yes
Top of Staff Salary Range: $96,000 (1988)
Meets NCIB Standards: Yes (2/15/89)

Purpose: To provide services and supplemental aid to cancer patients and their families in the New York-New Jersey-Connecticut area

Program: Information about fiscal 1988 activities was received too late for inclusion in NCIB's report. Fiscal 1987 activities included:
- Social Services (50%) - provision of information, referral services, counseling, group sessions, guidance and supplemental financial assistance to patients and families; presentation of community education programs and work-site workshops; seminars for professionals
- Community Services (11%) - expenses of 33 chapters which provide educational information, referral and support; publication of a quarterly paper for chapters

Comments: Although CCI describes itself as the "service arm" of NCCF in the New York City-New Jersey-Connecticut region, NCIB reports that, for all practical purposes, the two are a single organization with identical boards of directors. NCIB's report treats both organizations under the name of CCI.

CANCER FUND OF AMERICA

NCIB reports that, as of July 1, 1990, this organization has not, over a period of several years, furnished requested information sufficient to prepare a report.

CANCER RESEARCH COUNCIL (Preliminary Report)

4853 Cordell Avenue, Suite 11
Bethesda, MD 20814
(301) 654-7933

Year of Data: 1987
Expenditures $458,289
Percent to Program: 69%
Fund-raising Costs: N/A
Contributions Deductible: Yes
Top of Staff Salary Range: None
Meets NCIB Standards: No determination (6/30/88)

Purpose: To "investigate and promote the development, clinical testing and implementation of hormone associated therapy for all cancers...."

Comments: The editor deemed this organization too small (under $1 million in expenditures in the most recent year reported) to be given a complete listing.

CANCER RESEARCH FOUNDATION OF AMERICA (Preliminary Report)

700 Princess Street, Suite 5
Alexandria, VA 22314
(703) 836-4412

Year of Data: 1987
Expenditures: $446,717
Percent to Program: 70%
Fund-raising Costs: 26.2%
Contributions Deductible: Yes
Top of Staff Salary Range: $28,000 (1988)
Meets NCIB Standards: No determination (3/3/89)

Purpose: To fund "grants to individuals and organizations engaged in research and educational activities involving cancer, with specific emphasis placed on cancer prevention research and educational programs"

Comments: The editor deemed this organization too small (under $1 million in expenditures in the most recent year reported) to be given a complete listing.

CANCER RESEARCH INSTITUTE, INC.

133 East 58th Street
New York, NY 10022
(212) 688-7515 or (800) 992-2623

Year of Data: 1988
Expenditures: $4,146,394
Percent to Program: 85.5%
Fund-raising Costs: 6.1%
Contributions Deductible: Yes
Top of Staff Salary Range: $110,000 (1988)
Meets NCIB Standards: Yes (2/24/89)

Purpose: To effect the "complete control of cancer through the effective application of immunological principles"

Program: Fiscal 1988 activities included:
- Clinical and Laboratory Research (76%) - support for 88 fellows at 45 institutions in 13 states and two foreign countries; 15 research grants and seven "investigatorships;" sponsorship of workshops and conferences
- Medical Communications and Research Analysis (9%) - not described in CRI materials

Comments: CRI reports that its studies "lead us to believe that through immunotherapy alone or combined with surgery or radiation, the inadequate resistance of the body to cancer can be stimulated to combat the disease effectively, and thus create a lasting immunity."

CHEMOTHERAPY FOUNDATION

NCIB reports that, as of July 1, 1990, this organization has not, over a period of several years, furnished requested information sufficient to prepare a report.

LEUKEMIA SOCIETY OF AMERICA, INC.

733 Third Avenue
New York, NY 10017
(212) 573-8484

Year of Data: 1987
Expenditures: $27,597,335
Percent to Program: 69.7%
Fund-raising Costs: 22.6%
Contributions Deductible: Yes
Top of Staff Salary Range: $115,000 (1988)
Meets NCIB Standards: Yes (6/30/88)

Purpose: "To make grants of financial aid to hospitals and other institutions and individuals, for the study of, and research into, the causes of leukemia and its treatment and cure"

Program: Fiscal 1987 activities included:
- Research (23%) - grants in the form of five-year awards of $200,000 to researchers with "significant experience;" three-year awards of $87,000 to researchers who have completed at least three years of supervised postdoctoral research and are ready to begin independent research; and three-year grants of $70,500 to researchers beginning their postdoctoral work
- Public Health Education (17%) - preparation of print materials, a video for adolescent leukemia patients and a slide presentation; distribution of about one million pieces of education literature
- Patient Service (16%) - financial aid of up to $750 per year for more than 5,500 patients, to help them with the costs of drugs, processing of information for transfusions, transportation and initial induction x-ray therapy
- Professional Community Service (12%) - response to calls and letters seeking medical, psychological or financial help; 6,500 referrals to other agencies; participation in local science and health fairs
- Education (5%) - costs of a national symposium, workshops, local professional education programs and a nursing symposium

Comments: LSA recently reported 57 local chapters in 31 states and the District of Columbia. Local chapters are asked to contribute a percentage of their gross income to the National Headquarters. In fiscal 1987, about 42% of LSA's total support was "collected through chapters."

NATIONAL CANCER CENTER (formerly National Cancer Cytology Center)

88 Sunnyside Boulevard, Suite 204
Plainview, NY 11802
(516) 349-0610

Year of Data: 1986
Expenditures $605,121
Percent to Program: 52.2%
Fund-raising Costs: 71.6%
Contributions Deductible: Yes
Top of Staff Salary Range: N/A
Meets NCIB Standards: No: 4; inadequate information: 1-3, 5-8 (5/14/87)

Purpose: "To achieve earlier diagnosis of cancer through widespread use of cytology techniques, and to further the knowledge of cancer through research"

Comments: The editor deemed this organization too small (under $1 million in expenditures in the most recent year reported) to be given a complete listing.

NATIONAL CHILDREN'S CANCER SOCIETY, INC. (Preliminary Report)

18 Lindenwood Drive
Troy, IL 62294
(618) 667-9563 or (800) 622-0190

Year of Data: N/A
Expenditures N/A
Percent to Program: N/A
Fund-raising Costs: N/A
Contributions Deductible: Yes
Top of Staff Salary Range: N/A
Meets NCIB Standards: No: 1a, 4 (2/27/89)

Purpose: To provide financial assistance to "children stricken with life-threatening cancer"

Comments: The editor deemed this organization too small (under $1 million in expenditures in the most recent year reported) to be given a complete listing.

NATIONAL FOUNDATION FOR CANCER RESEARCH, INC.

7315 Wisconsin Avenue, Suite 332W
Bethesda, MD 20814
(301) 654-1250 or (800) 321-CURE

Purpose: To "support basic science cancer research projects including the theories of Dr. Albert Szent-Gyorgyi [the discoverer of Vitamin C] ...."

Comments: NCIB is currently preparing a new report on this organization.

PACIFIC WEST CANCER FUND (PRELIMINARY REPORT)

701 Fifth Avenue
Columbia Center 2601
Seattle, WA 98104
(206) 343-3114

Year of Data: 1988
Expenditures $376,000
Percent to Program: N/A
Fund-raising Costs: N/A
Contributions Deductible: Yes
Top of Staff Salary Range: $60,000 (1988)
Meets NCIB Standards: No: 1, 4, 5 (3/15/89)

Purpose: To "promote improved rates of survivability for persons with cancer through awareness education directed to the early detection and treatment of cancer and increased public awareness of the causes of cancer, [and to] support national programs which improve methods of treatment of cancer"

Comments: The editor deemed this organization too small (under $1 million in expenditures in the most recent year reported) to be given a complete listing.

PROJECT CURE

NCIB reports that, as of July 1, 1990, this organization has not, over a period of several years, furnished requested information sufficient to prepare a report.

DAMON RUNYON - WALTER WINCHELL CANCER RESEARCH FUND

131 East 36th Street
New York, NY 10016
(212) 532-7000

Year of Data: 1988
Expenditures: $2,585,848
Percent to Program: 79.8%
Fund-raising Costs: 12.7%
Contributions Deductible: Yes
Top of Staff Salary Range: $80,000 (1989)
Meets NCIB Standards: Yes (7/21/89)

Purpose: "Advancing cancer research" by encouraging "the nation's most promising young investigators to pursue careers in cancer research by funding initial postdoctoral fellowships"

Program: All of DR-WW's program funds go to fellowships for cancer research; in fiscal 1988, 88 grants, totalling $1,832,203, were awarded.

Comments: NCIB faults DR-WW for its fund-raising solicitations which speak of "the young scientists we have to turn away for lack of funds" at a time when the organization had $11,899,185 in available assets, about 4.6 times its current budget. The organization has agreed to change its appeals. NCIB recommends improvements in DR-WW's budget presentation.

STOP CANCER (Preliminary Report)

10889 Wilshire Blvd.
Suite 1445
Los Angeles, CA 90024
(213) 824-5200
or
1230 Avenue of the Americas, 16th Fl.
New York, NY 10020
(212) 586-4444

Year of Data: 1988
Expenditures: $1,117,657
Percent to Program: N/A
Fund-raising Costs: N/A
Contributions Deductible: Yes
Top of Staff Salary Range: $100,000 (1989)
Meets NCIB Standards: No determination
(10/16/89)

Purpose: To conduct a four-year campaign to raise $1 billion to be distributed by the National Cancer Institute, an agency of the U.S. Department of Health and Human Services, as grants to cancer research scientists. The National Cancer Institute's entire budget in 1988 was $1.4 billion.

Program: SC is a one-time campaign to raise $1 billion for cancer research, half of it from the private sector and half from matching federal dollars. Expenses during 1988 were primarily for promotion and advertising. SC reports that it has sent $408,472 to the National Cancer Institute; no federal money had yet been appropriated by the date of NCIB's report.

Comments: SC was incorporated in March 1988, and NCIB judged that it would be premature to make statements about its adherence to standards. NCIB recommends improvements in SC's audited financial statements.

WALKER CANCER RESEARCH INSTITUTE

NCIB reports that, as of July 1, 1990, this organization has not, over a period of several years, furnished requested information sufficient to prepare a report.

* **ACTION ON SMOKING AND HEALTH** (see HEALTH-GENERAL)

* **AMERICAN LIVER FOUNDATION** (see HEALTH-GENERAL)

* **AMERICAN LUNG ASSOCIATION** (see HEALTH-GENERAL)

* **CITY OF HOPE** (see HEALTH-GENERAL)

* **NATIONAL HOSPICE ORGANIZATION** (see HEALTH-GENERAL)

HEALTH - MENTAL HEALTH

research and care, autism

AMERICAN MENTAL HEALTH FUND
2735 Hartland Road, Suite 302
Falls Church, VA 22043
(703) 573-2200 or (800) 433-5959

Year of Data: 1988
Expenditures $749,587
Percent to Program: 83.6%
Fund-raising Costs: 13.8%
Contributions Deductible: Yes
Top of Staff Salary Range: $40,000 (1988)
Meets NCIB Standards: Yes (9/6/89)

Purpose: To publicize the facts and warning signals of mental illness and to support expanded research into its causes and cures

Comments: The editor deemed this organization too small (under $1 million in expenditures in the most recent year reported) to be given a complete listing.

AUTISM SOCIETY OF AMERICA (formerly National Society for Children and Adults with Autism)
1234 Massachusetts Ave., NW, Suite C-1-17
Washington, DC 20005
(202) 783-0125

Purpose: To "promote the general welfare, education and training of autistic children; and further the advancement of all study, research, therapy, care and cure of autistic children; and to serve as a clearinghouse for gathering and disseminating information"

Comments: NCIB is currently preparing a new report on this organization.

THE DEVEREUX FOUNDATION

19 South Waterloo Road
P.O. Box 400
Devon, PA 19333-0418
(215) 964-3000

Year of Data: **1985**
Expenditures $60,096,949
Percent to Program: 92.9%
Fund-raising Costs: 18.3%
Contributions Deductible: Yes
Top of Staff Salary Range: $120,000 (1985)
Meets NCIB Standards: Yes (10/2/86)

Purpose: "To provide high quality human services to children, adults and families with special needs which derive from behavioral, psychological, intellectual or neurological impairments"

Comments: The editor deemed NCIB's information about this organization too dated (1985 data or before) to give it a complete listing.

NATIONAL MENTAL HEALTH ASSOCIATION

1021 Prince Street
Alexandria, VA 22314
(703) 684-7722 or (800) 969-6642

Year of Data: 1987
Expenditures: $47,519,375
Percent to Program: 83%
Fund-raising Costs: 5%
Contributions Deductible: Yes
Top of Staff Salary Range: $75,000 (1988)
Meets NCIB Standards: Yes (6/15/89)

Purpose: "To develop a coordinated citizens voluntary movement to work for the improved care and treatment of the mentally ill and handicapped; for improved methods and services in research, prevention, detection, diagnosis and treatment of mental illnesses and handicaps; and for the promotion of mental health"

Program: In fiscal 1987, the national headquarters had total expenditures of $2,027,071, 85% of which was spent for program services. Activities of the national headquarters included:

- Public Health Education (34%) - including educating the general public about symptoms of mental disease, early detection and treatment, and unwarranted fears and misconceptions; promoting interest in fostering good mental health
- Community Services (25%) - including planning and improving community mental health services; study and surveys on the needs in the community; informing and educating legislators about needs
- Professional Education and Training (20%) - including assistance to affiliates in efforts to improve knowledge, skills and judgments of physicians, clergy, teachers, law enforcement officials and others regarding mental health concepts and practices

Comments: NMHA has 600 affiliates which provided about 31% of the national headquarters' total revenue of $2,231,558 in fiscal 1987. Total revenue for national and affiliates combined was $50,379,436, of which 25% came from government grants and 18% from program service revenue. NCIB recommends improvements in NMHA's annual report and budget presentation.

HOUSING

*equal and low-cost housing,
urban renewal*

FUND FOR AN OPEN SOCIETY

311 South Juniper Street, Suite 400
Philadelphia, PA 19107
(215) 735-6915

Year of Data: 1987
Expenditures $794,780
Percent to Program: 54.3%
Fund-raising Costs: 24.5%
Contributions Deductible: Yes
Top of Staff Salary Range: $30,200 (1987)
Meets NCIB Standards: No: 1g, 6a (9/28/88)

Purpose: "To advance the goal of equal housing opportunity without discrimination as to race, creed, national origin or sex" and "to grant mortgages at below market rates for people making pro-integration housing moves"

Comments: The editor deemed this organization too small (under $1 million in expenditures in the most recent year reported) to be given a complete listing.

HABITAT FOR HUMANITY, INC.

Habitat & Church Streets
Americus, GA 31709
(912) 924-6935

Year of Data: 1986
Expenditures: $5,132,710
Percent to Program: 39%
Fund-raising Costs: 16.8%
Contributions Deductible: Yes
Top of Staff Salary Range: $26,800 (1987)
Meets NCIB Standards: Yes (10/23/87)

Purpose: "To engage in sponsoring specific projects in habitat development globally, starting with the construction of modest but adequate housing. To implement the gospel of Jesus Christ throughout the United States and around the world by working with economically disadvantaged people to help them create a better human habitat in which to live and work. To cooperate with other agencies which are working to develop better habitat for economically disadvantaged people. To communicate the gospel of Jesus Christ by means of the spoken word and by distribution of Bibles and other Christian literature."

Program: In fiscal 1986, HFH devoted about 34% of its total expenditures to sponsored home-building projects, which built or repaired 290 houses in 18 foreign countries, and 17% to affiliate projects, which built or repaired housing for 273 families in North America. HFH's projects operate by building homes which are sold to poor families on the basis of need. Houses are sold at no profit and with a no-interest mortgage to be repaid over 15-25 years. The payments are "recycled" to build more houses. HFH publishes a quarterly newspaper.

Comments: HFH conducts both affiliate projects, which are located in the United States and which raise their own funds, and sponsored projects, which are located overseas and are funded primarily by HFH's international headquarters. NCIB's report concerns HFH's international headquarters and its 11 regional centers only; readers interested in local affiliated projects should examine their individual programs and finances. NCIB reports that while HFH expended only 39% of its total available support for program activities in 1986, it spent another 31% to reduce its 1985 deficit and purchase fixed assets; NCIB adjudges these expenditures as "reasonable" with regard to its Standard 4. NCIB expresses reservations about HFH's solicitation letters, some of which may blur the distinction between the International office and affiliate projects. NCIB also objects to HFH's use of "matching check" solicitations which do not give contributors the option of having their donations returned if the matching check challenge is not met. NCIB recommends improvements in HFH's annual report and audited financial statements.

LOCAL INITIATIVES SUPPORT CORPORATION

733 Third Avenue
New York, NY 10017
(212) 455-9800

Year of Data: 1988
Expenditures: $13,054,563
Percent to Program: 66.3%
Fund-raising Costs: 1.9%
Contributions Deductible: Yes
Top of Staff Salary Range: $140,000 (1989)
Meets NCIB Standards: No: 1e (9/25/89)

Purpose: To "combat poverty and community deterioration and to lessen neighborhood tensions, by encouraging growth of and providing support to neighborhood and community development organizations which foster improvement of economic conditions, housing and other physical facilities, improvement of amenities and services and other improvements to revitalize deteriorated communities and to prevent such deterioration." In 1987, LISC organized the National Equity Fund, Inc., "to create a national investment pool to aggregate and channel corporate equity investments into low-income housing developments," and the Local Initiatives Managed Assets Corporation, "to create a secondary market to buy [community development] loans from LISC and other intermediaries, in furtherance of its charitable purposes...."

Program: In general, LISC, in partnership with community development corporations (CDCs), develops property in low-income areas that are not adequately served by traditional financial institutions. In 1988, LISC devoted 27% of its expenditures to grants to local CDCs, making it feasible for them to raise and borrow funds in their communities. LISC also provided technical assistance to CDCs and has organized housing or neighborhood development programs for CDC staff in Boston, Los Angeles and Chicago.

Comments: LISC's practice of compensating board of directors members violates NCIB's Standard 1e. NCIB recommends improvements in LISC's budget presentation.

HUMAN SERVICE

counseling, food, clothing and shelter, disaster services, family services, equal opportunity

AMERICAN RED CROSS

17th and E Streets, NW
Washington, DC 20006
(202) 737-8300

Year of Data: 1988
Expenditures: $977,803,000
Percent to Program: 90.6%
Fund-raising Costs: 8.7%
Contributions Deductible: Yes
Top of Staff Salary Range: $240,000 (1989)
Meets NCIB Standards: Yes (6/29/89)

Purpose: "To improve the quality of human life, to enhance self-reliance and concern for others, and to help people avoid, prepare for, and cope with emergencies"

Program: Fiscal 1988 activities included:

- Blood Services (59%) - collection of 6,268,119 units of blood from an estimated 4,475,000 blood donors; the blood is processed at laboratories of the 56 regional Red Cross blood centers and supplied to hospitals for a processing fee which is generally passed on to the patient; this program is largely funded by these processing fees, income from distribution of plasma derivatives and federal and foundation grants
- Disaster Services (10%) - services meant to meet emergency needs of domestic and international disaster victims, pending follow-up help from government agencies; ARC estimated that it provided services to over 400,000 persons affected by 54,000 disaster situations
- Service to Members of the Armed Forces, Veterans and their Families (8%) - information and referral services; assistance with benefits; counseling in personal and family problems; financial assistance; and disaster assistance to members of the military and their families, veterans and civilians
- Health Services (8%) - provision of 745,184 courses to 9,290,934 persons, in such activities as water safety, cardiopulmonary resuscitation (CPR) and first aid; AIDS education events; health fairs; direct services to 4,459,097 persons through first aid/emergency aid stations, blood pressure and cholesterol screenings and health counseling and referral
- Community Volunteer Programs (5%) - support for the estimated 1,152,393 volunteers active in ARC activities, at all levels of the organization; blood services, nursing and health and youth services are among programs staffed substantially by volunteers

Comments: ARC is not a member of the International Committee of the Red Cross, the independent Swiss group which serves as an intermediary to protect victims of war, in accordance with the Geneva Conventions. ARC reports that 90% of funds raised in its annual fund campaign in fiscal 1988, amounting to over $222,000,000, was collected through a joint undertaking by 1,481 ARC chapters with United Way organizations. Another $518,084,000, 53% of the total revenues of the organization, came from blood services processing. By comparison, the expenses associated with blood services activities were $572,417,000. ARC received $36,496,914 in government funds.

ARC has over 2,800 chapters, which are responsible for local activities of the Red Cross within their territories, usually counties. NCIB's report concerns only the national headquarters. ARC reports that over half of the chapters are operated entirely by volunteer staff. NCIB suggests that, since about 66% of ARC's net contribution income is retained by local chapters, potential contributors may want to study in detail the operations of chapters in their communities. NCIB also notes that, unless otherwise directed by donors, ARC places legacies and bequests in its Endowment Fund. NCIB recommends improvements in ARC's budget presentation.

AMVETS NATIONAL SERVICE FOUNDATION

4647 Forbes Boulevard
Lanham, MD 20706
(301) 459-9600

Purpose: To be "of assistance in furthering the program and services of AMVETS National Service Department [and] furnish to those citizens who are not eligible for membership in AMVETS, an opportunity to support the service program of that organization"

Comments: NCIB is currently preparing a new report on this organization.

BUTTERFIELD YOUTH SERVICES

NCIB reports that, as of July 1, 1990, this organization has not, over a period of several years, furnished requested information sufficient to prepare a report.

CEDARS HOME FOR CHILDREN FOUNDATION, INC.

6601 Pioneers Boulevard
Lincoln, NE 68506
(402) 488-4067

Year of Data: **1985**
Expenditures: $1,117,946
Percent to Program: 57.6%
Fund-raising Costs: 46%
Contributions Deductible: Yes
Top of Staff Salary Range: $34,848 (1986)
Meets NCIB Standards: No: 1, 3, 4 (10/15/86)

Purpose: "To temporarily furnish a family type home for boys and girls who are in need of a home"

Comments: The editor deemed NCIB's information about this organization too dated (1985 data or before) to give the organization a complete listing.

CHILD FIND OF AMERICA, INC.

7 Innis Avenue
P.O. Box 277
New Paltz, New York 12561
(914) 255-1848 or (800) 426-5678

Year of Data: 1986
Expenditures $470,073
Percent to Program: 79%
Fund-raising Costs: 6.8%
Contributions Deductible: Yes
Top of Staff Salary Range: $50,000 (1986)
Meets NCIB Standards: Yes (7/8/87)

Purpose: To help find missing children and promote child safety

Comments: The editor deemed this organization too small (under $1 million in expenditures in the most recent year reported) to be given a complete listing.

CHILD WELFARE LEAGUE OF AMERICA, INC.

440 First Street, NW, Suite 310
Washington, DC 20001-2085
(202) 638-2952

Year of Data: 1988
Expenditures: $3,972,963
Percent to Program: 82.2%
Fund-raising Costs: 27%
Contributions Deductible: Yes
Top of Staff Salary Range: $115,000 (1989)
Meets NCIB Standards: Yes (7/20/89)

Purpose: To improve care and services for deprived, dependent and neglected children, youth and their families, through assistance to agencies which provide such services

Program: CWLA's reporting of its financial materials does not allow a detailed breakdown of its expenses. In fiscal 1988, CWLA activities included revising its standards on adoption and services for abused and neglected children and their families; developing and publishing guidelines for the care of HIV-infected children, children at risk and their families; training programs on AIDS prevention and treatment policies; lobbying for federal legislation to help children and their families; and drafting standards for independent living programs for youth who are about to leave the foster care system at age 18.

Comments: CWLA is a federation of about 535 affiliated agencies in the United States and Canada, public and private, sectarian and nonsectarian. Included are such groups as children's aid societies, children's institutions, child protective agencies, day nurseries and state, county and local public child welfare departments. CWLA claims to serve 2.3 million children and their families annually. NCIB recommends improvements in CWLA's annual report and budget presentation.

CHILDHELP USA

6463 Independence Avenue
Woodland Hills, CA 91367
(818) 347-7280

Year of Data: 1987
Expenditures: $6,884,965
Percent to Program: 85.1%
Fund-raising Costs: 12.2%
Contributions Deductible: Yes
Top of Staff Salary Range: $75,000 (1988)
Meets NCIB Standards: No: 1, 6b? (8/11/88)

Purpose: To meet "the physical, emotional, educational and spiritual needs of abused and neglected children"

Program: Fiscal 1987 activities included:
- Residential Treatment (60%) - "home-like treatment for abused and neglected children" who are referred by courts in six California counties; treatment takes place in CU's residential village for abused and neglected children near Beaumont, CA
- National Child Abuse Hotline (10%) - a counseling and referral service "receiving over 100,000 calls a year, 80% of which are from outside of California"
- Family Evaluation (7%) - a psychological assessment program to assist children and families referred to local dependency courts
- Public Education (6%) - a national campaign for the prevention of child abuse and neglect, including distribution of materials, public service announcements and speakers bureaus

Comments: In fiscal 1987, 41% of CU's revenues came from fees paid by such governmental units as the California State Department of Education and the County of Los Angeles Superior Court; an additional 17% came from "Group programs" income. CU's by-laws place control of the organization in its two founding members by giving them the right to designate and remove board members and of-

ficers. NCIB views this provision as limiting the board's ability to function as an independent governing body and as a violation of Standard 1. Because CU had been in a deficit situation in 1985-87, NCIB questions the organization's adherence to Standard 6b. NCIB recommends improvements in Childhelp's annual report.

CHRISTIAN APPALACHIAN PROJECT, INC.

322 Crab Orchard Road
Lancaster, KY 40446
(606) 792-3051

Purpose: To "alleviate the social and economic hardships of the people of Appalachia, primarily in eastern Kentucky, through education, economic opportunity and employment . . . a Christian service organization"

Comments: NCIB is currently preparing a new report on this organization.

CONCERN FOR DYING

250 W. 57th Street, Room 323
New York, NY 10107
(212) 246-6962

Year of Data: 1988
Expenditures: $1,147,969
Percent to Program: 73.9%
Fund-raising Costs: 32.7%
Contributions Deductible: Yes
Top of Staff Salary Range: $75,000 (1989)
Meets NCIB Standards: Yes (4/28/89)

Purpose: "To assure patient autonomy in regard to treatment during terminal illness; to prevent the futile prolongation of the dying process and needless suffering by the dying"

Program: Fiscal 1988 activities included:
- Student Programs (32%) - seminars for about 300 students and practitioners in medicine, nursing, law, social work, chaplaincy and other fields, who in turn presented educational programs to 5,000 other students and practitioners around the country
- Educational Materials (27%) - publication and distribution of "living wills" and informative literature about death and dying; maintenance of a library
- Legal and Legislative Programs (7%) - efforts by CFD's staff counsel to assist

the organization and its supporters in legal issues

- Public Awareness (5%) - provision of information and advice about treatment decisions to families of the terminally ill

Comments: CFD received support/revenue of $706,146 in fiscal 1988, but because of a $704,664 loss in security investments, had a net support/revenue of only $1,482.

COVENANT HOUSE
346 West 17th Street
New York, NY 10011-5002
(212) 727-4000

Year of Data: 1989
Expenditures: $68,392,109
Percent to Program: 69%
Fund-raising Costs: 19%
Contributions Deductible: Yes
Top of Staff Salary Range: $100,000 (1989)
Meets NCIB Standards: No: 1, 8? (3/30/90)

Purpose: Provides food, shelter, medical and counseling services to runaways and abandoned youth

Program: Fiscal 1989 activities included:
- Shelter and Crisis Care (37%) - provision of shelter, food, clothing, counseling, medical care and legal advice for over 1,400 adolescents per day in six states and four Central American countries
- Rights of Passage (12%) - provision of homes for up to 18 months for adolescents who need counseling regarding education, jobs and housing
- Public Education (8%) - efforts to inform and educate the public on how to identify potential runaway and "throwaway" adolescents, the public and private resources to help them, related family support services and "public services needed to provide productive environments" for them

Comments: CH was much in the news in early 1990, as its founder and staff head, Father Bruce Ritter, became the subject of allegations regarding sexual misconduct and financial irregularities. In the aftermath, Father Ritter and eight members of the Board of Directors resigned, the Board appointed a Special Oversight Committee and instituted reviews of internal financial controls, compensation and benefit practices. In June 1990, the *New York*

Times reported that the organization had suffered a sharp decline in contributions, had determined to cut its 460-member staff almost in half and planned to cut several programs. NCIB faults CH's former structure and by-laws, which gave Father Ritter the right to designate and remove Board members (Standard 1), and CH's loans and salary advances to Father Ritter and two senior staff members (Standard 1g). NCIB questions the accountability demonstrated by CH's Board regarding activities of the Franciscan Charitable Trust, a separate non-profit, of which Father Ritter was the sole trustee.

DISABLED AMERICAN VETERANS
P.O. Box 14301
Cincinnati, OH 45250
(606) 441-7300

Year of Data: 1987
Expenditures: $54,507,642
Percent to Program: 64.6%
Fund-raising Costs: 35.8%
Contributions Deductible: Yes
Top of Staff Salary Range: $130,000 (1988)
Meets NCIB Standards: Yes (3/14/89)

Purpose: "To provide for the rehabilitation and continuing welfare of the Nation's disabled veterans, their families, dependents, and survivors"

Program: Fiscal 1987 activities include:
- Services to Veterans and Dependents (46%) - efforts to assist veterans in obtaining benefits to which they are entitled, including maintenance of personnel at Veterans Administration facilities and offices, interviewing veterans and dependents and appearing before Veterans Administration boards; organization of a transport service for veterans; also included under this category are expenses of the DAV national convention and expenses of national commanders and staff
- Publications and Other Communications (7%) - publication of a monthly magazine and other communications for disabled veterans, in order to provide information about benefits and social activities
- Membership Services (7%) - coordination of DAV's state departments and

local chapters which "provide a social environment to aid the veterans in personal and social development"

- Other activities include provision of emergency relief grants and scholarships to veterans and dependents.

Comments: NCIB's report is about the DAV national headquarters only and does not include the activities or finances of its 2,750 local chapters. Potential contributors may wish to examine the programs and finances of local chapters. NCIB encourages DAV to prepare combined or compiled financial statements for the national headquarters and chapters in future years. NCIB recommends improvements in DAV's annual report and audited financial statements.

FAMILY SERVICE AMERICA

11700 West Lake Park Drive
Park Place
Milwaukee, WI 53224
(414) 359-1040

Year of Data: 1987
Expenditures: $5,693,310
Percent to Program: 84%
Fund-raising Costs: 6.8%
Contributions Deductible: Yes
Top of Staff Salary Range: $110,000 (1988)
Meets NCIB Standards: Yes (11/28/88)

Purpose: To strengthen family life in America, in part through assistance to agencies which provide family services

Program: Fiscal 1987 activities included:
- National Services to Industry (49%) - contracted assistance to major corporations, to enable employers and employees to resolve human problems that can disrupt family life and job performance
- Support of Member Agencies (22%) - consultation on research projects and statistical systems; referrals on vacancies at executive levels; guides for personnel policies; collection and analysis of operating data and reaccreditation services
- Professional Publications (7%) - costs of a monthly journal and publications on older women and on work and the family

Comments: FSA is a federation of 290 member agencies, religious and non-sectarian, public and private, located in 42 states and Canada. In fiscal 1987, about 54% of FSA's total support came from program service fees and about 30% from dues from member agencies. NCIB recommends improvements in FSA's annual report.

CAL FARLEY'S BOYS RANCH AND GIRLS CAMP

P.O. Box 1890
Amarillo, TX 79174
(806) 372-2341

Year of Data: 1985
Expenditures $9.108,248
Percent to Program: 72%
Fund-raising Costs: 19.2%
Contributions Deductible: Yes
Top of Staff Salary Range: $48,700 (1985)
Meets NCIB Standards: No: 3, 4 (6/26/86)

Purpose: To maintain "a home for troubled, confused, delinquent or problem boys"

Comments: The editor deemed this organization too small (under $1 million in expenditures in the most recent year reported) to be given a complete listing.

FATHER FLANAGAN'S BOYS' HOME (BOYS TOWN)

Boys Town, NE 68010
(402) 498-1674

Purpose: To "provide residential care, educational and other services for resident and day youths and to operate an institute for communications disorders in children, a center for the study of youth development, and an alternative high school program"

Comments: NCIB is currently preparing a new report on this organization.

NATIONAL ALLIANCE TO END HOMELESSNESS (formerly Committee for Food and Shelter, Inc.)

1518 K Street, NW, Suite 206
Washington, DC 20005
(202) 638-1526

Year of Data: 1987
Expenditures $392,909
Percent to Program: 82.6%
Fund-raising Costs: 6.8%
Contributions Deductible: Yes
Top of Staff Salary Range: $75,000 (1988)
Meets NCIB Standards: Yes (9/9/88)

Purpose: To "reinforce and encourage programs and initiatives to serve the nation's hungry and homeless and to link government and private resources to accomplish that purpose"

Comments: The editor deemed this organization too small (under $1 million in expenditures in the most recent year reported) to be given a complete listing.

NATIONAL ASSEMBLY OF NATIONAL VOLUNTARY HEALTH AND SOCIAL WELFARE ORGANIZATIONS, INC.

1319 F Street, NW, Suite 601
Washington, DC 20004
(202) 347-2080

Year of Data: 1986
Expenditures $266,502
Percent to Program: 73.4%
Fund-raising Costs: 0%
Contributions Deductible: Yes
Top of Staff Salary Range: $56,400 (1987)
Meets NCIB Standards: Yes (2/8/88)

Purpose: "To provide opportunities for the continuing development of knowledge, skills and values needed to effectively lead and manage national voluntary human service organizations and to promote sound public policy to areas relevant to its members and those they serve"

Comments: The editor deemed this organization too small (under $1 million in expenditures in the most recent year reported) to be given a complete listing.

NATIONAL BOARD OF THE YOUNG WOMEN'S CHRISTIAN ASSOCIATION OF THE U.S.A. (YWCA)

726 Broadway
New York, NY 10003
(212) 614-2700

Year of Data: **1985**
Expenditures $9,065,097
Percent to Program: 67.9%
Fund-raising Costs: 30.2%
Contributions Deductible: Yes
Top of Staff Salary Range: $80,000 (1986)
Meets NCIB Standards: Yes (6/3/87)

Purpose: "To meet the needs of women and to open new opportunities for them through delivery of programs and as an advocate for social change"

Comments: The editor deemed NCIB's information about this organization too dated (1985 data or before) to give the organization a complete listing.

NATIONAL COMMITTEE FOR ADOPTION

1930 17th Street, NW
Washington, DC 20009-6207
(202) 328-1200

Year of Data: 1987
Expenditures $399,568
Percent to Program: 73.1%
Fund-raising Costs: 2.6%
Contributions Deductible: Yes
Top of Staff Salary Range: $66,000 (1988)
Meets NCIB Standards: Yes (9/27/88)

Purpose: To support "adoption through licensed non-profit agencies to ensure the protection of children...."

Comments: The editor deemed this organization too small (under $1 million in expenditures in the most recent year reported) to be given a complete listing.

NATIONAL COUNCIL ON THE AGING

600 Maryland Avenue, SW
West Wing 100
Washington, DC 20024
(202) 479-1200 or (800) 424-9046

Year of Data: 1987
Expenditures: $35,392,889
Percent to Program: 94.5%
Fund-raising Costs: 10.5%
Contributions Deductible: Yes
Top of Staff Salary Range: $94,410 (1988)
Meets NCIB Standards: Yes (11/14/88)

Purpose: To "make our society more equitable for older persons, more caring and understanding of them so their rights are protected, opportunities are advanced and their needs are met in a humane, effective and efficient manner"

Program: In fiscal 1987, about 89% of expenditures went to programs placing older persons in jobs specifically designed for them; services are to community agencies, not to individuals. Small percentages of expenditures were devoted to member services, professional training, community health and social services and life enrichment programs.

Comments: In fiscal 1987, about 92% of NCA's support came from government grants. NCIB recommends improvements in NCOA's annual report and budget presentation.

NATIONAL URBAN COALITION, INC.

8601 Georgia Avenue, Suite 500
Silver Spring, MD 20910
(301) 495-4999

Year of Data: **1985**
Expenditures $1,466,197
Percent to Program: 55.3%
Fund-raising Costs: 16.1%
Contributions Deductible: Yes
Top of Staff Salary Range: $84,000 (1986)
Meets NCIB Standards: No: 3, 4, 7?(8/27/87)

Purpose: To bring together "representatives of business, labor, minorities, mayors, and leaders of civic, community, and religious organizations," and "to revitalize America's cities and enhance the quality of life of urban residents," through "programs in urban education, community and minority economic development, and health"

Comments: The editor deemed NCIB's information about this organization too dated (1985 data or before) to give the organization

a complete listing.

NATIONAL URBAN LEAGUE

500 East 62nd Street
New York, NY 10021
(212) 310-9000

Year of Data: 1987
Expenditures: $19,696,898
Percent to Program: 80.6%
Fund-raising Costs: 12.0%
Contributions Deductible: Yes
Top of Staff Salary Range: $101,100 (1986)
Meets NCIB Standards: Yes (4/7/88)

Purpose: To secure "equal opportunity for Blacks and members of other minority groups in all area of American life"

Program: The only major program expenditure in fiscal 1987 (57% of total expenditures) was for employment programs, including NUL's Business Careers Summer Internships, which provide minority undergraduate students with fellowships at participating corporations, and provision of subsidized training and job opportunities for more than 3,000 older adults and senior citizens. NUL devoted small amounts to governmental affairs, education and career development, research, public education, field services and training.

Comments: NUL recently reported 112 affiliates which remit 4% of their general budgets to the national headquarters and receive services in return. Affiliates generally do not solicit funds in the name of the national organization and NUL does not control or direct the affiliates' financial transactions. NCIB's report concerns only the national organization. In fiscal 1987, about 62% of NUL's support for current use came from government grants. Its percentage of government support has generally declined since 1980, when it stood at 75%. In June 1987, NUL had a deficit unrestricted fund balance of a little more than $1 million. NCIB recommends improvements in NUL's annual report.

OMAHA HOME FOR BOYS

NCIB reports that, as of July 1, 1990, this organization has not, over a period of several years, furnished requested information sufficient to prepare a report.

ROSEBUD EDUCATIONAL SOCIETY/ ST. FRANCIS INDIAN MISSION/ LITTLE SIOUX

P.O. Box 499
St. Francis, SD 57572
(605) 747-2361

Year of Data: 1988
Expenditures: $2,279,555
Percent to Program: 43%
Fund-raising Costs: 48%
Contributions Deductible: Yes
Top of Staff Salary Range: $26,200 (1989)
Meets NCIB Standards: No: 1f, 6a, 6b? (9/18/89)

Purpose: "To work for the benefit of the Sioux Indian people and others living among them, especially residents of the Rosebud Reservation in south central South Dakota"

Program: Fiscal 1988 activities included:

• Socio-Pastoral (30%) - operation and maintenance of five parishes and eight satellite chapels on the Rosebud Reservation; Christian programming for a radio station; operation and maintenance of an office of social concerns; operation of a program on chemical dependency; and grants to needy individuals

• Public Information and Education (8%) - informing and educating the general public about the Sioux Indian culture and people

Comments: RES fails to meet NCIB's Standard 1f because its board of trustees is comprised of paid staff members. It fails to meet Standard 6a because of low program expenses and high fund-raising costs. NCIB also raises a question about RES's adherence to Standard 6b in that the organization's assets available for use at the end of fiscal 1988 were 2.1 times its fiscal 1988 expenses, just over NCIB's standard of two times expenses. NCIB recommends improvements in RES's annual report and budget presentation.

RURAL ADVANCEMENT FUND OF THE NATIONAL SHARECROPPERS FUND

2128 Commonwealth Avenue
Charlotte, NC 28205
(704) 334-3051

Year of Data: 1988
Expenditures $776,953
Percent to Program: 73.3%
Fund-raising Costs: 6.3%
Contributions Deductible: Yes
Top of Staff Salary Range: $44,150 (1988)
Meets NCIB Standards: Yes (7/26/89)

Purpose: "To ensure equal rights for all rural people, and to promote a just, sustainable system of agriculture based on family farms and the wise stewardship of human and environmental resources"

Comments: The editor deemed this organization too small (under $1 million in expenditures in the most recent year reported) to be given a complete listing.

SECOND HARVEST (NATIONAL FOOD BANK NETWORK)

116 S. Michigan Ave., Suite 4
Chicago, IL 60603
(312) 263-2303

Year of Data: **1985**
Expenditures $976,822
Percent to Program: 64.3%
Fund-raising Costs: 9.5%
Contributions Deductible: Yes
Top of Staff Salary Range: $32,647 (1985)
Meets NCIB Standards: Yes (2/11/87)

Purpose: To feed the hungry by soliciting surplus food from America's food industry and distributing these donations to a nationwide network of certified food banks. The food banks in turn distribute the food to community charities and church groups with feeding programs for the needy.

Comments: The editor deemed NCIB's information about this organization too dated (1985 data or before) to give the organization a complete listing.

SOUTHWEST INDIAN FOUNDATION

100 West Coal
P.O. Box 307
Gallup, NM 87301

Purpose: To "help improve the quality of life for Indian people of the Southwestern U.S. and to stimulate cooperative efforts to build a sense of mutual help and community spirit"

Comments: NCIB is currently preparing a new report on this organization.

TEKAKWITHA INDIAN MISSION

NCIB reports that, as of July 1, 1990, this organization has not, over a period of several years, furnished requested information sufficient to prepare a report.

UNITED NEIGHBORHOOD CENTERS OF AMERICA

1319 F Street, NW, Suite 603
Washington, D.C. 20004
(202) 393-3929

Year of Data: **1985**
Expenditures $217,324
Percent to Program: 77.5%
Fund-raising Costs: 5.0%
Contributions Deductible: Yes
Top of Staff Salary Range: $52,000 (1985)
Meets NCIB Standards: Yes (10/3/86)

Purpose: To "promote the welfare of settlements and of the neighborhoods in which they are located and act on public matters of interest; to help neighbors, to motivate them to join forces in meeting their specific problems

Comments: The editor deemed NCIB's information about this organization too dated (1985 data or before) to give the organization a complete listing.

UNITED SERVICE ORGANIZATIONS, INC. (USO)

601 Indiana Avenue, NW
Washington, DC 20004
(202) 783-8121

Year of Data: 1986
Expenditures $13,871,954
Percent to Program: 74.5%
Fund-raising Costs: 36.6%
Contributions Deductible: Yes
Top of Staff Salary Range: $125,000 (1987)
Meets NCIB Standards: Yes (7/18/88)

Purpose: To "provide a voluntary civilian agency through which the people of this nation may, in peace or war, serve the religious, spiritual, social welfare, educational and entertainment needs of the men and women in the Armed Forces within or without the territorial limits of the United States, and in general, to contribute to the maintenance of morale of such men and women...."

Program: Virtually all of USO's fiscal 1986 program expenditures (67% of total expenditures) were devoted to services to military personnel, such as information and referral programs; inter-cultural understanding; community outreach; informal education; community involvement; recreation; religious understanding; social development; snack bars and gift shops; and recreation programs. Costs include operation of airport centers, naval fleet centers and family and community centers in 85 locations overseas.

Comments: NCIB's report concerns the national office and overseas operation only and does not include domestic USO's, which raise their own funds and are administered independently; contributors may wish to examine the individual programs and finances of domestic USO's. NCIB recommends improvements in USO's annual report.

VOLUNTEERS OF AMERICA

3813 N. Causeway Boulevard
Metairie, LA 70002
(504) 837-2652

Purpose: To "provide technical support to its local affiliates to help them serve the needs of America's underprivileged by providing food, shelter, clothing and job training"

Comments: NCIB is currently preparing its first report on this organization.

YMCA OF THE UNITED STATES

101 North Wacker Drive
Chicago, IL 60606
(312) 977-0031 or (800) USA-YMCA

Year of Data: 1987
Expenditures $25,135,421
Percent to Program: 83.3%
Fund-raising Costs: 14.4%
Contributions Deductible: Yes
Top of Staff Salary Range: $183,300 (1988)
Meets NCIB Standards: Yes (6/7/89)

Purpose: "Developing Christian personality and building a Christian society"

Program: Fiscal 1987 activities included:
- Field Services (39%) - management services to member associations and other branches
- National Support Activities (17%) - support for local Ys, such as fund-raising, volunteer recruitment, financial management, legal advice, property management, membership promotion, housing for the homeless and training and development
- International Division (10%) - programs in conjunction with Ys in 92 other countries, including global education, human development, youth exchanges, overseas personnel and partnerships between domestic and foreign Ys
- Special Services (9%) - capital campaigns, architectural and interior design and software services to member associations
- Program Services (9%) - help to local Ys in delivering their programs

Comments: The approximately 960 local YMCA's in the country are grouped into 63 "Clusters," comprising 10-15 associations each. In 1987, they served 5.8 million members and 8.2 million non-member participants. Total income was $1.13 billion. Local associations pay one to two percent of their gross income to support the National Council. Local associations do not solicit funds in the name of the national organization and YMCAUS does not control or direct the locals. NCIB's report concerns only the national organization. NCIB recommends improvements in the YMCAUS annual report.

- **AMERICA THE BEAUTIFUL FUND** (see THE ENVIRONMENT)
- **AMERICAN COUNCIL FOR NATIONALITIES SERVICE and U.S. COMMITTEE FOR REFUGEES** (see INTERNATIONAL)
- **AMERICAN FRIENDS SERVICE COMMITTEE** (see INTERNATIONAL RELIEF)
- **AMERICAN REFUGEE COMMITTEE** (see INTERNATIONAL RELIEF)
- **AMERICARES FOUNDATION, INC.** (see INTERNATIONAL RELIEF)
- **ASSOCIATION ON AMERICAN INDIAN AFFAIRS** (see SOCIAL ACTION)
- **CENTER FOR POPULATION OPTIONS** (see HEALTH-GENERAL)
- **CHILDREN, INCORPORATED** (see INTERNATIONAL RELIEF)
- **CHILDREN'S DEFENSE FUND** (see SOCIAL ACTION)
- **CHRISTIAN CHILDREN'S FUND, INC.** (see INTERNATIONAL RELIEF)
- **COMPASSION INTERNATIONAL, INC.** (see INTERNATIONAL RELIEF)
- **FREEDOM FROM HUNGER FOUNDATION** (see INTERNATIONAL RELIEF)
- **FUTURES FOR CHILDREN, INC.** (see INTERNATIONAL RELIEF)
- **HEIFER PROJECT INTERNATIONAL** (see INTERNATIONAL RELIEF)
- **INTERNATIONAL RESCUE COMMITTEE** (see INTERNATIONAL RELIEF)
- **MARTIN LUTHER KING, JR. CENTER FOR NONVIOLENT SOCIAL CHANGE, INC.** (see SOCIAL ACTION)
- **NATIONAL ALLIANCE OF BUSINESS, INC.** (see EMPLOYMENT)
- **NATIONAL LEAGUE OF FAMILIES OF AMERICAN PRISONERS AND MISSING IN SOUTHEAST ASIA** (see INTERNATIONAL)
- **NATIONAL LEGAL AID AND DEFENDER ASSOCIATION** (see CONSUMER PROTECTION)

- **ST. LABRE INDIAN SCHOOL EDUCATIONAL ASSOCIATION** (see EDUCATION)
- **SAVE THE CHILDREN FEDERATION, INC.** (see INTERNATIONAL RELIEF)
- **UNITED WAY OF AMERICA** (see COMMUNITY IMPROVEMENT)

INTERNATIONAL

exchanges and dialogue, refugee services, protection of freedoms, peace, cultural, educational and policy programs

AFS INTERCULTURAL PROGRAMS, INC. (Formerly AFS International/ Intercultural Programs, Inc.)

313 East 43rd Street
New York, NY 10017
(212) 949-4242

Year of Data: 1988
Expenditures: $34,803,694
Percent to Program: 90%
Fund-raising Costs: 32%
Contributions Deductible: Yes
Top of Staff Salary Range: $140,000 (1988)
Meets NCIB Standards: Yes (1/25/90)

Purpose: To "promote intercultural learning through worldwide exchange programs for students and educators"

Program: All of AFS's program expenditures for fiscal 1988 were to support its exchange programs, especially its programs for about 8,700 secondary school students, about 6,000 of whom lived with a family in a foreign country for one school year and the rest of whom participated for part of a year. AFS also conducted exchange programs for about 700 teachers, school administrators and other education professionals.

Comments: AFS maintains offices in about 50 countries. In fiscal 1988, about 83% of AFS's total revenues came from participant fees. NCIB recommends improvements in AFS's budget presentation. AFS stands for American Field Service.

AFRICAN-AMERICAN INSTITUTE

833 United Nations Plaza
New York, NY 10017
(212) 949-5666

Year of Data: 1987
Expenditures: $16,348,153
Percent to Program: 89.3%
Fund-raising Costs: 2.7%
Contributions Deductible: Yes
Top of Staff Salary Range: $97,450 (1985)
Meets NCIB Standards: Yes (5/16/88)

Purpose: To further African-American understanding and African development

Program: AAI's reporting of its activities does not allow a detailed breakdown of its programs. Fiscal 1985 activities included provision of education opportunities in the United States and Africa to African students destined for African university or civil service careers; aid to rural development activities; post-secondary education opportunities for refugees from Zimbabwe, Namibia and South Africa; programs to bring Africans to the United States to broaden their professional perspectives; conferences, seminars, press conferences and information activities; production of a bimonthly magazine and other publications; and exhibitions of African art.

Comments: In fiscal 1987, 72% of AAI's total support came from U.S. government agencies. NCIB recommends improvements in AAI's budget and audited financial statements.

AIESEC-UNITED STATES, INC.
(Association Internationale des Etudiants en Sciences Economiques et Commerciales)

841 Broadway
New York, NY 10003-3608
(212) 979-7400

Year of Data: 1986
Expenditures $536,889
Percent to Program: 70.3%
Fund-raising Costs: 15.9%
Contributions Deductible: Yes
Top of Staff Salary Range: $19,500 (1987)
Meets NCIB Standards: Yes (8/11/87)

Purpose: To further "international understanding and education within the various national business communities by means of an international exchange of paid commercial

traineeships [and] educational tours and seminars...."

Comments: The editor deemed this organization too small (under $1 million in expenditures in the most recent year reported) to be given a complete listing.

AMERICAN COUNCIL FOR NATIONALITIES SERVICE and its U.S. COMMITTEE FOR REFUGEES

95 Madison Avenue
New York, NY 10016
(212) 532-5858

Year of Data: 1987
Expenditures: $6,256,775
Percent to Program: 85.9%
Fund-raising Costs: 4.4%
Contributions Deductible: Yes
Top of Staff Salary Range: $76,000 (1987)
Meets NCIB Standards: No: 1d (6/8/89)

Purpose: To help "immigrants and refugees adjust to life in the United States," and to promote "inter-cultural dialogue and understanding" and "humane national and international policies for the treatment of refugees"

Program: Fiscal 1987 activities included:
* Refugee Resettlement and Other Government Programs (73%) - support for resettlement programs of local agencies, largely in behalf of Indochinese, Afghan, Ethiopian and Eastern European refugees; placement of refugees for sponsorship with cooperating member agencies; "work with national and international bodies in finding practical solutions for refugees in asylum situations;" immigration and legalization services in connection with the 1986 Immigration Reform and Control Act
* Public Information (13%) - publications, including USCR's monthly newsletter, and testimony and reports for congressional committees

Comments: USCR is ACNS's "public education, policy analysis, and advocacy" arm; it does not conduct direct relief services. In fiscal 1987, about 80% of ACNS's revenues came from restricted government grants; ACNS has stated that it is increasing its efforts to gain private funding. ACNS fails to meet NCIB's Standard 1d because it failed to attract a majority of members at any of its four board of directors meetings in fiscal 1988.

AMNESTY INTERNATIONAL OF THE U.S.A., INC.

322 Eighth Avenue
New York, NY 10001
(212) 807-8400
(800) 55-AMNESTY for membership

Year of Data: 1987
Expenditures: $12,667,897
Percent to Program: 56.8%
Fund-raising Costs: 29.4%
Contributions Deductible: Yes
Top of Staff Salary Range: $56,700 (1987)
Meets NCIB Standards: Yes (2/10/89)

Purpose: To work "for release of prisoners of conscience, for fair trials for political prisoners, and for an end to torture and the death penalty"

Program: Fiscal 1987 activities included:
- U.S. Program (26%) - special campaigns, emergency appeal cases, information for and training of new groups, all concerned with rights abuses in foreign countries and the abolition of the death penalty in the United States; work with the organization's networks (like the Urgent Action Network, the Freedom Writers Network, the Health Professionals Network and the Legal Support Network) whose members make personal appeals and offer services on behalf of people in danger of torture or execution or who need medical or legal assistance; work to promote U.S. ratification of the Genocide Convention
- International Program (21%, including assessment to Amnesty International) - research activities concerning political prisoners in Turkey and the Soviet Union, extra-judicial executions in Afghanistan, torture and disappearances in Ethiopia and human rights violations in many other countries
- Publications (5%) - including reports about conditions in various countries and about fact-finding missions by human rights experts
- Public Information (5%) - dissemination about AIUSA's concerns and organizational methods

Comments: AIUSA is affiliated with Amnesty International in London, to which it contributes an annual assessment ($3,098,000 in 1988). AIUSA has grown rapidly in recent years; its 1988 budget was about twice that of 1985. Part of its increasing visibility is the result of its series of concerts by rock and other musicians, especially in 1988. These concerts were intended to spread awareness of the organization and its concerns, rather than to raise money. AIUSA's program service expenses were about 59.5% of its total expenses in 1985, 62.4% in 1986 and 56.8% in 1987. NCIB advises that AIUSA needs to increase its program expense ratio in future years in order to meet Standard 6a. NCIB recommends improvements in AIUSA's annual report and budget presentation.

ASIA FOUNDATION

465 California Street
San Francisco, CA 94104
(415) 982-4640

Year of Data: 1987
Expenditures: $17,956,395
Percent to Program: 90.6%
Fund-raising Costs: 7.9%
Contributions Deductible: Yes
Top of Staff Salary Range: $80,000 (1987)
Meets NCIB Standards: Yes (2/10/89)

Purpose: To assist Asians "in the growth and development of their societies, to promote Asian regional cooperation, and to further Asian-American understanding, cooperation, and friendship"

Program: Fiscal 1987 activities included:
- Country Programs (45%) - grants of $8,127,381, directed at such areas as education; human resource development; law and judicial administration; government and civic affairs; public administration; economic development; free enterprise and business management; international relations and diplomacy; foreign trade and investment; communication and journalism; library development and books; and English for special purposes. Recipients are civic and community groups; universities and schools; professional societies; business associations; libraries and research centers; women's and

youth associations; semi-governmental agencies; governmental institutions; and regional organizations. Grants went to 16 countries, with the largest amounts going to Bangladesh, the Philippines, Thailand, Indonesia and Korea.

- Partners for International Education and Training (15%) - places and monitors Asian participants in education and training programs funded by the U.S. Agency for International Development

Comments: In addition to cash expenses, AF also distributed donated materials, chiefly books, valued at $9,765,453. In fiscal 1987, AF received about 89.5% of its total cash support from U.S. Government grants. This percentage is decreasing as AF expands its approach to the private sector. NCIB recommends improvements in AF's audited financial statements.

THE ASIA SOCIETY

725 Park Avenue
New York, NY 10021
(212) 288-6400

Year of Data: **1985**
Expenditures $6,771,310
Percent to Program: 78%
Fund-raising Costs: 10.6%
Contributions Deductible: Yes
Top of Staff Salary Range: $100,000 (1985)
Meets NCIB Standards: Yes (2/20/86)

Purpose: To deepen American understanding of Asia and promote "thoughtful trans-Pacific discourse"

Comments: The editor deemed NCIB's information about this organization too dated (1985 data or before) to give the organization a complete listing.

THE ATLANTIC COUNCIL OF THE UNITED STATES, INC.

1616 H Street, NW, 3rd Fl.
Washington, DC 20006
(202) 347-9353

Year of Data: 1986
Expenditures: $1,579,670
Percent to Program: 68.4%
Fund-raising Costs: 2.3%
Contributions Deductible: Yes
Top of Staff Salary Range: $70,000 (1987)
Meets NCIB Standards: Yes (12/23/87)

Purpose: To "enhance the dialogue and the mechanisms for achieving closer cooperation and a sense of community between the United States and the other developed democracies, and to promote a better public understanding of the profound interdependence which binds us to our friends and allies"

Program: ACUS's reporting of its activities does not allow a detailed breakdown of its programs. In general, ACUS operates through "Working Groups" to formulate "private and public recommendations to both elected and appointed officials on intergovernmental relations and on the parallel strengthening of mutually beneficial private lines across national boundaries." In 1986, ACUS's activities included Working Groups on such issues as "Long-Term U.S.-Soviet Relations," "Toward Strategic Stability for the Year 2000," "Western Interests and U.S. Policy Options in the Middle East," and "Mexico's Future and U.S. Policy Options." Its publications included its quarterly magazine, its bimonthly newsletter, a book and several papers. It also operated a NATO Information Office.

Comments: ACUS reports that U.S. Government grants or contracts are usually limited by ACUS's Board of Directors to less than half of the total cost of the project to which they are applied and that "governmental contributions are invariably limited to 30 percent or less of the Council's budget in any given year." NCIB recommends improvements in ACUS's audited financial statements and annual report.

BUSINESS COUNCIL FOR THE UNITED NATIONS

60 East 42nd Street
New York, NY 10165
(212) 661-1772

> Year of Data: 1987
> Expenditures $505,845
> Percent to Program: 64.3%
> Fund-raising Costs: 16.5%
> Contributions Deductible: Yes
> Top of Staff Salary Range: $83,000 (1988)
> Meets NCIB Standards: Yes (10/14/88)

Purpose: To "help establish in the United States and worldwide, through educational processes, the concept that the responsibility of all persons and groups extends to international relations, and specifically, to provide means whereby such persons and groups can improve their understanding of the principles of the United Nations as expressed in the preamble of its Charter and enable them to take an active role in developing commitment to and practice of such principles...."

Comments: The editor deemed this organization too small (under $1 million in expenditures in the most recent year reported) to be given a complete listing.

COUNCIL ON FOREIGN RELATIONS

58 East 68th Street
New York, NY 10021
(212) 734-0400

> Year of Data: **1984**
> Expenditures $6,539,500
> Percent to Program: 60.6%
> Fund-raising Costs: 16.8%
> Contributions Deductible: Yes
> Top of Staff Salary Range: N/A
> Meets NCIB Standards: Yes (6/27/86)

Purpose: To bring "together leaders from the academic, public, and private worlds" to "learn from each other, expand their perspectives, and develop their ideas about the shifting, complex fields of foreign relations"

Comments: The editor deemed NCIB's information about this organization too dated (1985 data or before) to give the organization a complete listing.

EISENHOWER EXCHANGE FELLOWSHIPS, INC.

256 South 16th Street
Philadelphia, PA 19102
(215) 546-1738

> Year of Data: 1987
> Expenditures: $1,368,654
> Percent to Program: 75.9%
> Fund-raising Costs: 16.1%
> Contributions Deductible: Yes
> Top of Staff Salary Range: $84,000 (1988)
> Meets NCIB Standards: No: 1d (10/13/88)

Purpose: "To promote understanding between the United States and other countries ... and in so doing to help develop in the most practical way the outstanding potential leaders in the field their country most needs"

Program: EEF's sole program is the award of Eisenhower Fellowships to men and women between 35 and 50 years of age from the United States and abroad. About 58% of fiscal 1987 expenditures supported awards to 28 fellows, each from a different country. These fellowships included a one-week orientation seminar, eight weeks of travel and professional consultations in the United States and a concluding seminar. About 16.7% of expenditures supported nine Korean fellows in a program of seminars and travel in the United States.

Comments: About 61% of EEF's revenues for fiscal 1987 came from government appropriations. NCIB faults EEF because it was unable to convene a majority of members at any of the meetings of its board of directors or executive committee (Standard 1d).

EXPERIMENT IN INTERNATIONAL LIVING

P.O. Box 676
Brattleboro, VT 05302
(802) 257-7751 or (800) 451-4465

> Year of Data: 1986
> Expenditures: $23,144,091
> Percent to Program: 74.7%
> Fund-raising Costs: 8.8%
> Contributions Deductible: Yes
> Top of Staff Salary Range: $75,000 (1987)
> Meets NCIB Standards: Yes (8/26/87)

Purpose: "To strengthen international understanding and service through . . . citizen exchange and language programs, career-oriented higher education, and field projects in international development and training"

Program: Fiscal 1986 activities included:

- Government and Private Contract Programs (45%) - programs teaching English and cultural awareness in such countries as Uganda, Thailand and Indonesia; government-sponsored high school exchange programs
- International Exchange Programs (14%) - programs, focusing on language and cross-cultural experiences, for American and foreign students; visits last from three weeks to one year
- School for International Training (12%) - a school in Brattleboro, VT, which focuses on world awareness, languages and international business

Comments: Of EIL's total revenues for fiscal 1986, 51% was from government grants and contracts, 40% from tuition and program fees and only 6% from private gifts and grants. NCIB recommends improvements in EIL's annual report.

FOREIGN POLICY ASSOCIATION

729 Seventh Avenue
New York, NY 10019
(212) 764-4050

Year of Data: 1987
Expenditures: $2,361,454
Percent to Program: 57.4%
Fund-raising Costs: 17.2%
Contributions Deductible: Yes
Top of Staff Salary Range: $100,000 (1988)
Meets NCIB Standards: Yes (8/12/88)

Purpose: To "help Americans gain a better understanding of significant issues in U.S. foreign policy and stimulate constructive and informed citizen participation in world affairs"

Program: Fiscal 1987 activities included:

- Publications (28%) - publication of an annual discussion of major issues in American foreign policy, a guide to careers in world affairs and a book and discussion guide on affairs concerning Europe and North America
- Community Programming (16%) - teacher training workshops, presentations at conventions, counseling adult groups in how to use FPA materials, development of media programs and

discussion programs for 250,000 adults and 50,000 students

- Meetings, Programs and Tours (14%) - costs of 55 meetings, at which 12,450 attendees heard prominent officials and authorities speak on world affairs

Comments: NCIB reports that FPA's low program service expenditures are due to special circumstances peculiar to fiscal 1987. NCIB recommends improvements in FPA's annual report and budget format.

FREEDOM HOUSE, INC. and WILLKIE MEMORIAL OF FREEDOM HOUSE, INC.

48 East 21st Street
New York, NY 10010
(212) 473-9691

Year of Data: 1986
Expenditures: $1,613,305
Percent to Program: 79.4%
Fund-raising Costs: 3%
Contributions Deductible: Yes
Top of Staff Salary Range: $70,000 (1987)
Meets NCIB Standards: Yes (6/26/87)

Purpose: "To strengthen the institutions of freedom"

Program: Fiscal 1986 activities included:

- Exchange Program (13%) - maintenance of a network of about 370 correspondents in 55 countries who contribute articles and other materials concerning problems of and opportunities for freedom, which FH translates and circulates for further publication and broadcast; a workshop on democracy for representatives of 14 Latin American countries
- Libro Libre (12%) - assistance for publication of Spanish-language books on democratic themes
- Freedom at Issue (11%) - publication of a bimonthly magazine
- International Cultural Program (7%) - assistance to *Encounter* magazine, a British journal of social, political and literary comment
- Comparative Survey of Freedom (6%) - production of a study of the state of freedom in the world and of a curriculum guide for high school social studies classes

Comments: Willkie Memorial of Freedom House is separately incorporated, but has the same board and executive director as Freedom House. NCIB reports that attendance at FH's board of directors meetings has been consistently low and that the Executive Committee of the organization should be regarded as the controlling board, with other directors serving primarily in an advisory capacity. NCIB recommends improvements in FH's annual report.

THE FUND FOR PEACE

345 E. 46th Street, Suite 810
New York, NY 10017
(212) 661-5900

Year of Data: 1987
Expenditures: $2,836,814
Percent to Program: 90.6%
Fund-raising Costs: less than 1%
Contributions Deductible: Yes
Top of Staff Salary Range: $61,000 (1988)
Meets NCIB Standards: Yes (11/23/88)

Purpose: To carry out "non-partisan research and public education on a broad range of topics in the areas of arms control, Third World development, regional conflict resolution, international environment issues, and human rights"

Program: Fiscal 1987 activities included:
- Center for National Security Studies (49%) - a center, co-sponsored with the American Civil Liberties Union Foundation, which conducts research and public education on the balance between national security needs and individual rights of citizens; including collection of documentary material on U.S. foreign policy and making them available to journalists, scholars and other organizations
- Center for International Policy (15%) - carries out research on international financial and developmental issues and their bearing upon human rights; including an Indochina Project, concentrating on political, economic and social trends in Southeast Asia
- Institute for the Study of World Politics (9%) - supports research by awarding doctoral and postdoctoral fellowships at U.S. universities on topics in arms control, international economic and social

issues, human rights and environmental protection
- Other Programs - including regional conferences on arms control issues; a conference for filmmakers and other media specialists from various countries concerning the media's treatment of war and peace issues; provision of materials on international affairs to schools, libraries and citizens groups

Comments: FP did not provide an annual report for NCIB review. NCIB recommends improvements in FP's budget presentation.

THE HUNGER PROJECT (formerly The Global Hunger Project)

1388 Sutter Street
San Francisco, CA 94109
(415) 928-8700 or (800) ACT-NOW1

Year of Data: 1987
Expenditures: $8,090,161
Percent to Program: 83.2%
Fund-raising Costs: 14.5%
Contributions Deductible: Yes
Top of Staff Salary Range: $95,000 (1989)
Meets NCIB Standards: Yes (4/21/89)

Purpose: To "educate and inform people about the problem of world hunger and to support them in participating effectively in its solution"

Program: Fiscal 1987 activities included:
- Educational Programs, Grants and Strategic Initiatives (28%) - sponsorship of a lecture; award of HP's annual "Africa Prize for Leadership;" training for 4,600 educators; grants of $264,000
- "Ending Hunger" Teleconference (25%) - expenses for a satellite teleconference linking 41,000 people in 16 countries (revenues for this event included a $1.5 million contribution from a Japanese donor and $779,000 in ticket sales)
- Global Operations and U.S. Volunteer Activities (16%) - activities to enroll individuals to make formal commitments to ending hunger through increasing opportunities for people in countries where hunger persists; enrollments are solicited through "a nationwide network of volunteers," who conduct one-to-one conversations, small group meetings and briefings; HP reports that

about 140,000 people "enrolled themselves" in 1987 and that total enrollment reached 5.2 million people in 152 countries

- Publications (15%) - including a newspaper distributed to 1.8 million people, a bi-weekly newsletter on international development, a monthly publication focusing on hunger in the United States and one of a series of papers on hunger and development issues

Comments: HP was founded in 1977 with strong initial support from the est Foundation and the for-profit est, An Educational Corporation. Werner Erhard, the founder of est and co-founder of HP is a member of HP's board of directors. NCIB points out that since one of HP's programs is the enrollment of people committed to ending hunger and one of the ways of expressing that commitment is a contribution to HP, it is sometimes difficult to distinguish the organization's enrollment program from its fund-raising activities. NCIB recommends improvements in HP's annual report.

INSTITUTE OF INTERNATIONAL EDUCATION

809 United Nations Plaza
New York, NY 10017
(212) 984-5440

Year of Data: 1987
Expenditures: $113,319,826
Percent to Program: 97.5%
Fund-raising Costs: 13.7%
Contributions Deductible: Yes
Top of Staff Salary Range: $155,000 (1988)
Meets NCIB Standards: Yes (12/9/88)

Purpose: "To develop better understanding and create goodwill between the people of the U.S. and the peoples of other countries through educational exchange programs for students, scholars, artists, leaders and specialists; to exchange ideas, knowledge and skills among individuals of all countries; to assist in developing educational programs to serve the economic and social needs of new and emerging nations"

Program: Fiscal 1987 activities included:
- Scientific Cooperation Activities (51%) - logistical support for agricultural research institutions; procurement functions for institutions and universities;

sponsors include the U.S. Agency for International Development, the U. S. Information Agency and the Harvard Institute for International Development

- International Exchange of Persons (39%) - usually academic exchanges between the U.S. and a foreign country or between two foreign countries; these programs include those sponsored by the U.S. Information Agency and the Ford Foundation

Comments: Of IIE's total support of $113,439,351 in fiscal 1987, over $108,000,000 was contract revenue for its "Sponsored Programs." Foundations and research organizations funded about 54% of these programs, and the U.S. government about 37%. The remainder of IIE's income, including $2,265,472 in contributions, funded such activities as counseling, information services, seminars, provision of loans to foreign students and publications. NCIB recommends improvements in IIE's annual report and budget.

INTERNATIONAL PEACE ACADEMY

777 United Nations Plaza
New York, NY 10017-3521
(212) 949-8480

Year of Data: 1987
Expenditures: $1,243,369
Percent to Program: 56.8%
Fund-raising Costs: 23.9%
Contributions Deductible: Yes
Top of Staff Salary Range: $100,000 (1988)
Meets NCIB Standards: Yes (9/9/88)

Purpose: To provide "practical mechanisms for the resolution of international conflicts ... and systematic training of career diplomats and military officers in the skills of peacekeeping and mediation"

Program: IPA's reporting of its expenditures does not allow a detailed breakdown of its programs. In general, 1987 activities included workshops and seminars on issues of peace, development, security, conflict resolution, negotiation and mediation; and publication of various reports and case studies. Topics of seminars and publications included regional concerns in the Caribbean Basin, Southern Africa, Southeast Asia, India and South America.

Comments: NCIB reports that although IPA's 1987 program expenditures were slightly below the threshold of Standard 6, particular circumstances regarding governmental support of its activities make this level "reasonable." NCIB recommends improvements in IPA's audited financial statements.

JAPAN SOCIETY, INC.

333 East 47th Street
New York, NY 10017
(212) 832-1155

Year of Data: 1986
Expenditures: $3,748,253
Percent to Program: 67.8%
Fund-raising Costs: 7.6%
Contributions Deductible: Yes
Top of Staff Salary Range: $68,135 (1986)
Meets NCIB Standards: Yes (2/24/87)

Purpose: To bring "the peoples of Japan and the United States closer together in understanding, appreciation and cooperation ... [through] discussions, exchanges and studies in areas of vital interest in both peoples"

Program: Fiscal 1986 activities included:
* Gallery (26%) - exhibitions of Japanese art at the Society's Japan House in New York City and associated lectures and discussions
* Public Affairs (15%) - conferences and seminars to introduce Americans to aspects of Japanese society, economics, politics and culture
* Film (7%) - presentation of Japanese films at Japan House and distribution of films, including documentaries, to American educational institutions and film centers
* Membership Activities (5%) - lectures on contemporary Japan and other topics
* Performing Arts (5%) - performances, demonstrations and lectures on dance, poetry and other arts

Comments: NCIB recommends improvements in JS's annual report and audited financial statements.

MEDICAL EDUCATION FOR SOUTH AFRICAN BLACKS, INC. (Preliminary Report)

4200 Wisconsin Ave., NW, Suite 300
Washington DC 20016
(202) 364-6727

Year of Data: 1987
Expenditures $172,246
Percent to Program: 75.5%
Fund-raising Costs: N/A
Contributions Deductible: Yes
Top of Staff Salary Range: $40,000 (1987)
Meets NCIB Standards: no determination (6/17/88)

Purpose: "To improve the health status of black South Africans" and to provide scholarships to black South Africans for training in the health professions

Comments: The editor deemed this organization too small (under $1 million in expenditures in the most recent year reported) to be given a complete listing.

NATIONAL LEAGUE OF FAMILIES OF AMERICAN PRISONERS MISSING IN SOUTHEAST ASIA (National League of POW-MIA Families)

1001 Connecticut Ave., NW Suite 219
Washington, DC 20036
(202) 223-6846

Purpose: To seek to "obtain the release of all prisoners, the fullest possible accounting for the missing and the repatriation of remains of those who died serving our nation" in Southeast Asia

Comments: NCIB is currently preparing a new report on this organization.

OVERSEAS DEVELOPMENT COUNCIL

1717 Massachusetts Ave., NW, Suite 501
Washington, DC 20036
(202) 234-8701

Year of Data: 1987
Expenditures: $1,374,227
Percent to Program: 57.9%
Fund-raising Costs: 2.3%
Contributions Deductible: Yes
Top of Staff Salary Range: $80,000 (1989)
Meets NCIB Standards: Yes (4/27/89)

Purpose: To increase "American understanding of the economic and social problems confronting the developing countries and of the interests of the United States in their development progress. Toward this end, the Council functions as a center for policy research and analysis, a forum for exchange of ideas, and a resource for public education."

Program: The largest category of ODC's program expenditures for fiscal 1987 (32% of total expenditures) was public education projects undertaken to increase the American public's understanding of the problems of development in low-income countries; included were two publications. Other activities included a research study of politics and economics of developing countries; a series of meetings for Congressional staff concerning food and development issues; a national public opinion survey about American attitudes toward development issues; and research, meetings and public education devoted to Mexico-United States relations.

Comments: NCIB reports that ODC's low (57.9%) program expenditures are the result of miscalculations and that the correct figure is within the requirements of Standard 6a. NCIB recommends improvements in ODC's annual report and budget presentation.

PEOPLE TO PEOPLE INTERNATIONAL

501 East Armour Boulevard
Kansas City, MO 64109
(816) 531-4701

Purpose: To "foster contact and exchange of ideas between the people of different countries with each other; improve individual understanding of cultures of the world; and establish a force of friendship to assist all mankind in its quest for world peace"

Comments: NCIB is currently preparing a new report on this organization.

UNITED NATIONS ASSOCIATION OF THE UNITED STATES OF AMERICA, INC.

485 Fifth Avenue, 2nd Fl.
New York, NY 10017
(212) 697-3232

Year of Data: 1986
Expenditures $3,032,507
Percent to Program: 71.4%
Fund-raising Costs: 15.9%
Contributions Deductible: Yes
Top of Staff Salary Range: $75,280 (1986)
Meets NCIB Standards: Yes (2/2/88)

Purpose: To "contribute to the strengthening of multilateral mechanisms and to encourage US leadership in solving global problems"

Program: Fiscal 1986 activities included:
- Policy Studies (20%) - costs of three programs of conferences, research papers and reports, which focus on political, economic and security issues in the United States' relationships with Japan, China and the Soviet Union; activities of an Economic Policy Council which orchestrates involvement in international economic problems by the American private sector
- Multilateral Issues and Institutions (19%) - including studies of the peaceful uses of outer space, of management and decision-making at the United Nations and of policy coordination among Western nations at the United Nations
- Chapters, Divisions and Memberships (5%) - costs of providing information, guidance and program materials to chapters and divisions

Comments: In 1988, UNA-USA reported 165 state and local chapters and divisions and about 20,000 members. NCIB recommends improvements in UNA-USA's annual report.

WORLD POLICY INSTITUTE, INC.

777 United Nations Plaza
New York, NY 10017
(212) 490-0010

Year of Data: 1986
Expenditures $1,233,223
Percent to Program: 78%
Fund-raising Costs: 7.5%
Contributions Deductible: Yes
Top of Staff Salary Range: $85,000 (1987)
Meets NCIB Standards: Yes (8/19/87)

Purpose: To address "both national and world economic and security issues through research, publishing and public education. The Institute seeks to develop and promote positive, practical policies for the United States and other concerned nations. Its policy recommendations stress: economic growth; conflict resolution through political and legal means; and thoughtful ways to reduce dependence on military force, especially nuclear weapons."

Program: WPI's reporting of its activities does not allow a detailed breakdown of its programs. In general, WPI commissions speeches and articles for its own and other publications on such subjects as military expenditures, military policy, domestic economic policies, international trade and finance matters and regional problems in Central America, the Middle East and Asia. WPI disseminates information in its quarterly journal, in mailings and in publications on such topics as world military and social expenditures, international law and sexism.

Comments: NCIB reports that the low attendance at meetings of WPI's Board of Directors suggests that the organization's Executive Committee is actually functioning as its controlling body, with the other trustees serving primarily in an advisory capacity. NCIB recommends improvements in WPI's annual report.

YOUTH FOR UNDERSTANDING, INC.

3501 Newark Street, NW
Washington, DC 20016
(202) 966-6800

Year of Data: 1987
Expenditures $20,507,475
Percent to Program: 86%
Fund-raising Costs: 12.7%
Contributions Deductible: Yes
Top of Staff Salary Range: $96,100 (1987)
Meets NCIB Standards: Yes (9/21/88)

Purpose: To increase understanding between people and cultures by providing opportunities for teenagers worldwide to experience family life in another country

Program: Fiscal 1987 activities included:
- Student Direct Services (52%) - direct expenses for 7,300 student exchanges, including travel, orientation and language tutoring; exchanges are of students 14-18 years of age and may be for a year, a semester, a summer, or in the case of sports exchanges, a month; YFU also administers government- and corporate-sponsored scholarships which support special exchanges like the Congress-Bundestag Youth Exchange
- Student Support (34%) - costs of support activities relating to student exchanges

Comments: YFU is an international organization with headquarters in Washington, DC, 13 regional offices in the U.S. and 26 national organizations around the world. In fiscal 1987, about 77% of YFU's support came from program fees from participants. NCIB recommends improvements in YFU's budget presentation and audited financial statements.

- **AFRICAN WILDLIFE FOUNDATION, INC.** (see ANIMAL-RELATED)
- **AMERICA THE BEAUTIFUL FUND** (see THE ENVIRONMENT)
- **AMERICAN FRIENDS SERVICE COMMITTEE** (see INTERNATIONAL RELIEF)
- **ASSOCIATION FOR VOLUNTARY SURGICAL CONTRACEPTION** (see HEALTH-GENERAL)
- **CLERGY AND LAITY CONCERNED and CLERGY AND LAITY CONCERNED FOUNDATION** (see SOCIAL ACTION)

- **CONSERVATION INTERNATIONAL FOUNDATION** (see THE ENVIRON-MENT)
- **DUCKS UNLIMITED, INC.** (see ANIMAL-RELATED)
- **FRIENDS OF THE EARTH, INC. and FRIENDS OF THE EARTH FOUNDA-TION** (see THE ENVIRONMENT)
- **GREENPEACE USA** (see THE ENVIRONMENT)
- **INTERACTION: AMERICAN COUNCIL FOR VOLUNTARY INTERNATIONAL ACTION** (see INTERNATIONAL RELIEF)
- **NATIONAL COUNCIL OF NEGRO WOMEN, INC.** (see SOCIAL ACTION)
- **NATIONAL 4-H COUNCIL** (see YOUTH DEVELOPMENT)
- **NATURAL RESOURCES DEFENSE COUNCIL, INC.** (see THE ENVIRONMENT)
- **THE NATURE CONSERVANCY** (see THE ENVIRONMENT)
- **HUGH O'BRIAN YOUTH FOUNDATION** (see YOUTH DEVELOPMENT)
- **POPULATION CRISIS COMMITTEE/ DRAPER WORLD POPULATION FUND** (see SOCIAL ACTION)
- **THE POPULATION INSTITUTE** (see SOCIAL ACTION)
- **STARLIGHT FOUNDATION** (see HEALTH-GENERAL)
- **UNION OF CONCERNED SCIENTISTS** (see THE ENVIRONMENT)
- **UNITARIAN UNIVERSALIST SERVICE COMMITTEE, INC.** (see INTER-NATIONAL RELIEF)
- **UNITED STATES OLYMPIC COM-MITTEE** (see RECREATION)
- **WORLD RESOURCES INSTITUTE and WORLD RESOURCES INSTITUTE FUND** (see THE ENVIRONMENT)
- **YMCA OF THE UNITED STATES** (see HUMAN SERVICES)

INTERNATIONAL RELIEF

food, medicine and technical aid, development, aid to refugees, child sponsorship, disaster relief

ACCION INTERNATIONAL

130 Prospect Street
Cambridge, MA 02139
(617) 492-4930

Year of Data: 1986
Expenditures: $1,324,582
Percent to Program: 88.3%
Fund-raising Costs: 16.2%
Contributions Deductible: Yes
Top of Staff Salary Range: $55,000 (1987)
Meets NCIB Standards: Yes (10/7/87)

Purpose: To combat "poverty and unemployment in Latin America and the Caribbean," through creation of jobs and increasing income of "the poorest of the economically active"

Program: Fiscal 1986 activities included:
- Foreign Micro Business program (75%) - creates and assists efforts to generate employment in very small businesses of the poor in the Caribbean and Latin America
- Public Education (6%) - efforts to educate the private sector on economic development

Comments: In 1986, about 57% of total cash support came from agencies of U.S. government. NCIB recommends improvements in AI's annual report and audited financial statements.

AFGHANISTAN RELIEF COMMITTEE

NCIB reports that, as of July 1, 1990, this organization has not, over a period of several years, furnished requested information sufficient to prepare a report.

THE AFRICA FUND (affiliated with AMERICAN COMMITTEE ON AFRICA)

198 Broadway
New York, NY 10038
(212) 962-1210

Year of Data: ACA: **1984**; AF: **1984**
Expenditures ACA: $121,997; AF: $233,721
Percent to Program: ACA: 84.5%; AF: 83.2%
Fund-raising Costs: ACA: 9.5%; AF: 13.2%
Contributions Deductible: ACA: No; AF: Yes
Top of Staff Salary Range: ACA: $10,742 (1985); AF:
$11,092 (1986)
Meets NCIB Standards: ACA: Yes (5/6/86); AF: Yes
(5/6/86)

Purpose: ACOA's purpose is to "support African independence and majority rule." AF "provides humanitarian aid to Africans struggling for independence and promotes public understanding of African issues...."

Comments: The editor deemed NCIB's information about this organization too dated (1985 data or before) to give the organization a complete listing.

AFRICAN ENTERPRISE

P.O. Box 727
Pasadena, CA 91017
(818) 357-8811

Year of Data: 1986
Expenditures: $1,276,670
Percent to Program: 80.3%
Fund-raising Costs: 9.6%
Contributions Deductible: Yes
Top of Staff Salary Range: $35,000 (1985)
Meets NCIB Standards: Yes (1/27/87)

Purpose: To "respond to the invitation of local African churches and groups of churches to assist them in evangelism, and—in that context—to also help them meet emergency human needs"

Program: Fiscal 1986 activities included:
- Evangelism and Ministry (58%) - outreach activities to churches, interchurch groups, universities and others for the purpose of "evangelism, discipling, and leadership training," primarily in Africa
- Relief Projects (12%) - provision of short-term supplies of food, clothing, medicine, immunization and shelter in Africa, where need arises due to such circumstances as war and natural disasters

- Mission Challenge and Publication (11%) - efforts to develop awareness in "the North American and European church of the ministry, needs and progress of Africa and ... on the work of the church in Africa"

Comments: NCIB reports that AE had a negative $5,233 in assets available for use as of June 30, 1986. NCIB recommends improvements in AE's annual report and audited financial statements.

AFRICARE

440 R Street, NW
Washington, DC 20001
(202) 462-3614

Year of Data: **1985**
Expenditures $8,132,839
Percent to Program: 83.6%
Fund-raising Costs: 2.5%
Contributions Deductible: Yes
Top of Staff Salary Range: $53,460 (1986)
Meets NCIB Standards: Yes (4/17/87)

Purpose: "To assist in the improvement of the health of the people of Africa, including improvement of health resulting from economic, agricultural, educational and social development in harmony with the environment"

Comments: The editor deemed NCIB's information about this organization too dated (1985 data or before) to give the organization a complete listing.

AMERICAN FRIENDS SERVICE COMMITTEE

1501 Cherry Street
Philadelphia, PA 19102-1479
(215) 241-7000 or (800) 342-5796

Year of Data: 1987
Expenditures: $18,842,354
Percent to Program: 73.9%
Fund-raising Costs: 11%
Contributions Deductible: Yes
Top of Staff Salary Range: $50,703 (1988)
Meets NCIB Standards: Yes (10/6/88)

Purpose: To promote "economic and social justice, international understanding, human rights and the relief of suffering, peace, reconciliation and disarmament" and other domestic and international concerns

Program: Fiscal 1987 activities included:
- International (26%) - including opening a center to support parents and teachers in the Gaza Strip; providing emergency shelter, food and medicines for displaced people in Lebanon; support for "small-scale irrigation projects" in Laos and Kampuchea; installing rice de-hullers in villages in Guinea-Bissau; shipping clothing, bedding, cloth and medical supplies to Mozambique; and shipping 6,000 pounds of school supplies donated by U.S. children to Nicaragua
- Peace Education (22%) - holding a seminar on Soviet-American relations; arranging for a speaking tour for three Nicaraguan teachers to publicize "the struggle in their country;" production of books on the Middle East and Korea and of a documentary on South Africa
- Community Relations (18%) - including opening a center for homeless women and children in Boston; speaking out in the media on welfare reform; immigration policy; "abuse of immigrant communities;" the "prolonged detention of Cubans in Atlanta and Louisiana;" the working environment in U.S.-owned corporations in Mexico; providing legal aid to Guatamalan and Salvadoran refugees; and teaching Indians in South Dakota about diet and disease

Comments: Though AFSC arose from and continues a close association with various bodies of the Religious Society of Friends (Quakers), it administers its welfare and relief services on a non-sectarian basis and regardless of the ideology of the government involved.

AMERICAN NEAR EAST REFUGEE AID, INC.
1522 K Street, NW, Suite 202
Washington, DC 20005
(202) 347-2558

Year of Data: 1988
Expenditures: $2,857,137
Percent to Program: 87.4%
Fund-raising Costs: 11.2%
Contributions Deductible: Yes
Top of Staff Salary Range: $71,000 (1988)
Meets NCIB Standards: Yes (2/16/89)

Purpose: To further American understanding of the Arab refugee problem and to support programs for needy individuals in the Near East, especially those aimed at "the long-term development needs of Palestinians and Lebanese"

Program: Fiscal 1988 activities included:
- Community and Economic Development (57%) - major projects included construction of slaughter houses and a wholesale produce market and training of personnel in the West Bank and Gaza; establishment of agricultural mechanized units with West Bank cooperatives; and support of dairy and livestock cooperatives in the West Bank
- Education (16%) - grants for scholarships for Lebanese and Palestinian university students and for orphaned, destitute and handicapped children in the West Bank and Lebanon; operational funds for education; grants for construction and the purchase of equipment
- Health Services (12%) - cash grants and in-kind grants of pharmaceuticals and medical supplies for hospitals and clinics in Lebanon; support for instruction and organization in health services; provision of food, shelter, clothing, blankets and clinic services to victims of conflict

Comments: ANERA solicits individual "sponsorships" of $85-100 per child for one-year scholarships. About 64% of ANERA's cash support in fiscal 1988 was from U.S. government grants.

AMERICAN REFUGEE COMMITTEE

2344 Nicollet Avenue South, Suite 350
Minneapolis, MN 55404
(612) 872-7060

Year of Data: 1987
Expenditures: $1,777,071
Percent to Program: 82.5%
Fund-raising Costs: 5.2%
Contributions Deductible: Yes
Top of Staff Salary Range: $82,600 (1989)
Meets NCIB Standards: Yes (1/18/89)

Purpose: To provide nutritional aid, medical care, training and related support services to refugees harbored in Thailand and Sudan and to operate educational and self-reliance programs in Minnesota and Chicago designed to help refugees adjust to life in the United States

Program: Fiscal 1987 activities included:

- International (68%) - administration of 14 projects in two refugee camps in Thailand and 14 projects in two camps in Sudan; services to 214,500 refugees, including 11,000 admissions to ARC hospitals and 278,000 refugee visits to ARC out-patient departments; supplemental food rations for 1,400 refugees in Sudan; publication and distribution of 6,500 copies of ARC's medic, nursing and health worker training manual

- Resettlement (15%) - operation of six projects in Minnesota and five in Illinois, serving over 4,700 refugees; services include physical and mental health information and support for education of refugees in "information, attitudes and skills needed to move toward self-sufficiency and become integrated with American mainstream society"

Comments: Approximately 38% of ARC's total revenue in 1987 was in government grants. The percentage of government support has generally declined in recent years; in 1985 it was 58%. NCIB recommends improvements in ARC's annual report.

AMERICARES FOUNDATION, INC.

161 Cherry Street
New Canaan, CT 06840
(203) 966-5195 or (800) 666-HOPE

Year of Data: 1988
Expenditures: $4,132,969
Percent to Program: 69.7%
Fund-raising Costs: 15.9%
Contributions Deductible: Yes
Top of Staff Salary Range: $90,000 (1989)
Meets NCIB Standards: Yes (1/26/90)

Purpose: To "provide medicines, pharmaceutical supplies and other needed items to people in crisis areas all over the world, and to help to ameliorate the suffering wherever and whenever disasters strike"

Program: AF reported all of its fiscal 1988 spending in a single program category, which included shipment of medicines and medical supplies to such disaster areas as Poland, Soviet Armenia, El Salvador, Guatemala, Honduras and Lebanon. This activity accounted for 70% of AF's cash expenditures, but involved delivery of $44 million worth of donated medical, food and disaster-relief supplies, equipment, facilities and services. Other activities included dispatch of doctors, medicines and equipment to treat emergency patients on a short-term voluntary basis; leprosy treatment projects in Venezuela and Brazil; and support for projects and individuals that work on behalf of disadvantaged people in the United States.

Comments: In addition to its cash income of $5,939,130 in fiscal 1988, AF reported over $41 million in donated medical, food and other disaster relief supplies and over $675,000 in contributed services, donated facilities and equipment.

THE PEARL S. BUCK FOUNDATION, INC.

Green Hills Farm
P.O. Box 181
Perkasie, PA 18944
(215) 249-0100

> Year of Data: **1985**
> Expenditures $3,111,491
> Percent to Program: 78.2%
> Fund-raising Costs: 14.9%
> Contributions Deductible: Yes
> Top of Staff Salary Range: $55,000 (1986)
> Meets NCIB Standards: Yes (3/18/87)

Purpose: To provide supplemental aid to Amerasian children in five Asian countries

Comments: The editor deemed NCIB's information about this organization too dated (1985 data or before) to give the organization a complete listing.

CARE, INC.

660 First Avenue
New York, NY 10016
(212) 686-3110 or (800) 242-GIVE

> Year of Data: 1987
> Expenditures: $116,065,000
> Percent to Program: 81.6%
> Fund-raising Costs: 41.7%
> Contributions Deductible: Yes
> Top of Staff Salary Range: $104,400 (1988)
> Meets NCIB Standards: Yes (4/27/89)

Purpose: To "help the developing world's poor in their efforts to achieve social and economic well-being"

Program: CARE's reporting of its activities does not allow a detailed breakdown of its programs. Fiscal 1987 activities included agricultural programs in Chad and Bangladesh; agroforestry projects involving planting 22 million seedlings in 23 countries; provision of food supplements to women and school children; promoting the health of mothers in 20 countries; vaccination programs in 17 countries; 29 small enterprise development projects; and emergency relief in countries experiencing calamities and political upheaval

Comments: CARE USA is a member of CARE International, an umbrella organization which coordinates activities of member organizations in eight countries. In fiscal 1987, CARE USA provided 93% of the support for CARE International. NCIB's report concerns CARE USA only. In fiscal 1987, about 59% of CARE's total cash support came from government grants. In addition, CARE received $172,548,000 in agricultural commodities and ocean freight and $11,857,000 in "contributions-in-kind" from the U.S. and other governments. NCIB recommends improvements in CARE's annual report.

CHILDREN, INCORPORATED

1000 Westover Road
P.O. Box 5381
Richmond, VA 23220
(804) 359-4562

> Year of Data: 1989
> Expenditures: $3,950,769
> Percent to Program: 80.6%
> Fund-raising Costs: 16.1%
> Contributions Deductible: Yes
> Top of Staff Salary Range: $65,000 (1989)
> Meets NCIB Standards: Yes (5/30/90)

Purpose: To assist "children of all races and creeds, administering to their physical, mental and spiritual needs"

Program: CI's reporting of its finances does not allow a detailed breakdown of expenses. In general, CI provides care and supplemental aid to children in orphanages, missions and schools that are administered and largely financed by others; in fiscal 1989, CI provided about $1.7 million (43% of its total expenditures) to 194 affiliated programs, aiding about 14,900 children in 24 countries, including the United States; funds assisted individuals (food, clothing, school supplies, medical needs and personal necessities) and communities (repair of buildings and equipment, provision of desks, physical training equipment, sanitary supplies and supplementary funds for teacher salaries)

Comments: CI offers sponsorships of children at $21 per month; it had obtained 13,624 sponsorships by June 30, 1989. The organization provides information to sponsors regarding gifts to sponsored children and helps make sure that the children spend any money sent according to the sponsor's wishes. NCIB recommends improvements in CI's annual report.

CHILDREN INTERNATIONAL (formerly Holy Land Christian Mission)

2000 East Red Bridge Road
Kansas City, MO 64131
(816) 942-2000

Year of Data: 1989
Expenditures: $23,247,933
Percent to Program: 73.3%
Fund-raising Costs: 17.2%
Contributions Deductible: Yes
Top of Staff Salary Range: $125,700 (1989)
Meets NCIB Standards: Yes (7/5/90)

Purpose: "Improving the quality of life and meeting the needs of orphans, widows, crippled children and other poor people throughout the world"

Program: Fiscal 1989 activities included:

- Children International Sponsorship (53%) - operation of a child sponsorship program for 104,000 children in Colombia, Guatemala, Ecuador, Honduras, Chile, Israel, India, the Philippines, Thailand and the Dominican Republic; provision of food, clothing, medical care, books, educational opportunities and community health programs; a Widow's Aid and Sponsorship program provides food, medicine and kerosene heater to help 400 widows
- Bethlehem Hospital and Orphan Home (14%) - costs of operating a fourteen-building complex in Bethlehem, Israel, including an orphanage, a 68-bed hospital, a Christian school and a church
- Mission Outreach (7%) - expenses of making Christian training and counseling available for the poor and needy in CI's projects; includes publication of quarterly newsletters

Comments: CI asks child sponsors to pay $12 per month to support one child.

CHILDREN'S AID INTERNATIONAL

6720 Melrose Avenue
P.O. Box 480155
Los Angeles, CA 90048
(213) 519-8923
(800) 842-2810 outside CA

Purpose: To "give emergency medical and nutritional support to children and their families displaced by war and turbulence; create and guide long-term programs for children and their families, especially in the Third World; and obtain maximum involvement of local professionals and organizations"

Comments: NCIB is currently preparing a new report on this organization.

THE CHILDREN'S MERCY FUND (COUNCIL FOR INTERNATIONAL DEVELOPMENT; formerly The Mercy Fund)

1000 Potomac Street, NW
Plaza 100
Washington, DC 20001
(202) 965-5404

Year of Data: 1986
Expenditures: $2,034,560
Percent to Program: 35.2%
Fund-raising Costs: 52.9%
Contributions Deductible: Yes
Top of Staff Salary Range: $77,760 (1986)
Meets NCIB Standards: No: 1, 4; insufficient information: 2-5, 6-8 (7/23/87)

Purpose: To "serve the disadvantaged by becoming involved in medical and humanitarian activities around the world.... [and to establish] a public donor information program to better acquaint the American public with the plight and needs of these disadvantaged people"

Program: CMF's reporting of its activities does not allow a detailed breakdown of its programs and expenses. In general its fiscal 1985 activities included distribution of over $450,000 worth of dried milk, clothing and medical supplies; programs to feed hungry children in Africa; and medical and humanitarian assistance to Afghans in Afghanistan and Pakistan.

Comments: CMF has solicited contributions in the names of The Mercy Fund and the Afghan Mercy Fund. NCIB reports that it had difficulties in receiving up-to-date information from CMF. It faults the organization for its high fund-raising costs and low program spending (Standard 4) and for questionable family and financial relationships centering on the group's chairman of the board (Standard 1). NCIB states that it could not determine the extent of CMF's participation in programs it claimed as its own in its descriptive and promotional materials. In 1987, CMF released a new statement of purpose.

CHRISTIAN CHILDREN'S FUND, INC.

Box 26511
Richmond, VA 23261
(804) 644-4654 or (800) 776-6767

Year of Data: 1988
Expenditures: $91,592,600
Percent to Program: 81.2%
Fund-raising Costs: 10%
Contributions Deductible: Yes
Top of Staff Salary Range: $100,000 (1988)
Meets NCIB Standards: Yes (7/24/89)

Purpose: To provide supplemental aid to homeless children and families with children in the United States and other countries

Program: CCF provided aid to over 1,400 projects in 23 countries during fiscal 1988; types of projects supported include day care centers, educational projects, community-based projects, residential projects and social service centers. Fiscal 1988 activities included:

- Services for Children's Support in the Family (68%) - assistance to children who have some degree of family affiliation
- Children's Education (12%) - assistance to projects which provide primary or secondary education to children

Comments: NCIB points out that CCF uses the appeal of person-to-person giving in its fund-raising; sponsors are asked to donate $21 per month for the sponsorship of an individual child. But CCF's program provides only supplementary financial aid to projects. All sponsored children are primarily supported by others and the CCF sponsor's gift does not generally provide enough help to care for a child in most countries.

COMPASSION INTERNATIONAL, INC.

3955 Cragwood Drive
P.O. Box 7000
Colorado Springs, CO 80933
(719) 594-9900

Year of Data: 1988
Expenditures: $26,628,845
Percent to Program: 80%
Fund-raising Costs: 14.2%
Contributions Deductible: Yes
Top Employee Salary: $75,000 (1988)
Meets NCIB Standards: Yes (7/7/89)

Purpose: To "help support needy children physically and spiritually in developing countries" and "to proclaim the Gospel of Jesus Christ"

Program: CII's reporting of its activities does not allow a detailed breakdown of its programs. Fiscal 1988 activities included child sponsorship programs in 29 countries, including the United States, providing 114,090 sponsored children with schooling, vocational training, religious education, food, clothing and medical care; a separate program providing meals for 10,874 needy children; a School Program which "allows children to attain a formal education by attending private evangelical Christian schools;" a Family Helper Program which supports education and other needs of children living at home; a Scholarship Program which helps students continue their education at schools distant from their home villages; Student Centers which assist children in evangelical churches with their formal and non-formal learning; Children's Homes which house orphans and abandoned children; and Special Care Centers which provide assistance to physically or mentally handicapped children in hospitals, clinics and day-care centers.

Comments: CII sponsors contribute $21 per month to provide for individual children; an $8 per month program provides meals; in 1988, sponsorship comprised 52% of income. CII provides sponsors with photographs and biographical information about children and encourages correspondence between sponsors and children.

DIRECT RELIEF INTERNATIONAL

Post Office Box 41929
Santa Barbara, CA 93103
(805) 687-3694 or (800) 422-9243

Year of Data: 1988
Expenditures $989,267
Percent to Program: 63.0%
Fund-raising Costs: 24.1%
Contributions Deductible: Yes
Top of Staff Salary Range: $28,761 (1989)
Meets NCIB Standards: Yes (11/28/89)

Purpose: To "assist people in medically less-developed areas to help themselves by supplying them with the means to improve health delivery systems; and to provide relief to victims of natural disaster, civil strife and economic displacement"

Comments: The editor deemed this organization too small (under $1 million in expenditures in the most recent year reported) to be given a complete listing.

THOMAS A. DOOLEY FOUNDATION/INTERMED - USA, INC.

420 Lexington Avenue, Suite 2428
New York, NY 10170
(212) 687-3620

Year of Data: 1986
Expenditures $495,370
Percent to Program: 47.1%
Fund-raising Costs: 24.2%
Contributions Deductible: Yes
Top of Staff Salary Range: $60,000 (1987)
Meets NCIB Standards: No: 1,3,4 (1/12/88)

Purpose: "Providing equipment, supplies, personnel and financial support for the improvement of the health services of underdeveloped countries with emphasis directed toward training and education"

Comments: The editor deemed this organization too small (under $1 million in expenditures in the most recent year reported) to be given a complete listing.

FOOD FOR THE HUNGRY, INC.

7729 E. Greenway Road
Scottsdale, AZ 85260
(602) 998-3100

Year of Data: **1984**
Expenditures $9,747,357
Percent to Program: 75.9%
Fund-raising Costs: 17.5%
Contributions Deductible: Yes
Top of Staff Salary Range: $42,000 (1985)
Meets NCIB Standards: Yes (3/25/86)

Purpose: "To provide food and material aid for disaster relief, to conduct ongoing relief and rehabilitation programs, to inform people about the problem of world hunger, to eliminate causes of hunger through development of projects aimed at self-reliance and to develop small scale technologies and educational programs concerning the needs of developing nations." Food for the Hungry states that it finds its "motivation and service example in the life and teaching of Jesus Christ;" it "seeks to satisfy both physical and spiritual hunger."

Comments: The editor deemed NCIB's information about this organization too dated (1985 data or before) to give the organization a complete listing.

FREEDOM FROM HUNGER FOUNDATION

1644 DaVinci Court
P.O. Box 2000
Davis, CA 95617
(916) 758-6200

Year of Data: 1987
Expenditures: $3,718,286
Percent to Program: 78%
Fund-raising Costs: 18%
Contributions Deductible: Yes
Top of Staff Salary Range: $85,000 (1988)
Meets NCIB Standards: Yes (11/4/88)

Purpose: "To improve the nutritional status of 0-5 year old children and pregnant and nursing women in developing communities overseas and in the U.S." and to "create opportunities for the hungry and poor to become part of the permanent solution to world hunger by establishing an on-going development process that is self-sustaining in the community...."

Program: Fiscal 1987 activities included:
• Latin America (22%) - programs in Honduras and Ecuador, including improv-

ing food production, processing and storage; developing agricultural cooperatives; training health center staff; training volunteers in health and sanitation; monitoring the health of children
- Africa (21%) - programs in Togo, Sierra Leone and Kenya, including organizing and training village development committees; training health workers; monitoring the health of children and pregnant women; vaccinating children; and assisting agricultural development
- Asia (11%) - programs in Nepal and Thailand, including training village volunteers in gardening, sanitation and child survival practices; funding for pit latrine construction; distributing seeds, chicks and ducklings; training in health, nutrition and family planning
- United States (8%) - programs in Arizona and Mississippi, including nutrition education programs; promoting coordination between poor rural communities and state agencies; promoting self-help and mutual-help solutions to nutrition and health problems

Comments: In fiscal 1987, about 31% of FHF's revenues came from the U.S. Agency for International Development. NCIB recommends improvements in FHF's audited financial statements.

FRIENDS OF SOS CHILDREN'S VILLAGES

NCIB reports that, as of July 1, 1990, this organization has not, over a period of several years, furnished requested information sufficient to prepare a report.

FUTURES FOR CHILDREN, INC.,
805 Tijeras NW
Albuquerque, NM 87102
(505) 247-4700 or (800) 545-6843

Year of Data: 1988
Expenditures: $969,288
Percent to Program: 80.6%
Fund-raising Costs: 9.7%
Contributions Deductible: Yes
Top of Staff Salary Range: $52,500 (1988)
Meets NCIB Standards: Yes (2/1/89)

Purpose: To "assist underprivileged families and communities [especially American Indian communities in the Southwest], by means of self-help projects, to help themselves to raise their standard of living and, therefore, better insure the futures of their children"

Comments: The editor deemed this organization too small (under $1 million in expenditures in the most recent year reported) to be given a complete listing.

HEIFER PROJECT INTERNATIONAL
1015 S. Louisiana
Little Rock, AR 72202
(501) 376-6836

Year of Data: 1988
Expenditures: $7,553,499
Percent to Program: 66%
Fund-raising Costs: 28.7%
Contributions Deductible: Yes
Top of Staff Salary Range: $61,000 (1988)
Meets NCIB Standards: Yes (5/1/90)

Purpose: To work "through livestock development programs to improve the nutrition and increase the resources of those most in need of freedom from hunger and the oppression of poverty"

Program: Fiscal 1988 activities included:
- Shipment of Animals, Semen, Equipment and Supplies (30%) - including distribution of 165 dairy cows, 390 dairy goats, 265 sheep, 241 hogs, over 16,000 chickens and 100 alpacas to farmers in Latin America and the Caribbean; and 110 beef cattle, 55 dairy cattle, 32 goats, 44 sheep, 218 swine and 58 rabbits to projects in the U.S. and Canada
- Public Education (14%) - costs of speakers, literature, books and workshops for curriculum and teacher development
- Project Administration (12%) - review,

design, administration and evaluation of projects

- International Learning and Livestock Center (7%) - production and preparation of animals for shipment; adaptive research on selected species

Comments: NCIB recommends improvements in HPI's annual report, budget presentation and audited financial statements.

INTERACTION: AMERICAN COUNCIL FOR VOLUNTARY INTERNATIONAL ACTION

200 Park Avenue South
New York, NY 10003
(212) 777-8210
or
815 H Street, NW, 11th Fl.
Washington, DC 20006
(202) 822-8429

Year of Data: **1983**
Expenditures $1,282,559
Percent to Program: 78.4%
Fund-raising Costs: 14%
Contributions Deductible: Yes
Top of Staff Salary Range: $55,000 (1985)
Meets NCIB Standards: Yes (6/3/85)

Purpose: To "complement and enhance the effectiveness of its member organizations," over 100 American private and voluntary organizations working in "international development, relief and reconstruction, migration and refugee assistance, public policy and federal relations and education on Third World development issues ... and to strengthen the capacity of the private and voluntary agency community as a whole"

Comments: The editor deemed NCIB's information about this organization too dated (1985 data or before) to give the organization a complete listing.

INTERAID INC./INTERAID INTERNATIONAL

5217 Verdugo Way, Suite A
Camarillo, CA 93012
(805) 987-8888

Year of Data: 1987
Expenditures: $2,600,923
Percent to Program: 43.6%
Fund-raising Costs: N/A
Contributions Deductible: Yes

Top of Staff Salary Range: $75,996 (1987)
Meets NCIB Standards: No: 1, 6a, 4?, 7a?, 7c?
(7/19/89)

Purpose: To "teach and disseminate the Gospel of Jesus Christ throughout the world for the advancement of the Christian religion and Christian religious education, to fulfill the Christian commitment to help the needy and hurting people of this world in both material and spiritual ways; to establish and operate a Christian church, including, without limitation, the conduct of Christian worship, the ordination of ministers, and the ministration of all sacraments and sacerdotal functions"

Program: InterAid Inc.'s reporting of its financial data is incomplete and confuses its activities with those of InterAid International. Programs for 1987 appear to have included "International Christian Aid," which provided food, clothing, medical assistance, shelter and other relief aid for refugees and victims of natural disasters in Southeast Asia, Portugal, the Philippines, Central America, Mexico and Africa; and a "Child Sponsorship Program," which provided monthly assistance to needy children around the world, though it did not involve a direct relationship between a donor and an individual child.

Comments: InterAid Inc. is the U.S. fundraising affiliate of InterAid International, an evangelical religious organization with fundraising offices in 13 other countries. Both are headquartered in the U.S. and have the same board of directors. InterAid International also has divisions called International Christian Aid and Underground Evangelism. NCIB's report is primarily about the activities of InterAid Inc.

NCIB faults InterAid Inc. because its chief operating officer is president of its board and has veto power over decisions of the board (Standard 1) and because NCIB's analysis shows that program expenses were only about 43.6% of total expenditures (Standard 6a). NCIB also questions InterAid's adherence to Standards 4, 7a and 7c because the organization's publications do not explain its relationship with InterAid International, because its annual report described activities which had been conducted primarily by InterAid International and because the annual report failed to notify readers that audited financial statements were available upon request. InterAid Inc.'s audited financial statements for 1987 report that the United States Attorney and Postal Inspector, in conjunction with a Federal Grand Jury, had commenced an investigation into the organization's activities between 1973 and 1985. InterAid Inc. pledged to cooperate fully and quoted its attorneys as believing that no judgment against the organization was likely to result. NCIB recommends improvements in InterAid's budget and audited financial statements.

INTERNATIONAL EXECUTIVE SERVICE CORPS

8 Stamford Forum
P.O. Box 10005
Stamford, CT 06904-2005
(203) 967-6000

Year of Data: 1987
Expenditures: $13,491,580
Percent to Program: 83.4%
Fund-raising Costs: 17.8%
Contributions Deductible: Yes
Top of Staff Salary Range: $90,000 (1986)
Meets NCIB Standards: Yes (6/30/88)

Purpose: To help "locally owned private enterprises, government entities, educational, health care and other organizations ... in developing countries to increase their productivity, upgrade their management skills and improve their basic technologies"

Program: IESC's reporting of its activities does not allow a detailed breakdown of its programs. In general, IESC recruits retired U.S. executives and technical advisors to share their experience with businesses in developing nations as short-term volunteers. The organization maintains a "Skills Bank" of about 9,600 experienced volunteers. In 1987, IESC completed 633 projects in 56 developing countries. IESC charges fees based on the ability to pay.

Comments: NCIB reports that about 59% of IESC's total cash support in 1987 was from grants from the U. S. Agency for International Development. NCIB recommends improvements in IESC's annual report and audited financial statements.

INTERNATIONAL INSTITUTE OF RURAL RECONSTRUCTION

475 Riverside Drive, Room 1270
New York, NY 10015
(212) 870-2992

Year of Data: 1987
Expenditures: $2,878,579
Percent to Program: 81.5%
Fund-raising Costs: 26.2%
Contributions Deductible: Yes
Top of Staff Salary Range: $65,000 (1988)
Meets NCIB Standards: Yes (12/2/88)

Purpose: To help "rural people to help themselves to a better life through tested and successful programs of rural reconstruction"

Program: Fiscal 1987 activities included:
- Emergency Food Aid to Negros (42%) - distribution of food to the Island of Negros in the Philippines, funded by a one-time grant from the German Freedom from Hunger Campaign
- International Leadership Training (16%) - graduate level training of rural development administrators and others from developing countries; seminars and workshops for personnel of agencies in the Philippines
- International Extension (12%) - assistance to leaders of developing countries to establish private rural reconstruction movements to help peasant people; technical assistance to affiliated national movements
- Field Operational Research (11%) - studies of economic and social problems of peasant people and search for new strategies and approaches for solving them

Comments: In 1987, about 18% of IIRR's cash support came from restricted government grants. NCIB recommends improvements in IIRR's annual report.

INTERNATIONAL RESCUE COMMITTEE

386 Park Avenue South
New York, NY 10016
(212) 679-0010

Year of Data: 1988
Expenditures: $28,874,352
Percent to Program: 93.4%
Fund-raising Costs: 10.4%
Contributions Deductible: Yes
Top of Staff Salary Range: $60,300 (1989)
Meets NCIB Standards: Yes (8/3/89)

Purpose: To help "refugees who escape from religious, racial and political persecution in their countries"

Program: Fiscal 1988 activities included:
- Asia and the Near East (40%) - medical aid, public health, sanitation, education and self-help services to Afghan refugees in Pakistan and Vietnamese refugees in Thailand
- Resettlement in the USA (23%) - resettlement of 10,930 refugees from 22 countries, about half of them from Vietnam, Cambodia and Laos
- Europe (8%) - registration of almost 8,000 people seeking resettlement in the U.S., including Poles, Hungarians, Czechs, Soviets, Rumanians, Iranians, Afghans and Ethiopians; IRC's Spanish Refugee Aid division provided aid to non-communist refugees from the Spanish Civil War and their families
- Africa (8%) - aid to Ethiopian refugees in the Sudan and to Mozambican refugees in Malawi
- Latin America (7%) - programs in El Salvador and Costa Rica, including aid to Nicaraguan refugees

Comments: In 1988, about 69% of IRC's total support came from government grants.

MAP INTERNATIONAL

Box 50
Brunswick, GA 31520
(912) 265-6010 or (800) 225-8550

Year of Data: 1987
Expenditures: $4,406,717
Percent to Program: 69.5%
Fund-raising Costs: 33%
Contributions Deductible: Yes
Top of Staff Salary Range: $60,935 (1988)
Meets NCIB Standards: Yes (1/20/89)

Purpose: To "distribute medicines, equipment and supplies to Christian medical institutions outside of the United States, to provide disaster relief to other countries, to provide assistance to missions and indigenous Christian organizations in the Third World Countries in the design and implementation of development assistance projects, and to provide short-term overseas service for medically-trained persons"

Program: Fiscal 1987 activities included:
- Hospital Supplies, Procurement and Distribution (31%) - distribution of over $34 million in donated medicines and supplies to mission hospitals and agencies in 75 countries
- Community Health Services (19%) - programs to help health workers overseas eliminate causes of disease and teach preventative practices, including 35 workshops in Latin America and 24 in Africa
- International Health Education (10%) - production and distribution of MAP publications to health workers, training of health practitioners, responding to field requests for information and serving as a consultant to affiliated agencies in the United States and abroad

Comments: NCIB notes a $400,000 deficit in MAP's unrestricted fund balance as of December 31, 1987 and cautions that adherence to Standard 6 will depend on what future financial statements reveal about this deficit. NCIB recommends improvements in MAP's annual report.

NEAR EAST FOUNDATION

342 Madison Avenue
New York, NY 10173
(212) 867-0064

Purpose: To "construct, operate, maintain and direct, either alone or in conjunction with other agencies and schools, agricultural schools, model farms, schools for artisans, orphanages, hospitals and clinics in the Near East and in countries adjacent thereto"

Comments: NCIB is currently preparing a new report on this organization.

OEF INTERNATIONAL

1815 H Street, NW, 11th Fl.
Washington, DC 20006
(202) 466-3430

Year of Data: 1987
Expenditures: $3,504,429
Percent to Program: 71%
Fund-raising Costs: 25%
Contributions Deductible: Yes
Top of Staff Salary Range: $72,000 (1988)
Meets NCIB Standards: Yes (8/30/88)

Purpose: To design and deliver "training and technical assistance programs which address the economic and social needs of low-income women in developing countries" and "to increase public awareness about the critical roles of Third World women in development"

Program: Virtually all of OEF's program expenditures for fiscal 1987 (70% of total expenditures) were devoted to overseas economic development. Activities stressed establishment of small enterprises and included training women how to affect policy and how to access or change laws; organizational development and management training of OEF's local staffs, indigenous organizations and women's groups; and dissemination of training manuals, publications and films on women and small enterprises.

Comments: In fiscal 1987, about 81% of OEF's support came from government grants. NCIB recommends improvements in OEF's annual report and audited financial statements. OEF stands for Overseas Education Fund.

OUR LITTLE BROTHERS AND SISTERS, INC.

1210 Hillside Terrace
P.O. Box 3134
Alexandria, VA 22302
(703) 836-1233

Year of Data: 1988
Expenditures: $5,359,196
Percent to Program: 66.9%
Fund-raising Costs: 33.5%
Contributions Deductible: Yes
Top of Staff Salary Range: None (1988)
Meets NCIB Standards: ?: 4 (2/6/90)

Purpose: To solicit and provide funds for the support of Nuestros Pequenos Hermanos (NPH), which operates orphanages and other child care/education facilities in Mexico, Honduras and Haiti

Program: Virtually all of fiscal 1988 program spending (59% of total expenditures) was in direct support of NPH, which provides food, clothing, housing and education for over 1,100 orphaned children and young adults at several locations; OLBS also publishes a newsletter informing the public about the plight of orphaned children in its areas of operation (8%).

Comments: Other organizations soliciting funds for NPH are Friends of Our Little Brothers, in Phoenix, AZ, and NPH itself. In fiscal 1986, OLBS raised about 26% of NPH's total revenues, while NPH itself generated an additional 27% and the remainder came from other organizations in the U.S. and Europe. OLBS's fund-raising costs are about 20.6% of related United States contributions and about 38% of related European contributions. NCIB questions whether OLBS's promotional materials, which imply that OLBS and NPH are the same organization, accurately describe the organization's identity and programs (Standard 4).

OXFAM AMERICA, INC.

115 Broadway
Boston, MA 02116
(617) 482-1211

Year of Data: 1986
Expenditures: $11,336,577
Percent to Program: 73.5%
Fund-raising Costs: 20.9%
Contributions Deductible: Yes
Top of Staff Salary Range: $59,000 (1987)
Meets NCIB Standards: Yes (9/3/87)

Purpose: Reduction of poverty and physical need, and the promotion of long-term, self-sustaining development throughout the world

Program: Fiscal 1986 activities included:
- Overseas Grants (66%) - grants and projects to aid in self-help in Asia, Africa, Latin America and the Caribbean; including provision of oxen, seeds and tools to famine-afflicted areas in Ethiopia; development projects to benefit indigenous Indian peoples in South America; a food program for sugar workers and their families on Negros Island in the Philippines; also, petitioning against the U.S. government's refusal to allow shipment of

farming and construction tools to displaced peasants in Nicaragua
- Education (8%) - promoting understanding of poverty and third world development problems; distribution of publications, films and slide shows

Comments: OA is one of seven autonomous Oxfam organizations and often cooperates with other Oxfams and other international voluntary agencies. NCIB recommends improvements in OA's annual report. Oxfam stands for the Oxford Committee for Famine Relief.

PAN AMERICAN DEVELOPMENT FOUNDATION, INC.
1889 F Street, NW
Washington, DC 20006
(202) 458-3969

Year of Data: 1987
Expenditures: $6,593,855
Percent to Program: 86%
Fund-raising Costs: 14.8%
Contributions Deductible: Yes
Top of Staff Salary Range: $65,000 (1988)
Meets NCIB Standards: Yes (8/17/88)

Purpose: To "strengthen the ability of the private sector of Latin America and the Caribbean to participate in economic and social development"

Program: Fiscal 1987 activities included:
- Development Foundations (38%) - efforts to encourage private sector leaders to become founders of national development foundations to provide business assistance and credit to low-income citizens; regional training seminars and forums for boards and staff of the foundations
- Income Generating Program (31%) - programs supported by the U.S. Agency for International Development for planting five million trees in Haiti and for training in resource development and conservation practices in the Dominican Republic; support for cocoa production and marketing projects in Central America and the Caribbean
- Health Services (10%) - distribution of donated medical equipment and supplies, valued at over 3.7 million, to hospitals and clinics in Latin America

and the Caribbean; assistance to vocational training institutions in Central America and the Caribbean for development of curriculum in the maintenance and repair of medical equipment
- Tools for Training Program (6%) - distribution of donated hand tools, heavy machinery, buses, boats, laboratory instruments, equipment and supplies, valued at over $2.2 million, to schools and vocational training centers

Comments: In fiscal 1987, about 58% of PADF's support came from "Grants, primarily U.S. government." NCIB recommends improvements in PADF's budget presentation and audited financial statements.

PARTNERS OF THE AMERICAS
(formerly National Association of the Partners of the Americas, Inc.)
1424 K Street, NW
Washington, DC 20005
(202) 628-3300

Year of Data: 1987
Expenditures: $6,533,777
Percent to Program: 94.8%
Fund-raising Costs: less than 1%
Contributions Deductible: Yes
Top of Staff Salary Range: $85,000 (1988)
Meets NCIB Standards: Yes (8/12/88)

Purpose: To promote "economic and social development throughout the Western Hemisphere"

Program: Fiscal 1987 activities included:
- Economic and Social Development (44%) - support for volunteer work to help local citizens enhance agricultural and rural development, small business opportunities, health care and nutrition and preparedness for natural and man-made disasters
- Partnership Development (27%) - managerial support, leadership training and guidance for the 60 affiliated partnerships
- Community Education (9%) - efforts to promote cooperative decision-making and the maximum use of human and financial resources to solve local problems
- Educational and Cultural Projects (8%) - educational, cultural and sports ex-

change programs, including promotion of exchanges of community leaders, youth and university professors
• Rehabilitation (6%) - international efforts to address human development needs of people with physical and mental handicaps

Comments: POA's headquarters office is supported by corporate, foundation and government funds and provides technical assistance and grants to affiliated Partners programs. The Partners raise 85-90% of their funds locally and get the rest from the national office. NCIB's report is about the national headquarters only, and does not concern the activities or finances of affiliated Partners. In fiscal 1987, about 73% of POA's support came from government grants. NCIB recommends improvements in POA's annual report.

PLAN INTERNATIONAL (U.S.A.) (formerly Foster Parents Plan, Inc. (U.S.A))

155 Plan Way
Warwick, RI 02886
(401) 738-5600 or (800) 556-7918

Year of Data: 1986
Expenditures: $21,267,604
Percent to Program: 71.7%
Fund-raising Costs: 21.2%
Contributions Deductible: Yes
Top of Staff Salary Range: $72,500 (1987)
Meets NCIB Standards: Yes (12/31/87)

Purpose: "Transmitting funds ... to provide material aid and services to Foster Children and families, assisting Foster Parents to develop meaningful relationships with their Foster Children, and conducting an educational program in the United States about the needs of the poor in developing countries"

Program: In fiscal 1986, about 70% of PI-USA's total expenditures went to Foster Parents Plan International, Inc. (PI), a separately governed affiliate "directly responsible for all program activities overseas." PI's programs are of three kinds. In the Family Development Model, field staff help an individual family set objectives for improvement and provide money or materials to help them accomplish it. In the Group Development Model, field staff provide guidance and material support to groups of families working together to pursue common

interests. In the Community Development Model, used in a few countries where closely knit communities are the center of society, staff works "with the entire community as an extended family." In fiscal 1986, PI had total expenditures of $48,249,786 and supported programs serving about 275,000 people in 21 countries. Of total expenditures, about 17% was for Health Services, 15% for Social Services, 11% for Family Assistance, 11% for Education, 9% for Resources and Skill Development, and 8% for Community Development.

Comments: In view of the relationship between PI-USA and PI, NCIB suggests that potential contributors may wish to request both organizations' annual reports. PI-USA asks its contributors to donate $22 per month to become a foster parent and provides the contributor with a photograph and case history of the sponsored child. Sponsors are encouraged to write to their foster child and are given an annual report from field staff about the child's progress. In fiscal 1986, PI received $54,697,402 in revenues from its national organizations, about 33% of it from Canada, 31% from the Netherlands, 27% from the United States and smaller amounts from Australia, the United Kingdom, Japan and other countries. NCIB recommends improvements in PI-USA's audited financial statements.

PROJECT CONCERN INTERNATIONAL

3550 Afton Road
P.O. Box 85323
San Diego, CA 92138
(619) 279-9690

Year of Data: **1985**
Expenditures $3,272,026
Percent to Program: 73.6%
Fund-raising Costs: 29.4%
Contributions Deductible: Yes
Top of Staff Salary Range: $40,000 (1985)
Meets NCIB Standards: Yes (12/19/86)

Purpose: To promote child survival through self-help projects in nutrition, immunization, maternal child health and hygiene education, and by training health volunteers to take responsibility for their communities

Comments: The editor deemed NCIB's information about this organization too dated (1985 data or before) to give the organization a complete listing.

PROJECT HOPE/PEOPLE-TO PEOPLE HEALTH FOUNDATION

Carter Hall
Millwood, VA 22646
(703) 837-2100

Year of Data: 1988
Expenditures: $21,203,000
Percent to Program: 82.1%
Fund-raising Costs: 9.2%
Contributions Deductible: Yes
Top of Staff Salary Range: $195,000 (1989)
Meets NCIB Standards: Yes (9/6/89)

Purpose: "To improve health care in developing areas of the world by teaching techniques of medical science to physicians, dentists, nurses and allied health personnel in those areas"

Program: PH's reporting of its activities does not allow a detailed breakdown of its programs and expenses. Fiscal 1988 activities included programs in 17 foreign countries and the United States, such as sponsoring training in hospital administration for 13 Chinese graduate students; establishing a national nursing education center in Beijing; distributing textbooks to libraries and resource centers in 14 countries; disseminating information on AIDS prevention; assisting in training emergency medical technicians in Costa Rica; providing medical supplies and basic health services in El Salvador; coordinating the transfer of Salvadoran children to the United States for medical care related to war injuries; and sponsoring a nursing conference in Poland.

Comments: Prior to 1974, the principal activity of PH was the operation of *S.S. Hope*, a hospital ship. About 58% of PH's total revenue for fiscal 1988 came from U.S. government grants and 39% from donated "publications, equipment and supplies." NCIB recommends improvements in PH's annual report and audited financial statements.

SAVE THE CHILDREN FEDERATION, INC.

54 Wilton Road
Westport, CT 06880
(203) 226-7272

Year of Data: 1987
Expenditures: $65,863,000
Percent to Program: 81%
Fund-raising Costs: 23%
Contributions Deductible: Yes
Top of Staff Salary Range: $148,000 (1988)
Meets NCIB Standards: Yes (8/16/88)

Purpose: To "improve the lives of children by increasing the self-sufficiency of the communities in which they live"

Program: In fiscal 1987, SCF devoted about 30% of its expenditures to programs in the Middle East/North Africa, 20% to the rest of Africa, 13% to the United States, 11% to Latin America/Caribbean, 10% to refugee programs in Indonesia and Thailand, 9% to Asia/Pacific, and 6% to American Indian nations. Activities included:

- Refugees and Disaster Relief (26%) - assistance sometimes in the form of provision of food, clothing and housing, but more often in the form of long-term development activities, such as job and skills training, health and nutrition education and growing food
- Human Resources Development (14%) - promotion of activities in child day care and feeding, recreation, community organization and leadership development; emphasis is on women and children
- Education/Training (12%) - formal and informal educational services and construction of educational facilities
- Health/Nutrition (10%) - health care services, emphasizing maternal and child health, nutrition, potable water and water resource development, construction of health care facilities and sanitation systems
- Small Scale Industry and Crafts (8%) - activities designed to produce income for community groups and individuals
- Community Improvement (7%) - construction, maintenance and improvement of such community facilities as access roads, parks and aqueducts
- Agriculture (5%) - activities relating to

production and improvements in crops, livestock and fish ponds; construction of storage facilities; forestation

Comments: SCF emphasizes that its child sponsorship programs provide services to communities, not directly to children. SCF offers two sponsorship programs. In the "One-to-One" program, sponsors contribute $20 per month and receive a brief history and photograph of the child and family, plus information about the community and local SCF projects which will benefit the family. In the "Lifeline" program, sponsors contribute $14 per month and receive information about a child chosen by SCF to represent the community, as well as reports on the progress of community projects. About 34% of SCF's revenue for fiscal 1987 came from "sponsorships" and about 50% from government grants. NCIB recommends improvements in SCF's budget presentation and audited financial statements.

TECHNOSERVE

148 East Avenue
Norwalk, CT 06851
(203) 852-0377 or (800) 99WORKS

Year of Data: 1987
Expenditures $6,032,372
Percent to Program: 80.6%
Fund-raising Costs: 20.2%
Contributions Deductible: Yes
Top of Staff Salary Range: $78,000 (1988)
Meets NCIB Standards: Yes (2/22/89)

Purpose: To provide "technical and management assistance to community-based enterprises, such as cooperatives, farmer associations and savings and credit associations, which are owned by groups of rural people. These in turn help farmers to grow more food, generate jobs and increase their incomes, leading to improved health and nutrition, greater access to education, better living conditions and strong local economies, without creating dependence on outside assistance."

Program: Fiscal 1987 activities included providing assistance to about 126 community-based enterprises, projects and related institutions in such areas as organization and administration, finance and accounting, production, marketing and evaluation. The bulk of the funds were devoted to El Salvador (17% of total expenditures), Rwanda (13%), Zaire (9%),

Panama (7%), Peru (7%), Kenya (6%), Sudan (5%) and Ghana (5%).

Comments: In fiscal 1987, about 64% of Technoserve's support came from the U.S. Agency for International Development.

UNITARIAN UNIVERSALIST SERVICE COMMITTEE, INC.

130 Prospect Street
Cambridge, MA 02139
(617) 868-6600

Year of Data: 1988
Expenditures $2,567,360
Percent to Program: 72%
Fund-raising Costs: 19.9%
Contributions Deductible: Yes
Top of Staff Salary Range: $68,825 (1988)
Meets NCIB Standards: Yes (1/31/89)

Purpose: To "seek a more just and human society by: providing experiences that promote self-determination and humane freedom; resisting and changing oppressive institutions and practices; educating and mobilizing individuals and groups for service and actions; and bringing occasional emergency direct relief where human dignity and rights are violated"

Program: Fiscal 1988 activities included:
- Africa (17%) - support for 14 projects to improve health care, agriculture, access to water, education, leadership development and job skills; emergency famine relief to Ethiopia
- Human Rights Education (14%) - sponsorship of both a Congressional and an educational fact-finding mission to assess human rights and the impact of U.S. foreign policy in Central America; publication of a study guide to Central America
- Volunteer Network and Units (9%) - support for volunteers who work in Unitarian Universalist congregations to promote UUSC and its programs; support for grass roots social action groups working on local and national issues with other organizations
- Unitarian Universalist Peace Network (7%) - support for a coalition of six Unitarian Universalist organizations which publishes educational materials and organizes workshops and social ac-

tion events concerned with nuclear disarmament and world peace

- Latin America (7%) - support for Mexican groups working to improve health care, literacy, leadership skills and community organizing; training for community development leaders in Guatemala, El Salvador and Honduras; support for health care personnel and other health projects in Nicaragua, particularly in the "war zone;" publication of a magazine for community development leaders in Central America
- Criminal Justice (7%) - efforts to involve citizens in monitoring court and prison policies to promote a more humane system and to develop alternatives to incarceration
- India (6%) - support for ten projects, concerning health care, education and leadership training, primarily for women

Comments: NCIB recommends improvements in UUSC's annual report.

UNITED STATES COMMITTEE FOR UNICEF

331 East 38th Street
New York, NY 10016
(212) 686-5522

Year of Data: 1989
Expenditures: $22,319,000
Percent to Program: 64%
Fund-raising Costs: 25.5%
Contributions Deductible: Yes
Top of Staff Salary Range: $160,000 (1989)
Meets NCIB Standards: Yes (5/31/90)

Purpose: To "support child relief and rehabilitation in foreign countries" and to act as "the United States representative for the United Nations Children's Fund (UNICEF)"

Program: Fiscal 1989 activities included:
- Grants to UNICEF Assisted Projects (50%) - support, including the proceeds from sales of greeting cards, for UNICEF programs, like those involving child nutrition, community and family-based services for children, child health, emergency relief, water supplies and sanitation
- State and Local Representation (10%) - operation of a congressional relations

office in Washington and seven full-time regional offices to serve as liaisons between the national headquarters, area committees, advisory councils and community groups

Comments: USC/UNICEF is one of 34 committees around the world concerned with increasing financial support for UNICEF. NCIB does not report about UNICEF itself because it is not a U.S. organization; direct contributions to UNICEF are not tax deductible for the same reason. In fiscal 1989, about 23% of USC/UNICEF's support came from sales of greeting cards and related items; another 21% consisted of gifts in kind. NCIB recommends improvements in USC/UNICEF's audited financial statements.

VITA (VOLUNTEERS IN TECHNICAL ASSISTANCE, INC.)

1815 North Lynn Street, Suite 200
Arlington, VA 22209
(703) 276-1800

Year of Data: 1986
Expenditures $4,113,528
Percent to Program: 69.1%
Fund-raising Costs: 2.1%
Contributions Deductible: Yes
Top of Staff Salary Range: $70,000 (1988)
Meets NCIB Standards: Yes (3/10/88)

Purpose: "To provide technical assistance for those peoples of the world who, either directly or indirectly, seek aid and consultation in advancing and improving their status; to utilize the skills and knowledge of its participants for the betterment and advancement of those peoples of the world who need and seek technical assistance; to promote the exchange among its participants of ideas concerned with international development; to foster research and study technical needs of the less developed areas of the world...."

Program: VITA's reporting of its activities does not allow a detailed breakdown of its programs. Fiscal 1986 activities included computerization of management information systems of a community health program in Bangladesh; assistance to the Thai Ministry of Science, Technology and Industry; reducing food loss to rodents in the Central African Republic; loans and technical assistance to small businesses and farms in Chad; and helping Chinese manufacturers modernize their facilities. Under a five-year grant from the U.S. Agency for International Development, VITA promotes low cost energy projects in developing countries, such as Djibouti, Honduras and Mali. VITA also maintains an information service and publishes books.

Comments: In fiscal 1986, about 74% of VITA's support came from government contracts. NCIB recommends improvements in VITA's annual report and audited financial statements.

WORLD CONCERN (Division of CRISTA Ministries)

19303 Fremont Avenue North
Seattle, WA 98133
(206) 546-7201

Purpose: To provide "humanitarian relief, rehabilitation and development programs in the developing world." The purpose of CRISTA Ministries is to "demonstrate Christ's love to all people and use every method so that the people of the world may hear the gospel and accept Christ as their personal Saviour."

Comments: NCIB is currently preparing a new report on this organization.

WORLD EDUCATION, INC.

210 Lincoln Street
Boston, MA 02111
(617) 482-9485

Year of Data: 1989
Expenditures: $2,976,976
Percent to Program: 77%
Fund-raising Costs: 19.3%
Contributions Deductible: Yes
Top of Staff Salary Range: $55,608 (1989)
Meets NCIB Standards: Yes (6/5/90)

Purpose: To "promote, encourage, aid, sponsor, and operate educational (including literacy) programs, institutions, and projects in various countries of the world for the purposes of improving the material and cultural conditions of the people of such countries, and for creating better mutual understanding and appreciation between the people of different countries"

Program: Fiscal 1989 activities included:
- Africa Programs (48%) - including training and evaluation for a project to

review "Band Aid" funded projects in Mali, Chad, Sudan, Ethiopia and Burkina Faso; development of literacy materials for small business programs in Kenya; and introducing business skills and leadership training in support of the development of women's businesses in Swaziland
- Asia Programs (21%) - including help for Southeast Asian refugees in Thailand; developing materials for a literacy campaign in Nepal; and development of curriculum for a project involving agriculture, forestry and animal husbandry in China
- Domestic Programs (6%) - including support for an effort to provide volunteer tutors in a literacy project in Massachusetts; assistance to a project to provide literacy and parenting skills to mothers of disadvantaged families in Rhode Island; and help for a project to improve the quality of federally-funded job training programs for disadvantaged youth in California

Comments: In fiscal 1989, about 72% of WEI's support came from governmental and intergovernmental agencies.

WORLD MERCY FUND, INC.

121 South St. Asaph Street
Alexandria, VA 22314
(703) 548-4646

Year of Data: 1989
Expenditures: $4,721,904
Percent to Program: 57.1%
Fund-raising Costs: 46%
Contributions Deductible: Yes
Top of Staff Salary Range: $60,000 (1989)
Meets NCIB Standards: No: 6a, 4?, 8? (5/23/90)

Purpose: To "alleviate the suffering of the world," with emphasis on "providing medical facilities and support; water; education; knowledge of modern methods of agriculture; self-help assistance and support as needed to improve the well- being of those in need"

Program: WMF reported all of its program expenditures for fiscal 1989 under a single heading (57% of total expenditures), about two-thirds of which was for "projects directly funded." These included funding to 21 adult education projects in 15 countries; 47 health programs in 18 countries; and 28 development and agricultural programs in 19 countries. Countries receiving the most aid were Nigeria, Sierra Leone, Senegal, Ireland and Ghana.

Comments: WMF has chapters in Australia, Switzerland, Germany and Ireland which are controlled through the Alexandria headquarters. In fiscal 1989, these chapters provided about 68% of WMF's total support. WMF's fiscal 1989 expenditures of $4,721,904 apparently includes an undisclosed amount of in-kind expenses; the organization reported receiving $225,570 in donated materials, but did not report corresponding expenditures. NCIB faults WMF for its high fund-raising and low program expenditures (Standard 6a). NCIB questions WMF's practice of soliciting funds for emergency relief efforts while expending funds primarily for non-emergency, ongoing programs (Standard 4) and WMF's failure to explain its allocation of $1,060,854 in printing and direct mail costs to "Health, education and transportation," rather than to the more usual fund- raising category (Standard 8).

WORLD NEIGHBORS, INC.

5116 North Portland Avenue
Oklahoma City, OK 73112
(405) 946-3333 or (800) 242-6387

Year of Data: 1988
Expenditures $2,797,286
Percent to Program: 74.7%
Fund-raising Costs: 16.8%
Contributions Deductible: Yes
Top of Staff Salary Range: $70,000 (1988)
Meets NCIB Standards: Yes (2/10/89)

Purpose: To "mobilize the constructive resources of mankind; to discover, and/or train specialists (usually indigenous personnel) ... to assist ... peoples of underdeveloped areas in the attainment of ultimate self-sufficiency; and to build, in that process, improved relationships between peoples and nations. To provide such information and programs as may help Americans and others to understand more fully their international responsibilities and opportunities"

Program: Fiscal 1988 activities included:
- Foreign Projects and Direct Grants (45%) - efforts to establish or assist self-help programs in food production, agriculture, health education, family

planning and small business enterprise; areas aided, in order of the greatest spending, were Central and South America, Africa and Asia
- Supplementary Services (26%) - costs of providing "counsel, advice, and inspiration" to overseas programs; production and distribution of village-oriented training materials and training local people how to use them; "cross-fertilization" of ideas, through travel, conferences and training opportunities

Comments: NCIB recommends improvements in WN's annual report and budget presentation.

WORLD REHABILITATION FUND, INC.

400 East 34th Street
New York, NY 10016
(212) 340-6062

Year of Data: 1987
Expenditures $1,209,635
Percent to Program: 84%
Fund-raising Costs: 9.8%
Contributions Deductible: Yes
Top of Staff Salary Range: $67,000 (1988)
Meets NCIB Standards: No: 1d (12/29/88)

Purpose: "Assisting governmental and voluntary agencies worldwide to establish, improve and expand rehabilitation services for the disabled through such media as technical assistance, training, exchange of experts and information, and supplies and equipment"

Program: Fiscal 1987 activities included:
- General Programs (46%) - assistance to underdeveloped nations to improve and expand their rehabilitation services for the physically handicapped, including support for residency programs in the Philippines; an exchange program between Spanish and American hospitals; establishment of a Latin American Regional Training center for Prosthetics/Orthotics in the Dominican Republic; provision of medical equipment and supplies to Lebanon and El Salvador; training conferences for the establishment of community-based rehabilitation services in South America and the Caribbean; and support for

rehabilitation work in India, Haiti and South Korea
- Department of Education (20%) - spending associated with a U.S. Department of Education grant for an international exchange of experts on rehabilitation
- Agency for International Development (17%) - spending associated with a multi-year grant from A.I.D. for training in all rehabilitation disciplines for Lebanese professionals

Comments: In fiscal 1987, about 33% of WRF's support came from government grants. NCIB faults WRF for poor attendance at its board of director meetings (Standard 1d). NCIB recommends improvements in WRF's annual report.

WORLD VISION, INC.

919 W. Huntington Drive
Monrovia, CA 91016
(818) 357-7979

Year of Data: 1989
Expenditures: $136,064,000
Percent to Program: 64.9%
Fund-raising Costs: 25.1%
Contributions Deductible: Yes
Top of Staff Salary Range: $111,060 (1989)
Meets NCIB Standards: Yes (6/22/90)

Purpose: To "glorify God by enabling people, through giving and serving, to follow Jesus Christ in meeting the spiritual and material needs of the poor throughout the world"

Program: Fiscal 1989 activities, conducted primarily by World Vision International, included:
- Childcare Ministries (35%) - operation of a child sponsorship program, which collects $20 per month from sponsors for the benefit of 404,638 children in 52 countries; types of aid include Christian schooling, case worker visits, food, vitamins, health care and family community assistance
- Relief, Development and Christian Leadership Ministries (23%) - including costs of 169 emergency relief projects aiding 1.4 million people in 49 countries

Comments: WV is the United States fund-raising affiliate of World Vision International (WVI), an evangelical religious organization which conducts social welfare programs internationally. WV distributed $131,694,000, or about 70% of its total expenses, to WVI and other ministries in fiscal 1989. NCIB cautions that all WV publications should explain the relationship between the organization and WVI. In addition to its cash expenditures in 1989, WV received and distributed gifts-in-kind which it valued at $51.7 million. NCIB objects to WV's use of "matching check" solicitations which do not give contributors the option of having their donations returned if the matching check challenge is over- or under-matched. NCIB recommends improvements in WV's annual report.

- **AFRICAN-AMERICAN INSTITUTE** (see INTERNATIONAL)
- **AMERICAN LEPROSY MISSIONS** (see HEALTH-GENERAL)
- **AMERICAN RED CROSS** (see HUMAN SERVICE)
- **COVENANT HOUSE** (see HUMAN SERVICE)
- **HABITAT FOR HUMANITY** (see HOUSING)
- **INTERNATIONAL EYE FOUNDATION** (see HEALTH-VISUAL HANDICAPS)
- **HELEN KELLER INTERNATIONAL, INC.** (see HEALTH-VISUAL HANDICAPS)
- **NEW EYES FOR THE NEEDY** (see HEALTH-VISUAL HANDICAPS)

MINORITIES

*civil rights, education,
social action, human service*

- **AMERICAN INDIAN GRADUATE CENTER** (see EDUCATION)
- **AMERICANS FOR INDIAN OPPORTUNITY** (see SOCIAL ACTION)
- **ARROW, INC.** (see SOCIAL ACTION)
- **ASPIRA OF AMERICA, INC.** (see EDUCATION)
- **ASSOCIATION ON AMERICAN INDIAN AFFAIRS, INC.** (see SOCIAL ACTION)
- **CONGRESS FOR RACIAL EQUALITY** (see SOCIAL ACTION)
- **COUNCIL ON CAREER DEVELOPMENT FOR MINORITIES, INC.** (see EMPLOYMENT)
- **INTERRACIAL COUNCIL FOR BUSINESS OPPORTUNITY** (see SOCIAL ACTION)
- **MARTIN LUTHER KING, JR. CENTER FOR NONVIOLENT SOCIAL CHANGE, INC.** (see SOCIAL ACTION)
- **MAINSTREAM, INC.** (see SOCIAL ACTION)
- **MEXICAN AMERICAN LEGAL DEFENSE AND EDUCATIONAL FUND, INC.** (see SOCIAL ACTION)
- **NAACP LEGAL DEFENSE AND EDUCATIONAL FUND and EARL WARREN LEGAL TRAINING PROGRAM, INC.** (see SOCIAL ACTION)
- **NAACP SPECIAL CONTRIBUTION FUND** (see SOCIAL ACTION)
- **NATIONAL ACTION COUNCIL FOR MINORITIES IN ENGINEERING, INC.** (see EDUCATION)
- **NATIONAL COUNCIL OF NEGRO WOMEN, INC.** (see SOCIAL ACTION)
- **NATIONAL HISPANIC SCHOLARSHIP FUND** (see EDUCATION)

- **NATIONAL MERIT SCHOLARSHIP CORPORATION** (see EDUCATION)
- **NATIONAL URBAN COALITION, INC.** (see HUMAN SERVICE)
- **NATIONAL URBAN FELLOWS, INC.** (see EDUCATION)
- **NATIONAL URBAN LEAGUE** (see HUMAN SERVICE)
- **NATIVE AMERICAN RIGHTS FUND** (see SOCIAL ACTION)
- **NOW LEGAL DEFENSE AND EDUCATION FUND, INC.** (see SOCIAL ACTION)
- **PUERTO RICAN LEGAL DEFENSE AND EDUCATION FUND, INC.** (see SOCIAL ACTION)
- **PUSH FOR EXCELLENCE** (see EDUCATION)
- **RED CLOUD INDIAN SCHOOL** (see EDUCATION)
- **ROSEBUD EDUCATIONAL SOCIETY/ ST. FRANCIS INDIAN MISSION/LITTLE SIOUX** (see HUMAN SERVICE)
- **ST. JOSEPH'S INDIAN SCHOOL** (see EDUCATION)
- **ST. LABRE INDIAN SCHOOL EDUCATIONAL ASSOCIATION** (see EDUCATION)
- **SER/JOBS FOR PROGRESS, INC.** (see EMPLOYMENT)
- **SOUTHERN CHRISTIAN LEADERSHIP CONFERENCE** (see SOCIAL ACTION)
- **SOUTHERN CHRISTIAN LEADERSHIP FOUNDATION** (see SOCIAL ACTION)
- **SOUTHWEST INDIAN FOUNDATION** (see HUMAN SERVICE)
- **TEKAKWITHA INDIAN MISSION** (see HUMAN SERVICE)
- **UNITED NEGRO COLLEGE FUND** (see EDUCATION)

PHILANTHROPY

giving to colleges, voluntarism, gifts in kind, federations

COUNCIL FOR AID TO EDUCATION (formerly Council for Financial Aid to Education)

51 Madison Avenue, Suite 2200
New York, NY 10010
(212) 689-2400

Year of Data: 1986
Expenditures: $1,223,337
Percent to Program: 72.9%
Fund-raising Costs: 5.2%
Contributions Deductible: Yes
Top of Staff Salary Range: $75,000 (1987)
Meets NCIB Standards: Yes (3/30/87)

Purpose: "To encourage the widest possible voluntary support of institutions of higher learning, especially by business"

Program: Fiscal 1986 activities include:

- Consultations and Meetings (35%) - provision of free consulting services to corporations on how they can best assist higher education; sponsorship of seminars and workshops
- Research Activities (31%) - preparation of "definitive" reports on voluntary support for higher education
- Advertising and Public Information (7%) - a national advertising campaign to encourage giving (CFAE's familiar slogan is "Give to the college of your choice"); newsletters, reports, and manuals about planning and implementing aid to higher education

Comments: The Council "promotes, but neither solicits nor disburses, funds for higher education." It has reported more than 350 corporate supporters.

FOUNDATION FOR INDEPENDENT HIGHER EDUCATION (formerly Independent College Funds of America)

Five Landmark Square, Suite 330
Stamford, CT 06901-2502
(203) 353-1544

Year of Data: 1988
Expenditures: $2,518,781
Percent to Program: 82%
Fund-raising Costs: 12%
Contributions Deductible: Yes
Top of Staff Salary Range: $125,000 (1988)
Meets NCIB Standards: Yes (8/7/89)

Purpose: To encourage "contribution of unrestricted funds for distribution by its [39] member associations to their [600] colleges and universities"

Program: FIHE's reporting of its activities does not allow a detailed breakdown of its programs and expenses. In fiscal 1988, FIHE distributed about 64% of its total expenditures to its member associations. It also presented "Distinguished Donor Awards" to corporations for "significant volunteer leadership and financial support" and "Distinguished Performance Awards" to acknowledge outstanding efforts by associations in raising funds for their member colleges and universities.

Comments: FIHE has 39 member state and regional college associations which in turn raise funds for 600 member colleges and universities. NCIB's report concerns FIHE only. NCIB recommends improvements in FIHE's annual report, budget presentation and audited financial statements.

GIFTS IN KIND AMERICA

700 North Fairfax Street, Suite 300
Alexandria, VA 22314
(703) 836-2121

Year of Data: 1989
Expenditures: $1,064,658
Percent to Program: 87.4%
Fund-raising Costs: 3%
Contributions Deductible: Yes
Top of Staff Salary Range: $67,000 (1989)
Meets NCIB Standards: Yes (6/6/90)

Purpose: To "support and encourage corporate in-kind contributions to the nonprofit community ... and improve the operating capacity of nonprofit health and human care organizations nationwide and across the globe"

Program: GIKA reported all of its program expenditures for fiscal 1989 under a single heading (87% of total expenditures) covering costs of identifying qualified recipients and administering the details of donations, including coordination, scheduling, transportation and record keeping. This activity resulted in the acquisition of 303 donations and distribution of such products as facsimile machines, photocopiers, telephone systems, telephone answering machines, computer software packages, personal care products, small home appliances, writing supplies, video tapes and film to over 50,000 voluntary agencies.

Comments: GIKA was created in 1984 by the United Way of America, employees of which manage the organization under a contractual agreement. In fiscal 1989, GIKA received about 37% of its total support from United Way of America and local United Ways. About 50% of total support came from administrative fees paid by donors to facilitate distribution of donated products. GIKA reports that during fiscal 1989, the organization assisted in the direct transfer of over $21 million in goods from donors to donees. NCIB recommends improvements in GIKA's audited financial statements.

NATIONAL COMMITTEE FOR RESPONSIVE PHILANTHROPY

NCIB reports that, as of July 1, 1990, this organization has not, over a period of several years, furnished requested information sufficient to prepare a report.

NATIONAL EXECUTIVE SERVICE CORPS

257 Park Avenue South
New York, NY 10010
(212) 529-6660

Year of Data: 1986
Expenditures: $1,606,991
Percent to Program: 70.1%
Fund-raising Costs: 16.4%
Contributions Deductible: Yes
Top of Staff Salary Range: $50,000 (1986)
Meets NCIB Standards: Yes (1/4/88)

Purpose: To "provide management assistance to U.S. not-for-profit institutions [and, in certain circumstances, to governmental agencies, other public entities and commercial enterprises] in the fields of education, health, religion, social services and the arts ..." in order to "improve ... efficiency and effectiveness of their operations"

Program: NESC's reporting of its activities does not allow a detailed breakdown of its programs. Fiscal 1986 activities included provision of consultant and volunteer services by retired business executives to non-profit clients, about 48% of which were civic and social service agencies, 24% health agencies, 14% educational institutions, 12% arts and humanities groups, and 2% religious institutions. Assistance to nonprofits included consultation regarding accounting systems and controls, board development, business plans, communications, feasibility studies, financial planning, fund-raising, management information systems, marketing, personnel, public relations and strategic planning. NESC also published a newsletter and conducted a study to determine the degree of interest among technically educated industry and military personnel in becoming secondary school teachers after retirement.

Comments: NESC charges its non-profit clients consulting fees, which are negotiable and based on their ability to pay. NCIB recommends improvements in NESC's annual report and audited financial statements.

VOLUNTEER - THE NATIONAL CENTER

1111 North 19th Street, Suite 500
Arlington, VA 22209
(703) 276-0542

Purpose: "Promoting and supporting more effective volunteering, with the goal of involving more people, more effectively in addressing human and social problems"

Comments: NCIB is currently preparing a new report on this organization.

- **INTERACTION: AMERICAN COUNCIL FOR VOLUNTARY INTERNATIONAL ACTION** (see INTERNATIONAL RELIEF)
- **NATIONAL ASSEMBLY OF NATIONAL VOLUNTARY HEALTH AND SOCIAL WELFARE ORGANIZATIONS, INC.** (see HUMAN SERVICE)
- **UNITED NEGRO COLLEGE FUND** (see EDUCATION)
- **UNITED WAY OF AMERICA** (see COMMUNITY IMPROVEMENT)

PUBLIC POLICY

think-tanks, policy institutes

AMERICAN ENTERPRISE INSTITUTE

NCIB reports that, as of July 1, 1990, this organization has not, over a period of several years, furnished requested information sufficient to prepare a report.

COMMITTEE FOR ECONOMIC DEVELOPMENT, INC.

477 Madison Avenue
New York, NY 10022
(212) 688-2063

Year of Data: **1984**
Expenditures $3,384,820
Percent to Program: 68.4%
Fund-raising Costs: 12.1%
Contributions Deductible: Yes
Top of Staff Salary Range: $187,500 (1984)
Meets NCIB Standards: No: 1 (9/23/85)

Purpose: To "develop business and public policy proposals that will significantly improve the country's long-range economic progress and to speak out for their adoption"

Comments: The editor deemed NCIB's information about this organization too dated (1985 data or before) to give the organization a complete listing.

ETHICS AND PUBLIC POLICY CENTER

1030 15th Street, NW, Suite 300
Washington, DC 20005
(202) 682-1200

Year of Data: 1987
Expenditures: $1,439,028
Percent to Program: 63.9%
Fund-raising Costs: 3.8%
Contributions Deductible: Yes
Top of Staff Salary Range: $100,000 (1988)
Meets NCIB Standards: Yes (4/12/88)

Purpose: "To clarify and reinforce the bond between the Judeo-Christian moral tradition and domestic and foreign policy issues"

Program: The nature of EPPC's presentation of its financial materials does not allow a detailed breakdown of programs and expenses. In general, EPPC conducts a program of research, writing, publication and conferences "to encourage debate on domestic and foreign policy issues among religious, educational, academic, business, political, and other leaders." Its four primary areas of research are Religion and Society, Business and Society, Education and Society and Foreign Policy. In fiscal 1987, EPPC held five conferences on such topics as "Crisis in Central America," "Future of Korea" and "New Approaches to Poverty and Self-Respect." EPPC publishes a quarterly newsletter, various studies and both original and reprinted essays.

Comments: NCIB recommends improvements in EPPC's annual report and audited financial statements.

THE HERITAGE FOUNDATION

214 Massachusetts Avenue, NE
Washington, DC 20002
(202) 546-4400

Year of Data: **1985**
Expenditures $8,974,647
Percent to Program: 73.4%
Fund-raising Costs: 16.8%
Contributions Deductible: Yes
Top of Staff Salary Range: $156,575 (1985)
Meets NCIB Standards: Yes (2/2/87)

Purpose: To support "free enterprise, individual liberty, limited government and a strong national defense"

Comments: The editor deemed NCIB's information about this organization too dated (1985 data or before) to give the organization a complete listing.

INSTITUTE FOR HUMANE STUDIES

NCIB reports that, as of July 1, 1990, this organization has not, over a period of several years, furnished requested information sufficient to prepare a report.

THE INSTITUTE OF CULTURAL AFFAIRS

4750 North Sheridan Road
Chicago, IL 60640
(312) 769-6363

Year of Data: **1985**
Expenditures $2,102,001
Percent to Program: 86.6%
Fund-raising Costs: 5.5%
Contributions Deductible: Yes
Top of Staff Salary Range: $19,000 (N/A)
Meets NCIB Standards: No: 3, 1?, 5? (3/10/87)

Purpose: "To foster human development in all sectors of society through providing methods to individuals, communities and organizations"

Comments: The editor deemed NCIB's information about this organization too dated (1985 data or before) to give the organization a complete listing.

PACIFIC RESEARCH INSTITUTE FOR PUBLIC POLICY

177 Post Street, Suite 500
San Francisco, CA 94108
(415) 989-0833

Year of Data: 1986
Expenditures $631,044
Percent to Program: 68.5%
Fund-raising Costs: 15.0%
Contributions Deductible: Yes
Top of Staff Salary Range: $80,000 (1987)
Meets NCIB Standards: Yes (6/3/88)

Purpose: To "broaden public understanding of the nature and effects of market processes and government policy through various media programs and book publications"

Comments: The editor deemed this organization too small (under $1 million in expenditures in the most recent year reported) to be given a complete listing.

- **THE ATLANTIC COUNCIL OF THE UNITED STATES, INC.** (see INTERNATIONAL)

- **CATALYST** (see SOCIAL ACTION)

- **COUNCIL ON ECONOMIC PRIORITIES** (see SOCIAL ACTION)

- **COUNCIL ON FOREIGN RELATIONS** (see INTERNATIONAL)

- **ETHICS RESOURCE CENTER** (see EDUCATION)

- **FOREIGN POLICY ASSOCIATION** (see INTERNATIONAL)

- **FREEDOM HOUSE, INC. and WILLKIE MEMORIAL OF FREEDOM, INC.** (see INTERNATIONAL)

- **THE FUND FOR PEACE** (see INTERNATIONAL)

- **INVEST-IN-AMERICA NATIONAL COUNCIL** (see EDUCATION)

- **LEAGUE OF WOMEN VOTERS EDUCATION FUND and LEAGUE OF WOMEN VOTERS OF THE U.S.** (see SOCIAL ACTION)

- **NATIONAL ASSEMBLY OF NATIONAL VOLUNTARY HEALTH AND SOCIAL WELFARE ORGANIZATIONS, INC.** (see HUMAN SERVICES)

- **NATIONAL COUNCIL ON CRIME AND DELINQUENCY** (see CRIME PREVENTION)

- **OVERSEAS DEVELOPMENT COUNCIL** (see INTERNATIONAL)

- **POPULATION REFERENCE BUREAU** (see EDUCATION)

- **UNITARIAN UNIVERSALIST SERVICE COMMITTEE, INC.** (see INTERNATIONAL RELIEF)

- **UNITED NATIONS ASSOCATION OF THE UNITED STATES OF AMERICA, INC.** (see INTERNATIONAL)

- **WORLD POLICY INSTITUTE, INC.** (see INTERNATIONAL)

- **WORLD RESEARCH, INC.** (see EDUCATION)

RECREATION

NATIONAL RECREATION AND PARK ASSOCIATION

3101 Park Center Drive
Alexandria, VA 22302
(703) 820-4940

Year of Data: 1987
Expenditures: $3,836,499
Percent to Program: 73.5%
Fund-raising Costs: 2.4%
Contributions Deductible: Yes
Top of Staff Salary Range: $82,500 (1987)
Meets NCIB Standards: Yes (4/27/88)

Purpose: To "promote an adequate system of parks and recreation areas, to improve recreation and park leadership for service to people, and to educate the public on recreation and park matters beneficial to the community and the nation"

Program: NRPA's reporting of its activities does not allow a detailed breakdown of its programs. Fiscal 1987 activities included programs to promote the benefits of recreation, park and leisure services, including publication of a monthly magazine, a monthly newsletter and two quarterly journals for park and recreation professionals and citizens; public policy programs, including monitoring the work and recommendation of the president's Commission on Americans Outdoors; professional and citizen development programs; sponsorship of a leisure research symposium; and maintenance of a library and information center.

Comments: NRPA consists of a national headquarters, five regional offices and 60 affiliated state and regional organizations. NCIB recommends improvements in NRPA's annual report and audited financial statements.

SPECIAL OLYMPICS INTERNATIONAL (formerly Special Olympics, Inc.)

1350 New York Ave., NW, Suite 500
Washington, DC 20005
(202) 628-3630

Purpose: To "sponsor solely, promote and conduct athletic activities for the mentally retarded (children and adults) on a year-round basis"

Comments: NCIB is currently preparing a new report on this organization.

UNITED STATES OLYMPIC COMMITTEE

1750 East Boulder Street
Colorado Springs, CO 80909
(719) 632-5551

Year of Data: 1985-87
Expenditures $97,884,268
Percent to Program: 73.6%
Fund-raising Costs: 18.7%
Contributions Deductible: Yes
Top of Staff Salary Range: $175,000 (1988)
Meets NCIB Standards: Yes (11/14/88)

Purpose: To promote and maintain the interest of the people of the United States in, and obtain their support for, creditable and sportsmanlike participation and representation of the United States in Olympic and Pan American games

Program: USOC's reporting of its activities does not allow a detailed breakdown of its expenses and programs. In general, its activities include operating training centers; providing room, board and other support for athletes at the centers; sponsoring a U.S. Olympic Festival for more than 2,600 athletes in non-Olympic years; and operating a Job Opportunities Program to provide employment to athletes with high potential.

Comments: USOC consists of 39 national sports governing bodies responsible for selection of team members for the Olympic and Pan American Games; 12 multi-sport organizations; 8 affiliated sport organizations; seven national organizations for the handicapped; and representatives from 54 state or area fund-raising organizations. USOC uses a unique "Quadrennial Accounting Period," in which activities are organized in four-year cycles ending the year that the Olympic Games are held. NCIB's report concerns the first three years of the 1985-88 period. In 1984, USOC established the United States Olympic Foundation, "to provide a permanent endowment for amateur sports in the United States." USOC transferred $82,110,474 to the Foundation as of December 31, 1987. NCIB asked USOC for, but did not receive, information about the program and fiscal activities of the Foundation. NCIB recommends improvements in USOC's annual report.

- **52 ASSOCIATION, INC.** (see HEALTH-GENERAL)
- **NATIONAL PARKS AND CONSERVATION ASSOCIATION** (see THE ENVIRONMENT)
- **SIERRA CLUB** (see THE ENVIRONMENT)
- **THE SIERRA CLUB FOUNDATION** (see THE ENVIRONMENT)
- **YOUTH FOR UNDERSTANDING** (see INTERNATIONAL)

RELIGIOUS ORGANIZATIONS

Although the NCIB does not generally undertake to report about religious organizations, several organizations included in this directory do have religious or sectarian affiliations or goals. For the reader's ease, those organizations are cross-referenced below.

- **AFRICAN ENTERPRISE** (see INTERNATIONAL RELIEF)
- **AMERICAN FRIENDS SERVICE COMMITTEE** (see INTERNATIONAL RELIEF)
- **AMERICAN LEPROSY MISSIONS** (see HEALTH-GENERAL)
- **CHILDREN INTERNATIONAL** (see INTERNATIONAL RELIEF)
- **CHRISTIAN APPALACHIAN PROJECT, INC.** (see HUMAN SERVICE)
- **CHRISTIAN RECORD SERVICES, INC.** (see HEALTH-VISUAL HANDICAPS)
- **CLERGY AND LAITY CONCERNED and CLERGY AND LAITY CONCERNED FOUNDATION** (see SOCIAL ACTION)
- **COMPASSION INTERNATIONAL, INC.** (see INTERNATIONAL RELIEF)
- **FOOD FOR THE HUNGRY, INC.** (see INTERNATIONAL RELIEF)
- **HABITAT FOR HUMANITY** (see HOUSING)
- **INSTITUTE OF CULTURAL AFFAIRS** (see PUBLIC POLICY)
- **INTERAID, INC./INTERAID INTERNATIONAL** (see INTERNATIONAL RELIEF)
- **MAP INTERNATIONAL** (see INTERNATIONAL RELIEF)
- **NATIONAL CONFERENCE OF CHRISTIANS AND JEWS** (see SOCIAL ACTION)
- **RELIGION IN AMERICAN LIFE** (see SOCIAL ACTION)

- **ST. LABRE INDIAN SCHOOL EDUCATIONAL ASSOCIATION** (see EDUCATION)
- **SOUTHERN CHRISTIAN LEADERSHIP CONFERENCE** (see SOCIAL ACTION)
- **SOUTHERN CHRISTIAN LEADERSHIP FOUNDATION** (see SOCIAL ACTION)
- **UNITARIAN UNIVERSALIST SERVICE COMMITTEE, INC.** (see INTERNATIONAL RELIEF)
- **WORLD CONCERN** (see INTERNATIONAL RELIEF)
- **WORLD VISION, INC.** (see INTERNATIONAL RELIEF)

SOCIAL ACTION, ADVOCACY

civil rights, social analysis, advocacy and advancement, legal defense, political activity

ACCURACY IN MEDIA, INC.

1275 K Street, NW
Washington, DC 20005
(202) 371-6710

Year of Data: 1987
Expenditures: $1,276,212
Percent to Program: N/A
Fund-raising Costs: N/A
Contributions Deductible: Yes
Top of Staff Salary Range: $38,500 (1987)
Meets NCIB Standards: No: 1, 7; insufficient information: 4 (12/4/87)

Purpose: To "help raise the standards of news reporting by the correction of serious errors and/or omissions in the news media so that the public will be presented with all pertinent facts on important issues and thereby be able to reach intelligent conclusions"

Program: AIM's reporting of its activities does not allow a detailed breakdown of its programs. Fiscal 1987 activities included publication of a bimonthly magazine, distributtion of books and sponsorship of conferences and speaking events. Recent magazine articles have included "You Pay for Red Propaganda," "The Media as Drug Promoters," "Investigate PBS!," "Is the Left Hijacking UPI?" and "North Saves the Freedom Fighters." Conferences in fiscal 1987 included "The Media: Law Enforcers and Law Observers" and "Impact of the Media on Public Policy."

Comments: NCIB faults AIM for paying compensation to three members of its Board of Directors (Standard 1) and for failing to provide an annual report for fiscal 1987 (Standard 7). Because AIM's audited financial statements failed to identify program, management and fund-raising expenses, NCIB could not calculate figures necessary to evaluate the organization with respect to Standard 4. NCIB advises contributors that AIM donated services and office space to two affiliated organizations, the Council for the Defense of Freedom and Accuracy in Academia.

AMERICAN CIVIL LIBERTIES UNION and AMERICAN CIVIL LIBERTIES UNION FOUNDATION

132 West 43rd Street
New York, NY 10036
(212) 944-9800

Purpose: "To maintain throughout the United States and its possessions, the rights of free speech, free press, free assemblage and other civil rights, and to take all legitimate action in furtherance of such purposes"

Comments: NCIB is currently preparing a new report on this organization.

AMERICANS FOR INDIAN OPPORTUNITY

NCIB reports that, as of July 1, 1990, this organization has not, over a period of several years, furnished requested information sufficient to prepare a report.

ARROW, INC.

1000 Connecticut Ave., NW, Suite 1206
Washington, DC 20036
(202) 296-0685

Year of Data: 1988
Expenditures $150,477
Percent to Program: 90%
Fund-raising Costs: 2.5%
Contributions Deductible: Yes
Top of Staff Salary Range: $42,100 (1987)
Meets NCIB Standards: Yes (7/21/88)

Purpose: To promote "the advancement of Indian welfare and education"

Comments: The editor deemed this organization too small (under $1 million in expenditures in the most recent year reported) to be given a complete listing.

ASSOCIATION ON AMERICAN INDIAN AFFAIRS, INC.

95 Madison Avenue, Suite 1407
New York, NY 10016
(212) 689-8720

Year of Data: 1988
Expenditures: $1,269,136
Percent to Program: 68%
Fund-raising Costs: 21%
Contributions Deductible: Yes
Top of Staff Salary Range: $75,000 (1988)
Meets NCIB Standards: Yes (1/17/90)

Purpose: To "promote the welfare of American Indians and Alaska Natives by supporting efforts to sustain their sovereignty, constitutional, legal and human rights, and natural resources; to improve their health, education, and economic and community development"

Program: Fiscal 1988 activities included:
- Youth and Child Welfare Development (17%) - including assistance to tribes regarding agreements on Indian child welfare with the states of Alaska, California and Washington; an investigation of the Bureau of Indian Affairs' implementation of the Omnibus Drug and Alcohol Abuse Prevention Act
- Economic Community Development (10%) - technical services to seven tribes and organizations; an "Arts and Crafts Resource Guide" for Native American small craft producers; and a "Socio-Economic Data Project" to aid tribes in economic planning
- Education (10%) - promotion of Indian parent input into their children's education; participation in the National Indian Dialogues; assistance to an inter-tribal council regarding claims of mismanagement at an Indian school
- Scholarships (9%) - award of $108,800 in scholarships, including emergency aid grants, health aid grants, graduate fellowships and a nursing fellowship
- Legal Affairs (9%) - support for efforts to protect Indian religious freedom rights; support for tribes in the process of writing or revising their constitutions and codes
- Health (8%) - working for passage of Indian Health Care Improvement Act amendments; support for a video on teen alcohol and drug abuse and suicide

prevention; beginning production of a video in the Lakota language about AIDS and its prevention
- Public Education (6%) - development of a "Tribal Bond Handbook," a guide on Native American tax status and business development on reservations, and publication of a newsletter

Comments: None

CATALYST

250 Park Avenue South
New York, NY 10003-1459
(212) 777-8900

Year of Data: 1989
Expenditures: $1,823,784
Percent to Program: 72%
Fund-raising Costs: 18%
Contributions Deductible: Yes
Top of Staff Salary Range: $103,000 (1989)
Meets NCIB Standards: Yes (4/13/90)

Purpose: To work "within the corporate community to foster the full participation of women in business and professional life by furthering their upward mobility, expanding career options, and helping to reconcile the needs of the workplace and the family"

Program: Fiscal 1989 activities included:
- Corporate Programs (26%) - including provision of advisory services and environmental assessments of workplaces; operation of the Corporate Board Resource, which assists companies in identifying qualified women for their boards of directors
- National Education (17%) - participation in panel discussions and research conferences; operation of an active public relations campaign; publication of a monthly magazine and reports about the organization
- Publications (15%) - reports on such topics as flexible work arrangements and building effective corporate women's groups; updating of a 1987 publication on resources for parents
- Library and Information Services (7%) - operation of a national clearinghouse of books and periodicals on issues related to women in corporate management and an associated on-line data base
- Career and Family (6%) - continuation

of a study and report on flexible work arrangements; assistance to companies studying maternal leave policies

Comments: None

CHILDREN'S DEFENSE FUND

122 C Street, NW
Washington, DC 20001
(202) 628-8787

Year of Data: 1988
Expenditures: $6,217,789
Percent to Program: 80.7%
Fund-raising Costs: 13%
Contributions Deductible: Yes
Top of Staff Salary Range: $70,950 (1988)
Meets NCIB Standards: Yes (5/11/90)

Purpose: To "provide systematic and long-range advocacy on behalf of children"

Program: Because CDF's annual report described fiscal 1988 activities under different headings than those used in its audited financial statements, NCIB was unable to provide detailed information about the organization's program expenditures. CDF reported expenditures under headings including Public Affairs and Publications (23% of total expenditures), State and Local Affairs (12%), State Offices (10%), Health (7%) and Child Development (6%). In general, CDF gathers data, publishes reports and provides information on issues affecting children; monitors the development and implementation of federal and state policies; provides information, technical assistance and support to a network of state and local child advocates, organizations and public officials; and pursues advocacy before Congress and state and federal courts. In 1988, these activities contributed to institution of Minnesota's Child Health Plan; expansion of medical coverage for 30,000 poor pregnant women and children in Texas and implementing child care services for nearly 6,000 Ohio children in families leaving welfare for employment. CDF also distributed over 15,000 copies of its *A Children's Defense Budget*, helped in congressional negotiations regarding appropriation levels for children's programs and assisted five major religious denominations and organizations in developing community campaigns or institutional strategies related to children and poverty.

Comments: In fiscal 1988, about 64% of CDF's total revenues came from foundation and corporate grants. NCIB recommends improvements in CDF's budget presentation.

CLERGY AND LAITY CONCERNED and CLERGY AND LAITY CONCERNED FOUNDATION

198 Broadway, Suite 302
New York, NY 10038
(212) 964-6730

Purpose: To "bring religious witness to bear on questions of international affairs"

Comments: NCIB is currently preparing a new report on this organization.

CONGRESS FOR RACIAL EQUALITY (CORE)

NCIB reports that, as of July 1, 1990, this organization has not, over a period of several years, furnished requested information sufficient to prepare a report.

COUNCIL ON ECONOMIC PRIORITIES

30 Irving Place
New York, NY 10003
(212) 420-1133 or (800) 822-6435

Year of Data: 1987
Expenditures $920,452
Percent to Program: 73%
Fund-raising Costs: 19.7%
Contributions Deductible: Yes
Top of Staff Salary Range: $60,000 (1987)
Meets NCIB Standards: Yes (9/7/88)

Purpose: "To enhance corporate performance as it affects society in the critically important areas of energy, the costs and consequences of military spending, political influence, fair employment practices, and environmental impact"

Comments: The editor deemed this organization too small (under $1 million in expenditures in the most recent year reported) to be given a complete listing.

FEDERATION FOR AMERICAN IMMIGRATION REFORM

1666 Connecticut Ave., NW, Suite 400
Washington, DC 20009
(202) 328-7004

Purpose: To "develop a better understanding of immigration through research and policy analysts; inform leaders as well as the public at large; and influence public policy directly by lobbying and by litigation"

Comments: NCIB is currently preparing a new report on this organization.

GRAY PANTHERS PROJECT FUND

1424 16 Street, NW, Suite 602
Washington, DC 20036
(202) 387-3111

Purpose: To work for the "prevention of age discrimination as it affects people of all ages"

Comments: NCIB is currently preparing a new report on this organization.

INTERRACIAL COUNCIL FOR BUSINESS OPPORTUNITY

51 Madison Avenue, Suite 2212
New York, NY 10010
(212) 779-4360

Year of Data: 1986
Expenditures $889,351
Percent to Program: 79.7%
Fund-raising Costs: 9.5%
Contributions Deductible: Yes
Top of Staff Salary Range: $85,000 (1987)
Meets NCIB Standards: Yes (4/27/88)

Purpose: "To help minority businesses get started and be competitive at the local community level" and to help "more sophisticated minority-owned businesses; those that would have regional as well as community economic impact"

Comments: The editor deemed this organization too small (under $1 million in expenditures in the most recent year reported) to be given a complete listing.

MARTIN LUTHER KING, JR. CENTER FOR NONVIOLENT SOCIAL CHANGE, INC.

449 Auburn Avenue, NE
Atlanta, GA 30312
(404) 524-1956

Year of Data: 1986
Expenditures: $3,091,700
Percent to Program: 79.8%
Fund-raising Costs: 6.2%
Contributions Deductible: Yes
Top of Staff Salary Range: $85,000 (1986)
Meets NCIB Standards: Yes (6/26/87)

Purpose: "To preserve and advance Dr. King's unfinished work through teaching, interpreting, advocating and promoting nonviolently the elimination of poverty, racism, violence and war...."

Program: Fiscal 1986 activities included:

* Community Services (53%) - organization of activities in celebration of Dr. King's birthday; work with the Department of the Interior in support of a National Historic Site to memorialize Dr. King; comprehensive child care services to 75 children and their families; a single parents program, which provides housing assistance, job training and placement, child care, counseling, leadership development and other training to help 70 single-parent households make the transition to productive employment
* Education and Training (20%) - education and training in Dr. King's nonviolent methods and techniques; development and distribution of training manuals, reading materials and slide and film presentations on nonviolence training; training in nonviolent conflict resolution for correctional workers in two prisons; an internship program for students from the United States and abroad; cultural programs, including theatre, musical concerts, dance, poetry, visual arts, films, workshops and conferences
* Research (6%) - maintenance of the Center's King Library and Archives

Comments: NCIB notes that five members of the King family are among the 49 members of the organization's board of directors, and a sixth is a paid employee of the Center. NCIB recommends improvements in the Center's annual report.

LEAGUE OF WOMEN VOTERS EDUCATION FUND and LEAGUE OF WOMEN VOTERS OF THE UNITED STATES

1730 M Street, NW
Washington, DC 20036
(202) 429-1965

Year of Data: 1988
Expenditures: LWVUS: $3,359,035;
LWVEF $4,423,848
Percent to Program: LWVUS: 63%; LWVEF: 74%
Fund-raising Costs: LWVUS: 19%; LWVEF: 20%
Contributions Deductible: LWVUS: No; LWVEF: Yes
Top of Staff Salary Range: LWVUS: N/A;
LWVEF: $70,000 (1988)
Meets NCIB Standards: LWVUS: Not reported;
LWVEF: Yes (9/21/89)

Purpose: LWVUS's purpose is "to encourage informed and active participation of all citizens in government and politics;" LWVEF is a research and education organization that "offers citizens reliable, impartial information about national issues."

Program: LWVUS fiscal 1988 activities included membership and development expenditures to improve operation of the national office and various state and local programs (40% of total expenditures); communications (11%); and programs to promote political awareness (9%). LWVEF did not provide NCIB with information about specific programs, but listed such themes as public and private responsibilities for providing food, shelter, health care and a basic income level; the role of the federal government in agriculture; the changing role of the federal government; national security issues; environmental health issues; economic equity for women; and promoting interest and participation in elections.

Comments: LWVUS and LWVEF share identical boards of directors and certain expenses; LWVUS sometimes makes contributions to LWVEF. LWVUS recently reported about 1,200 local leagues and about 105,000 male and female members. NCIB's report is chiefly about the LWVEF. NCIB recommends improvements in LWVEF's budget and audited financial statements.

MAINSTREAM, INC.

1030 15th Street, NW, Suite 1010
Washington, DC 20005
(202) 898-1400

Year of Data: 1986
Expenditures $559,145
Percent to Program: 57.1%
Fund-raising Costs: 13.2%
Contributions Deductible: Yes
Top of Staff Salary Range: $45,000 (1987)
Meets NCIB Standards: Yes (1/20/87)

Purpose: To "conduct and furnish educational and consulting activities and services for the purpose of assisting persons, corporations, businesses and entities to comply with federal laws bearing upon discrimination, with special reference to the avoidance and prevention of discrimination against handicapped persons"

Comments: The editor deemed this organization too small (under $1 million in expenditures in the most recent year reported) to be given a complete listing.

MEXICAN AMERICAN LEGAL DEFENSE AND EDUCATIONAL FUND INC.

634 South Spring Street, 11th Fl.
Los Angeles, CA 90014
(213) 629-2512

Year of Data: **1985**
Expenditures $3,107,640
Percent to Program: 71.5%
Fund-raising Costs: 17%
Contributions Deductible: Yes
Top of Staff Salary Range: $60,000 (1986)
Meets NCIB Standards: Yes (10/28/86)

Purpose: "To provide legal action and legal education on behalf of the many millions of Mexican Americans in this country"

Comments: The editor deemed NCIB's information about this organization too dated (1985 data or before) to give the organization a complete listing.

NAACP LEGAL DEFENSE AND EDUCATIONAL FUND, INC., and EARL WARREN LEGAL TRAINING PROGRAM, INC.

99 Hudson Street
New York, NY 10013
(212) 219-1900

Year of Data: 1988
Expenditures: $8,262,679
Percent to Program: 78%
Fund-raising Costs: 19%
Contributions Deductible: Yes
Top of Staff Salary Range: $144,000 (1988)
Meets NCIB Standards: Yes (5/1/90)

Purpose: To "render legal aid gratuitously to such Negroes as may appear to be worthy thereof, who are suffering legal injustices by reason of race or color and are unable to employ and engage legal aid assistance on account of poverty." EWLTP's purpose is "to increase the availability of educational facilities and programs" and to provide and develop programs for financial assistance for black law students "who have been denied educational opportunities for legal training by reason of race, color, economic deprivation or overly restrictive admission policies."

Program: Fiscal 1988 activities included:
- Legal (61%) - work of 24 staff lawyers to provide legal assistance in the areas of education, administration of criminal justice and capital punishment, voting rights, fair employment and affirmative action, poverty and justice and fair housing; in 1988, there were over 500 cases on docket and over 100 in active participation
- Public Information (7%) - activities by social scientists and other specialists to assemble data relevant to organizational programs and present it to the public
- Herbert Lehman Education Fund (7%) - award of $327,600 for 175 undergraduate and 122 law scholarships

Comments: LDEF is a separate corporation, not associated with the National Association for the Advancement of Colored People or the NAACP Special Contribution Fund. NCIB recommends improvements in LDEF's budget presentation and annual report.

NAACP SPECIAL CONTRIBUTION FUND

4805 Mt. Hope Drive
Baltimore, MD 21215-3297
(301) 358-8900

Year of Data: 1987
Expenditures: $6,061,291
Percent to Program: 76%
Fund-raising Costs: 17%
Contributions Deductible: Yes
Top of Staff Salary Range: $72,000 (1988)
Meets NCIB Standards: Yes (4/14/89)

Purpose: To "support [NAACP's] program in its striving to eliminate all forms of discrimination from American society through legal action and economic and social programs"

Program: Fiscal 1987 NAACP activities, supported by NAACP/SCF, included:
- Legal (22%) - costs of suits and investigations involving discrimination in education, employment, voting and housing
- Youth (13%) - costs of maintaining the Youth and College Division, which has about 36,000 members in 500 local units; sponsorship of leadership training workshops, a "Back to School/Stay in School" program and an academic competition involving 735 youngsters from 450 cities
- Economic Development (12%) - negotiation and monitoring of "fair-share" agreements, by which corporations commit themselves to increase hiring and promotion of minorities and to increase business with minority-owned companies; sponsorship of minority franchise seminars and trade shows

Comments: NAACP/SCF provides the funding for virtually all of NAACP's national program efforts as well as some local programs and projects. NAACP created the NAACP/SCF in 1964 as a "tax-deductible vehicle." Since that date, contributions to NAACP itself have become tax deductible and the parent organization is studying ways to merge the two entities. Contributions to local NAACP units are not tax deductible. NCIB recommends improvements in NAACP/SCF's annual report.

NATIONAL CONFERENCE OF CHRISTIANS AND JEWS

71 Fifth Avenue, Suite 1100
New York, NY 10003
(212) 206-0006

Year of Data: 1987
Expenditures: $9,725,176
Percent to Program: 82%
Fund-raising Costs: 9.9%
Contributions Deductible: Yes
Top of Staff Salary Range: $140,000 (1988)
Meets NCIB Standards: Yes (1/20/89)

Purpose: To "promote individual and group dignity, cooperation, mutual understanding and respect among all peoples,...to eliminate prejudices which disfigure and distort religious, business, social and political relations, [and]...to achieve a society in which the ideals of equity and justice shall become the standards of human relationships"

Program: Fiscal 1987 activities included:
- Community Activities (36%) - activities such as involvement in helping to plan local observances of Martin Luther King Jr. Day; police-community relations programs; a national institute on law enforcement and criminal justice; production of a videotape about the difficulties experienced by minorities and women in trying to move into middle and upper management positions; and a seminar on educational systems and workforce needs; issues addressed included Soviet Jewry, South African apartheid, bilingual education, child advocacy, victim/witness services, AIDS education for clergy and bio-medical ethics
- Children and Young Adults (32%) - activities such as distribution of 75,000 learning modules about the "initiative, compromise and sense of responsibility necessary for diverse citizens to operate a democratic nation together;" residential camps or institutes for high school students; school-based human relations training for elementary students; and distribution of 50,000 copies of a brochure about understanding other people
- Interreligious Relations (14%) - programs which bring clergy and laymen from different religions together for exploration of issues of faith and society

Comments: NCIB recommends improvements in NCCJ's budget.

NATIONAL COUNCIL OF NEGRO WOMEN, INC.

1211 Connecticut Ave., NW, Suite 702
Washington, DC 20036
(202) 659-0006 or (800) 762-7988

Purpose: To undertake "program activities which attempt to effect changes in the community through the advancement of the economic, social, educational, and cultural welfare of black women on both a national and international level"

Comments: NCIB is currently preparing a new report on this organization.

NATIONAL RIGHT TO WORK LEGAL DEFENSE FOUNDATION

NCIB reports that, as of July 1, 1990, this organization has not, over a period of several years, furnished requested information sufficient to prepare a report.

NATIVE AMERICAN RIGHTS FUND

1506 Broadway
Boulder, CO 80302
(303) 447-8760

Year of Data: 1986
Expenditures: $3,455,662
Percent to Program: 76.4%
Fund-raising Costs: 28.8%
Contributions Deductible: Yes
Top of Staff Salary Range: $68,714 (1987)
Meets NCIB Standards: Yes (10/16/87)

Purpose: "Protection of Indian Rights and ... orderly development of the massive body of law affecting Native American People ... [with emphasis on] preservation of Indian tribal existence and resources and the fulfillment of the nation's long standing obligations to Indian People"

Program: Fiscal 1986 activities included:
• Litigation and Client Services (71%) - costs of research, negotiation, litigation and legislative advocacy necessary to providing and securing rights of tribal and individual Indian clients; cases tend to preserve tribal existence and

authority, protect tribal natural resources and promote such human rights as religious freedom, voting rights and education
• National Indian Law Library (5%) - maintenance of a national repository and clearing house for materials on Indian law; publication of a catalogue as a resource guide to these materials

Comments: NARF is a national Indian law firm, with an average annual docket of 200 client matters. In fiscal 1986, about 46% of its support came from government grants.

NOW LEGAL DEFENSE AND EDUCATION FUND, INC.

99 Hudson Street
New York, NY 10013
(212) 925-6635

Year of Data: 1986
Expenditures: $1,727,533
Percent to Program: 69.3%
Fund-raising Costs: 22.1%
Contributions Deductible: Yes
Top of Staff Salary Range: $60,000 (1988)
Meets NCIB Standards: Yes (5/16/88)

Purpose: To "secure equal justice for all women by undertaking precedent-setting sex discrimination litigation and by investigation into and dissemination of information about the root causes and practice of sex discrimination"

Program: Fiscal 1986 activities included:
• Legal Research and Litigation (30%) - a National Judicial Education Program, which provides programs, technical assistance and information to members of the American judiciary about such issues as treatment of female plaintiffs, defendants, lawyers, witnesses and jurors or the process of judicial decision-making in cases involving divorce, spousal abuse, custody and rape; a Family Law Project, which seeks to establish recognition of marriage as an equitable economic partnership through litigation, education programs for judges and lawyers and proper use of new laws regarding distribution of marital property after divorce; an Economic Rights Program, which includes research, public education,

litigation and technical assistance to lawmakers concerning women in poverty, the need for sex-neutral policies for determining insurance rates and benefits and equal opportunity in education, the workplace and the family
- Project on Equal Education Rights (23%) - support for educational equity for women in elementary and secondary schools, including advocacy of equal access to computer education; helping parent and community groups promote equal education goals in their schools; efforts to end sex and race stereotypes that encourage early parenting
- Public Information and Education (17%) - including a campaign to improve the image of women in the mass media, increase employment of women in the communications industry and inform women on economic policy issues affecting them

Comments: Contributions to NOW LDEF are deductible for federal income tax purposes; contributions to NOW itself are not. NOW stands for National Organization for Women.

THE PATHFINDER FUND

9 Galen Street, Suite 217
Watertown, MA 02172
(617) 924-7200

Year of Data: **1985**
Expenditures $10,003,646
Percent to Program: 80%
Fund-raising Costs: 18.6%
Contributions Deductible: Yes
Top of Staff Salary Range: $85,000 (1985)
Meets NCIB Standards: No: 1 (7/25/86)

Purpose: "To increase the recognition that population growth must be limited; to make contraception available to people willing to use it; and to accelerate the social changes that will bring population stabilization"

Comments: The editor deemed NCIB's information about this organization too dated (1985 data or before) to give the organization a complete listing.

PEOPLE FOR THE AMERICAN WAY, INC. and PEOPLE FOR THE AMERICAN WAY ACTION FUND

2000 M Street, NW, Suite 400
Washington, DC 20036
(202) 467-4999

Year of Data: 1986
Expenditures: $8,088,582
Percent to Program: 40.1%
Fund-raising Costs: 43.4%
Contributions Deductible: PFAW: Yes; PFAWAF: No
Top of Staff Salary Range: $90,000 (1987)
Meets NCIB Standards: No: 1, 4, 7? (11/20/87)

Purpose: "To educate citizens about the need to actively maintain a society that allows for diverse views, guarantees the civil and equal rights of all Americans, and that protects the majority from attempts by any minority to impose its will or infringe on the rights of others." PFAWAF supplements the educational activities of PFAW through legislative and policy advocacy work.

Program: Fiscal 1986 activities included:
- Public Policy Programs (11%) - expenses of field offices, including cataloging "far right" censorship attempts, monitoring racial and religious bigotry in election campaigns, designing and implementing programs and communicating positions to selected leaders and the public
- Communications (9%) - generation of news and commentary through print and broadcast media on issues such as book censorship, the "religious right" and the role of an independent judiciary; help in producing and sponsoring a series of three-minute radio spots on "Voices of Freedom"
- Program Management and Development (8%) - planning and management of the organization; meetings with press and opinion leaders; testimony before Congress
- Issues Development (8%) - publications and papers on history textbooks and on religion and education; work on publications and papers on government and civics textbooks, textbook censorship issues and a survey on the issue of an independent judiciary

Comments: NCIB considers PFAW and PFAWAF as a single organization for purposes of its report. NCIB faults PFAW for providing compensation for three of its board members (Standard 1) and for its low program and high fund-raising expenditures (Standard 4). NCIB questions PFAW's allocations of costs of certain activities in its audited financial statements (Standard 7).

POPULATION CRISIS COMMITTEE/ DRAPER WORLD POPULATION FUND

1120 19th Street, NW, Suite 550
Washington, DC 20036
(202) 659-1833

Year of Data: **1985**
Expenditures $2,797,242
Percent to Program: 86.1%
Fund-raising Costs: 6%
Contributions Deductible: Yes
Top of Staff Salary Range: $112,500 (1986)
Meets NCIB Standards: Yes (4/14/87)

Purpose: "To generate knowledge, understanding, and support for efforts throughout the world to bring birth rates into balance with lowered death rates at the earliest possible time"

Comments: The editor deemed NCIB's information about this organization too dated (1985 data or before) to give the organization a complete listing.

THE POPULATION INSTITUTE

110 Maryland Avenue, NE
Washington, DC 20002
(202) 544-3300

Year of Data: 1988
Expenditures: $1,352,216
Percent to Program: 73%
Fund-raising Costs: 8.7%
Contributions Deductible: Yes
Top of Staff Salary Range: $90,000 (N/A)
Meets NCIB Standards: Yes (12/11/89)

Purpose: To "create awareness about the world population problem and its relationship to resource shortages and environmental deterioration and establish appropriate leadership to deal with these problems"

Program: Fiscal 1988 activities included:
- Information and Education (38%) - publication of a bimonthly newspaper, a public affairs series for national and

international policy makers and journalists and a news service report which provides information about population issues to the media
- Community Leaders (26%) - activities to recruit and train volunteers, including 525 presentations on world population growth, resulting in the recruitment of about 12,000 volunteers; recruitment of 12 university students to participate in PI's Future Leaders of America six-month intern program

Comments: None

POPULATION REFERENCE BUREAU, INC.

777 14th Street, NW, Suite 800
Washington, DC 20005
(202) 639-8040

Year of Data: 1988
Expenditures: $2,524,806
Percent to Program: 79%
Fund-raising Costs: 1.3%
Contributions Deductible: Yes
Top of Staff Salary Range: $76,156 (1988)
Meets NCIB Standards: Yes (2/2/90)

Purpose: To develop public understanding of the problems posed by the rapid growth of population in relation to natural resources, by compiling data on worldwide population trends and what they mean in terms of foreign and domestic policy, city and community planning, marketing and family living

Program: Fiscal 1988 activities included:
- International Projects (50%) - activities of PRB's Innovative Materials for Population Action Project, designed to bring population research findings to Third World policymakers, including production of information packets on contraceptive safety
- Policy Studies (13%) - including initiation of a project to explain how changing U.S. demographics are affecting the capacity of federal, state and local officials to govern
- Publications (11%) - publication of periodicals, data sheets and education modules
- Information and Education (6%) - production of teaching/learning materials for use by teachers; operation of an

audiovisual lending library; teacher training activities; and consultation on population education methods and materials

Comments: In fiscal 1988, about 62% of PRB's support came from government grants and contracts. In the same year, PRB used $145,529 of its revenues to cover operating losses of its wholly-owned, for-profit subsidiary, Decision Demographics, which provides demographic analysis on a fee basis. Decision Demographics produced revenues of $447,723 and had expenses of $593,252, including $154,709 paid to PRB for supporting services. NCIB recommends improvements in PRB's budget presentation.

PUERTO RICAN LEGAL DEFENSE AND EDUCATION FUND, INC.

99 Hudson Street, 14th Fl.
New York, NY 10013
(212) 219-3360

Year of Data: **1984**
Expenditures $947,033
Percent to Program: 66.9%
Fund-raising Costs: 15.2%
Contributions Deductible: Yes
Top of Staff Salary Range: $55,000 (1985)
Meets NCIB Standards: Yes (7/26/85)

Purpose: "To help the Puerto Rican community achieve equal rights and opportunities by providing legal representation and promoting legal education"

Comments: The editor deemed NCIB's information about this organization too dated (1985 data or before) to give the organization a complete listing.

RELIGION IN AMERICAN LIFE

2 Queenston Place, Room 200
Princeton, NJ 08540
(609) 921-3639

Year of Data: 1987
Expenditures $400,881
Percent to Program: 61.0%
Fund-raising Costs: 9.4%
Contributions Deductible: Yes
Top of Staff Salary Range: $50,000 (1987)
Meets NCIB Standards: Yes (7/28/88)

Purpose: "To build support for America's religious institutions;" "To strengthen the moral

climate of America;" "To give public relations assistance to America's religious community"

Comments: The editor deemed this organization too small (under $1 million in expenditures in the most recent year reported) to be given a complete listing.

SOUTHERN CHRISTIAN LEADERSHIP CONFERENCE

NCIB reports that, as of July 1, 1990, this organization has not, over a period of several years, furnished requested information sufficient to prepare a report.

SOUTHERN CHRISTIAN LEADERSHIP FOUNDATION

NCIB reports that, as of July 1, 1990, this organization has not, over a period of several years, furnished requested information sufficient to prepare a report.

SOUTHERN POVERTY LAW CENTER

400 Washington Avenue
P.O. Box 2087
Montgomery, AL 36101
(205) 264-0286

Purpose: To educate "the economically and educationally deprived of their rights under the Constitution and to mobilize resources and provide services and assistance which give promise of progress towards equal justice for the poor"

Comments: NCIB is currently preparing a new report on this organization.

ZERO POPULATION GROWTH, INC.

1400 16th Street, NW, Suite 320
Washington, DC 20036
(202) 332-2200

Year of Data: 1988
Expenditures $1,046,889
Percent to Program: 68%
Fund-raising Costs: 13%
Contributions Deductible: Yes
Top of Staff Salary Range: $57,000 (1989)
Meets NCIB Standards: Yes (12/4/89)

Purpose: To "achieve a sustainable balance of population, resources, and the environment both in the U.S. and worldwide"

Program: Fiscal 1988 activities included:
- Public Education (30%) - efforts to educate the general public about population issues and to encourage support for ZPG projects and programs; includes publication of a book and a bimonthly newsletter
- Membership Services (12%) - activities designed to keep members informed on population issues and involved in ZPG programs
- Population Education (11%) - training aids, curricular materials, a quarterly publication and workshops for teachers interested in introducing population studies into their classrooms
- Field Services (8%) - information, services, materials and grants to ZPG chapters and federations and to other activists, including a quarterly newsletter; support for a 4,000-member volunteer network
- Public Policy (7%) - monitoring population-related legislation and promotion of domestic and international population stabilization policies

Comments: ZPG has nine local chapters, one each in Florida, Minnesota, Oregon, Washington and Utah and four in California.

- **ACTION FOR CHILDREN'S TELEVISION** (see ARTS)
- **AMERICAN COMMITTEE ON AFRICA and THE AFRICA FUND** (see INTERNATIONAL RELIEF)
- **AMERICAN FARMLAND TRUST** (see THE ENVIRONMENT)

- **AMERICAN FRIENDS SERVICE COMMITTEE** (see INTERNATIONAL RELIEF)
- **AMERICAN HUMANE ASSOCIATION** (see ANIMAL-RELATED)
- **AMERICAN NEAR EAST REFUGEE AID, INC.** (see INTERNATIONAL RELIEF)
- **AMNESTY INTERNATIONAL OF THE U.S.A., INC.** (see INTERNATIONAL)
- **ASPIRA OF AMERICA, INC.** (see EDUCATION)
- **CHILDREN'S LEGAL FOUNDATION** (see CRIME PREVENTION)
- **EPILEPSY FOUNDATION OF AMERICA** (see HEALTH-GENERAL)
- **FRIENDS OF ANIMALS** (see ANIMAL-RELATED)
- **HALT (HELP ABOLISH LEGAL TYRANNY)** (see CONSUMER PROTECTION)
- **HUMANE SOCIETY OF THE UNITED STATES** (see ANIMAL-RELATED)
- **MORALITY IN MEDIA** (see CRIME PREVENTION)
- **NATIONAL ACTION COUNCIL FOR MINORITIES IN ENGINEERING, INC.** (see EDUCATION)
- **NATIONAL ANTI-VIVISECTION SOCIETY** (see ANIMAL-RELATED)
- **NATIONAL CIVIC LEAGUE** (see COMMUNITY IMPROVEMENT)
- **NATIONAL FEDERATION OF THE BLIND** (see HEALTH-VISUAL HANDICAPS)
- **NATIONAL URBAN COALITION, INC.** (see HUMAN SERVICE)
- **NATIONAL WILDLIFE FEDERATION** (see ANIMAL-RELATED)
- **PUSH FOR EXCELLENCE** (see EDUCATION)
- **UNITARIAN UNIVERSALIST SERVICE COMMITTEE, INC.** (see INTERNATIONAL RELIEF)

VETERANS

care for disabled and hospitalized veterans, POW-MIAs, services to military

- **AMERICAN RED CROSS** (see HUMAN SERVICE)
- **AMVETS NATIONAL SERVICE ASSOCIATION** (see HUMAN SERVICE)
- **BLINDED VETERANS ASSOCIATION** (see HEALTH-VISUAL HANDICAPS)
- **DISABLED AMERICAN VETERANS** (see HUMAN SERVICE)
- **HELP HOSPITALIZED VETERANS** (see HEALTH-GENERAL)
- **NATIONAL LEAGUE OF FAMILIES OF AMERICAN PRISONERS MISSING IN SOUTHEAST ASIA** (see INTERNATIONAL)
- **PARALYZED VETERANS OF AMERICA** (see HEALTH-GENERAL)

YOUTH DEVELOPMENT

scouts, youth clubs, relationships with adults, education and experience

AMERICAN HUMANICS, INC.
4601 Madison Avenue, Suite B
Kansas City, MO 64112
(816) 561-6415 or (800) 343-6466

Year of Data: 1986
Expenditures: $1,008,354
Percent to Program: 45.8%
Fund-raising Costs: 27.6%
Contributions Deductible: Yes
Top of Staff Salary Range: $80,000 (1987)
Meets NCIB Standards: No: 4 (12/21/87)

Purpose: To provide "career-oriented college education for men and women who aspire to professional employment in youth and human service leadership and administration"

Program: AH's reporting of its activities did not include program descriptions. Fiscal 1986 activities included the "Relationship" Program, for "maintaining contact and rapport with various youth agencies" (17%), Co-Curricular Program (14%), Recruiting (10%) and Placement (5%). In general, AH contracts and operates with three-year agreements with its affiliated colleges and universities to establish programs in youth agency administration. AH provides a co-curricular program, which may include field trips to youth agencies, workshops conducted by agency executives, summer employment, internships, counseling and career placement. Students share the expenses of co-curricular activities but pay no fee; the colleges pay about 25% of the on-campus costs of the program. At the end of fiscal 1986, campus enrollment in AH's program totaled 440; program graduates numbered 68.

Comments: NCIB faults AH for low program expenses and high "management and general" and fund-raising expenses in fiscal 1986 (Standard 4). AH also had an excess of revenue over expenses of $359,892, or about 26%. NCIB recommends improvements in AH's annual report.

BIG BROTHERS/BIG SISTERS OF AMERICA

230 North 13th Street
Philadelphia, PA 19107
(215) 567-2748

Year of Data: 1988
Expenditures: $2,811,258
Percent to Program: 78.2%
Fund-raising Costs: 19.8%
Contributions Deductible: Yes
Top of Staff Salary Range: $86,000 (1988)
Meets NCIB Standards: Yes (2/5/90)

Purpose: To provide "children in need with positive interpersonal relationships which provide the nurturing necessary to achieve a well-adjusted adulthood"

Program: Because BB/BSA's annual report described fiscal 1988 activities under different headings than those used in its audited financial statements, it is not possible to provide detailed information about the organization's program expenditures. BB/BSA reported expenditures under the headings of Field Services (39%), Program Development (25%) and Member Communications (14%). In assisting its local agencies, BB/BSA "coordinates publicity and volunteer recruiting efforts, produces ... publications, provides fund-raising assistance, service delivery and administrative counsel, and offers opportunities for professional development." In 1988, the organization developed and tested programs on child sexual abuse prevention and AIDS education; further developed a program matching mature high school seniors with younger children; and began a two-year project to increase minority participation in five local agencies in California.

Comments: In 1989, there were about 460 local agencies affiliated with BB/BSA. These agencies are autonomous but must meet minimum standards for membership in the national organization. NCIB reports that local agencies pay dues to BB/BSA, producing about one-third of its total revenues, but apparently do not solicit funds on behalf of the national organization. NCIB's report concerns only the national organization. In fund-raising activities, BB/BSA participates in numerous partnerships with for-profit corporations; one of these involves telemarketing of magazine subscriptions by DialAmerica Marketing, Inc., which describes the work of BB/BSA and advises prospective customers that the charity will receive 12.5% of the purchase price of magazines ordered. NCIB recommends improvements in BB/BSA's annual report and budget presentation.

BOY SCOUTS OF AMERICA

1325 Walnut Hill Lane
Irving, TX 75038-3096
(214) 580-2000

Year of Data: 1986
Expenditures: $49,740,000
Percent to Program: 80%
Fund-raising Costs: 7.0%
Contributions Deductible: Yes
Top of Staff Salary Range: $153,900 (1987)
Meets NCIB Standards: Yes (10/16/87)

Purpose: To "promote, through organization, and cooperation with other agencies, the ability of boys to do things for themselves and others, to train them in Scoutcraft, and to teach them patriotism, courage, self-reliance, and kindred virtues, using the methods which are now in common use by Boy Scouts"

Program: BSA's reporting of its activities does not allow a detailed breakdown of its programs. Fiscal 1986 expense categories included Field Operations (31%), Program and Program Delivery (24%), Insurance and Benefit Costs for Local Councils (17%) and Personnel and Training (5%). Activities included provision of services to local councils (including recruitment and training of adult leaders, research and direct service in the areas of finance, membership, camp development and fund-raising); publishing three magazines, official handbooks and merit badge pamphlets; sponsorship of the National Scout Jamboree; and sales of uniforms, equipment and supplies.

Comments: About 45% of BSA's revenues in 1986 came from member dues, local council fees and other fees; only about 11% came from contributions and bequests. The national office of BSA charters local Scout councils, which serve and supervise Scout units in their areas. In 1986, there were 411 councils serving 132,126 units with over 4,000,000 members. The councils, which receive support primarily from United Ways, pay assessments to BSA which, in turn, provides services to them. The councils do not solicit funds in the name of the national organization, and BSA does not control or direct the councils' financial transactions. NCIB's report concerns only the national organization and does not include local Boy Scout councils. NCIB recommends improvements in BSA's annual report, budget presentation and audited financial statements; NCIB made similar recommendations to BSA in 1983 and 1986, but notes no improvement.

BOYS AND GIRLS CLUBS OF AMERICA (formerly Boys Clubs of America)

771 First Avenue
New York, NY 10017
(212) 351-5900

Year of Data: **1984**
Expenditures $10,878,821
Percent to Program: 68.2%
Fund-raising Costs: 30.4%
Contributions Deductible: Yes
Top of Staff Salary Range: $86,176 (1984)
Meets NCIB Standards: Yes (3/4/86)

Purpose: "To promote the health, social, educational, vocational and character development of boys [and girls] through development of local clubs. The program is focused on age groups 6 to 18, and includes recreation, health, education, leadership development, and other programs directed to specific youth difficulties."

Comments: The editor deemed NCIB's information about this organization too dated (1985 data or before) to give the organization a complete listing.

CAMP FIRE, INC.

4601 Madison Avenue
Kansas City, MO 64112
(816) 756-1950

Year of Data: 1988
Expenditures: $3,829,920
Percent to Program: 87%
Fund-raising Costs: 8.8%
Contributions Deductible: Yes
Top of Staff Salary Range: $110,000 (1989)
Meets NCIB Standards: Yes (10/18/89)

Purpose: To "provide, through a program of informal education, opportunities for youth to realize their potential and to function effectively as caring, self-directed individuals responsible to themselves and to others; and as

an organization, to seek to improve those conditions in society which affect youth"

Program: Fiscal 1988 activities of CFI included:

- Development Services (32%) - "research, development and maintenance of programs and management systems for councils and the national organization," including publication of a newsletter on management of councils
- Consultation Services (30%) - services to councils to improve management and facilitate extension of quality programs
- Materials Distribution (13%) - distribution of uniforms, supplies and publications, including services to 51 stores
- Democratic Process (7%) - including annual meeting

Comments: About 57% of CFI's revenues for fiscal 1988 came from membership dues and charter fees; an additional 19% came from sales of uniforms and other merchandise; only about 7% came from contributions. CFI sets policies and standards for its nearly 300 chartered local councils and licensed membership associations. In 1988, local councils served 500,000 members. Local councils receive much of their support from United Ways and pay dues to CFI. The councils do not solicit funds in the name of the national organization, and CFI does not control or direct the councils' financial transactions. NCIB's report concerns only the national organization and does not include local Camp Fire councils. NCIB recommends improvements in CFI's budget presentation.

GIRL SCOUTS OF THE U.S.A., INC.

830 Third Avenue
New York, NY 10022
(212) 940-7500 or (800) 223-0624

Year of Data: 1987
Expenditures: $23,895,000
Percent to Program: 72.2%
Fund-raising Costs: 24.5%
Contributions Deductible: Yes
Top of Staff Salary Range: $105,000 (1988)
Meets NCIB Standards: Yes (1/13/89)

Purpose: To offer "a program of informal education, relevant to living in the contemporary world, that will attract girls, retain their interest, and help them achieve full potential"

Program: Fiscal 1987 activities included:

- Field Services (27%) - direct consultation and technical assistance services to all councils
- National Centers Administration (17%) - costs of delivering "operational program and training opportunities for girls and adults" at three centers
- Communications (12%) - communications with the membership and the general public; publication of a leadership magazine for adult members; development of public relations and other materials for use by councils
- Program and Training Development (10%) - design, development and evaluation of training for volunteers and staff

Comments: GSUSA provides services to 335 local councils, which had 2,274,000 members in 1987. Volunteers comprise more than 99% of adult membership. GSUSA does not receive an assessment from the councils, but derives most of its revenue from the annual dues paid by members (35%) and proceeds from the sale of uniforms, equipment, accessories and publications (42%). Local councils derive their income from product sales (especially cookies and calendars), program services, United Way campaigns and other sources. councils do not solicit funds in the name of the national organization, and GSUSA does not control or direct the councils' financial transactions. NCIB's report concerns only the national organization and its affiliate, New York Girl Scouts, Inc.; it does not include local Girl Scout councils. NCIB recommends improvements in GSUSA's annual report and audited financial statements.

GIRLS, INC. (formerly Girls Clubs of America, Inc.)

30 East 33rd Street
New York, NY 10016
(212) 689-3700 or (800) 221-2606

Year of Data: 1987
Expenditures: $2,591,299
Percent to Program: 79.7%
Fund-raising Costs: 5.2%
Contributions Deductible: Yes
Top of Staff Salary Range: $82,833 (1988)
Meets NCIB Standards: Yes (12/9/88)

Purpose: "To assist Girls Clubs in effectively meeting the needs of girls in their communities; to help girls to overcome the effects of discrimination and to develop their capacity to be self-sufficient, responsible members of the community; and to serve as a vigorous advocate for girls, focusing attention on their special needs"

Program: GI's reporting of its activities does not allow a detailed breakdown of its programs and expenses. In general terms, GI offers technical assistance to member clubs through a toll-free telephone line, consultation and on-site visits. GI provides the clubs with program development and evaluation activities, training programs and special assistance to newly employed executive directors. In 1987, the national organization developed or assisted with the implementation of programs concerning careers in science, mathematics and technological fields; adolescent pregnancy; and sports and fitness.

Comments: In 1988 there were about 240 local groups affiliated with GI. Local clubs are autonomous but must meet minimum standards for membership in the national organization. Local clubs pay dues to GI, but do not generally solicit funds on behalf of the national organization. NCIB's report concerns only the national organization and its four offices; it does not include local Girls Clubs. NCIB recommends improvements in GI's annual report.

JUNIOR ACHIEVEMENT INC.

45 E. Clubhouse Drive
Colorado Springs, CO 80906
(719) 540-8000

Year of Data: 1988
Expenditures: $7,594,607
Percent to Program: 69%
Fund-raising Costs: 27%
Contributions Deductible: Yes
Top of Staff Salary Range: $150,000 (1989)
Meets NCIB Standards: Yes (6/9/89)

Purpose: "To enhance America's economic vitality by providing our young people and the changing work force with experience-based economic education through partnerships responsive to business, education and community needs"

Program: JAI's fiscal 1988 activities were virtually all dedicated to support of four franchise programs in economic education: "Business Basics" for younger students; "Project Business" for junior high school students; "Applied Economics" for senior high school students; and the "Junior Achievement Company Program," in which high school students work with volunteers from the business community to learn how to organize a corporation and raise capital. The national office's activities in support of these franchise-funded programs included such field services as data processing, finance, communications, marketing and training (33% of total expenditures); research and development concerning new economic education programs (14%); human resource services (14%); and communications and marketing services, including publication of a magazine (13%).

Comments: JAI consists of a national office and three regional service centers; JAI issues franchises to local Junior Achievement organizations, which numbered 237 and enrolled about 1,057,000 students in fiscal 1988. The franchises pay "participation fees" to JAI in return for a number of services; these fees amounted to 41% of JAI's total support in 1988. Local franchises do not solicit funds in the name of the national organization, and JAI does not control or direct the franchises' financial transactions. NCIB's report concerns only the national organization. NCIB recommends improvements in JAI's annual report.

NATIONAL FFA FOUNDATION (formerly Future Farmers of America Foundation, Inc.)

5632 Mt. Vernon Memorial Hwy.
Alexandria, VA 22309
(703) 360-3600

Year of Data: **1982**
Expenditures $1,200,826
Percent to Program: 75%
Fund-raising Costs: 16.1%
Contributions Deductible: Yes
Top of Staff Salary Range: $45,000 (1983)
Meets NCIB Standards: Yes (10/16/84)

Purpose: To offer "prizes and awards to deserving students of vocational agriculture who have achieved distinction in their Future Farmer and agricultural activities," to stimulate interest in agricultural leadership and to "promote the interests of students of vocational agriculture and of members of FFA"

Comments: The editor deemed NCIB's information about this organization too dated (1985 data or before) to give the organization a complete listing.

NATIONAL 4-H COUNCIL

7100 Connecticut Avenue
Chevy Chase, MD 20815
(301) 961-2800

Year of Data: 1987
Expenditures: $14,455,630
Percent to Program: 88.6%
Fund-raising Costs: 11.6%
Contributions Deductible: Yes
Top of Staff Salary Range: $115,000 (1987)
Meets NCIB Standards: Yes (11/30/87)

Purpose: To "help expand and strengthen the 4-H program"

Program: Fiscal 1987 activities included:
- Educational Programs (45%) - domestic programs, including citizenship programs, leadership development programs, state and county achievement awards and staff development and training; international programs, including youth exchanges involving 2,500 youth participants and 3,500 host families
- National 4-H Center (21%) - operation of an educational facility which provided lodging, meals and conference facilities for 33,000 participants
- National 4-H Supply Service (18%) -

provision of 1,600 items used for awards and for visibility of 4-H programs; revenues from the service were less than its costs

Comments: NCIB recommends improvements in 4-H's annual report and audited financial statements.

HUGH O'BRIAN YOUTH FOUNDATION

10880 Wilshire Blvd., Suite 900
Los Angeles, CA 90024
(213) 474-4370

Year of Data: 1987
Expenditures: $1,481,992
Percent to Program: 60.6%
Fund-raising Costs: 13.2%
Contributions Deductible: Yes
Top of Staff Salary Range: $86,400 (1987)
Meets NCIB Standards: Yes (7/11/88)

Purpose: To "seek out, recognize, and reward leadership potential of high school sophomores here and abroad; to encourage and assist members of this formative age group in their quest for self-identification and self-development; to interface these potential leaders with recognized leaders in business, industry, government, science, and education through give-and-take discussion sessions; and to present through this exposure a keen exploration of the American economic incentive system and our democratic process"

Program: Fiscal 1987 activities included:
• State Seminars (36%) - three- to four-day seminars held in all 50 states, plus several foreign countries, attended by about 10,600 students; seminars have the theme of "America's Incentive System" and feature workshops and meetings with leaders in business, industry, government, education and the professions; funds for these seminars are raised by volunteer state committees, with some assistance from the national headquarters
• International Leadership Seminar (19%) - an eight-day seminar held for 183 students from 50 states and 20 foreign countries
• Alumni Association (9%) - participation of about 600 students in a "college and career fair;" production of a satellite

broadcast to 7,500 people; and other services related to 2,600 dues-paying alumni members

Comments: NCIB's report concerns HOBY's national headquarters only and does not include consideration of separately incorporated state committees. Contributors interested in state committees should examine their individual programs and finances. NCIB recommends improvements in HOBY's audited financial statements.

UP WITH PEOPLE

3103 N. Campbell Avenue
Tucson, AZ 85719
(602) 327-7351

Purpose: To "provide students with an effective work-learning experience" by means of a touring entertainment show

Comments: NCIB is currently preparing a new report on this organization.

• **AMERICAN RED CROSS**
  (see HUMAN SERVICE)
• **FATHER FLANAGAN'S BOYS' HOME**
  (see HUMAN SERVICE)
• **NATIONAL BOARD OF THE YOUNG WOMEN'S CHRISTIAN ASSOCIATION OF THE U.S.** (see HUMAN SERVICE)
• **STARR COMMONWEALTH SCHOOLS**
  (see EDUCATION)
• **UNITED WAY OF AMERICA** (see COMMUNITY DEVELOPMENT)
• **YMCA OF THE U.S.A.** (see HUMAN SERVICE)

APPENDIX A

National Charities Information Bureau
"Basic Standards in Philanthropy"*
Highlights of Version In Effect Before July 1988

Philanthropic organizations have a high degree of responsibility because of the public trusteeship involved. Compliance with the following standards with reasonable evidence supplied on request, is considered essential by the NCIB.

1. Board - An active and responsible governing body, holding regular meetings, whose members have no material conflict of interest and serve without compensation.

2. Purpose - A clear statement of purpose in the public interest.

3. Program - A program consistent with the organization's stated purpose and its personnel and financial resources, and involving inter-agency cooperation to avoid duplication of work.

4. Expenses - Reasonable program, management, and fundraising expenses.

5. Promotion - Ethical publicity and promotion excluding exaggerated or misleading claims.

6. Fund-raising - Solicitation of contributions without payment of commissions or undue pressure, such as mailing unordered tickets or merchandise, general telephone solicitation and use of identified government employees as solicitors.

7. Accountability - An annual report available on request that describes program activities and supporting services in relation to expenses and that contains financial statements comprising a balance sheet, a statement of support/revenue and expenses and changes in fund balances, a statement of functional expenses, and notes to financial statements, that are accompanied by the report of an independent public accountant. National organizations operating with affiliates should provide combined or acceptably compiled financial statements prepared in the foregoing manner. For its analysis, NCIB may request disclosure of accounting treatment of various items included in the financial statements.

8. Budget - Detailed annual budget approved by the governing body in a form consistent with annual financial statements.

* Reprinted with permission of National Charities Information Bureau.

National Charities Information Bureau "Standards in Philanthropy"* Current Version (In Effect Since July 1988)**

Preamble

The support of philanthropic organizations soliciting funds from the general public is based on public trust. The most reliable evaluation of an organization is a detailed review. Yet the organization's compliance with a basic set of standards can indicate whether it is fulfilling its obligations to contributors, to those who benefit from its programs, and to the general public.

Responsibility for ensuring sound policy guidance and governance and for meeting these basic standards rests with the governing board, which is answerable to the public.

The National Charities Information Bureau recommends and applies the following nine standards as common measures of governance and management.

NCIB Standards

Governance, Policy and Program Fundamentals

1. **Board Governance:** The board should be an independent, volunteer body. It is responsible for policy setting, fiscal guidance, and ongoing governance, and should regularly review the organization's policies, programs and operations. The board should have

   a. a minimum of 5 voting members;

   b. [an individual attendance policy;]

   c. [specific terms of office for its officers and members;]

NCIB Interpretations and Applications

Fiscal guidance includes responsibility for investment management decisions, for internal accounting controls, and for short and long-term budgeting decisions.

Many organizations need more than five members on the board. Five, however, is seen as the minimum required for adequate governance.

Board membership should be more than honorary, and should involve active participation in the board meetings.

d. in-person, face-to-face meetings, at least twice a year, with a majority of voting members in attendance at each meeting;

Many board responsibilities may be carried out through committee actions, and such additional active board involvement should be encouraged. No level of committee involvement, however, can substitute for the face-to-face interaction of the full board in reviewing the organization's policy-making and program operations. As a rule, the full board should meet to discuss and ratify the organization's decisions and actions at least twice a year. If, however, the organization has an executive committee of at least five voting members, then three meetings of the executive committee, evenly spaced, with a majority in attendance, can substitute for one of the two full board meetings.

e. no fees to members for board service, but payments may be made for costs incurred as a result of board participation;

Organizations should recruit board members most qualified, regardless of their financial status, to join in making policy decisions. Costs related to a board member's participation could include such items as travel and daycare arrangements. Situations where board members derive financial benefits from board service should be avoided.

f. no more than one paid staff person member, [usually the chief staff officer, who shall not chair the board or serve as treasurer;]

g. no material conflicts of interest involving board or staff, and [policy guidelines to avoid such conflicts;]

In all instances where an organization's business or policy decisions can result in direct or indirect financial or personal benefit to a member of the board or staff, the decisions in questions must be explicitly reviewed by the board with the members concerned absent.

h. [a policy promoting pluralism and diversity within the organization's board, staff, and constituencies.]

Organizations vary widely in their ability to demonstrate pluralism and diversity. Every organization should establish a policy that fosters such inclusiveness. An affirmative action program is an example of fulfilling this requirement.

2. **Purpose:** The organization's purpose, approved by the Board, should be formally and specifically stated.

The formal or abridged statement of purpose should appear with some frequency in organization publications and presentations.

3. **Programs:** The organization's activities should be consistent with its statement of purpose.

4. Information: Promotion, fund-raising, and public information should describe accurately the organization's identity, purpose, programs, and financial needs.

Not every communication from an organization need contain all this descriptive information, but each one should include all accurate information relevant to its primary message.

There should be no material omissions, exaggerations of fact, misleading photographs, or any other practice which would tend to create a false impression or misunderstanding.

5. Financial Support and Related Activities: The board is accountable for all authorized activities generating financial support on the organization's behalf:

a. Fund-raising practices should encourage voluntary giving and should not be intimidating.

b. Descriptive and financial information for all substantial income and for all revenue-generating activities conducted by the organization should be disclosed on request.

Such activities include, but are not limited to, fees for service, related and unrelated business ventures, and for-profit subsidiaries.

c. Basic descriptive and financial information for income derived from authorized commercial activities, involving the organization's name, which are conducted by for-profit organizations, should be available. All public promotion of such commercial activity should either include this information or indicate that it is available from the organization.

Basic descriptive and financial information may vary depending on the promotional activity involved. Common elements would include, for example, the campaign time frame, the total amount or the percentage to be received by the organization, whether the organization's contributor list is made available to the for-profit company, and the campaign expenses directly incurred by the organization.

6. Use of Funds: The organization's use of funds should reflect

a. reasonable annual program, management/general, and fund-raising expenses, with at least 60% of annual expenses applied to program;

The distribution of non-program funds between fund-raising and management/general expense should be reasonable over time. Recognizing that all resources applied to management/general and fund-raising are not available for program, an organization should exercise great care to ensure that such expenses are appropriate to the organization's sound operations.

Fund-raising methods available to organizations vary widely and often have very different costs. Overall, an organization's fund-raising expense should be reasonable in relation to the contributions received, which could include indirect contributions (such as federated campaign support), be-

b. consideration of current and future needs and resources in planning for program continuity. Usually, the organization's net assets available for the following fiscal year should not be more than twice the higher of the current year's expenses or the next year's budget. There should not be a persistent and/or increasing deficit in the unrestricted fund balance.

Reporting and Fiscal Fundamentals

7. **Annual Reporting:** An annual report, or equivalent package of documentation, should be available on request, and should include

a. an explicit narrative description of the organization's major activities, presented in the same major categories and covering the same fiscal period as the audited financial statements;

b. a list of board members;

c. audited financial statements or, at a minimum, a comprehensive financial summary that 1) reflects all revenues, 2) reports expenses in the same program, management/general, and fund-raising categories as in the audited financial statements, and 3) reports all ending balances. (When the annual report does not include the full audited financial statements, it should indicate that they are available on request.)

8. **Accountability:** Complete financial statements should be prepared in conformity with

quests (generally averaged over five years), and government grants.

Reserve Funds

Unless specifically told otherwise, most contributors believe that their contributions are being applied to the current program needs identified by the organization.

Organizations may accumulate reserve funds in the interest of prudent management. Reserve funds in excess of the standard may be justified in special circumstances.

In all cases the needs of the constituency served should be the most important factor in determining and evaluating the appropriate level of available net assets.

Deficits

An organization which incurs a deficit in its unrestricted fund balance should make every attempt to restore the fund balance as soon as possible. Any organization sustaining a substantial and persistent, or an increasing, deficit is at least in demonstrable financial danger, and may even be fiscally irresponsible. In its evaluations, NCIB will take into account evidence of remedial efforts.

generally accepted accounting principles (GAAP), accompanied by a report of an independent certified public accountant, and reviewed by the board.

A statement of functional allocation of expenses should be available on request, if this is not required by generally accepted accounting principles to be included among the financial statements.

Combined financial statements for a national organization operating with affiliates should be prepared in the foregoing manner.

9. **Budget:** The organization should prepare a detailed annual budget consistent with the major classifications in the audited financial statements, and approved by the board.

To be able to make its financial analysis, NCIB may require more detailed information regarding the interpretation, applications and validation of GAAP guidelines used in the audit. Accountants can vary widely in their interpretations of GAAP guidelines, especially regarding such relatively new practices as multi-purpose allocations. NCIB may question some interpretations and applications.

Program categories can change from year to year; the budget should still allow meaningful comparison with the previous year's financial statements recast if necessary.

NCIB believes the spirit of these standards to be universally useful for all nonprofit organizations. However, for organizations less than three years old or with annual budgets of less than $100,000, greater flexibility in applying some of the standards may be appropriate.

APPENDIX B

Council of Better Business Bureaus Standards*

Introduction

The Council of Better Business Bureaus promulgates these standards to promote ethical practices by philanthropic organizations. The Council of Better Business Bureaus believes that adherence to these standards by soliciting organizations will inspire public confidence, further the growth of public participation in philanthropy, and advance the objectives of responsible private initiative and self-regulation.

Both the public and soliciting organizations will benefit from voluntary disclosure of an organization's activities, finances, fundraising practices, and governance—information that donors and prospective donors will reasonably wish to consider.

These standards apply to publicly soliciting organizations that are tax exempt under section 501(c)(3) of the Internal Revenue Code, and to other organizations conducting charitable solicitations.

While the Council of Better Business Bureaus and its member Better Business Bureaus generally do not report on schools, colleges, or churches soliciting within their congregations, they encourage all soliciting organizations to adhere to these standards.

These standards were developed with professional and technical assistance from representatives of soliciting organizations, professional fund raising firms and associations, the accounting profession, corporate contributions officers, regulatory agencies, and the Better Business Bureau system. The Council of Better Business Bureaus is solely responsible for the contents of these standards.

For the Purposes of These Standards:

1. "Charitable solicitation" (or "solicitation") is any direct or indirect request for money, property, credit, volunteer service or other thing of value, to be given now or on a deferred basis, on the representation that it will be used for charitable, educational, religious, benevolent, patriotic, civic, or other philanthropic purposes. Solicitations include invitations to voting membership and appeals to voting members when a contribution is a principal requirement for membership.

2. "Soliciting organization" (or "organization") is any corporation, trust, group, partnership or individual engaged in a charitable

solicitation; a "solicitor" is anyone engaged in a charitable solicitation.

3. The "public" includes individuals, groups, associations, corporations, foundations, institutions, and/or government agencies.

4. "Fund raising" includes a charitable solicitation; the activities, representations and materials which are an integral part of the planning, creation, production and communication of the solicitation; and the collection of the money, property, or other thing of value requested. Fund raising includes but is not limited to donor acquisition and renewal, development, fund or resource development, member or membership development, and contract or grant procurement.

Public Accountability

1. Soliciting organizations shall provide on request an annual report.

The annual report, an annually-updated written account, shall present the organization's purposes; descriptions of overall programs, activities and accomplishments; eligibility to receive deductible contributions; information about the governing body and structure; and information about financial activities and financial position.

2. Soliciting organizations shall provide on request complete annual financial statements.

The financial statements shall present the overall financial activities and financial position of the organization, shall be prepared in accordance with generally accepted accounting principles and reporting practices, and shall include the auditor's or treasurer's report, notes, and any supplementary schedules. When total annual income exceeds $100,000, the financial statements shall be audited in accordance with generally accepted auditing standards.

3. Soliciting organizations' financial statements shall present adequate information to serve as a basis for informed decisions.

Information needed as a basis for informed decisions generally includes but is not limited to: a) significant categories of contributions and other income; b) expenses reported in categories corresponding to the descriptions of major programs and activities contained in the annual report, solicitations, and other informational materials; c) a detailed schedule of expenses by natural classification (e.g., salaries, employee benefits, occupancy, postage, etc.), presenting the natural expenses incurred for each major program and supporting activity; d) accurate presentation of all fund-raising and administrative costs; and e) when a significant activity combines fund-raising and one or more other purposes (e.g., door-to-door canvassing combining fund raising and social advocacy, or television broadcasts combining fund raising and religious ministry, or a direct mail campaign combining fund raising and public education), the financial statements shall specify the total cost of the multi-purpose activity and the basis for allocating its costs.

4. Organizations receiving a substantial portion of their income through the fund-raising activities of controlled or affiliated entities shall provide on request an accounting of all income received by and fund-raising costs incurred by such entities.

Such entities include committees, branches or chapters which are controlled by or affiliated with the benefiting organization, and for which a primary activity is raising funds to support the programs of the benefiting organization.

Use of Funds

1. A reasonable percentage of total income from all sources shall be applied to programs and activities directly related to the purposes for which the organization exists.

2. A reasonable percentage of public contributions shall be applied to the programs and activities described in solicitations, in accordance with donor expectations.

3. Fund raising costs shall be reasonable.

4. Total fund raising and administrative costs shall be reasonable.

Reasonable use of funds requires that a) at least 50% of total income from all sources be spent on programs and activities directly related to the organization's purposes; b) at least 50% of public contributions be spent on the programs and activities described in solicitations, in accordance with donor expectations; c) fund-raising costs not exceed 35% of related contributions; and d) total fund-raising and administrative costs not exceed 50% of total income.

An organization which does not meet one or more of these percentage limitations may provide evidence to demonstrate that its use of funds is reasonable. The higher fund raising and administrative costs of a newly created organization, donor restrictions on the use of funds, exceptional bequests, a stigma associated with a cause, and environmental or political events beyond an organization's control are among the factors which may result in costs that are reasonable although they do not meet these percentage limitations.

5. Soliciting organizations shall substantiate on request their application of funds, in accordance with donor expectations, to the programs and activities described in solicitations.

6. Soliciting organizations shall establish and exercise adequate controls over disbursements.

Solicitations and Informational Materials

1. Solicitations and informational materials, distributed by any means, shall be accurate, truthful and not misleading, both in whole and in part.

2. Soliciting organizations shall substantiate on request that solicitations and informational materials, distributed by any means, are accurate, truthful and not misleading, in whole and in part.

3. Solicitations shall include a clear description of the programs and activities for which funds are requested.

Solicitations which describe an issue, problem, need or event, but which do not clearly describe the programs or activities for which funds are requested will not meet this standard. Solicitations in which time or space restrictions apply shall identify a source from which written information is available.

4. Direct contact solicitations, including personal and telephone appeals, shall identify a) the solicitor and his/her relationship to the benefiting organization, b) the benefiting organization or cause and c) the programs and activities for which funds are requested.

5. Solicitations in conjunction with the sale of goods, services or admissions shall identify at the point of solicitation a) the benefiting organization, b) a source from which written information is available and c) the actual or anticipated portion of the sales or admission price to benefit the charitable organization or cause.

Fund Raising Practices

1. Soliciting organizations shall establish and exercise controls over fund raising activities conducted for their benefit by staff, volunteers, consultants, contractors, and controlled or affiliated entities, including commitment to writing of all fund raising contracts and agreements.

2. Soliciting organizations shall establish and exercise adequate controls over contributions.

3. Soliciting organizations shall honor donor requests for confidentiality and shall not publicize the identity of donors without prior written permission.

Donor requests for confidentiality include but are not limited to requests that one's name not be used, exchanged, rented or sold.

4. Fund raising shall be conducted without excessive pressure.

Excessive pressure in fund raising includes but is not limited to solicitations in the guise of invoices; harassment; intimidation or coercion, such as threats of public disclosure or economic retaliation; failure to inform recipients of unordered items that they are under no obligation to pay for or return them; and strongly emotional appeals which distort the organization's activities or beneficiaries.

Governance

1. Soliciting organizations shall have an adequate governing structure.

Soliciting organizations shall have and operate in accordance with governing instruments (charter, articles of incorporation, bylaws, etc.) which set forth the organization's basic goals and purposes, and which define the organizational structure. The governing instruments shall define the body having final responsibility for and authority over the organization's policies and programs (including authority to amend the governing instruments), as well as any subordinate bodies to which specific responsibilities may be delegated.

An organization's governing structure shall be inadequate if any policy-making decisions of the governing body (board) or committee of board members having interim policy-making authority (executive committee) are made by fewer than three persons.

2. Soliciting organizations shall have an active governing body.

An active governing body (board) exercises responsibility in establishing policies, retaining qualified executive leadership, and overseeing that leadership.

An active board meets formally at least three times annually, with meetings evenly spaced over the course of the year, and with a majority of the members in attendance (in person or by proxy) on average.

Because the public reasonably expects board members to participate personally in policy decisions, the governing body is not active, and a roster of board members may be misleading, if a majority of the board members attend no formal board meetings in person over the course of a year.

If the full board meets only once annually, there shall be at least two additional, evenly spaced meetings during the year of an executive committee of board members having interim policy-making authority, with a majority of its members present in person, on average.

3. Soliciting organizations shall have an independent governing body.

Organizations whose directly and/or indirectly compensated board members constitute more than one-fifth (20%) of the total voting membership of the board or of the executive committee will not meet this standard. (The ordained clergy of a publicly soliciting church, who serve as members of the church's policy-making governing body, are excepted from this 20% limitation, although they may be salaried by or receive support or sustenance from the church.)

Organizations engaged in transactions in which board members have material conflicting interests resulting from any relationship or business affiliation will not meet this standard.

APPENDIX C

State Offices of Charity Regulation and Solicitation Disclosure Requirements*

Alabama

Attorney General
Consumer Protection Division
11 South Union Street
Montgomery, AL 36130
205-242-7334

Solicitors must disclose name, professional status, % of funds going to organization.

Alaska

Attorney General, Dept. of Law
1031 W. 4th Avenue, Suite 200
Anchorage, AK 99501
907-276-3550

None

Arizona

Attorney General
1275 West Washington
Phoenix, AZ 85007
602-542-1719

None

Arkansas

Secretary of State
Trademarks Department
256 State Capitol
Little Rock, AR 72201
501-682-1010

Solicitors must disclose % of gross proceeds allocated to charity.

California

Registry of Charitable Trusts
1718 3rd Street
Sacramento, CA 95814
916-445-2021

"Solicitation or Sale for charitable Purpose Card" must be shown prior to any solicitation. Solicitors must make oral and written disclosures as required by CA Bus & Prof. Code section 17510.3.

Colorado

Attorney General, Dept. of Law
1525 Sherman Street
Denver, CO 80203
303-866-3611

None

Connecticut

Attorney General, Public Charities Unit
55 Elm Street
Hartford, CT 06106
203-566-5836

Paid non-employee solicitors must disclose name of the soliciting firm, that firm is paid to solicit.

---

* Reprinted from *Giving USA Update*, Winter 1990 by permission. © 1990 AAFRC Trust for Philanthropy

Delaware

Attorney General, Civil Division
820 N. French Street
Wilmington, DE 19801
302-571-2528

None

District of Columbia

Dept. of Consumer & Regulatory Affairs
614 H. Street NW
Washington, DC 20001
202-727-7086

Solicitor must present to prospective donor a solicitation information card issued by Department.

Florida

Department of Agriculture
Division of Consumer Services
Mayo Building
Tallahassee, FL 32399-0800
904-488-2221

Solicitor must disclose name and relationship to charitable organization, and, upon request, furnish organization's financial statement.

Georgia

Secretary of State
Business Services and Regulation
2 Martin Luther King Drive
West Tower, Suite 315
Atlanta, GA 30334
404-656-4910

Organization must disclose to donor names of solicitor and organization. If telephone solicitation, the location of the caller; that full description of charitable program and financial statement are available upon request.

Hawaii

Dept. of Commerce & Consumer Affairs
P.O. Box 40
Honolulu, HI 96810
808-548-5319

Solicitor must furnish authorization on request.

Idaho

Attorney General
Business Regulation Division
Statehouse, Room 210
Boise, ID 83720
208-334-2400

None

Illinois

Attorney General
Charitable Trust Division
100 West Randolph, 12th Floor
Chicago, IL 60601-3175
312-814-2595

None

Indiana

Attorney General
Consumer Protection Div.
219 State House
Indianapolis, IN 46204
317-232-4522

Name of charitable organization, that solicitor is professional and is paid to solicit.

Iowa

Attorney General
Consumer Protection Div.
1300 East Walnut
Hoover State Office Bldg.
Des Moines, IA 50319
515-281-5926

None

Kansas

Secretary of State
Judicial Center - 2nd Floor
301 West 10th Street
Topeka, KS 66612
913-296-3751

Name and address of charity & professional solicitor; that information is filed with Secretary of State.

Kentucky

Attorney General
Division of Consumer Protection
209 St. Clair Street
Frankfort, KY 40601
502-564-2200

Opinion of Attorney General: Solicitors not employed by the charitable organization must disclose % of proceeds allocated to charity if so requested by solicitee.

Louisiana

Attorney General's Office
Consumer Protection Div.
P.O. Box 94095
Capital Station
Baton Rouge, LA 70804
504-342-7013

None

Maine

Dept. of Business
Occupational & Professional Regulation
State House Station 35
Augusta, ME 04333
207-582-8700

Solicitors and professional solicitors must disclose the name and address of charitable organization and of professional fund-raiser respectively. Professional solicitor must state the she "is a professional charitable fund-raiser."

Maryland

Secretary of State
Charitable Division
State House
Annapolis, MD 21401
301-974-5534

Written solicitations must state that documents and information under the Maryland charitable organizations laws can be obtained from the Secretary of State.

Massachusetts

Attorney General
Division of Public Charities
One Ashburton Place
Boston, MA 02108
617-727-2200

Solicitor must disclose name of organization, that she is a paid solicitor, what funds will be used for, minimum % of gross receipts allocated to charity. If the solicitation is for advertising, the geographic circulation of publication must be disclosed.

Michigan

Attorney General
Charitable Trust Section
P.O. Box 30214
Lansing, MI 48909
517-373-1152

None

Minnesota

Attorney General
Charities Division
340 Bremer Tower
7th Place & Minnesota St.
St. Paul, MN 55101
612-297-4613

Solicitation card must be shown prior to solicitation. Solicitor must disclose identity of charity, tax deductibility of contribution, description of charitable program, name, that she is a professional fund-raiser.

Mississippi

Attorney General
Carroll Gartin Justice Bldg.
P.O. Box 220
Jackson, MS 39205-0220
601-359-3680

None

Missouri

Attorney General
P.O. Box 899
Jefferson City, MO 65102
314-751-8769

Solicitors must disclose that she is a professional fund-raiser working on behalf of charitable organization; name of organization.

Montana

Secretary of State
Room 225, Capitol Station
Helena, MT 59620
406-444-3665

None

Nebraska

Secretary of State
2300 State Capitol
Lincoln, NE 68509
402-471-2554

Solicitor must show certificate, and issue receipts for donations of more than $2.00.

Nevada

Attorney General
Capitol Complex
Carson City, NV 89710
702-687-4170

None

New Hampshire

Attorney General
Charitable Trust Div.
State House Annex
25 Capitol Street
Concord, NH 03301-6397
603-271-3591

Solicitor must disclose name, that she is a paid solicitor.

New Jersey

Charities Registration Section
1100 Raymond Blvd., Room 518
Newark, NJ 07102
201-648-4002

Telephone solicitors must disclose name and address of organization; tax exempt status, if any, % of donation tax deductible.

New Mexico

Office of the Attorney General
Charitable Organization Registry
P.O. Drawer 1508
Sante Fe, NM 87504-1508
505-827-6060

Solicitor must disclose that she is a professional fund-raiser on behalf of organization, state % to go to charity upon request. No disclosure requirements for written solicitators.

New York

Office of Charities Registration
Department of State
162 Washington Avenue
Albany, NY 12231
518-474-3820

Solicitations must state that upon request, a person may obtain from the organization or from the secretary, a copy of the last annual report filed by the organization with the secretary. The statement shall specify the address of the organization and the address of the secretary in Albany, to which such request should be addressed and in the case of a written solicitation, must be placed conspicuously in the material with print no smaller than 10 point bold face type or, alternative, no smaller than the size print used for the most number of words in the statements.

North Carolina

Solicitation Licensing Branch
701 Balbour Drive
Raleigh, NC 27603
919-733-4510

Professional solicitors must disclose name, professional status.

North Dakota

Secretary of State
Capitol Bldg.
600 E. Boulevard Avenue
Bismarck, ND 58505-0500
701-224-2905

None

Ohio

Attorney General
Charitable Foundation Section
State Office Tower
30 East Broad Street, 15th Floor
Columbus, OH 43266-0410
614-466-4462

None

Oklahoma

Income Tax Division
Oklahoma Tax Commission
2501 Lincoln Blvd.
Oklahoma City, OK 73194-0009
405-521-2617

Receipts must be given in duplicate for contributions over $2. Annual report may be obtained from the Oklahoma Tax Commission.

Oregon

Attorney General
Administrator of Charitable Trusts
1515 S.W. 5th Avenue, Suite 410
Portland, OR 97201
503-229-5548

Solicitor must disclose professional status; within 10 days of solicitation, must disclose in writing the % allocated to charity.

Pennsylvania

Dept. of State
Bureau of Charitable Organizations
Room 308, North Office Bldg.
Harrisburg, PA 17120
717-783-1720

Solicitor must disclose professional status in oral solicitations pursuant to case law.

Rhode Island

Dept. of Business Regulations
Charitable Organization Section
233 Richmond Street
Providence, RI 02903
401-277-2416

Solicitor must show ID card for each solicitation; card must contain name and address of organization, purpose for which contribution is solicited, tax exempt status, % of contribution tax deductible.

South Carolina

Secretary of State
Dir. of Public Charities
P.O. Box 11350
Columbia, SC 29211
803-734-2169

None

South Dakota

Attorney General
500 E. Capitol
Pierre, SD 57501-5070
605-773-3215

None

Tennessee

Secretary of State
Division of Charitable Solicitations
James K. Polk Bldg., Suite 500
Nashville, TN 37243-0308
615-741-2555

Identification must be presented upon demand. Disclosure of professional status, and percent that the professional solicitor receives. Financial records are on file with secretary of state's office and available to the public.

Texas

Attorney General
Charitable Trust Section
P.O. Box 12548
Austin, TX 78711
512-463-2018

Name, address of solicitor, or law enforcement organization, purpose for which funds are solicited.

Utah

Dept. of Business Regulation
Div. of Consumer Protection
P.O. Box 45802
Salt Lake City, UT 84145-0801
801-530-6601

Professional solicitor must present permit card to donor upon request. In telephone solicitation, the information contained on the card must be read only upon request of any person solicited.

Vermont

Attorney General
109 State Street
Montpelier, VT 05602
802-828-3171

None

Virginia

Division of Consumer Affairs
P.O. Box 1163
Richmond, VA 23209
804-786-1343

Solicitor must disclose name, employer, that she is a paid solicitor. In writing, must disclose that financial statements are available from the State and Office of Consumer Affairs.

Washington

Charities Division
Legislative Building, (AS-22)
Office of the Secretary of State
Olympia, WA 98504-0422
206-753-7121, 1-800-332-4483 (in state only)

Solicitor must disclose name, organization, purpose of solicitation, name of charity, whether organization is registered

West Virginia

Secretary of State
Charitable Organizations
State Capitol Complex
Charleston, WV 25305
304-345-4000

Wisconsin

Dept. of Regulation & Licensing
P.O. Box 8935
Madison, WI 53708
608-266-0829

Wyoming

Secretary of State
Charities Division
Capitol Bldg.
200 W. 24th
Cheyenne, WY 82002-0020
307-777-7378

Every printed solicitation should include the following statement: "West Virginia residents may obtain a summary of the registration and financial documents from the secretary of state, State Capitol, Charleston, WV 25305. Registration does not imply endorsement."

Sale of product using charitable appeal must include disclosure of amount going to charity.

None

APPENDIX D

America's One Hundred Largest Charities
*(The NonProfit Times 100)**

*All figures are in millions and from
1988 (unless otherwise stated)*

ORGANIZATION	Public Support	Govt.	Investment	Members, Fees	Other	TOTAL
1. Young Men's Christian Association	$250.48	—	$21.19	$914.38	$18.06	$1,204.11
2. Lutheran Social Ministry Organizations	N.A.	N.A.	N.A.	N.A.	N.A.	1,027.00
3. American Red Cross	315.37	—	26.79	544.86	98.16	985.18
4. Salvation Army (1986 Data)	473.00	$92.00	N.A.	N.A.	300.00	865.00
5. Catholic Charities	203.15	396.10	N.A.	178.50	73.10	850.00
6. UNICEF	168.82	496.30	N.A.	N.A.	43.88	709.00
7. Goodwill Industries of America	41.60	103.00	—	384.20	26.20	555.00
8. Shriners Hospitals for Crippled Children	162.13	2.22	203.03	0.22	5.03	372.64
9. Boy Scouts of America	180.11	—	27.08	115.95	47.73	370.86
10. United Jewish Appeal	360.91	—	—	—	0.19	361.10
11. JWB (Jewish Welfare Board)	90.30	12.25	—	209.65	37.80	350.00
12. American Cancer Society	301.04	—	32.72	—	1.99	335.76
13. CARE Inc.	35.05	209.61	1.09	74.28	1.07	321.09
14. United Cerebral Palsy Associations	90.43	208.37	—	—	14.48	308.06
15. Planned Parenthood Federation of America	72.50	106.50	—	104.20	19.90	303.10
16. Catholic Relief Services	190.91	91.18	5.08	—	1.14	288.30
17. Evangelical Lutheran Good Samaritan Society	2.30	—	8.25	266.92	0.70	276.77
18. Association for Retarded Citizens (1986/87 Data)	31.79	193.49	3.48	37.66	6.46	272.89
19. National Easter Seal Society	85.70	62.88	9.30	44.66	27.41	229.96
20. Boys Clubs of America (est.)	N.A.	N.A.	N.A.	N.A.	N.A.	223.49
21. American Heart Association	188.18	0.98	14.98	8.20	4.85	217.19
22. Volunteers of America	22.12	89.43	2.07	69.12	26.11	208.85
23. World Vision	159.48	6.63	—	—	2.16	168.26

* Reprinted with permission of the *NonProfit Times*, Hopewell, NJ.

ORGANIZATION	Public Support	Sources of Income				
		Govt.	Investment	Members, Fees	Other	TOTAL
24. Nazareth Literary and Benevolent Inst. (1985 Data)*	0.29	0.27	3.09	147.28	3.00	153.92
25. Rotary Foundation	118.18	0.99	17.32	—	0.52	135.98
26. City of Hope	31.80	—	—	66.03	28.13	125.96
27. March of Dimes	111.52	3.01	3.36	—	1.76	119.66
28. Visiting Nurse Service of New York	—	—	—	110.26	3.24	113.50
29. Muscular Dystrophy Association	105.05	—	—	—	6.34	111.40
30. New York Blood Center	0.67	5.48	—	101.78	2.38	110.32
31. American Lung Association (1986/87 Data)	80.95	0.81	9.94	7.18	4.67	103.55
32. American Lebanese Syrian Associated Charities	73.35	—	2.65	13.63	13.16	102.79
33. Christian Children's Fund	84.68	—	1.32	—	6.70	92.71
34. Legal Aid Society	5.86	77.69	0.73	0.47	4.18	88.93
35. Save the Children Federation	61.49	22.14	0.56	1.04	0.66	85.88
36. Father Flanagan's Boys Home	22.82	—	47.10	10.77	0.50	81.18
37. U.S. Olympic Committee	37.29	—	1.42	38.79	2.21	79.70
38. Nature Conservancy	60.13	1.87	7.79	4.43	0.25	74.47
39. Special Olympics (Est.)	N.A.	2.00	N.A.	N.A.	N.A.	73.90
40. Ducks Unlimited	40.45	3.29	1.74	22.25	2.86	70.59
41. Natl. Benevolent Assn. of Christ. Church	11.93	—	6.90	49.73	—	68.96
42. Covenant House	67.98	2.39	1.90	—	-0.11	68.36
43. Consumers Union of the United States	2.79	—	3.44	61.33	0.42	67.97
44. National Wildlife Federation	11.09	—	1.77	51.78	2.24	66.88
45. National Multiple Sclerosis Society	53.90	1.18	1.43	1.84	0.33	58.67
46. Metro NY Coord. Council on Jewish Poverty	1.08	54.44	0.06	0.23	0.05	55.83
47. Arthritis Foundation	51.22	0.21	2.37	1.73	—	55.53
48. Big Brothers/Big Sisters of America (Est.)	N.A.	N.A.	N.A.	N.A.	N.A.	50.00
49. Children's Television Workshop	7.56	7.98	3.57	16.04	13.31	48.43
50. Jewish Board of Family, Children's Services	9.65	—	0.47	37.14	0.40	47.66
51. AmeriCares Foundation	47.07	0.43	0.13	—	—	47.63
52. United Negro College Fund	40.79	—	5.36	0.06	—	46.21
53. Camp Fire (Est.; 1986/87 Data)	N.A.	N.A.	N.A.	N.A.	N.A.	46.20

* *NonProfit Times* reports that this organization has restructured and no longer qualifies as one of the 100 largest charities

Sources of Income

ORGANIZATION	Public Support	Govt.	Investment	Members, Fees	Other	TOTAL
54. American Diabetes Association	30.58	0.22	1.48	13.04	0.65	45.96
55. Cystic Fibrosis Foundation	42.63	—	0.64	—	1.11	44.38
56. Lutheran World Relief	11.28	25.29	0.18	—	6.70	43.47
57. National Council on the Aging	1.20	37.33	—	1.46	0.43	40.41
58. Experiment in International Living	1.99	0.14	0.16	36.07	—	38.37
59. Larry Jones Ministries/Feed the Children	37.80	—	—	—	0.28	38.08
60. Girls Clubs of America	21.34	3.52	2.06	7.33	1.58	35.82
61. MAP International	33.21	0.26	—	0.68	0.13	34.28
62. Greenpeace USA	29.13	—	0.39	2.60	1.82	33.93
63. Church World Service	26.86	5.71	0.32	—	0.95	33.84
64. Hadassah: Women's Zionist Org. of Am.	27.76	—	—	5.59	0.02	33.37
65. Project HOPE	18.37	13.62	—	—	1.39	33.37
66. Mothers Against Drunk Driving	32.20	—	0.36	0.30	0.07	32.94
67. National Audubon Society	10.68	—	3.68	17.29	0.92	32.57
68. American Field Service Intercultural Program	4.13	0.64	0.66	27.04	0.10	32.57
69. Compassion International	32.15	—	0.15	—	—	32.30
70. Mennonite Central Committee	26.86	—	—	4.01	1.28	32.15
71. Girl Scouts of the USA (Nat'l Office only)	3.47	—	3.33	24.96	0.15	31.92
72. Leukemia Society of America	28.70	—	0.50	—	0.01	29.21
73. International Rescue Committee	8.19	—	0.24	20.57	0.14	29.13
74. National Church Residences	—	—	1.28	26.29	0.64	28.21
75. Jewish Child Care Association of New York	1.40	25.67	—	0.60	—	27.67
76. Central Blood Bank	—	—	0.44	23.71	3.33	27.49
77. Children's Aid Society	5.02	2.02	3.72	12.66	3.60	27.01
78. Population Council	21.13	—	3.85	0.92	-0.02	25.88
79. Foster Parents Plan	24.99	—	0.67	—	—	25.66
80. National Safety Council	—	—	—	24.09	0.79	24.89
81. Youth for Understanding International Exchange	2.74	1.54	0.56	19.70	0.13	24.67
82. National Trust for Historic Preservation	13.91	—	1.54	6.29	2.50	24.24
83. Juvenile Diabetes Foundation	21.71	—	1.40	0.63	0.32	24.05
84. World Wildlife Fund	18.91	1.43	2.25	—	0.76	23.34
85. National Urban League	8.44	12.42	0.88	1.33	0.04	23.11
86. American Friends Service Committee	17.54	0.22	4.15	0.83	0.28	23.03

ORGANIZATION	Public Support	Govt.	Investment		Other	Members, Fees
TOTAL						
87. Epilepsy Foundation of America (1986/87 Data)	13.81	5.68	0.41	2.68	0.40	22.98
88. Joslin Diabetes Center	6.01	5.57	1.26	9.81	-0.13	22.51
89. Food for the Hungry	15.64	5.17	—	—	0.07	20.88
90. World Relief	6.04	11.73	—	—	1.92	19.68
91. Christian Appalachian Project	16.55	0.78	0.39	1.80	0.13	19.66
92. Holy Land Christian Mission/ Children International	19.14	—	—	—	0.10	19.24
93. Perkins School for the Blind	2.03	0.89	4.91	10.76	0.35	18.94
94. Blood Systems Incorporated	—	—	0.76	17.49	0.21	18.46
95. Interchurch Medical Assistance	17.21	—	0.01	0.23	—	17.45
96. Braille Institute	10.55	0.72	4.96	0.88	0.16	17.27
97. Amnesty International	16.38	—	0.45	0.21	—	17.03
98. Jewish Guild for the Blind	1.85	—	0.20	14.43	—	16.48
99. American Printing House for the Blind	1.71	0.55	1.49	12.38	0.36	16.47
100. American Institute for Cancer Research	14.96	—	0.13	—	0.90	15.99

Sources of Income

APPENDIX E

Budgeting Your Contributions

There are several good reasons for budgeting your contributions. One is, of course, to have a complete record of your giving for tax purposes. Another is to have easy access to information about when you last gave so you can make the appropriate response when solicitors say it's time to renew your membership or give again.

But the most important reason for budgeting your giving is that it forces you to go through a thoughtful process, using the information you have learned about in this book. In other words, the best way to give wisely is to plan your giving in an organized manner, to set down a wide range of possible charities in a variety of areas, and then to make choices among them when you have the time and the information in front of you. Through the process of budgeting your giving, you can see clearly what the alternatives are and make decisions you'll be happy with.

There is no best way of budgeting your charity. Any method that organizes your decision-making is better than giving haphazardly. One way is to start at the most general level. First, decide how much you want to give to charities in the particular calendar year. Then divide that amount among the various categories on a Contributions Budgeting Sheet like the one below. At this level, you decide how much to give to particular types of charity; how much to give locally versus nationally; and how much to give to your own groups (e.g., your alma maters, place of worship, or scout troup) versus to those that support other social classes or other nationalities. At this point, you might start jotting down possible charities under each of the categories, so that you can have a more concrete idea of where each category's money will go.

As a next step, list under the relevant category *every* charity in that category that you would consider giving to. This sounds like a major chore, and it is the first time you do it. After that, all you need to do is add any new charities you have discovered and remove those you have a change of attitude about.

To put together your list, go through this book, examine your checkbook or recent tax returns and think of local charities that fit into each category, even if you've never given to them before (try the phone book and other methods discussed in this book). It's always best to start with too many charities and then winnow them down, not least because it will give you a list for future years, when your interests and priorities may change.

The last step (before actually writing checks) is to divide your charity money among the particular organizations. You might find that you want to give more (or less) to a category than you had decided before listing the charities in that area; don't hesitate to go back and redivide the allotted money among the categories. You might want to consider giving more money to fewer organizations every other year; this will mean lower administrative costs for the charities and less check writing for you. The next year, your budget will show you quickly which organizations you didn't give to the year before.

The most important thing in budgeting your contributions is that the method you choose should work for you. Whatever process will best enable you to make rational decisions among the wide range of potential charities is the right one. Try the method suggested here, adapt it or try one of your own. And remember that even if the first time is tough, it will lay an excellent foundation for wise giving in the future.

Here is a sample budget form, followed by a blank form that you may duplicate. The organizations and types of organization on the sample sheet were chosen solely to provide a range of typical organizations and are not recommendations of any kind.

Sample Contributions Budgeting Sheet

Name of Organization	Date of Contribution	Amount of Contribution

Arts and Humanities $300
theater, orchestra, dance and opera companies, museums,
historical preservation, public tv and radio, publications, united arts funds

Municipal Theater	March 1	$50
State Symphony Orchestra	December 15	60
City Museum of Art		
County Historical Society	December 15	30
Channel 23	May 15	75
WJZZ-FM	August 15	50
Poetry Journal	December 15	35
Modern Dance Society		

Disaster Relief
unplanned gifts when disasters strike
locally, nationally, or internationally

Oxfam America (Iran earthquake)
Red Cross (Caribbean hurricane)

Education - Alma Maters
Van Buren University
State University

Education - Other
community, scholarship funds, libraries, literacy

Local Community College
Local High School
United Negro College Fund
Town Library
Literacy Volunteers of America

The Environment
environmental protection, energy use and conservation, resources
management, land and wildlife preservation, recycling

Natural Resources Defense Council
Nature Conservancy
World Wildlife Fund
Local Recycling Group

Health - Community
local hospitals and senior citizen homes,
schools for the handicapped, combined health appeal

     County Hospital
     Area Retirement Home
     Local Health Clinic
     Metropolitan Combined Health Appeal

Health - National
research, care and rehabilitation, education

     American Heart Association
     National Hospice Organization
     American Cancer Society
     St. Jude's Children's Research Hospital
     National Hemophilia Foundaton

Health - Handicapped
services, special education, research, disabled veterans,
publications, recordings and dogs for the blind

     Association for Retarded Citizens
     Goodwill Industries of America
     Muscular Dystrophy Association
     Paralyzed Veterans of America
     American Printing House for the Blind

Human Service - Community
counseling, food, clothing and shelter, housing, employment,
community improvement, consumer protection, legal aid, equal
opportunity, volunteer fire and first aid squads

     Family Service Association
     County Legal Services Association
     State Big Brothers, Big Sisters
     Nearby Settlement House
     Local Red Cross
     Jobs for Youth
     Local Group for the Homeless
     Town Volunteer Fire Dept.
     Local Urban League

Human Service - National
     Consumers Union
     Public Citizen
     American Red Cross
     Habitat for Humanity

Human Service and Youth Development - Membership Organizations

Y's, Scouts, Camp Fire, Youth Clubs, 4-H, Junior Achievement

>Local YWCA
>Town Boy Scout Troop
>Town Camp Fire Group
>County 4-H Council

International Relief

food, medicine and technical aid, aid to refugees and political prisoners, development, child sponsorship

>CARE
>American Friends Service Committee
>Project HOPE
>Amnesty International
>International Rescue Committee
>Compassion International

International - Other

exchanges and dialogue, refugee services, protection of freedoms, peace and security, public policy

>Youth for Understanding
>AFS International
>International Peace Academy
>United Nations Association of the U.S.

Multipurpose Drives and Community Foundations

United Way, Combined Federal Campaigns, community foundations, Black United Funds, Community Shares, local alternative funds

>Metropolitan United Way
>City Foundation
>Tri-State Black Charities
>State Community Shares
>State Women's Way

Public and Societal Benefit

social advocacy, civil rights, voting, animal protection, public policy and protection voluntarism, crime prevention

>League of Women Voters Education Fund
>NAACP Legal Defense Fund
>Gray Panthers Project Fund
>American Humane Association
>Local Volunteer Center
>National Crime Prevention Council

Recreation
Olympics, parks

    U.S. Olympic Committee
    County Parks Association

Religion - Place of Worship
including local religious education

Religion - Other
affiliated charities and social services, interreligious relations,
scholarship funds, missionary organizations

    Catholic Charities
    United Jewish Appeal
    Lutheran Social Ministry
    National Conference of Christians & Jews

Contributions Budgeting Sheet

Name of Organization	Date of Contribution	Amount of Contribution

Arts and Humanities
theater, orchestra, dance and opera companies, museums,
historic preservation, public tv and radio, publications, united arts funds

Disaster Relief
unplanned gifts when disasters strike
locally, nationally, or internationally

Education - Alma Maters

Education - Other
community, scholarship funds, libraries, literacy

The Environment
environmental protection, energy use and conservation, resources
management, land and wildlife preservation, recycling

Health - Community
local hospitals and senior citizen homes,
schools for the handicapped combined health appeal

Health - National
research, care and rehabilitation, education

Health - Handicapped
services, special education, research, disabled veterans,
publications, recordings and dogs for the blind

Human Service - Community
counseling, food, clothing and shelter, housing, employment, community
improvement, consumer protection, legal aid, equal opportunity,
volunteer fire and first aid squads

Human Service - National

Human Service and Youth Development - Membership Organizations
Y's, Scouts, Camp Fire, Youth Clubs, 4-H, Junior Achievement

International Relief
food, medicine and technical aid, aid to refugees and political prisoners, development, child sponsorship

International - Other
exchanges and dialogue, refugee services, protection of freedoms, peace and security, public policy

Multipurpose Drives and Community Foundations
United Way, Combined Federal Campaigns, community foundations,
Black United Funds, Community Shares, local alternative funds

Public and Societal Benefit
social advocacy, civil rights, voting, animal protection, public policy
and protection voluntarism, crime prevention

Recreation
Olympics, parks

Religion - Place of Worship
including local religious education

Religion - Other
affiliated charities and social services, interreligious relations,
scholarship funds, missionary organizations

SUGGESTIONS FOR FURTHER READING

Both the National Charities Information Bureau (NCIB) and the Philanthropic Advisory Service of the Council of Better Business Bureaus (CBBB) publish pamphlets and booklets relating to prudent philanthropy. Useful NCIB publications include *The 1, 2, 3 of Evaluation: An Introduction to Three Basic Tools* and *The Volunteer Board Member in Philanthropy*.

CBBB pamphlets that you may find informative include "Tips on Charitable Giving: How to Give But Give Wisely"; "Tips on Solicitations by Police and Firefighter Organizations"; "Tips on Tax Deductions for Charitable Contributions"; "Tips on Handling Unwanted Direct Mail from Charitable Organizations" and "The Responsibilities of a Charity's Volunteer Board." CBBB also publishes a quarterly newsletter called *Insight*, which presents useful feature articles on a variety of topics in philanthropy.

The Givers Guide may have encouraged you to read further about some of the topics it raises. If you want to know more about the nature and amount of American philanthropy, the authoritative source is the most recent edition of *Giving USA: The Annual Report for Philanthropy*, published by the AAFRC Trust for Philanthropy in New York City. For polling data, see Virginia A. Hodgkinson, Murray S. Weitzman and The Gallup Organization, *Giving and Volunteering in the United States* (Washington: Independent Sector), 1988.

It is difficult to recommend materials on planned giving, because changes in the tax codes can render the best book obsolete overnight. There is no substitute for consulting a well-reputed attorney, accountant or financial advisor, but a little advance study may reduce the time you will need to spend with him or her. Two places to start are the most recent annual update of Conrad Teitell's *Charitable Lead Trusts — Explanation, Specimen Agreements, Forms* (Old Greenwich, CN: Taxwise Giving) and the 1989 edition of David M. Donaldson's *The Harvard Manual: Tax Aspects of Charitable Giving* (Boston: Ropes and Gray).

On corporate matching gifts of individual companies, see the most recent edition of *Matching Gift Details: Guidebook to Corporate Matching Gift Programs*, published by the Council for the Advancement and Support of Education in Washington, DC. CASE also publishes two pamphlets encouraging matching gift programs, "The Merits of Matching Gifts to Education" and "The Merits of Matching Gifts to Cultural, Civic, Health, and Social Service Organizations."

On volunteering, see Brian O'Connell and Ann Brown O'Connell, *Volunteers in Action* (New York: Foundation Center), 1989; Bill McMillon, *Volunteer Vacations: A Directory of Short-Term Adventures That Will Benefit You … and Others,* 2nd ed. (Chicago: Chicago Review Press), 1989; Harriet Clyde Kipps, ed., *Volunteerism: The Directory of Organizations, Training and Publications, 1990-91,* 3rd ed. (New York: Bowker), 1990. College students may want to examine *Break Away: A Guide to Organizing an Alternative Spring Break* (St. Paul: Campus Outreach Opportunity League), 1990. A book especially for pre-college youth is Sara D. Gilbert, *Lend A Hand: The How, Where, and Why of Volunteering* (New York: Morrow), 1988.

For books and articles relating to other topics, consult Margaret Derrickson, *The Literature of the Nonprofit Sector: A Bibliography with Abstracts* (New York: Foundation Center), 1989.

Finally, to keep current on developments concerning charities, governmental regulators and new reports from NCIB and CBBB, the essential periodical is the bi-weekly *Chronicle of Philanthropy* (P.O. Box 1989, Marion, OH 43305); also informative is the well-designed and breezily written monthly, *The NonProfit Times* (P.O. Box 408, Hopewell, NJ 08525).

INDEX TO TEXT

INDEX TO DIRECTORY OF CHARITABLE ORGANIZATIONS